Immigrant Voices

Critical Perspectives Series

Series Editor: Donaldo Macedo, University of Massachusetts, Boston

A book series dedicated to Paulo Freire

Immigrant Voices

In Search of Educational Equity

Edited by
Enrique (Henry) T. Trueba
and Lilia I. Bartolomé

ROWMAN & LITTLEFIELD PUBLISHERS, INC.
Lanham • Boulder • New York • Oxford

ROWMAN & LITTLEFIELD PUBLISHERS, INC.

Published in the United States of America
by Rowman & Littlefield Publishers, Inc.
4720 Boston Way, Lanham, Maryland 20706
http://www.rowmanlittlefield.com

12 Hid's Copse Road, Cumnor Hill, Oxford OX2 9JJ, England

Chapter 3 appeared in a slightly different version in the *Journal of Bilingual Education and Bilingualism* 2, no. 2 (1999).

Portions of chapter 14 have appeared or will appear in: Lilia I. Bartolomé. 2000. Democratizing Bilingualism: The Role of Critical Teacher Education. In *Lifting Every Voice: Pedagogy and Politics of Bilingualism*, pp. 167–186, Zeynep F. Beykont, ed. Cambridge, Mass.: Harvard Education Publishing Group; and Lilia I. Bartolomé and María Balderrama. In press. The Need for Politically and Ideologically Clear Educators: Providing Our Children with "The Best." In *The Best for Our Children: Latina/Latino Views on Literacy*. New York: Teachers College Press.

British Library Cataloguing in Publication Information Available

Library of Congress Cataloging-in-Publication Data
Immigrant voices : in search of educational equity / edited by Enrique (Henry) T. Trueba and Lilia I. Bartolomé.
    p. cm.
    Includes bibliographical references and index.
    ISBN 0-7425-0040-3 (cloth : alk. paper) — ISBN 0-7425-0041-1 (pbk. : alk. paper)
    1. Children of immigrants—Education—Social aspects—United States.
    2. Critical pedagogy—United States. 3. Multicultural education—United States. I. Trueba, Enrique T., 1931– II. Bartolomé, Lilia I.
LC3746 . I6 2000
    371.826′91′0973—dc21
                           99-057221

Printed in the United States of America

⊚ ™The paper used in this publication meets the minimum requirements of American National Standard for Information Sciences—Permanence of Paper for Printed Library Materials, ANSI Z39.48-1992.

We want to dedicate these pages,
first, to all the immigrant children in the United States,
especially those who feel lost, sad, and marginalized.
Second, to their teachers—may they discover their students'
many talents, the beauty and value of their languages
and cultures, and the potential bright futures ahead of them.
Finally, these pages are also dedicated to Laura, Phillip, and Alejandro Donaldo—
your presence in our lives gives us hope for a more humane tomorrow.

Contents

Series Foreword

Beyond Psychologizing Multiculturalism

Donaldo Macedo

The authors of *Immigrant Voices: In Search of Educational Equity* cogently teach us about the arduous and complex process of coming to voice, a process that invariably involves tensions, contradictions, fears, doubts, hopes, and dreams. Unlike the liberal educators who often reduce the process of coming to voice to facile propositions such as "we need to give them voice" or "we need to empower immigrants," these authors, by and large, attempt to demonstrate that the emergence of submerged voices almost always involves political clarity, pain, and hope. In other words, voice is not something to be given by those in power, for if you have the power to give voice, you also maintain the power to take it away. What is important to understand is that voice requires a struggle and the understanding of both its possibilities and limitations. For most immigrants and other subordinated groups in the United States, coming to voice represents a process through which they come to know what it means to be at the periphery of the intimate and yet fragile relationship between the colonizer and the colonized. It also means that the colonized becomes fully aware that voice is not something to be given by the colonizer. Voice is a human right. Voice is a democratic right. Although many readers of this book may object to the term *colonialism* to characterize the asymmetrical coexistence between the dominant and subordinated groups in the United States, it is important that we not lose sight that "the legacy of colonialism lives on today, still extracting surplus labor from workers, burdened by the baggage of white supremacy and self-interest in reproducing colonialism, and reaping the benefits of belonging to the capitalist class."

As a colonized person, who experienced firsthand the discriminatory policies of Portuguese colonialism, I can readily see many similarities between the colonial ideology and the dominant values that inform vicious attacks on the culturally different, immigrants, and those designated as "others." Colonialism imposes "distinction" as an ideological yardstick against which all other cultural values are measured, including one's humanity. On the one hand, this ideological yardstick serves to overcelebrate the dominant groups' values to a level of mystification (i.e., viewing English as education itself and measuring the success of bilingual programs only in terms of success in English acquisition), and, on the other hand, it devalues the worth of the cultures of nonwhite people who now populate most urban areas. The vicious attacks on people of color, the demonization of immigrants, the dismantling of affirmative action, and the assault on welfare programs for the poor are part and parcel of the unapologetic dominant ideology that was unleashed during the Reagan administration. It is the same ideology that has positioned itself against all public institutions, particularly those sectors that are perceived to serve mostly the poor and people of color. For example, public education in urban areas that now serves mostly nonwhite and poor students is under siege, as public housing is struggling to survive its so-called reform. If we analyze closely the ideology that informs the present assault on subordinated people in the United States, we can begin to see and understand that the ideological principles that sustain the constant devaluation of other cultures are consonant with the structures and mechanisms of a colonial ideology as succinctly described as follows:

> Culturally, colonialism has adopted a negation to the [native culture's] symbolic systems [including the native language], forgetting or undervaluing them even when they manifest themselves in action. This way, the eradication of past and the idealization and the desire to relive the cultural heritage of colonial societies constitute a situation and a system of ideas along with other elements situate the colonial society as a class.[1]

If it were not for the colonial legacy, how could we explain the U.S. educational policies in the Philippines and Puerto Rico. English was imposed as the only language of instruction in the Philippines, while the imposed American textbook presented the American culture not only as superior but as a "model par excellence for the Philippine society."[2] This type of miseducation was so prevalent that it led T. H. Pardo de Tavera, an early collaborator with U.S. colonialism, to write the following in a letter to general Douglas MacArthur: "After Peace is established all our efforts will be directed to Americanizing ourselves, to cause a knowledge of the English language to be extended and generalized in the Philippines, in order that through its agency we may adopt its principles, its political customs, and its peculiar civilization that our redemption may be complete and radical."[3] It is the same complete and radical redemption that the United States hoped to achieve in Puerto Rico when Theodore Roosevelt's commissioner of education there, Roland M. Faulkner, mandated in 1905 that instruction in public schools had to be conducted in English and made Puerto Rican schools "agencies of Americanization in the entire country, and where [schools] would present the American ideal to our youth. Children born under the American soil should have constantly present this ideal, so that they can feel proud of their citizenship and have the flag that represents the true symbol of liberty."[4]

By leaving our colonial legacy unexamined, most educators blindly embrace psychological models of analysis that not only depoliticize the complex and contradictory relationship between the dominant and the subordinated groups but also create spaces whereby ideology is erased from the discussion and psychological manifestations are reduced to biology. Even psychological models that are sometimes espoused as "progressive" because they include "subjective" variables such as race and class generally reduce these variables to the level of a footnote. In other words, researchers often make claims that they incorporate the variable "race" in their analyses so as to absolve themselves from criticism. At the same time, they straightjacket the variable race to a mere psychologization of manifestations of racism. By this process, these seemingly progressive educators achieve, at least, two fundamental objectives: (1) they create the illusion of a progressive posture while reproducing the dominant racist ideology, and (2) they prevent the interrogation of the white supremacist ideology that gave rise to the very racist manifestations they psychologize. As a result, their analyses brook no critical discussion concerning the white supremacy ideology and its relationship with the psychological profile empirically documented by these so-called progressive educators. In addition, models that psychologize seldom interrogate the descriptive nature of the discourse on race and ethnicity in order to unveil how the description hides the fact that, for example, "ethnicity has become displacement of class."[5] The models of analysis that psychologize never explain how "cultural differences are purged and social practices are reshaped around a racial identity, [giving rise to] a hierarchy that sub-categorizes while devaluing groups of people that are designated 'racial others,' 'ethnics,' 'outsiders.'"[6] Simply put, these facile empirical models never capture the complexity of the relationship between the present racist assault on immigrants at the level of language and the experience of racism. For example, presidential candidate Patrick Buchanan's call for the end of illegal immigration, even if it means putting the National Guard all along the southern frontier,[7] constitutes a form of racism at the level of language. However, this language-based racism has had the effect of licensing institutional discrimination, whereby both documented and undocumented immigrants materially experience the loss of their dignity, the denial of their humanity, and, in many cases, outright violence as witnessed by the cruel beatings of a Mexican man and woman by the border patrol. This incident was captured on videotape and outraged the Mexican communities in the United States as well as in Mexico, leading to a number of demonstrations in Los Angeles. Language, such as "border rats," "wetbacks," "aliens," "illegals," "welfare queens," and "nonwhite hordes," used by the popular press not only dehumanizes other cultural beings; it also serves to justify the violence perpetrated by white supremacists against subordinated immigrant groups. Documenting empirically the victims' attitudes and behaviors without interrogating the white supremacist ideology constitutes yet another mechanism to reproduce the dominant ideology. It is for this reason that most researchers who blindly embrace a positivistic mode of inquiry conveniently fail to understand that, according to Linda Brodkey, "scientific objectivity has too often and for too long been used as an excuse to ignore social and hence, political practice in which women and people of color, among others, are dismissed as legitimate subject of research."[8] The blind belief in objectivity not only provides pseudoscientists with a safe heaven from which they can attempt to prevent the emergence of counterdiscourses that interrogate "the hegemony of positivism and empiricism";[9] it is also a practice that generates a form of folk theory concerning objectivity believed only by nonscientists. In other words, as Brodkey so eloquently puts it, "any knowledge, including that arrived at empirically, is necessarily partial, that is, both an incomplete and an interested account of whatever is envisioned."[10]

What these educators fail to realize is that often the psychological profile they empirically document is a direct manifestation of the white supremacist ideology. Thus, in order to fully understand the multiplicity of reactions to a white supremacy ideology (which includes behaviors that range from accommodation to resistance), educators would be better served if they would reinsert their models of analysis within the very ideology that produces it. That is to say, the very model of analysis is ideologically shaped to the degree that "ideology is located . . . both in structures which constitute the outcome of past events and the conditions for current events, and in events themselves as they reproduce and transform their conditioning structures."[11] It is to this dialectical relationship that progressive educators need to turn their attention if they are to fully understand the intimate and yet oppressive relationship between the dominant and subordinated groups. In this respect, the characteristics and manifestations of this relationship are not too dissimilar from the contradictory codependency between the colonizer and the colonized as brilliantly discussed by Albert Memmi.[12]

By accepting our colonial legacy in the reproduction of the dominant ideology and the production of subordinated ideology manifested through accommodation, development of survival skills, and resistance, progressive educators will understand that, for example, the promotion of assimilation as common sense cannot escape the colonial legacy that gives it shape and sustains it. Assimilation is, according to Amilcar Cabral, nothing more and nothing less than an attempt by the dominant cultural group to achieve cultural hegemony; it either (1) liquidates "practically all the population of the dominated country, thereby eliminating the possibilities for cultural resistance or (2) succeeds in imposing itself without damage to the culture of the dominated people—that is, harmonizes economic and political domination of these people with their cultural personality."[13]

The first strategy was used to a great extent by European colonizers in their quasi genocide of Native Americans. Even though presently we are not engaged in direct genocide, the principles of the first strategy are, nevertheless, present in the laws promulgated to limit or eliminate immigration, particularly for groups that have been designated hard to assimilate, mainly nonwhites. The second strategy provides the basis for the melting pot theory, which differs little from "the imperialist colonial domination [that] tried to create theories which, in fact, are only gross formulations of racism, and which, in practice, are translated into permanent state of siege on the indigenous populations."[14]

In other words, the melting pot theory, or the "progressive assimilation of the [immigrant] population[,] turns out to be only a more or less violent attempt to deny the culture of the people in question."[15] Progressive educators need to unveil the white supremacist ideology instead of allowing pseudoprogressive educators to obfuscate it through models that overpsychologize so as to depoliticize. In this sense, the authors of *Immigrant Voices: In Search of Educational Equity*, with great political clarity, move their discussions of multiculturalism beyond the binaristic position of Western heritage versus multiculturalism. The issue is not multiculturalism versus our Western values. The real issue is cultural domination and white supremacy. In fact, it is an oxymoron to speak of American democracy and our "common culture" in view of the quasi-apartheid conditions that have predominated in the United States and the vicious attacks on immigrants and other subordinated groups. It is precisely because of the power inherent in a return to the cultural source that educators who are apologists seek refuge and legitimization in models of analysis that psychologize in order to depoliticize. The reading of *Immigrant Voices* makes it hard to accommodate to the comfort of a refugee camp of white supremacy. Reading this book enables us to understand that behind the empirical data are human faces with fractured identities, dreams, and aspirations, which are seldom captured through models that psychologize and sentence colonized cultural beings to a silenced culture, as is painfully recounted by Gloria Anzaldúa:

> El Anglo con cara de inocente nos arranco la lengua . . .
> Ahogados escupimos el oscuro.
> Luchando con nuestra propia sombra el silencio nos sepulta.
> [The Anglo with the innocent face has yanked our tongue . . .
> Drowned, we spit darkness.
> Fighting with our very shadow we are buried by silence.][16]

NOTES

1. Geraldo Navas Davilla, *La Dialectica del Desarollo Nacional: El Caso de Puerto Rico* (San Juan: Editorial Universitaria, 1987), 27.

2. Renato Constantino, *Neocolonial Identity and Counter-Consciousness* (London: Merlin, 1978), 66.

3. Ibid., 67.

4. Maria M. Lopez Lagunne, *Bilingualismo en Puerto Rico: Actitudes Sociolinguisticas del Maestro* (San Juan: M.I.S.C.E.S., Corp., 1989), 17.

5. Stanley Aronowitz, "Ethnicity and Higher Education in the U.S.," in *Tongue Tying Multiculturalism*, ed. Donaldo Macedo (forthcoming).

6. Pepi Leistyna, *Presence of Mind: Education and the Politics of Deception* (Boulder: Westview, 1999).

7. Adam Pertman, "Buchanan Announces Presidential Candidacy," *Boston Globe*, 15 December 1991, 13.

8. Linda Brodkey, *Writing Permitted in Designated Areas Only* (Minneapolis: Minnesota University Press, 1996), 10.

9. Ibid., 8.

10. Ibid.

11. Norman Fairclough, *Language and Power* (New York: Addison-Wesley, 1996).

12. For a detailed discussion concerning the relationship between the colonizer and the colonized, see Albert Memmi, *The Colonizer and the Colonized* (Boston: Beacon, 1991).

13. Amilcar Cabral, *Return to the Source: Selected Speeches of Amilcar Cabral* (New York: Monthly Review, 1973), 40.

14. Ibid.

15. Ibid.

16. Gloria Anzaldúa, *Borderlands: The New Mestiza* (San Francisco: Spinster/Aunt Lute, 1987).

Introduction

Democracy Sabotaged by Democracy: Immigration under Neoliberalism

Peter McLaren

> The tradition of the oppressed teaches us that the "state of emergency" in which we live is not the exception but the rule. We must attain to a conception of history that is in keeping with this insight. Then we shall clearly realize that it is our task to bring about a real state of emergency.
>
> —Walter Benjamin, 1969, 27

If we were to write the real history of the United States, the centerpiece of such a history would be inescapable—it would be the implacably brutal story of violence and the fundamental role that it has played in creating and preserving the "American way of life." Although the immigrants to this country most assuredly would be relegated to minor supporting roles among the cast of world-historical characters and events, theirs would be the *real* story of the United States, in the epochal shaping of social, cultural, and economic life. Immigration has a varied history, not all of it ending in the Panglossian fable known as the "American Dream." Among the earliest that made their way to these shores were European settlers. "Settlerism" in this case turned out to be little more than a form of decaffeinated imperialism. This is not to mention unspeakable acts of genocide whose haunting memories still cause the earth to groan beneath our feet. Regrettably, the legacy of colonialism lives on today, with wealthy elites—the "minority of the opulent"—still extracting surplus labor from workers, still armed by the weapons of white supremacy and all-consuming self-interest, still bent on reproducing colonialist formations, and still reaping the benefits of belonging to the capitalist class. Colonialism—which continues to advance the centrality of European values and European history—was parented historically by the marriage of capitalist social relations with the transatlantic slave trade, a concupiscent relationship if there ever was one.

1

The legacy of racism—from the views of nineteenth-century anthropology; to the Congressional eugenics experts at the dawn of the twentieth century whose mandate was the improvement of the "inborn qualities" of "the human breed"; to the racist views of Thomas Jefferson, Abraham Lincoln, Henry Cabot Lodge, Theodore Roosevelt, and Woodrow Wilson; and finally to the recent draconian laws against immigrants (such as California's infamous Propositions 187 and 229)—is largely with us today, ghosted into our economies of power and privilege, into our systems of intelligibility, even into the very structures of Western subjectivity itself. For centuries, immigrants have been the object of the state's panoptic gaze par excellence, and state bureaucrats have routinely placed them under militant scrutiny, in the crosshairs of their paranoid gaze. In recent years, politicians have used them unapologetically as cannon fodder in their public missives and have recycled and exploited—if not actually created—the immigrant "crisis" during election campaigns. In San Diego, signs depicting silhouettes of immigrant families in flight across highways reduce immigrants to the status of beasts. News videotapes of policemen beating undocumented Mexicans have become part of the public address system for the state's official anti-immigrant ideology. Undocumented immigrants are routinely displayed as a special breed of "aliens," so much so that they might as well be pickled in formaldehyde like body parts in the Gothic photographs of Joel-Peter Witkin.

Immigrants are the first to be blamed when the economy is doing poorly and the last to be praised when the economy is doing well. They are the most convenient scapegoats when crime statistics are on the rise or when Scholastic Aptitude Test scores are counted. Their presence in neighborhoods is consistently blamed for decreasing property values, and they are disproportionately held responsible for the conditions in the nation's urban ghettoes. These perceptions persist despite the fact that the vast majority of immigrants in the United States enjoy a legal status and are less likely to commit crimes and abuse publically funded services than nonimmigrants (Suárez-Orozco, this volume). In a society that is supposedly run by a democratic process that can empower citizens and ensure popular control over political institutions, why has the social contract between the people and the government never fully materialized? Why have so many immigrants had little more than formal access to civil rights? Why are there so few posteducational opportunity structures for immigrants within advanced capitalism, especially for those who live in neighborhoods with hypersegregated, deep-poverty schools? Why has the Left in this country largely abandoned internationalist struggles against capitalism—especially at a time when capitalism has mutated into a more deadly form of pathogen in which simmers the germ of social disintegration on an apocalyptic scale—and reduced its political vision to a type of Jacuzzi socialism? These are the larger questions that must be addressed before we can fully appreciate the struggles in this country around immigrant rights, civil rights, bilingual education, affirmative action, educational reform, and the revival of democracy.

In a society that canonizes individualism, immigrants are seen as fundamentally "cliquish"; their supposed "wolf-pack mentality" renders them hopelessly unable to socialize with groups in the mainstream. They are only perceived as worthwhile to the extent that they can be made over to serve the interests of the Euro-American majority population. Hence, the continuing lumping together and criminalization of people of color (African Americans and Latinos especially) persists into the present day. Immigrants—especially those who are nonwhite—run the most risk of becoming "stranded populations" of the "ruined poor."

The larger backdrop against which any story dealing with immigration, public schooling, and students of color must be played out—and this is certainly the case in this present historical conjuncture—is the competition among national economies and nation-states, the rapid movement of capital across national boundaries, and diasporic movements of peoples across various national borders. In other words, any consideration of issues of immigration, multiculturalism, and schooling must take into account dramatic shifts within the history of capitalism, including the ferocious juggernaut of finance capitalism, careening across the contemporary horizon in reckless abandonment to the forces of the unfettered market and bringing with it a form of low-overhead "pushcart capitalism," the McDominization of the cultural landscape and WalMartization of the American Dream.

In the current historical interregnum—that deadening lull of sheer intensity between the modernist quest for certainty and the postmodern celebration of uncertainty—we face a seismic shift in global capitalist relations. Capital acceleration and the social transformation that has followed in its wake have had devastating consequences for the poor. The self-propelling character of contemporary goon-squad capitalism has been dramatically enhanced by neoliberal policies that have savaged those already vulnerable and powerless. It is in the context of the historical development of capitalism that one of the most urgent struggles over subjectivity takes place.

Capitalism—the "now sole proprietor of this world and those who inhabit it" (Forrester 1999, 125)—is so predatory today that it would not be beneath it even to market and sell the tears of the poor. Viviane Forrester writes,

> Whatever the history of barbarism over the centuries, human beings until now were always given a guarantee they were essential to the function of the planet as well as to productivity, and to the exploitation of the instruments of profit—of which they themselves were part. So many elements that protected them. For the first time, the mass of humanity is no longer materially necessary to the small number holding power, and for whom human lives outside their private circle have nothing to recommend them, even have no existence—it is more obvious every day—but as utilitarian assets. [1999, 126]

The ruling class and its weapons of power did not suddenly rise to preeminence, purloining wealth with impunity and appropriating all manner of riches in a swift, kleptomaniac maneuver. First, it had to establish a "globalized apathy" within multiple public spaces throughout the nation-state. Forrester describes capitalism's fatal strategy of manufacturing indifference on a global scale through the production of specific forms of civic inattention—a "peaceful blindness" in which inattention itself goes unmarked and the history of exploitation remains camouflaged as the present remains inexorably locked within a "fait accompli." So effective is this process that "political and economic landscapes have been able to metamorphose in full view of all, but unperceived by anyone, without attracting attention, still less arousing concern" (Forrester 1999, 36).

According to David McNally, "Having vanquished all challengers, having apparently tamed labor, anti-imperialist, and radical social movements, [capitalism] can now calmly go about the business of making us all rich" (1999, 134). Of course, sustaining the present system of capitalist exploitation is only possible when hegemony functions as a type of social amnesia. McNally writes,

> The current bout of millennial exuberance suggests a manic desire on the part of the triumphalists to forget the past (and present) of their own system. "Wherever there is a symptom there is also an amnesia," wrote Freud. And this psychoanalytic insight—which joins the Marxian insistence on the anti-historical character of bourgeois thought—seems especially appropriate at the moment. After all, at its core mainstream ideology seeks to deny the historicity of capitalism by pretending that "there has been history, but there is no longer any." Pro-capitalist ideology thus betrays a remarkable amnesia about capitalism itself: it forgets its bloody past, its recurrent crises; it denies everything that hints at the historically specific limits of the capitalist mode of production. [1999, 135]

What must, of course, be kept in mind in our discussions of immigration and multicultural education is that imperialism today (what we have euphemistically renamed as "globalization") is no longer a matter of direct colonial domination, as Ellen Meiksins Wood points out, "but a relation between national entities" (1999, 10). She underscores the presence of new forms of imperial domination that include debt and financial manipulation or foreign direct investment exercised by nation-states directly or through international agencies. Wood also argues that afoot today is a perniciously new type of militarism, one that does not put particular nation-states or geographical boundaries in its sights but, rather, seeks "boundless hegemony over the global economy" (1999, 10). She writes that, "instead of absorbing or annexing territory, this imperialist militarism typically uses massive displays of violence to assert the dominance of global capital—which really means exercising the military power of specific nation-states to assert the dominance of capital based in a few nation-states, or one in particular, the United States, enforcing its freedom to navigate the global economy without hindrance" (1999, 10). In the case of the United States, there exists no real community to discipline and to normalize—just groups flung about by the giddy winds of the market. Groups today are forced to discipline themselves to the dictates of the market, and in the unlikely event that foreign governments refuse to heed the directives of Western bureaucrats, then the North Atlantic Treaty Organization or other military forces can be called in to make the world safe for the capitalist market to move about unhindered and unimpeded.

Currently in the United States we are experiencing (1) the ascendancy of neoliberalism and an enormous shift in money and political power toward capital, as First World countries gain at the expense of Third World countries, and (2) a climate in which owners are prospering while workers' salaries are remaining stationary. Doug Henwood reports that unemployed people still "blame themselves or their résumés, not the systemic allocation of scarcity" (1999, 132). The greater the shift of political power to capital, the greater the growth in unemployment; and the more rampant the dismantling of social programs, the less likely U.S. society will be able to meet the basic needs of its most vulnerable victims of racism, sexism, and capitalist exploitation.

Neoliberalism—"capitalism with the gloves off"—not only supports profit making as the pinnacle of democracy but also encourages the savage annihilation of nonmarket forces. Its fundamental message is that there is no alternative to the capitalist present. Hiding behind the façade of formal electoral democracy— whereby market forces are ordained with the task of determining resource production and distribution, whereby businesses seize those available spaces that enable them to codify and consolidate their political power in all public and private arenas, whereby the cutting of federal regulatory programs is accompanied by a dramatic proliferation in the number of prisons and the continued institutionalization and legalization of government corruption and corporate crime (Winslow 1999, 260), and whereby "the population is diverted from the information, access, and public forums necessary for meaningful participation in decision making" (Winslow 1999, 9)—the defenders of neoliberalism struggle to increase the corporate domination of the whole of society under the mandate of "socialism for the rich" (Chomsky 1999, 39). Robert McChesney describes neoliberalism as "the immediate and foremost enemy of genuine participatory democracy, not just in the United States but across the planet, . . . for the foreseeable future" (1999, 11).

According to Burbach and Robinson (1999), immigration has been a story wreaked by contradictions, and this is no less true during the present period of extraordinary conflict and upheaval: when transnational capital enjoys an unprecedented structural power over popular classes worldwide. Objective disparities in socioeconomic conditions remain fundamental for understanding how immigrants and people of color in general are positioned within and throughout U.S. society.

The feral politics of blaming immigrants rarely acknowledges that those who are both creating and destroying the lives of vast populations of the poor and powerless are those who are leaving the country, not emigrating to it. I am referring to capital flight and those businesses that leave a country in order to relocate somewhere where it is easier to exploit workers and where the cost of labor and work is minimal. And few people appear to acknowledge that those who are emigrating to our shores are leaving countries whose natural resources have already been savaged by our own economic beast. Forrester writes,

> Public opinion is far more concerned (and vehemently so) with the presence of "foreigners"—that is to say, poor foreigners—who are assumed to be grabbing non-existent jobs, swindling native born workers out of them and scrounging social welfare. Down with immigrants coming in, good luck to capital going out! It is easier to take it out on the weak who are arriving, or are already there, or who even arrived long ago, than on the mighty who are deserting. Let's not forget that if these immigrants emigrate to more prosperous countries, these same countries, including ours, have gone to their countries, and still do; and not only because of low wages. But to exploit their raw materials and natural resources, when they have not already used them up. Not to give away or distribute wealth is one thing; but to swipe the goods and deprive those areas of their advantages, lay claim to them on the pretext of being better qualified to exploit them (to benefit other regions) is another. [1999, 93]

The market value of an immigrant's labor is increasingly becoming a central concern in the debates over multiculturalism. For instance, what good is pluralism if it remains trapped in the politics of capitalist one-dimensionality (Hirsch 1999)? These, and related issues, are provocatively unelaborated in most books dealing with multicultural issues. The model of multiculturalism typical of educational research is placed under pressure by questions such as these.

As a blonde-haired and blue-eyed anglophone immigrant from Canada, I do not have to face the daily violence endured by some of my *compañeros/compañeras* (comrades), whose parents and grandparents immigrated from south of *la línea* (the border) in Latin America. Although they were born in this country (whereas I emigrated in 1985 and became a U.S. citizen in 1998), they are nonetheless treated more like immigrants, like outsiders, like subalterns, than I am. And yet academic researchers—as well as public opinion makers—are now telling us that we are living at the "end of history" and entering a new interregnum in which systematic practices of oppression on the basis of race, class, and gender have been all but eliminated. Such a position turns into rubbish the history of the civil rights movement, not to mention continuing antiracist struggles. A judicious application of political makeup has transformed capitalist social relations of exploitation into a Hallmark card version of romantic innocence. What now concerns us as a public should give rise to national shame: the reportedly dire effects of decades of affirmative action on the life chances of white men. That we should now focus our attention on the putative oppression of the most privileged group in history tells us something about the current political climate of the United States. Clarence Lusane writes,

> Academic charlatans now argue that we have seen "the end of racism," that a color-blind society has magically appeared in the last ten years or so. These bogus and hypocritical arguments are then used to justify any kind of institutional racism (which is apparently okay as long as nobody uses any racial slurs). This reconstruction of the racial paradigm, far from resolving America's great dilemma, has in fact exacerbated

the nation's racial cleavage. It has also put identity politics on the defensive, because for the most part identity movements lack a political program beyond better treatment for their particular constituents. [1996, 2]

Today we are called on by our identity theorists in the metropolitan academy to rethink our multicultural society in ways that will break the stereotypes of the immigrant and "minority" student and build a more tolerant, inclusive social order. While this is a good thing as far as it goes, postmodern theorists who self-style hybridity as the prerogative of the Anglo border crosser leave the following question largely unanswered: Why can some groups cross certain borders more freely than others? If, in this postmodern cultural milieu, we need only to proclaim the hyphenated immanence of all identity, why do some immigrants end up heading multinational corporations and others end up in the sweatshops of East Los Angeles? And why do the majority of financially successful immigrants have European backgrounds and white skin? And why has hyperindividualism dipped in the elixir of consumer culture become the default politics of a society in dire need of collective struggle against conditions brought about by the social relations of production? These and related questions are brought to light and examined in *Immigrant Voices*.

As I have argued in *Revolutionary Multiculturalism* (McLaren 1997), despite the pronouncements of the postmodern Left that we are all "postethnic multiculturalists" or "hybrid subjects" now in this putative "postcolonial" society, it remains the case that the official history of the United States suppresses the fact that racialized minorities still exist as internally colonized political subjects contained by contemporary practices of institutionalized racism. The Euro-American Great Delusion—the celebration of the pastness of racial oppression—plummets U.S. society back into the deep well of the mythic past, into that primordial moment before contact with people of color, when "racial problems" did not exist. This condition constitutes, in my mind, the Grand Denial of Race and Racism in contemporary society. As Tim Libretti notes, "The nomenclature of postethnicity with its implicit panglossian optimism threatens to obscure the persistence and re-ritualization of racial oppression and internal colonization in the U.S. through asserting the postmodern idealism of a harmony achieved through hybridity and heterogeneity" (1999, 9). Libretti rightly notes that the current focus on hybridity or border crossing constitutes, on the one hand, a "rehearsal of useless, bankrupt, and unviable conceptions of race and ethnicity" and, on the other hand, offers a position that opposes the "melting pot" paradigm of generalizable and uniform assimilation (1999, 9). But is the notion of *mestizaje*, or hybridity, or border crossing all that much more effective? In the final instance, Libretti argues that the position in favor of hybridity and postethnicity is "merely an amnesic rehearsal of bankrupt rhetorical solutions to racial oppression and division throughout U.S. history" (1999, 9). He writes,

The postethnic position, favoring the postmodern fetish of hybridity, refigures the melting pot ideal by envisioning the effective disappearance, negation, or mooting of

racial and ethnic identities through radical racial and cultural mixtures, the dissolv-
ing of distinctions through cultural and even biological amalgamation. . . . In the theorized postethnic society, the charged significance of racial, ethnic, or cultural differences is effectively disarmed as we all become even within our own individuated
cultural selves defined by difference, multiplicity, heterogeneity, hybridity—the
whole arsenal of postmodernist lingo. The hybrid putatively makes ethnic or racial
identity meaningless because difference becomes the hallmark of a generalizable
"American" cultural identity. [1999, 9]

Does the new "border crossing" motif obviate the need for moving "beyond the
color line"? Libretti considers that the "postmodernist version of multiculturalism, summed up in the term 'hybridity,' paves the way for the postethnic society
through an inflationary valuation of racial, ethnic, or cultural differences that renders them worthless and insignificant except as decorative and immaterial badges
of identity" (1999, 12). As I have argued elsewhere (McLaren 1997), postmodern
multiculturalism dovetails with liberal pluralism insofar as it creates an architec-
tonic of difference in which difference is effectively deculturalized or drained of
meaningful cultural differences. In other words, postmodern multiculturalism pos-
tulates an optic of difference expunged of the type of difference that makes a difference. In all of our racialized and culturalized differences, we remain standardized by the logic of capital and the (white supremacist) values and ideals that
shape U.S. culture. Instead, what I believe is needed is a form of revolutionary
multiculturalism, in which alliances must be forged through concrete and mate-
rialist political and social struggles in order to develop transnationalist politics of
social justice and political transformation. I have suggested that such struggles—
those, for instance, of the Zapatistas in Chiapas—set the stage for a revolutionary
transnationalism in their fight for the material evenness of global society and
against privileging hierarchies of domination and oppression. We must avoid
what Libretti calls "a hurried idealist and abstract internationalism that glosses
over the unique historical and cultural conditions of specific populations" (1999,
17) and assert the necessity of the Third World national political subject. In other
words, some provisional notion of nationalism is indispensable for the eventual
realization of a transnational politics. At the present moment, we need to effectively counter the liberal pluralist fantasy of a world without borders because such
a world is always already shot through with the logic of white supremacist cap-
tialist patriarchy (McLaren 1997).

I have placed a poster by the renowned Chicana artist Yolanda Lopez in the
corridor directly outside of my office, so that I see it each time I enter and leave.
It is a black-and-white drawing of an Aztec warrior crumpling up in his left hand
some papers labeled "immigration plans" and pointing the index finger of an
extended right arm directly at the viewer as he angrily poses the question, "Who's
the illegal alien pilgrim?" The poster reminds me that the ancestors of my com-
pañeros/compañeras were not the ones who crossed the border into the United
States; rather, the border crossed them. In other words, colonialism invaded their

world, creating a violent upheaval in their geographical, political, cultural, spiritual, moral, and epistemological universe. There are multiple internal colonies within the United States proliferating today, held together by white epistemologies linked to the imperatives of capital accumulation. The poster is there to remind me and visitors to my office of the dangers of what Guillermo Gómez-Peña calls "the error of compassion fatigue where the dangerous implications of appropriation are no longer there and the critical multicultural text is no longer present, [where] people are more willing to engage in culturally insensitive behavior" (cited in Kun 1999, 196).

In truth, Mexicans were demonized by the United States decades before Mexican families began entering into the United States in large numbers after 1907–08, settling into *colonias* across the Southwest and Midwest. As Gilbert Gonzalez (1999) notes, after the American "Gilded Age" came to a close, a major economic invasion of Mexico by U.S. capital investments began (i.e., in mining and railroad operations), and accompanying praise for the open-door investment policy of President Porfirio Diaz was an imperial vision of Mexicans (those who did not belong to the *hacendado* class) that consisted of an unending litany of pathologies. Mexicans were demonically constructed as the exemplification of the worst traits of both "the Indian and the European": the unwashed, uncivilized, and compulsively hypersexualized "Other." To this day, the United States does not envision equality between colonizer and colonized but, rather, continually positions itself as the ethical steward and cultural redeemer of the global subaltern. The juggernaut of Americanization, made possible by capital investment, is still seen today as a way of promoting the "civilizing mission" of the United States, putting down *pronunciamentos*, and ensuring via a politics whereby the United States plays the role of the global "alpha male" the reproduction of existing social relations of domination and subordination and the recapitulation of unequal and exploitative economic relations (Gonzalez 1999; McLaren 1997).

Because transnational globalization is marked by a growing social division at the national level and expanding diasporic movements across international borders, the editors of this volume are keenly aware that the study of immigrants and immigration must place at the forefront of analysis a recognition of the centrifugal hierarchies generated and sustained by global capitalism and its freshly minted imperial corps and reproduced by the ideological apparatuses of the state. Many theories of multicultural education lack explanatory efficacy and relevance precisely because they avoid dealing specifically with issues of immigration and the immigrant experience. Many of the essays contained in this important volume have distilled out issues urgently pertaining to our understanding of the relationship among race, ethnicity, class, immigration, and schooling.

The study of immigrants within mainstream educational discourse has been mired in what Gómez-Peña calls the "Northern multicultural model," a "Danteian model" that takes one from the center to the margins and back again. According to Gómez-Peña, "You leave the self-proclaimed center, and from the center you either descend to the seven rings of hell or you go to the margins. And in the process of 'descending' or going towards the margins, you find enlightenment. Then you come back to the center and speak about it. Or you 'discover' an exciting type of otherness, which later on you will sponsor, emulate, or be a ventriloquist of" (cited in Kun 1999, 197). As he further notes, this model is about the "other" performing for the mainstream—"about the much touted 'other' explaining itself to the mainstream in hopes of being 'discovered,' accepted, and eventually included" (cited in Kun 1999, 198). By contrast, the Latin American model of multiculturalism advocated by Gómez-Peña is about taking power away from those who have it and then occupying the center. It is about moving away from the margins to "occupy in the center, de-centering it" (cited in Kun 1999, 198). The Latin American model described by Gómez-Peña is similar to the model that I have called "revolutionary multiculturalism" (see McLaren 1997). It includes, but also exceeds, the task of trying to add more "ethnicities" to the center and, further, concentrates on interrogating the center for its allegiance to white supremacy, to global capitalist social relations of exploitation, and to imperial tropes and conceits.

Immigrant Voices: In Search of Educational Equity is a pathbreaking book that moves outside of the Northern multicultural model, advocating instead a critique of power relations and social practices that continue to racialize and ethnicize groups according to the imperatives of the hegemonic center. What is important to remember is that the global restructuring of capital is collapsing the distinctions north–south, core–periphery, and First World–Third World, for these distinctions, once held to be mainly geographic, are now becoming more social class oriented in character as the global economy creates new asymmetries of power and privilege that cut across nations and regions (Burbach and Robinson 1999). According to Burbach and Robinson,

> The trend is one in which there is ever growing poverty and marginalization in the First World, while the Third World has a large number of *nouveau riche* who are able to buy and sell in the global economy, creating vast fortunes that match or rival many in the First World. And in global capitalism's newest playground, the former Second World, it is obvious to all that the end of socialism has brought dramatic increases in poverty along with the creation of a new rich and ostentatious upper class. [1999, 28]

The United States has experienced a growing polarization and marked decrease in the influence of working-class constituencies. Trade unions have been in decline, and to a large extent the United States is in the process of being "Third Worldized" because of increasing marginalization, a downward leveling of the economy, and a cheapening and casualization of the workforce because of the globalization of capitalism (Burbach and Robinson 1999). Of course, it is in the interest of the capitalist class to reproduce this marginalization and the continued exploitation of the workforce.

According to the Federal Reserve's most recent survey of household finances, whites, African Americans, and Asians have all gained ground from the recent economic expansion in the United States, whereas Latinos have seen their household net worth fall by 24 percent (Walsh 2000). The median net worth of Latino households was $12,170 in 1995 but only $9,200 in 1998. Yet the average Latino household income had risen from $61,000 in 1995 to $86,000 in 1998. It is the accumulation of wealth by the richest Latino families that is pulling up the overall average. This pattern is consistent with the growing disparity in income between the working class and the capitalist class throughout the United States and the entire world. In the same period that Latino wealth was falling, the median Latino household income rose by almost 16 percent (Walsh 2000). In the face of this evidence of harsh economic realities suffered by Latino populations, when we learn that Latino students are twice as likely as African Americans and three times as likely as whites to drop out of high school, or that, in 1997, 25.3 percent of Latinos aged sixteen to twenty-four dropped out of high school compared with 13.4 percent of African Americans and 7.6 percent of whites (McQueen 2000), should we be surprised? Factors associated with the globalization of capital, such as the current bureaucratic-authoritarian restructuring under neoliberalism as well as the expansion of finance and industrial capital, have greatly enabled the widening of the already vast chasm between the rich and the poor. The internationalization of capital, allowing for the concentration and centralization of capital and production, has had dire consequences for the Latino working class.

The labor unions have a great challenge ahead of them in organizing the new U.S. immigrant labor force. While some small ethnic firms that are not union friendly have provided significant obstacles, the major barrier has been a racist immigration policy. Robin D. G. Kelley writes,

> Organizing the new immigrant labor force is perhaps the fundamental challenge facing the labor movement. For one, a substantial proportion of immigrant workers is employed by small ethnic firms with little tolerance for labor unions. Besides obvious language and cultural barriers, union leaders are trying to tackle the Herculean task of organizing thousands of tiny, independent, sometimes transient firms. Immigrants are also less represented in public sector jobs, which tend to have a much higher percentage of unionized employees. (Indeed, the heavy concentration of native-born black people in public sector jobs partly explains why African Americans have such a high unionization rate.) The most obvious barrier to organizing immigrant workers, however, has been discriminatory immigration policy. Even before Proposition 187 got on the ballot, the 1986 Immigration Reform and Control Act imposed legal sanctions against employers of "aliens" without proper documents. Thus, even when unions were willing to organize undocumented workers, fear of deportation kept many workers from joining the labor movement. [1997, 128]

Unions are not always innocent, however. Union leaders especially have to share some of the blame for the sorry state of labor organizing among immigrant workers, much of it the result of stereotyping immigrant workers. Kelley further notes that until recently, union leaders too often assumed that Latino and Asian workers were unorganizable or difficult to organize—arguments that have been made about women and African American workers in the past. [T]he American labor movement has a long and tragic history of xenophobia, racism, and anti-immigrant sentiment. Therefore, even when union organizers were willing to approach undocumented workers, they often operated on the assumption that immigrants were easily manipulated by employers, willing to undercut prevailing wages, or were "target workers" whose goal was to make enough money to return to their place of origin. [1997, 128–29]

One example of a powerful and important social movement that is helping to revitalize the labor movement through gaining the recognition of unions and fighting for a workforce made up of primarily Latino/ Latina immigrants, has been Justice for Janitors. Justice for Janitors has successfully undertaken community-based organizing and civil disobedience in cities throughout the country not only as a means of increasing unionized custodial employees but as a broad-based civil rights strategy to fight social injustice for all exploited workers.

The authors in *Immigrant Voices* are aware that immigrants and students of color in general are not the products of postmaterial society but, rather, are implicated in a transnational ideology of accumulation in which immigrants and subaltern groups are transformed into racialized and ethnicized collectivities of human capital in a climate in which racism and Latinophobia have become dangerously commonplace. The term *racialization* frames group origin in natural terms and defines "race" by means of a polarity between dominant and subordinate groups, whereas *ethnicization* frames group origin in cultural terms and gives order and shape to difference in such a way as to link it to the idea of class mobility (Urciuoli 1996). The baseline or standard marker for the practices of both racialization and ethnicization is the normative or generic white, middle-class, English-speaking heterosexual male. The entire process of "marking" race and ethnicity in this way constitutes a "cultural default setting" in U.S. society (Urciuoli 1996, 16). Racializing discourses are dangerous markers and equate language difference with disorder. Racialized groups are often perceived as unindividuated collectivities that hold fundamental differences from whites in values, habits, language, character, and aspirations. Ethnicized discourses, on the other hand, mediate the polarities between the middle-class Anglo and the nonwhite, poor, and culturally/linguistically "deficient" (Urciuoli 1996). The term *ethnicity* locates a group's origin as "pedigreed by an external high culture that validates their difference because it somehow makes them act like Americans in crucial ways" (Urciuoli 1996, 16). Urciuoli notes correctly that race and class are conflated in Western culture such that an imbalance is usually implied with somebody "higher" and somebody "lower." Class is measured by what individuals are or have, is linked to possessive individualism, and is focused on types of persons rather than on social conditions or one's relationship to the means of production. Consequently, African Americans, Latinos, or Puerto Ricans are constructed as metonyms for the "subaltern" class or "underclass" and are morally marked in such a way that dropping out of school, becoming teenaged mothers, taking drugs, and so on become habitually associated with people of color. *White* has become metonymous with *American*. As a result, people of color are often relegated to the status of a "subculture." Alicia Gaspar de Alba proposes that we rethink cultures that are racially and ethnically different from the dominant one as "altercultures" (which issues from the Latin word for "other") rather than "subcultures," a term that is linked to an ethnocentric ideology and reinforces the connection between people of color and inferiority (1998, 16). The authors in *Immigrant Voices* are especially perceptive about and attentive to those "altercultural" voices in U.S. society rendered the most mute and deprived of historical force as a result of the deracinating and imperializing imperatives of Western identity politics.

In a culture prone to racialization and ethnicization around an unmarked center of the white social universe, what is needed is a type of citizenship that speaks to the issue of multicultural, anticapitalist, and antiracist solidarity, an unvarnished version of citizenship that does not arch toward a common culture but, rather, establishes a common ground of struggle. Kobena Mercer is worth quoting on this issue: "In my view solidarity does not mean that everyone thinks in the same way, it begins when people have the confidence to disagree over issues of fundamental importance precisely because they 'care' about constructing pluralized and diversified forms of contemporary democracy that the issue of alliances needs to be rethought through an expanded and modernized concept of citizenship" (1990, 68).

What is important here is to understand that while objectively shared experiences are important, the creation of a revolutionary citizenship or internationalist collectivity does not stipulate a shared identity politics so much as a shared vision of the future. Such a vision of the future must be both local and international in scope. Comments by Joachim Hirsch are apposite here:

> If a new class of politics is to emerge under these social conditions it will develop on the basis, not so much of objectively given experiences, but rather, of a politically constructed vision and project. What is necessary, first and foremost, is a search for visions of a better world in which the bonds of dependency, instrumentalism, and extra-human modes of coordination may be broken. Traditional models of social democracy offer no answer to this problem. It is no longer merely a question of material prosperity and distribution, but also one of freedom and human dignity. A new "International" must therefore take the form of a radical movement for democracy and human rights. [1999, 289]

We need to smuggle into educational practice a pedagogy of trangression that defies the injunction to remain passive in a sea of misery where even "the molested masses are no longer necessary to the purposes of their tormentors" (Forrester 1999, 127), a contraband pedagogy that speaks to a politics of solidarity without sameness. Contraband educators do not operate so much as social agents that speak truth to power as much as they engage in speaking truth to the powerless so that the powerless themselves can create the conditions from the standpoint of those most exploited (Harstock 1983). Speaking truth to the powerless—through revolutionary praxis—means challenging power collectively, around a unified anticapitalist project of class struggle. We need a politics of identity and difference, not an identity politics; a community of dissent, not a common culture; a praxis of transformation, not the practice of reform; a struggle against capital itself and not just capitalism. We need to revolutionize pedagogy, but we also need to make the revolution pedagogical. We need to do more than substitute one type of hegemonic power for another—we need to reinvent power.

Immigrant Voices constitutes an urgent educational project that is long overdue. It raises important issues and courageously advances dangerous questions that will enlarge and deepen the struggle for liberation and human dignity.

REFERENCES

Burbach, Roger, and William Robinson. 1999. "The Fin de Siècle Debate: Globalization as Epochal Shift." *Science & Society* 63, no. 1 (spring): 10–39.

Chomsky, Noam. 1999. *Profit over People: Neoliberalism and Global Order*. New York: Seven Stories.

Forrester, Viviane. 1999. *The Economic Horror*. Cambridge: Polity.

Gaspar de Alba, Alicia. 1998. *Chicano Art: Inside/Outside the Mater's House*. Austin: University of Texas Press.

Gonzalez, Gilbert G. 1999. "American Writers and the Ideology of Empire: The U.S. and Mexico, 1880–1930." Working Papers Series in Cultural Studies, Ethnicity, and Race Relations, Department of Comparative American Cultures, no. 9, 1–24. Pullman: Washington State University.

Harstock, Nancy. 1983. *Money, Sex and Power: Toward a Feminist Historical Materialism*. Boston: Northeastern University Press.

Henwood, Doug. 1999. "Booming, Borrowing, and Consuming: The U.S. Economy in 1999." *Monthly Review* 51, no. 3 (July–August): 120–33.

Hirsch, Joachim. 1999. Globalization, Class and the Question of Democracy. In *Socialist Register 1999*, ed. Leo Panitch and Colin Leys, 278–93. New York: Monthly Review.

Kelley, Robin D. G. 1997. *Yo' Mama's Disfunktional! Fighting the Culture Wars in Urban America*. Boston: Beacon.

Kun, Josh. 1999. "Multiculturalism without People of Color: An Interview with Guillermo Gómez-Peña." *Aztlan: A Journal of Chicano Studies* 24, no. 1 (spring): 187–99.

Libretti, Tim. 1999. "Leaping over the Color Line: Postethnic Ideology and the Evasion of Racial Oppression." Working Papers Series in Cultural Studies, Ethnicity, and Race Relations, Department of Comparative American Cultures, no. 5, 1–20. Pullman: Washington State University.

Lusane, Clarence. 1996. Foreword. In *Emerging Social Justice Movements in Communities of Color*, ed. John Anner, 1–4. Boston: South End.

McChesney, Robert. 1999. Introduction. In *Profit over People: Neoliberalism and Global Order*, Noam Chomsky, 7–16. New York: Seven Stories.

McLaren, Peter. 1997. *Revolutionary Multiculturalism*. Boulder: Westview.

McNally, David. 1999. "The Present as History: Thoughts on Capitalism at the Millennium." *Monthly Review* 51, no. 3 (July–August): 135–45.

McQueen, Anjetta. 2000. "Dropout Rate of Latino Students Rises," *Daily Bruin News*, 16 March, 8, 14.

Urciuoli, Bonnie. 1996. *Exposing Prejudice: Puerto Rican Experiences of Language, Race, and Class*. Boulder: Westview.

Walsh, Mary Williams. 2000. "Hispanics Missing Economic Boom," *Fresno Bee*, 25 March, 1, 16.

Winslow, George. 1999. *Capital Crimes*. New York: Monthly Review.

Wood, Ellen Meiksins. 1999. "Unhappy Families: Global Capitalism in a World of Nation-States." *Monthly Review* 51, no. 3 (July–August): 1–12.

1

Some Conceptual Considerations in the Interdisciplinary Study of Immigrant Children

Marcelo Suárez-Orozco and Carola Suárez-Orozco

Immigration has emerged as an important topic of global concern at the end of the millennium. Since 1965 the United States has formally admitted over 20 million new immigrants. The vast majority of new immigrants to the United States are non-English-speaking people of color coming from the Afro-Caribbean basin, Asia, and Latin America. New research suggests that there are between 2 and 4 million "undocumented" immigrants living in the United States; an estimated 200,000 to 400,000 undocumented immigrants enter the United States every year (National Research Council 1997). This post-1965 wave of immigration is the driving force behind a significant transformation that will have profound implications for the remaking of U.S. democracy, society, and economy (M. Suárez-Orozco 1998).

Immigrant children make up the fastest growing sector of the U.S. child population (Landale and Oropesa 1995). Roughly one in six children in the United States today lives in an immigrant-headed household. Immigrant children are now present in substantial numbers in school districts throughout the country. In California, they now make up approximately 20 percent of the California school population. While California leads the nation in terms of numbers of immigrant students, no area of the country is unaffected by immigration. Today, in New York City public schools 48 percent of all children come from immigrant households speaking over one hundred different languages. Even if immigration tends to be highly concentrated in a handful of states (such as California, New York, Florida, Texas, and Illinois), immigrant youth are found in all areas of the nation and in diverse school systems. Forty-two percent of all schoolchildren enrolled in Dodge City, Kansas, come from immigrant backgrounds. Indeed, we are not in Kansas anymore.

Chapter 1

THEORETICAL CONSIDERATIONS IN THE
STUDY OF THE NEW IMMIGRATION

In recent years the study of immigration has been dominated by labor economists, sociologists, demographers, and—to a lesser extent—cultural anthropologists. While some topics, such as the economic causes and consequences of immigration, have generated a great deal of work, other areas remain virtual terra incognita. The effect of immigration on children is one such neglected area. Although in recent years there have been a few excellent studies of immigration and children, many areas of the problem remain underexplored and undertheorized.

In the area of theory building, important work remains to be done. The foundational theoretical work on immigration to the United States has been largely based on the experiences of European immigrants entering the country in the earlier decades of this century (Portes 1997). Much of this work came to privilege concepts such as "assimilation" and "acculturation" (see Alba and Nee 1997; Gordon 1964; Park and Burgess 1969). Assimilation, for example, was said to proceed along various paths on what was depicted as a generally upwardly mobile journey. As Robert Bellah once noted, "The United States was planned for progress" (quoted in Williamson 1996, 175), and each wave of immigrants was said to recapitulate the national destiny. The argument was elegant in its simplicity: the longer immigrants were in the United States, the more Americanized they became, the better they would do in terms of schooling, health, and income.

In recent years a number of distinguished social theorists have observed that the conceptual apparatus based on an earlier era of immigration may no longer be adequate to address the experiences of new immigrants. Some have argued that immigration is now structured by powerful but little understood forms of transnationalism, requiring new categories of understanding and conceptual approaches (see Basch et al. 1995; Levitt 1998). A number of prominent sociologists, including Gans (1992), Portes and Zhou (1993), Rumbaut (1996), and Waters (1996), have further argued that a new hourglass "segmentation" in U.S. economy and society has been shaping new patterns of immigrant insertion into American life.

This new research suggests what might be broadly termed a "trimodal" pattern of adaptation. Some immigrants today are achieving extraordinary patterns of upward mobility—quickly moving into the well-remunerated knowledge-intensive sectors of the economy in ways never seen before in the history of U.S. immigration. On the opposite side of the hourglass economy, large numbers of low-skilled immigrants of color find themselves in increasingly segregated sectors of the economy and society—locked into low-skill service jobs without much promise of status mobility (Portes and Zhou 1993). In between these two patterns are yet other immigrant groups that approximate the norms of the majority population—"disappearing" into U.S. institutions and culture without much notice.

This trimodal socioeconomic pattern seems to have an isomorphic relation to how the children of today's immigrants tend to do in school. In the last few years there have been a number of studies on the performance of immigrant children in schools. The data suggest a complex picture. Some immigrant children seem to do quite well in schools, surpassing native-born children in terms of grades, performance on standardized tests, and attitudes toward education (Kao and Tienda 1995). Other immigrants tend to overlap with native-born children (see Rumbaut 1995, 22–27; Waters 1996). Yet others tend to achieve below their native-born peers (Kao and Tienda 1995; Portes and Hao 1998; Rumbaut 1995).

In general, studies examining patterns that lead to school success tend to emphasize "the ideologies of opportunity" and "cultures of optimism" that motivate immigrant parents to migrate (Gibson 1988; Kao and Tienda 1995; Suárez-Orozco 1989; Tuan 1995). Some scholars have argued that successful adaptations among immigrants may relate to the patterns of cultural, economic, and social capital immigrants are able to deploy in the new land. Other scholars more specifically single out immigrant "cultural values" said to promote educational success (Sue and Okazaki 1990). Yet others suggest that some immigrant families succeed by developing culturally specific strategies that inoculate their children against the hostilities and negative attitudes they encounter in the new culture (De Vos 1992). Other studies note that successful immigrant parents are able to maintain social control by orienting the children away from various negative interpersonal and cultural aspects of the host culture (Zhou and Bankston 1998). This line of work suggests that immigrant parents who are able to maintain their own cultural patterns of social sanctioning and who actively resist a whole array of dystopian cultural practices and beliefs in the host country—specifically attitudes toward authority, discipline, homework, peer relations, and dating—tend to have children who are more successful in schools.

A number of studies have concentrated on school failure among the children of immigrants. Scholars working in the area of immigrant school underachievement have explored a variety of relevant factors. Some scholars have examined the structural barriers to advancement facing many immigrants of color today (Orfield 1998). Others have emphasized the sociocultural and linguistic practices involved in the schooling of children in poor and highly segregated inner-city schools—the schools at which many newly arrived immigrants, especially those from Afro-Caribbean and Latin American regions, tend to enroll (Trueba 1998).

A PARADOX IN SEARCH OF EXPLANATION

The issue of variability in school adaptations and outcomes among ethnic and immigrant groups has received some attention in the scholarly literature (Gibson and Ogbu 1991; Jacob and Jordan 1993; Ogbu and Simons 1998). Yet some recent data suggest an unsettling pattern in search of further robust empirical and theoretical treatment: among many immigrant groups today, length of residence in the United States seems associated with *declining* health, school achievement, and aspirations (see Kao and Tienda 1995; Rumbaut 1995; Steinberg 1996; Suárez-Orozco and Suárez-Orozco 1995; Vernez, Abrahamse, and Quigley 1996). A recent large-scale National Research Council (NRC) study considers a variety of measures of physical health and risk behaviors among children and adolescents from immigrant families—including general health, learning disabilities, obesity, emotional difficulties, and risk behaviors, among others. The NRC researchers found that immigrant youth were healthier than their counterparts from nonimmigrant families. The researchers point out that these findings are "counterintuitive" in light of the racial or ethnic minority status, overall lower socioeconomic status, and higher poverty rates that characterize many of the immigrant children and families that they studied. They also found that the longer youth were in the United States, the poorer was their overall physical and psychological health. Furthermore, the more "Americanized" they became, the more likely they were to engage in risky behaviors such as substance abuse, violence, and delinquency (Hernandez and Charney 1998).

Rubén Rumbaut working with Alejandro Portes found a similar pattern in a survey of over 15,000 seniors, juniors, and sophomores in San Diego, California, and Dade County, Florida. He reports a

> negative association of length of residence in the United States with both GPA [grade point average] and aspirations. Time in the United States is, as expected, strongly predictive of improved English reading skills; but despite that seeming advantage, longer residence in the United States and second-generation status (that is, being born in the United States) are connected to declining academic achievement and aspirations. [1995, 46–48]

In a different voice, the Reverend Virgil Elizondo, rector of the San Fernando Cathedral in San Antonio, articulates the same point: "I can tell by looking in their eyes how long they've been here. They come sparkling with hope, and the first generation finds hope rewarded. Their children's eyes no longer sparkle" (quoted in Suro 1998, 13). While the work of Portes and Rumbaut (see Rumbaut 1995), Steinberg (1996, 97–98), Kao and Tienda (1995), and others independently report similar findings, more sophisticated longitudinal data are needed to explore this important issue. While many immigrant children do brilliantly in schools, others over time seem to display more dystopian adaptations.

CONCEPTUAL THEMES IN THE STUDY OF IMMIGRANT CHILDREN

In order to examine the multiple paths immigrant children are able to make for themselves in their new country, we devised an interdisciplinary, longitudinal, and comparative study of the adaptations of immigrant children in U.S. schools. The Longitudinal Immigrant Adaptation Study (LISA) (inaugurated in 1997 at Harvard University, with generous funding from the National Science Foundation, W. T. Grant Foundation, and Spencer Foundation) is an experience-near psychosocial study of the factors involved in shaping the changing lives of immigrant children. Our sample consists of 400 youth from Central American (including El Salvador, Guatemala, Honduras, and Nicaragua), China (originating in Hong Kong, mainland China, and Taiwan), the Dominican Republic, Haiti, and Mexico. The study is structured around an interdisciplinary psychosocial methodology that deploys a number of research tools borrowed from cultural anthropology and cultural psychology (see Suárez-Orozco and Suárez-Orozco 1995).

Any systematic study of immigrant children that is nonreductionistic must contend with the problems inherent in multilevel psychosocial analyses (De Vos and Suárez-Orozco 1990). Yet multilevel, interdisciplinary strategies are needed because single-factor studies seem doomed to reduce extremely complex processes to disciplinary clichés. Reducing the experiences of immigrant children to the class backgrounds of their parents is a good example. A class-based argument fails to address some critical questions such as why some children from poor immigrant groups do much better than others (see Zhou and Bankston 1998). Such an approach also fails to explain why, when class differences are held constant, immigrant children constantly do better in schools than their nonimmigrant peers.

Our current research is guided by a multilevel conceptual framework that takes into consideration both "incoming resources" and a variety of "host culture variables" (see figure 1). The variables outlined in our conceptual framework—in various ways and with various force—are the major vectors that structure the schooling experiences and outcomes of immigrant youth. These factors help mold the emerging attitudes, identities, and behaviors of immigrant students. They are codeterminants of the youth's evolving cultural models and social practices regarding schooling.

Under "incoming resources" we include the usual predictors of schooling outcomes such as socioeconomic status, parental literacy, and education. Previous physical and psychological health, as well as previous schooling experiences and English proficiency, are also relevant to an immigrant's subsequent adaptation. A very powerful variable mediating school outcomes—a factor that, incredibly, is nearly always neglected in the literature—is the child's immigrant legal status.

Under "host culture variables" we include a series of factors known to be relevant to the schooling strategies of youth. What are the occupational opportunities available to immigrants in their local settings? What structural barriers do immigrants encounter? Are they penetrating the knowledge-intensive sectors of the economy? Are they recruited by co-ethnics into an ethnic enclave? Are they finding work in the low-skill service sector? Are they finding work in the underground economy? How does the changing relationship between schooling outcomes and the economic opportunity structure affect the cultural models and social practices deployed by immigrant families and communities?

Recently, Dowell Myers (1998) found a worrisome trend: while Mexican immigrant youth have in recent years made impressive gains in their educational adap-

Figure 1.1 Conceptual Framework

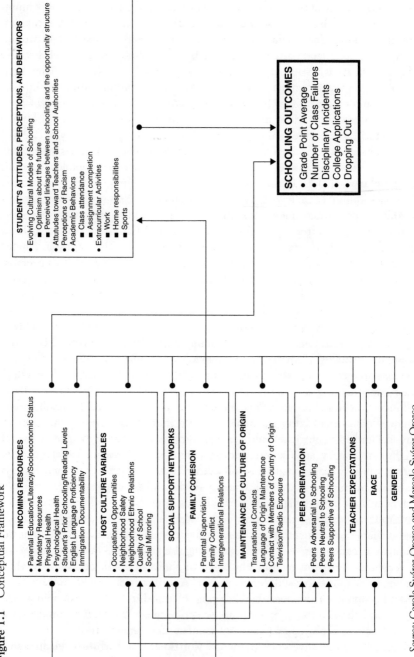

Source: Carola Suárez-Orozco and Marcelo Suárez Orozco.

tations, they are facing a pattern of declining returns to education in terms of the wages they are able to command in the posteducational opportunity structure. John Ogbu and his colleagues have argued that when there is a decoupling between efforts and outcomes in schools and the reward system in the opportunity structure, sooner or later, many children give up on schools as the principal route for status mobility (Ogbu and Simons 1998).

While the dialectic between schooling and the opportunity structure is highly relevant, other host culture variables must not be overlooked. Among many immigrants today neighborhood safety is an important concern. For many children the fear of violence is ever present.

A number of children participating in the LISA project told us of the violence they had witnessed in their neighborhoods since they had migrated—including several murders. As one twelve-year-old Mexican girl told us, "If you go out in the United States, you are always afraid of everything." A thirteen-year-old Chinese girl told us, "I have seen gang activities near my house. . . . I am afraid to go out— I don't feel safe." For poor immigrants from Latin America, the statistical likelihood of enrolling in hypersegregated, deep-poverty schools is astonishingly high (Orfield 1998; Trueba 1998). The stresses associated with immigration (see Aronowitz 1984; Padilla et. al 1988; Rumbaut 1977; Shuval 1980; C. Suárez-Orozco 1998), especially when compounded by violence and poverty, make for less than optimal schooling experiences for many children today.

Social support networks can play a critical role in mediating the stresses of immigration (Cobb 1976; Willis 1985). Such networks—which might include extended family and fictive kin, as well as cultural associations—can facilitate how immigrants navigate their new environments. They can make available resources (ranging from emergency loans to free baby-sitting), critical cultural information (for example, about corporal punishment in the new land or what courses are needed in high school to attend the better colleges), and job contacts. The emotional support generated by such social networks is equally important, particularly during the earliest phases of immigration when immigrants face the emotional losses and cultural disorientation that always accompany immigration (see Ainslie 1998; Garcia-Coll and Manuson 1997; C. Suárez-Orozco 1998).

Immigration is a process that deeply transforms the family system (Shuval 1980; Sluzki 1979). In our conceptual model, "family cohesion" refers to the interpersonal atmosphere or "ethos" in the immigrant family. We include patterns of intergenerational relations—particularly important in multigenerational immigrant families—parental supervision, and family conflict. As immigrant youth begin to attempt to navigate the complex, often contradictory waters of "home" and "host" culture, socially constructed hierarchies of authority are often disrupted. The paternal voice may be silenced. Gender scripts often need to be rewritten. Family conflicts often result as immigrants deal with the stresses of uprooting and resettling in the new land.

A number of scholars have argued that new transnational impulses are structuring the journeys of new immigrants in ways that are decidedly different from the experiences of earlier waves of immigrants from Europe and Asia (see M. Suárez-Orozco 1998). New technologies of communication—including computers, discount telephone cards, and faxes—and easier and more affordable systems of mass transportation, along with new social practices and cultural models celebrating ethnic and cultural difference, seem to subvert the sharp break with the country of origin that was said to characterize earlier waves of European immigration to the United States (Ainslie 1998). Many immigrants today are apt to remain players both "here" and "there," circuiting back and forth between the country of their birth and the country of their choice (Portes 1998).

To date there is no systematic research on how these new transnational practices affect the experiences of immigrant children. In our conceptual model, "maintenance of culture of origin" refers broadly to the nature and intensity of these transnational activities. How is schooling negotiated among youth engaged in intense transnationality—such as new immigrants from the Dominican Republic? How much contact is there with co-ethnics, versus members of other ethnic minorities, versus members of the dominant culture? Are immigrant youth maintaining the language of origin, or are they rapidly shifting into English only (Portes and Hao 1998; Wong-Fillmore 1991)? What structures are there in the child's social milieu to support linguistic practices in the first language?

The peer group has been generally neglected in the social science research on immigrant and ethnic minority children (De Vos 1992, 233–65). Yet in many cases it is the peer group, not the adult group, that is "in charge" in the lives of youth. When immigrant parents are not available to their children—because they face intense work schedules and other stresses—the peer group can become critical. For many youth, the peer group not only is the primary point of reference for values and tastes; it also provides social and emotional support, economic resources, and safety. Peer group orientation can be critical in the schooling strategies deployed by immigrant youth. Is the peer group supportive of school? Can a young person turn to her or his peers for help with homework? Can he or she turn to them for advice on what school to chose or what courses to take? Or, conversely, is the peer group in an adversarial relation to school? Are good students sanctioned for doing well in school? Is doing well in school constructed as "acting white"? Because of the emotional relevance of the peer group, the interpersonal tone set by peers is an important variable in the adaptation of immigrant children.

Teacher expectations, likewise, are quite relevant because of the important "social mirroring" functions that teachers perform (see below). Do teachers expect less or more from their immigrant students than from their nonimmigrant students? Do teachers have the same expectations of all immigrant students, or are there group-specific expectations? Do they expect that their immigrant students will go on to college? drop out of school? get into gangs? Do some immigrant children benefit from a "halo effect"? Or, conversely, are some immigrant children "brought down" because of negative teacher expectations toward their own immigrant groups?

Although teacher expectations have been singled out as important (see Rosenthal and Jacobson 1968), the more general prevailing attitudes of members of the host society toward immigrants are also highly relevant to the experiences of immigrant children. How public opinion and general attitudes toward immigration affect the children of immigrants has been neglected in the scholarly literature. Yet we know that in recent years attitudes toward immigration have become increasingly charged.

Public opinion data suggest that there has been widespread concern about the large influx of new immigrants (Espanshade and Belanger 1998). In their sophisticated study of national public opinion polls, Princeton scholars Espanshade and Belanger found that many perceive that immigrants (1) have a negative economic impact, (2) drain the social service system, and (3) contribute to crime with little prospect of assimilation into the mainstream. Though not founded on empirical evidence—the vast majority of immigrants in the United States are here legally, are less likely to commit crimes, and are less likely to abuse publicly funded services than nonimmigrants (Suárez-Orozco and Suárez-Orozco 1995)—these prevailing beliefs and sentiments have surely contributed to several dramatic anti-immigrant initiatives.

Historically there has been a very strong correlation between anti-immigrant sentiment and economic anxiety, particularly around unemployment rates. Espanshade and Belanger (1998) also found that fear of the cultural dilution of the country's Anglo-Saxon institutions and values is an enduring concern. Citizens today tend to feel more positive about immigrants from Europe than they do about immigrants from Latin America and the Caribbean. Immigrants who do not speak English and who "look" different from the dominant Anglo-European make many nonimmigrants uncomfortable.

Adults are not the only members of U.S. society who share negative attitudes toward immigrants. Nonimmigrant, nonminority students in a public high school in Northern California had the following thoughts to share with educational researcher Laurie Olsen: "They [immigrants] come to take our jobs, and are willing to break their backs for shit pay, and we can't compete"; another said, "These Chinese kids come over here and all they do is work and work and work. . . . No one can compete any more"; still another summed up a prevailing fear, "They just want to take over " (1998, 68).

In recent years, this anti-immigrant climate has resulted in a range of policies aimed at excluding immigrants (especially undocumented immigrants) from accessing a variety of publicly funded services. Immigration controls have moved slowly over the years from the border to the classroom (Proposition 187), the hospital (see Brown et. al 1998), and the welfare agency (see Hagan 1998).

In times of economic uncertainty, anti-immigrant sentiments and policies are prevalent and are often voiced with little sense of concern for either political fallout or the feelings of the targets. Anti-immigrant xenophobia appears to endure as the "last frontier" to openly vent racial and ethnic hostilities with little risk of sanctioning. While overt and blatant racism is today largely confined to the fringes of society, anti-immigrant sentiments seem to be more freely indulged in in public opinion, policy debates, and other social forums.

SOCIAL MIRRORING

The structural exclusion suffered by immigrants—whether documented or undocumented—is detrimental to their ability to participate in the opportunity structure of their new society. Furthermore, we argue that hostile attitudes and social exclusion also play a toxic role in the psychosocial lives of immigrant children. How does a child incorporate the notion that he or she is "an alien," an "illegal," unwanted, and not deserving of the most basic rights such as education and health care? Even if the immigrants are not undocumented, the hostility prevalent in the current climate radiates to all children with accents and darker complexions. How do these charged attitudes affect the developing identities of the children of immigrants? A first point to consider is whether or not immigrant youth are aware of these hostilities.

As part of the data collection for the LISA project, we asked our informants what was the hardest thing about immigration. The following statements are representative of the kinds of responses we received. A twelve-year-old Central American girl said, "One of the most difficult things about immigrating is that people make fun of me here. People from the United States think that they are superior to you." A thirteen-year-old Chinese girl told us, "[Americans] discriminate. They treat you badly because you are Chinese or black. I hate this most." We also asked all of our informants to complete the sentence "Most Americans think [people from my country of origin] are _____." Mexican children were asked, "Most Americans think Mexicans are _____," Dominicans were asked, "Most Americans think Dominicans are _____," and so forth. Strikingly, for Latino and Haitian immigrants, the most common response was "Most Americans think that we are bad." Overwhelmingly, the children perceived that "Americans" had negative perceptions about them. Below are other responses we received:

"Most Americans think that we are stupid." [ten-year-old Haitian girl]
"Most Americans think that we can't do the same things as them in school or at work." [ten-year-old Mexican girl]
"Most Americans think that we are good for nothing." [fourteen-year-old Central American boy]
"Most Americans think that we are garbage." [fourteen-year-old Dominican boy]
"Most Americans think that we are members of gangs." [nine-year-old Central American girl]
"Most Americans think that we are thieves." [thirteen-year-old Haitian girl]

"Most Americans think that we are lazy, gangsters, drug addicts that only come to take their jobs away." [fourteen-year-old Mexican boy]
"Most Americans think that we are bad like all Latinos." [twelve-year-old Central American boy]
"Most Americans think that we don't exist." [twelve-year-old Mexican boy]

These alarming data suggest that immigrant youth are well aware of the prevailing ethos of hostility and anti-immigrant sentiment. What do children do, psychologically, with this reception? Are these attitudes ignored, or are they internalized, and how so?

The British object-relations theorist D. W. Winicott (1971) articulated a theory of "mirroring" in self-other relations. Winicott focused much of his writing on the relationship between the mother and infant, adding greatly to our understanding of the significance of this relationship in the formation of identity and the "sense of self." A critical concept in object-relations theory is that of "mirroring." According to Winicott, "The mother functions as a mirror, providing the infant with a precise reflection of his own experience and gestures. . . . Imperfections in the reflected rendition mar and inhibit the child's capacity for self-experience and integration" (Greenberg and Mitchell 1983, 192–93).

The infant is highly dependent on the reflection of the experience he or she receives from the mothering figure. The mother provides clues about the environment. In determining whether he or she need be frightened by new stimuli, the infant will first look to the mother's expression and response. An expression of interest or calm will reassure the infant, whereas an expression of concern will cause alarm. Even more crucial is the mother's response to the infant's actions. Does the mother show delight when the infant reaches for an object, or does she ignore it or show disapproval? No one response (or nonresponse) is likely to have much effect, but the *accumulation of experiences* is significant in the formation of the child's sense of self. A child whose accomplishments are mirrored favorably is likely to feel more valued than the child whose accomplishments are either largely ignored or, worse still, denigrated.

Although the idea of "mirroring"—along with a number of his other concepts—is an important contribution to our understanding of the developing child, Winicott, like many of his psychoanalytic colleagues, failed to fully acknowledge the powerful force of social systems and culture in shaping self-other relationships. Particularly as the child grows, the mirroring function is by no means the exclusive domain of maternal figures. In fact, with the exception of individuals falling on the autistic spectrum, all human beings are dependent on the reflection of themselves mirrored back to them by others. "Others" include nonparental relatives, adult caretakers, siblings, teachers, peers, employers, people on the street, and even the media. When the reflected opinion is generally positive, the individual (adult or child) will be able to feel that he or she is worthwhile and competent. When the reflection is generally negative, it is extremely difficult to maintain an unblemished sense of self-worth for very long.

These reflections can be accurate or inaccurate. In some cases, the reflection can be a positive distortion; the response to the individual may be out of proportion to his or her actual contribution or achievement. In the most benign case, positive expectations can be an asset. In the classic "Pygmalion in the Classroom" study (Rosenthal and Jacobson 1968), when teachers believed that certain children were brighter than others (based on the experimentor randomly assigning some children that designation, unsubtantiated in fact), they treated those children more positively and assigned them higher grades. It is possible that some immigrants, such as some Asian groups, benefit somewhat from positive expectations of their competence as a result of being members of a "model minority"— though no doubt at a cost (Takaki 1989).

We are more concerned here, however, with negative distortions. What happens to a youth who receives social mirroring that is predominantly negative and hostile? When the assumptions about her or him include expectations of sloth, irresponsibility, low intelligence, and even danger, the outcome can be toxic. When these reflections are received in a number of mirrors including the media, the classroom, and the street, the outcome can be devastating (Adams 1990). Even when the parents provide positive mirroring, it is often insufficient to compensate for the distorted mirrors that children encounter in their daily lives. In some cases, the immigrant parent is considered "out of touch" with reality. Even when the parental opinion is considered valid, it may not be enough to compensate for the intensity and frequency of the distortions of the House of Mirrors the children encounter in their everyday lives. The statements made by the children in our study demonstrate that they are intensely aware of the hostile reception that they are encountering.

What can a child do with these hostilities? There are several possible responses. The most positive possible outcome is to be goaded—"I'll show you. I'll make it in spite of what you think of me." This response, while theoretically possible, is relatively infrequent. Others might attempt to defend themselves by denying the negative attitudes and hostilities they encounter. More likely, youth respond with self-doubt and shame, in some cases setting low aspirations in a kind of self-full-filling prophecy: "They are probablly right. I'll never be able to do it." Yet another response is one of "You think I'm bad. Let me show you how bad I can be."

IDENTITIES AND STYLES OF COPING

It is clear, then, that "incoming resources" and "host culture variables" help us a great deal in telling the story of the paths immigrant children are able to make for themselves in the new country. However, that tells only a partial story. Identity and agency, including changing social practices and cultural models, must also be factored into any satisfactory accounting of the immigrant experience.

A generation ago the study of identity was dominated by a handful of subdisciplines—dominant among them developmental psychology (Erikson 1968). Today significant numbers of social scientists in anthropology, sociology, and political science—along with scholars in the humanities—have begun, seemingly en masse, to caliber their various disparate analytical tools to examine this most modern of topics (Kagan, Appiah, and Noam 1998).

Traditionally, psychologists theorized "identity" in the singular (Phinney 1998). On the other hand, the new work by anthropologists and sociologists highlights plural "identities"—underscoring a desire to distance their work from what they see as the old Freudian/Eriksonian master narrative depicting a unilinear developmental epic journey of separation and individuation into maturity, autonomy, and coherence. In the words of Kagan, "the error in the elaborations of the Eriksonian concept of identity was to assume that each person had a fixed identity that remained relatively unchanged across varied social contexts and that this hypothetical structure was unified in some way" (Kagan, Appiah, and Noam 1998, 1). The one-size-fits-all approach to identity ran its course as concerns over reductionism and essentialism took center stage in the social sciences.

In our research we situate the study of identities in various fields of power—fields structured by the complex and often contradictory workings of class, religion, race and color, gender and sex, age, and disabilities. We approach the study of immigrant identities in the context of contexts: as multiple and fluid constructions in constant formation and transformation as children attempt to manage their daily "migrations" from the world of home and neighborhood to the world of peers and schools and, eventually, the world of work.

We suggest that as youth attempt to transverse these substantially discontinuous cultural, political, and economic spaces they struggle to develop identities gravitating toward one of three dominant styles of adaptation: (1) an "ethnic flight style," (2) an "adversarial style," and (3) a "bicultural style." We view these styles of adaptation as ideal types. A single child, depending on her or his age at migration, race, and socioeconomic background and, very importantly, the context of resettlement in the United States, may first gravitate to one style of adaptation but eventually, as contexts change and as the child matures, may develop another dominant style of adaptation. We do not see these styles as fixed or mutually exclusive. We hypothesize that contexts, opportunities, and networks act as powerful gravitational fields shaping the adaptation styles of immigrant children.

ETHNIC FLIGHT STYLES

Youth clustering around the "ethnic flight style" often struggle to "mimic" the dominant group and may attempt to join it, leaving their own ethnic groups behind. These youth tend to deny or minimize the negative social mirroring they might encounter. Many immigrant youth who deploy this style may feel more comfortable networking with peers from the dominant culture. For these youth, learning standard English not only may serve instrumental purposes but also often may become an important symbolic act of identification with the dominant culture. Among these youth, success in school may be seen as a route for instrumental mobility but also as a way to symbolically and psychologically dissemble and gain distance from the world of family and ethnic group.

These are immigrants who travel their journey with light affective baggage. The idiom that "making it" takes for these youth tends to be independence and individualistic self-advancement. These students may "imprint" with the cultural styles and attitudes of their peers from the dominant society, which may be a less than optimal strategy for school success (see Steinberg 1996; Suárez-Orozco and Suárez-Orozco 1995).

Among these youth, typically, the culturally constituted patterns of parental authority lose legitimacy—for them, parents are "out of it" and their ways, moral codes, values, and expectations are rejected as anachronistic and out of current in the new country. While this style of adaptation might have been consciously and unconsciously deployed by earlier waves of immigrants—especially those from Europe for whom their phenotype allowed them the option of "passing"—from the vantage point of late-20th-century immigration, we are witnessing, in the words of George De Vos, "the passing of passing" (1992, 266–99). For many immigrants of color today, this option is simply not a "viable ethnic option" (Waters 1990).

ADVERSARIAL STYLES

Youth clustering around "adversarial styles" of adaptation structure their identities around rejection by the institutions of the dominant culture—including schools and the formal economy. These are children who are pushed out and drop out of schools at a time when the U.S. economy is generating virtually no meaningful jobs for those without formal schooling (Orfield 1998). Among these youth, the culturally constituted function of parental authority is typically severely corroded. These youth, therefore, tend to have serious problems with their own parents and relatives (see Vigil 1988) and tend to gravitate toward those sharing their predicament—their peers. In many such cases, peer groups, not the elders, are in charge in the lives of these children.

Negative social mirroring may result in an attitude of "Let me show you how bad I can be." Luis Rodriguez, the child of Mexican immigrants in Southern California, recalls his early experiences in school as follows:

> You were labeled from the start. I'd walk into the counselor's office for whatever reason and looks of disdain greeted me—one meant for a criminal, alien, to be feared. Already a thug. It was harder to defy this expectation than just accept it and fall into the trappings. It was a jacket I could try to take off, but they kept putting it back on.

The first hint of trouble and preconceptions proved true. So why not be proud? Why not be an outlaw? Why not make it our own? [1993, 84]

From this situation typically emerge "gangs" structured around the margins of the dominant society and constructing spaces of competence in the underground or alternative economy and the counterculture. Ogbu and his colleagues have argued that in contexts of severe inequality and ethnic antagonism among many youth staying in school, learning standard English and school success may elicit severe peer group sanctioning when it is labeled a wish to "act white" or be a "coconut" (Ogbu and Simons 1998).

BICULTURAL STYLES

Youths clustering around "bicultural styles" deploy what we have termed "transnational strategies." These children typically emerge as "cultural brokers" mediating the often conflicting cultural currents of home culture and host culture. These youth respond to negative mirroring by identifying it, naming it, and resisting it. These youth craft their identities in "the hyphen," linking aspects of the discontinuous, and at times incommensurable, cultural systems they find themselves inhabiting. Some of these youth will achieve bicultural and bilingual competencies as an integral part of their identities. These are youth for whom the culturally constructed social strictures and patterns of social control of immigrant parents and elders maintain a degree of legitimacy. These will be youth who network among members of their own ethnic groups and with students and teachers of other backgrounds with equal ease.

Among those who are successful and "make it" in the idioms of the dominant society, issues of "reparation" often become important components of their life trajectories. In some such cases, when one's success appears in the context of the sacrifice of loved ones—who struggled to give them opportunities in the new land—feelings of reparative guilt are quite common (Suárez-Orozco 1989). Among many such youth, success in school will have not only instrumental meanings—for example, to achieve self-advancement, better paying opportunities, and independence—but also important "expressive" meanings (i.e., making the parental sacrifices "worthwhile" by "becoming a somebody," etc.). To "make it" for these students may well take the idiom of "giving back" to parents, siblings, peers, and other members of the community.

CONCLUDING THOUGHTS

In surveying the recent scholarship in the field of immigration, it becomes obvious that a critical but understudied and undertheorized aspect of immigration today is the experiences of children. During the 1960s there was concentrated research effort on issues of race, poverty, and education, mostly focused on African Americans and poor whites. Since the 1980s, at a time when immigration to U.S. cities was intensifying, there has been an erosion of progress in basic research on urban issues. We know much about some topics and next to nothing about others. Much of the work on immigration today is superficial and contradictory— such as the work on the fiscal consequences of immigration. In the area of children the research is quite scattered: there is some work on bilingual education, some work on the law, some work on health, some work on students in high school, and some work on the transition to college and the world of work. But there is a lack of basic research on a variety of problems.

[Immigration will continue to be a powerful vector of change] We need a better understanding of how immigration is transforming the United States and the world. We need a major research agenda to examine the long causes and consequences of immigration to the United States. We need better theoretical understandings of multiple paths taken by immigrants in their long-term adaptations. We need more interdisciplinary dialogue.

NOTE

Acknowledgments. The research reported in this essay was made possible by generous grants from the National Science Foundation, W. T. Grant Foundation, and Spencer Foundation.

REFERENCES

Adams, P. L. 1990. Prejudice and Exclusion as Social Traumata. In *Stressors and the Adjustment Disorders*, ed. J. D. Noshpitz and R. D. Coddington. New York: John Wiley and Sons.

Ainslie, R. C. 1998. Cultural Mourning, Immigration, and Engagement: Vignettes from the Mexican Experience. In *Crossings: Mexican Immigration in Interdisciplinary Perspectives*, ed. M. M. Suárez-Orozco, 285–305. Cambridge, Mass.: Harvard University Press.

Alba, R., and V. Nee. 1997. Rethinking Assimilation Theory for a New Era of Immigration. *International Migration Review* 31: 826–74.

Andreas, P. 1998. The US Immigration Control Offensive: Constructing an Image of Order on the Southern Border. In *Crossings: Mexican Immigration in Interdisciplinary Perspectives*, ed. M. M. Suárez-Orozco, 343–56. Cambridge, Mass.: Harvard University Press.

Aronowitz, M. 1984. The Social and Emotional Adjustment of Immigrant Children: A Review of the Literature. *International Review of Migration* 18: 237–57.

Brown, E. R., R. Wyn, H. Yu, A. Valenzuela, and L. Dong. 1998. Access to Health Insurance and Health Care for Mexican American Children in Immigrant Families. In

Crossings: Mexican Immigration in Interdisciplinary Perspectives, ed. M. M. Suárez-Orozco, 227–47. Cambridge, Mass.: Harvard University Press.

Cobb, S. 1976. Social Support as a Moderator of Life Stress. *Psychosomatic Medicine* 3, no. 5: 300–14.

De Vos, G. 1992. *Social Cohesion and Alienation: Minorities in the United States and Japan.* Boulder: Westview Press.

De Vos, G., and M. M. Suárez-Orozco. 1990. *Status Inequality: The Self in Culture.* Newbury Park, Calif.: Sage Press.

Erikson, E. 1968. *Identity, Youth and Crisis.* New York: W. W. Norton.

Espanshade, T., and M. Belanger. 1998. Immigration and Public Opinion. In *Crossings: Mexican Immigration in Interdisciplinary Perspectives*, ed. M. M. Suárez-Orozco, 365–403. Cambridge, Mass.: Harvard University Press.

Gans, H. 1992. Second-Generation Decline: Scenarios for the Economic and Ethnic Futures of the Post-1965 Immigrants. *Ethnic and Racial Studies* 15 (April): 173–92.

Garcia-Coll, C., and K. Manuson. 1997. The Psychological Experience of Immigration: A Developmental Perspective. In *Immigration and the Family: Research and Policy on U.S. Immigrants*, ed. A. Booth, A. Crouter, and N. Landale, 91–132. Mahwah, N.J.: Lawrence Erlbaum Associates.

Gibson, Margaret. 1988. *Accommodation without Assimilation: Sikh Immigrants in an American High School.* Ithaca, N.Y.: Cornell University Press.

Gibson, Margaret, and John Ogbu, eds. 1991. *Minority Status and Schooling: A Comparative Study of Immigrant and Involuntary Minorities.* New York: Garland Press.

Gordon, M. 1964. *Assimilation in American Life.* New York: Oxford University Press.

Greenberg, J. R., and S. A. Mitchell. 1983. *Object Relations in Psychoanalytic Theory.* Cambridge, Mass.: Harvard University Press.

Grinberg, Leon, and Rebecca Grinberg. 1989. *Psychoanalytic Perspectives on Migration and Exile.* New Haven, Conn.: Yale University Press.

Hagan, J. 1998. Commentary on the U.S. Immigration Control Offensive. In *Crossings: Mexican Immigration in Interdisciplinary Perspectives*, ed. M. M. Suárez-Orozco, 357–61. Cambridge, Mass.: Harvard University Press.

Hernandez, Donald, and Evan Charney, eds. 1998. *From Generation to Generation: The Health and Well-Being of Children in Immigrant Families.* Washington, D.C.: National Academy Press.

Immigration and Naturalization Service. 1998. *Statistical Yearbook.* Washington, D.C.: U.S. Government Printing Office.

Jacob, E., and C. Jordan, eds. 1993. *Minority Education: Anthropological Perspectives.* Norwood, N.J.: Ablex Publishing.

Kagan, J., A. Appiah, and G. Noam. 1998. *Identity.* Unpublished MS, Harvard Project on Schooling and Children, Harvard University.

Kao, G., and M. Tienda. 1995. Optimism and Achievement: The Educational Performance of Immigrant Youth. *Social Science Quarterly* 76, no. 1: 1–19.

Landale, N. S., and R. S. Oropesa. 1995. *Immigrant Children and the Children of Immigrants: Inter and Intra Ethnic Group Differences in the United States.* Population Research Group Research Paper, 95–2. East Lansing: Institute for Public Policy and Social Research, Michigan State University Press.

Levitt, Peggy. 1998. Commentary on Cultural Mourning, Immigration, and Engagement: Vignettes from the Mexican Experience. In *Crossings: Mexican Immigration in Inter-*

disciplinary Perspectives, ed. M. M. Suárez-Orozco, 301–05. Cambridge, Mass.: Harvard University Press.

Myers, D. 1998. Dimensions of Economic Adaptation by Mexican-Origin Men. In *Crossings: Mexican Immigration in Interdisciplinary Perspectives*, ed. M. M. Suárez-Orozco, 159–200. Cambridge, Mass.: Harvard University Press.

National Research Council. 1997. *The New Americans: Economic, Demographic, and Fiscal Effects of Immigration*. Washington, D.C.: National Academy Press.

Ogbu, J., and H. D. Simons. 1998. Voluntary and Involuntary Minorities: A Cultural-Ecological Theory of School Performance with Some Implications for Education. *Anthropology and Education Quarterly* 29, no. 2: 155–88.

Olsen, L. 1998. *Made in America: Immigrant Students in Our Public Schools*. New York: The New Press.

Orfield, G. 1998. Commentary on the Education of Mexican Immigrant Children. In *Crossings: Mexican Immigration in Interdisciplinary Perspectives*, ed. M. M. Suárez-Orozco, 276–80. Cambridge, Mass.: Harvard University Press.

Padilla, A., R. Cervantes, M. Maldonado, and R. Garcia. 1988. Coping Responses to Psychosocial Stressors among Mexican and Central American Immigrants. *Journal of Community Psychology* 16: 418–27.

Park, R., and E. Burgess. 1969 [1921]. *Introduction to the Science of Sociology*. Chicago: University of Chicago Press.

Phinney, J. 1998. Ethnic Identity in Adolescents and Adults. In *Readings in Ethnic Psychology*, ed. P. Organista, K. Chun, and G. Marín, 73–99. New York: Routledge.

Portes, Alejandro. 1997. Immigration Theory for a New Century: Some Problems and Opportunities. *International Migration Review* 31: 799–825.

———. 1998. Globalization: The Rise of Transnational Communities. Paper presented at the David Rockefeller Center for Latin American Studies, Harvard University, 2 April.

Portes, A., and L. Hao. 1998. E Pluribus Unum: Bilingualism and Loss of Language in the Second Generation. *Sociology of Education* 71, no. 4 (October): 269–94.

Portes, A., and M. Zhou. 1993. The New Second Generation: Segmented Assimilation and Its Variants. *The Annals of the American Academy* 530 (November): 74–96.

Rodriguez, Luis. 1993. *Always Running*. New York: Touchstone Books.

Rosenthal, R., and L. Jacobson. 1968. *Pygmalion in the Classroom: Teacher Expectations and Pupils' Intellectual Development*. New York: Holt, Rinehart and Winston.

Rumbaut, R. D. 1977. Life Events, Change, Migration, and Depression. In *Phenomenology and Treatment of Depression*, ed. W. E. Fann, I. Karocan, A. D. Pokorny, and R. L. Willimas. New York: Spectrum.

———. 1995. The New Californians: Comparative Research Findings on the Educational Progress of Immigrant Children. In *California's Immigrant Children*, ed. R. D. Rumbaut and W. Cornelius. La Jolla, Calif.: Center for U.S.–Mexican Studies.

———. 1996. Becoming American: Acculturation, Achievement, and Aspirations among Children of Immigrants. Paper presented at the Annual Meeting of the American Association for the Advancement of Science, Baltimore, Md., 10 February.

Shuval, J. 1980. Migration and Stress. In *Handbook on Stress and Anxiety: Contemporary Knowledge, Theory, and Treatment*, I. L. Kutasshm, L. B. Schlesinger, et al., eds. San Francisco: Jossey-Bass.

Sluzki, Carlos. 1979. Migration and Family Conflict. *Family Process* 18, no. 4: 379–90.

Steinberg, S. 1996. *Beyond the Classroom: Why School Reform Has Failed and What Parents Need to Do*. New York: Simon and Schuster.

Suárez-Orozco, Carola. 1998. The Transitions of Immigration: How Do Men and Women Differ? *David Rockefeller Center for Latin American Studies News*, Harvard University (winter): 6–7.

Suárez-Orozco, Carola, and Suárez-Orozco, M. M. 1995. *Transformations: Family Life and Achievement Motivation among Latino Youth*. Palo Alto: Stanford University Press.

Suárez-Orozco, M. M. 1989. *Central American Refugees and U.S. High Schools: A Psychosocial Study of Motivation and Achievement*. Stanford: Stanford University Press.

———. 1996. California Dreaming: Proposition 187 and the Cultural Psychology of Ethnic and Racial Exclusion. *Anthropology and Education Quarterly* 27, no. 2: 151–67.

Suárez-Orozco, M. M., ed. 1998. *Crossings: Mexican Immigration in Interdisciplinary Perspectives*. Cambridge, Mass.: Harvard University Press.

Sue, S., and S. Okazaki. 1990. Asian-American Educational Achievement: A Phenomenon in Search of an Explanation. *American Psychologist* 45, no. 8: 913–20.

Suro, R. 1998. *Strangers among Us: How Latino Immigration Is Transforming America*. New York: Alfred Knopf.

Takaki, R. 1989. *Strangers from a Different Shore*. New York: Penguin.

Trueba, E. 1998. The Education of Mexican Immigrant Children. In *Crossings: Mexican Immigration in Interdisciplinary Perspectives*, ed. M. M. Suárez-Orozco, 253–75. Cambridge, Mass.: Harvard University Press.

Tuan, Mia. 1995. Korean and Russian Students in a Los Angeles High School: Exploring the Alternative Strategies of Two High-Achieving Groups. In *California's Immigrant Children*, ed. R. D. Rumbaut and W. Cornelius, 107–30. La Jolla, Calif.: Center for U.S.–Mexican Studies.

Vernez, G., A. Abrahamse, and D. Quigley. 1996. *How Immigrants Fare in US Education*. Santa Monica, Calif.: Rand.

Vigil, Diego. 1988. *Barrio Gangs: Street Life and Identity in Southern California*. Austin: University of Texas Press.

Waters, M. 1990. *Ethnic Options: Choosing Identities in America*. Berkeley: University of California Press.

———. 1996. West Indian Family Resources and Adolescent Outcomes: Trajectories of the Second Generation. Paper presented at the Annual Meeting of the American Association for the Advancement of Science, Baltimore, Md., 10 February.

Williamson, C., Jr. 1996. *The Immigration Mystique*. New York: Basic Books.

Willis, Paul. 1977. *Learning to Labour: How Working Class Kids Get Working Class Jobs*. Farnborough, U.K.: Saxon House.

Willis, T. A. 1985. Supportive Functions of Interpersonal Relationships. In *Social Support and Health*, ed. S. Cohen and S. L. Symee. Orlando: Academic Press, Inc.

Winicott, D. W. 1971. *Playing and Reality*. Middlesex, U.K.: Penguin.

Wong-Fillmore, L. 1991. When Learning a Second Language Means Losing the First. *Early Childhood Research Quarterly* 6: 323–46.

Zhou, M., and C. Bankston III. 1998. *Growing Up American: How Vietnamese Children Adapt to Life in the United States*. New York: Russell Sage Foundation.

2

Critical Ethnography for the Study of Immigrants

Enrique (Henry) T. Trueba and Peter McLaren

We can argue that, in a strictly historical sense, the first critical ethnographies were constructed by the oppressed. For example, in 1542 Francisco Tenamaztle, an Indian from central Mexico who had led the revolt against the Spaniards in Jalisco, Michoacán, Colima, and other central Mexican states, was exiled to Spain. There, assisted by Fray Cristóbal de las Casas, he defended the human rights of all the Indians by stating, "Los indios tienen por ley natural, divina y humana [el derecho] de los hacerpedazos [a los blancos barbudos], sifuerzas y armas tuvieren, y echarlos de sus tierras" [The Indians have, by natural and divine law, (the right) to cut in pieces (the white bearded), if they (the Indians) had the strength and weapons, and to throw them (the bearded whites) away from their land] (cited in León-Portilla 1995, 30).

In a strict and more technical sense, critical ethnography has deep roots in psychological anthropology, and it was later refined in sociology and philosophy with the seminal work of Paulo Freire. The ideas of early anthropologists to improve the schooling and overall human development of all children were revealed in a conference held at Stanford University on 9–14 June 1954, organized by George Spindler. Renowned scholars such as Solorn T. Kimball, Alfred L. Kroeber, Dorothy Lee, Margaret Mead, Felix M. Keesing, John Gillin, and Cora DuBois shared their concerns relating to the overall development of all children, the preparation of ethnically diverse children, and the need to pursue pedagogically appropriate methods of teaching (Spindler 1955).

THE NATURE OF CRITICAL ETHNOGRAPHY

A modern concept of critical ethnography as a research methodology stresses the notion that *all* education is intrinsically political, and consequently critical

37

ethnography must advocate for the oppressed by (1) documenting the nature of oppression; (2) documenting the process of empowerment—a journey away from oppression; (3) accelerating the conscientization of the oppressed and the oppressors—without this reflective awareness of the rights and obligations of humans there is no way to conceptualize empowerment, equity, and a struggle of liberation; (4) sensitizing the research community to the implications of research for the quality of life—clearly linking intellectual work to real life conditions; and (5) reaching a higher level of understanding of the historical, political, sociological, and economic factors supporting the abuse of power and oppression, of neglect and/or disregard for human rights, and of the mechanisms to learn and internalize rights and obligations. Ultimately, the above draws attention to the importance of the intimate relationship between the intellectual activity of research and the *praxis* of the daily lives of researchers. Praxis (in Freire's sense of political commitment to struggle for liberation and in defense of human rights) is the ultimate goal of critical ethnography. This praxis must encompass a global and cross-cultural commitment to advocate for the rights of all humankind and, thus, to create human solidarity against oppression. For most critical theorists, oppression is not only the result of class oppression by the capitalist ruling elite but the result of structural elements perpetuated through cultural patterns leading to the perpetuation of economic, political, and other semiotic systems that violate human rights, especially the right to learn. Culture comes into the picture, not only from the standpoint of the oppressor's lifestyle, values, and the assumptions of "superiority" over "others" but as a socially and historically structured set of relationships, expectations, and accepted practices. Ultimately, reigning discourses *of* and *about* culture "justify" the presumed "rights" of the oppressor to perpetuate his or her position of power over the oppressed and rationalize the role of the oppressed in his or her own oppression. However, we must change our definitions of culture. What is culture? What is not culture?

In the early 1960s the classical definitions of culture included a complex set of values, traditions, lifestyles, and behavior patterns characterizing particular human groups and distinguishing them from each other; furthermore, culture was observable and transmitted from one generation to another. In the late 1960s and early 1970s culture became an integral part of the *cognitive revolution*, which explored various conceptual configurations. Under the editorship of George Spindler, the journal *American Anthropologist* published a number of new methodological studies in ethnoscience, ethnosemantics, the ethnography of law, ethnobotany, ethnolinguistics, and so forth. The new generation of linguist-ethnographers transformed ethnographic research into a very sophisticated instrument via discourse analysis in the study of diverse cultures. These studies became cross-cultural and more detached from any implications for praxis. Comparative cross-cultural ethnographic approaches are not all critical. They become "critical" only when their goal, ultimate purpose, direction, and expected outcomes constitute the *praxis* of the ethnographer, that is, a praxis of equity, a commitment for life to pursue equity and to struggle for the liberation of all humankind through ethnographic research. Yes, critical ethnography is advocacy oriented, but not all advocacy research is critical. This is one of the crucial elements of critical ethnography; one could say that its raison d'être is to transform society via conscientization and social change.

There are serious challenges involved in doing critical ethnographic research as a means of inquiry and as a means of transformation. In fact, some view it as inherently "colonizing" and "exploitative." In some sense all social science research is suspect of being hegemonic and colonizing—and even of objectifying and "orientalizing" people while it attempts to understand them: "This contradiction (between ethnography's "exemplary status" and its "colonial nature") instantiates the more generalized social division of intellectual and manual labor [whereby] research is posited only as the professional activity of the privileged minority" (De Genova 1997, 1). The historical changes in the concept of culture—from something out there to observe to something in people's heads, or cognitive configurations—affected anthropology, linguistics, and psychology (Shweder 1996, 25). Emphasis moved from observed behavior to the study of language as a window to understand cognitive structures. In other words, what Richard Shweder calls "mental-state language," dealing with beliefs, desires, plans, wants, emotions, goals, feelings, and so on, revealed a code and set of values that permitted ethnographers to make inferences. Ethnographers had to use mental-state language as accessible and public experiences (rather than inaccessible and private experiences), subject to external and intersubjective interpretation (Shweder 1996, 26).

The two revolutions, the "cognitive revolution," which was "pro-mentalistic," and the reaction against solipsism, which was anti-mentalistic, became compatible in the practice of ethnography conceptualized as an interpretive study of behavior sanctionable by members of a community (a "moral community" according to Shweder 1996, 26). In other words, ethnography is seen as the interpretive act of discourse and praxis about beliefs, desires, and other mental-state language to render observed behavior intelligible. This is clearly an effort to cross cultural (and cognitive) boundaries. Informants' reports about their own behavior are neither necessary nor sufficient to construct hypotheses about observed behavior. We know that culture is acquired by doing, acting, or performing our praxis (practicing our values) and that it is through communication (dialogical , reciprocal) that we manage to change and re-create our configurations of culture and values. Ultimately, culture is the set of principles, norms of behavior, exhibited in everyday life and everyday evaluative discourse, beginning in the small moral community of the family.

The cohesiveness of a moral community is maintained through "evaluative discourse," which reflects the agreed-on norms of behavior. But in the context of several moral communities in contact (as is the case of plural societies), there exist many evaluative discourses and plural sets of principles, norms, and value systems.

The prevalence of one evaluative discourse means oppression; freedom of evaluative discourses means liberation. Awareness of plural discourses is the start in the struggle for liberation because it facilitates the acquisition of "emancipatory knowledge." McLaren and da Silva feel that "emancipatory knowledge is never realized fully, but is continually dreamed, continually revived, and continually transformed in the heart of our memories, the flames of our longing and the passion of our struggle" (1993, 59). Critical ethnography permits us to get into the emancipatory knowledge that motivates ethnic minority students' resistance to the dominant culture in the United States. By retaining and affirming their ethnic identity, they feel empowered to resist racial and ethnic prejudicial policies and practices. Critical ethnography also permits us to reexamine cultural hegemony and the nature of cultural conflict as a drama taking place right in the classroom via reflection on historical factors of ethnic/racial legitimacy, reproduction of the social order, and the right to a voice in one's own language (Leistyna, Woodrum, and Sherblom 1996, 334).

Critical ethnography has many defining characteristics too numerous to fully elaborate here. A broad sweep of its development over the last several decades would undeniably identify as one of its preferred theoretical protocols a trenchant ability to produce a thick description of classroom activities set within the wider context of postindustrial capitalist society (McLaren 1993; Wexler 1992; Willis 1977). Employing a critical epistemology developed largely out of the hermeneutical philosophical traditions, critical ethnographers seek validity claims that inhere in structures of communication. Produced by sign and symbol systems that are mediated by power relationships, validity claims are derived from the truth claims of social actors. Judged to be true or false, correct or incorrect, right or wrong, truth claims are understood by critical ethnographers to be always related to and conditioned by processes in which social actors reach consensus and group consent is secured (Carspecken 1996).

The central questions posed by the critical ethnographer involve the way in which objective realms of social life are presupposed by certain types of truth claims. Critical ethnographers reject the notion of "objective" science in favor of understanding claims to objectivity, neutrality, impartiality, and balance on the part of the mainstream ethnographer as cultural fictions, as principles that essentially support the status quo and militate against the consideration of counterhegemonic viewpoints. Critical ethnographers employ a critical epistemology in order to develop "an understanding of the relationship between power and thought and power and truth claims" (Carspecken 1996, 107). For critical ethnographers, values and epistemologies are not constructed by means of visual metaphors but, rather, perception itself is considered to be structured by culturally given typifications, expectations, and shared understandings. Carspecken maintains that in the case of critical ethnography, "fundamental value orientations (for democracy, equality, and human empowerment)" are able "to fuse with epistemological imperatives" (1996, 21). In other words, critical ethnographers attempt to make tacit comparisons between normative realms familiar to them and normative realms that actors appear to validate through their actions. Put another way, the critical ethnographer is interested in distinguishing how both the subject and the object of research are interpellated or "written into" the ideologies of his or her cultural site through an acquisition of their systems of language, regimes of discourse, cultural arrangements, and microphysics of power. In addition, there also exists on the part of the critical ethnographer an abiding interest in how the researcher has been "sutured" into both a particular relationship to dominant analytic-descriptive models of research and an uncomplicated relationship to dominant ideological imperatives of the larger discipline of anthropology and academic culture in general. Ethnography itself is understood to contain forms of episodic thinking and taken-for-granted elements and, as such, is implicated in a complex process of social construction and legitimation that often serves the given dispositions of class, power, and authority that exist in the larger social order. For instance, in mainstream research on schooling, the larger social order of capitalist social relations often remains unremarked upon and taken for granted. In this case, such a structured silence or motivated amnesia may in fact advance a tacit proposition that supports the superiority of capitalism over other social systems (such as socialism, for instance).

Consequently, a major distinguishing trait of critical ethnography is that it attempts to analyze social class relations that are not empirically immediate. Critical ethnographers do this by operationalizing forms of macro- and microsociological theory (Fine 1991, 1992; McLaren 1993, 1995; Weis 1990; Weis and Fine 1993; Willis 1977). A major challenge for critical ethnography is to achieve a micro/macro-integration of analysis. As George Marcus notes, it is difficult to discuss macrostructures without reifying them. Marcus calls for the creation of mixed-genre texts that challenge the holism of realist ethnography, that are sensitive to both the inner lives of subjects and the nature of world historical political economy, and that include a reciprocity of perspectives, multiple authorial voices, a dialogical context of fieldwork, and polyglossic, interreferential voices (Marcus and Fischer 1986, 192). The techniques used in critical ethnography can be traced not only to Marxist anthropology but also to what Marcus and Fischer (1986) describe as the anthropological tradition of epistemological critique and cross-cultural juxtaposition. Underlying both of these practices is a strategy known as "defamiliarization" or the disruption of common sense. This technique—often used in the arts—can be found in surrealist artwork and literature (such as that of the Situationists) and in the theater of the oppressed. Practices of defamiliarization are designed to "raise havoc with our settled ways of thinking and conceptualization" (Marcus and Fischer 1986, 138). Such practices serve, in effect, to revise the ideological coordinates that distinguish the cultural center from the periphery.

Accompanying new modes of critical ethnography has been a proliferation of deconstructive and reflexive approaches. In her book *Fictions of Feminist Ethnog-*

raphy (1994), Kamala Visweswaran maintains that reflexive ethnography, like normative ethnography, rests on the "declarative mode" of imparting knowledge to a reader whose identity is anchored in a shared discourse. Deconstructive ethnography, in contrast, enacts the "interrogative mode" through a constant deferral or a refusal to explain or interpret. Within deconstructive ethnography, the specified identity of the reader is discouraged. Reflexive ethnography maintains that the ethnographer is not separate from the object of investigation, but the ethnographer is still viewed as a unified subject of knowledge that can make hermeneutic efforts to establish identification between the observer and the observed (as in modernist interpretive traditions). Deconstructive ethnography, in contrast, often disrupts such identification in favor of articulating a fractured, destabilized, multiply positioned subjectivity (as in postmodernist interpretive traditions). Whereas reflexive ethnography questions its own authority, deconstructive ethnography forfeits its authority. Both approaches to critical ethnography can be used to uncover the clinging Eurocentric authority employed by ethnographers in the study of Latino populations. The goal of both these approaches is criticalist in nature: that is, to free the object of analysis from the tyranny of fixed, unassailable categories and to rethink subjectivity itself as a permanently unclosed, always partial, narrative engagement with text and context. Such an approach can help the ethnographer to caution against the damaging depictions propagated by some Anglo observers about Mexican immigrants. As Ruth Behar notes,

> In classical sociological and ethnographic accounts of the Mexican and Mexican American family, stereotypes similar to those surrounding the black family perpetuated images of the authoritarian, oversexed, and macho husband and the meek and submissive wife surrounded by children who adore their good and suffering mother. These stereotypes have come under strong critique in the last few years, particularly by Chicana critics, who have sought to go beyond the various "deficiency theories" that continue to mark the discussion of African-American and Latina/Latino family life. [1993, 276]

The conception of culture advanced by critical ethnographers generally unpacks culture as a complex circuit of production that includes a myriad of dialectically reinitiating and mutually informing sets of activities such as routines, rituals, action conditions, systems of intelligibility and meaning making, conventions of interpretation, systems relations, and conditions both external and internal to the social actor (Carspecken 1996). In her recent ethnographic study *A Space on the Side of the Road*, Kathleen Stewart cogently illustrates the ambivalent character of culture, as well as its fluidity and ungraspable multilayeredness, when she remarks,

> Culture, as it is seen through its productive forms and means of mediation, is not, then, reducible to a fixed body of social value and belief or a direct precipitant of lived

experience in the world but grows into a space on the side of the road where stories weighted with sociality take on a life of their own. We "see" it only by building up multilayered narratives of the poetic in the everyday life of things. We represent it only by roaming from one texted genre to another—romantic, realist, historical, fantastic, sociological, surreal. There is no final textual solution, no way of resolving the dialogic of the interpreter/interpreted or subject/object through efforts to "place" ourselves in the text, or to represent "the fieldwork experience," or to gather up the voices of the other as if they could speak for themselves. [1996, 210]

According to E. San Juan (1996), a renewed understanding of culture—as both discursive and material—becomes the linchpin for any emancipatory politics. He writes that the idea of culture as social processes and practices that are thoroughly grounded in material social relations—in the systems of maintenance (economics), decision (politics), learning and communication (culture), and generation and nurture (the domain of social reproduction)—must be the grounding principle, or paradigm if you like, of any progressive and emancipatory research approach (1996, 177).

Rejecting the characterization of anthropologists as either "adaptationalists" (e.g., Marvin Harris) or "ideationalists" (e.g., cognitivists, Levi-Straussian structuralists, Schneiderian symbolists, Geertzian interpretivists), E. Valentine Daniel has remarked in his new ethnography, *Charred Lullabies: Chapters in an Anthropology of Violence*, that culture is "no longer something out there to be discovered, described, and explained, but rather something into which the ethnographer, as interpreter, enter[s]" (1996, 198). Culture, in other words, is cocreated by the anthropologist and informant through conversation. Yet even this semiotic conceptualization of culture is not without its problems. As Daniel himself notes, even if one considers oneself to be a "culture co-making processualist" in contrast to a "culture-finding essentialist," one still has to recognize that one is working within a logocentric tradition that, to a greater or lesser extent, privileges words over actions. Critical ethnography has benefited from this new understanding of culture and from the new hybridic possibilities for cultural critique that have been opened up by the current blurring and mixing of disciplinary genres—those that emphasize experience, subjectivity, reflexivity, and dialogical understanding. The advantage that follows such perspectives is that social life is not viewed as preontologically available for the researcher to study. It also follows that there is no perspective unspoiled by ideology from which one may study social life in an antiseptically objective way. Investigative journalist Juan Gonzalez (a founding member of the Young Lords Party in New York City) recognizes the profoundly partisan nature of all investigation in his book *Roll Down Your Window: Stories from a Forgotten America* (1995). A Puerto Rican who writes from the position of someone "whose homeland had been invaded and permanently occupied by Anglo-Americans, its wealth exploited to make fortunes for hundreds of U.S. corporations, its patriots persecuted and jailed," Gonzalez offers a description of the journalist that could equally apply to the critical ethnographer:

Each set of journalistic eyes is conditioned and shaped by family upbringing, church and school training; is invariably limited by time, place, and the specific condition of the writer's social development; and is inevitably stamped with the unconscious imprint of his or her class, race, and gender. Each set of eyes necessarily becomes a flawed prism, partial or subjective by its very nature, through which the writer filters and then re[-]creates an exceedingly complex reality. The battle to record history as it happens—from a divergent, sometimes unpopular view rather than from a consensus perspective already diluted by self-censorship—is the essential challenge to journalists in a modern capitalist democracy. [1995, xxiv–xxv]

What is important to note here is the stress placed on the ideological situatedness of any descriptive or socioanalytical account of social life. We wish to discuss this and other features of critical ethnography that translate into praxis or a way of life exhibited by researchers in accordance with their commitment to liberation in light of ongoing efforts to construct critical ethnographic practices for the study of immigrants. However, a critical ethnography for the study of immigrants must begin with a clear understanding that white privilege frequently has been mirrored in ethnographic research accounts, biases, goals, and purposes.

TOWARD A CRITICAL ETHNOGRAPHY FOR THE STUDY OF IMMIGRANTS

The fact that academia has been controlled primarily by whites and that the legitimacy of ethnographic research is determined by those in control of academia requires some reflection on the "whiteness of ethnography." Society is always willing to sacrifice the rights of black people to protect important economic or political interests of whites. The classic example is the Framers' decision to ignore the contradiction posed by the Constitution in guaranteeing freedom to all while containing provisions recognizing and protecting slavery that were accepted to insure the support of slave owners. The Hayes–Tilden Compromise is another example of this phenomenon. To resolve a serious dispute between the North and the South over which candidate had won the presidential election of 1876, a special commission negotiated a settlement that awarded the presidency to Rutherford B. Hayes while returning political control to the South and thus ending Reconstruction. The plan averted a renewal of the Civil War but sacrificed the newly gained rights of Southern blacks. Bell writes,

The laws—and society—recognize the rights of blacks and other people of color only when such recognition serves some economic or political interest of greater importance to whites than helping members of minority groups. Lincoln's reluctant issuance of the Emancipation Proclamation to help the faltering effort to save the Union is an example of this in action. . . . Disenchantment set in when [in the 1960s] it became obvious that racial equality for blacks meant more than merely condemning blatant segregation in Deep South towns. It meant, as well, adopting remedies requiring some whites to surrender their expectations of racial privilege. [1997, 134]

Whites are easily persuaded that their economic well-being is eroding because immigrants and people of color are abusing the system or not carrying their own load, though not because corporations downsize labor in order to increase profits (Bell 1997, 134). According to Bell,

> Even if the Supreme Court does not ban all affirmative action in the next few years, it is likely to continue tightening the scope of such programs. This will certainly not lessen, and could swell, the hostility that many whites feel toward minorities, immigrants, and the poor. . . . Throughout the nation's history, making minority groups and immigrants scapegoats has served as a convenient and comforting substitute for the economic well-being and social status that most whites lack. [1997, 135]

Judicial support for affirmative action in the past was misinterpreted by advocates as a total victory and a permanent acceptance by society. Victory in litigation in many instances led to passivity. In turn, loss in current litigation should lead to a collective will to struggle. However, in the end, as Bell points out, "The challenge is to undergird our commitment not to one strategy—affirmative action—but rather to the goal of helping anyone excluded from social opportunity because of a disadvantaged background" (1997, 135)

Recent studies of the social construction of whiteness have suggested some implications for the practice of ethnography (Frankenberg 1993; Ignatiev 1995; Ignatiev and Garvey 1996; Lopez 1996; Roediger 1994; Yúdice 1995). We are using *whiteness* to refer to a material and discursive space that is inflected by nationhood and informed by discursive practices of masculinity and femininity (Frankenberg 1993). A sociohistorical form of consciousness, whiteness serves as the unmarked marker from which Anglo researchers often judge the cultural practices of nonwhite groups. Whiteness is linked to the expansion of capitalism, social practices of assimilation and cultural homogenization, modes of naming culture and difference associated with Western European colonialist expansion, and myths of European superiority. In this sense, whiteness operates by means of its condition as a universalizing authority by which the hegemonic white bourgeois subject appropriates the right to speak on behalf of everyone who is nonwhite while denying voice and agency to Others in the name of civilized humankind. Whiteness is fundamentally Euro- or Western-centric in its episteme and is articulated in complicity with the pervasively imperializing logic of empire. It is also linked geopolitically to historically specific acts of imperialism that are often connected to current forms of capitalist accumulation through the "globalization" process. As a type of articulatory practice that can be located in the convergence of colonialism, capitalism, and subject formation, whiteness both fixes and sustains discursive regimes that represent the self and other; that is, whiteness represents a regime of differences that produces and racializes an "abject" other. In other words, whiteness serves as a discursive regime that has serious—and sometimes fatal—consequences. It displaces blackness and brownness—specific forms of nonwhiteness—into signifiers of deviance and criminality within social, cultural, cognitive, and political contexts. Whiteness is not only mythopoetical in the sense that it constructs a totality of illusions formed around the ontological superiority of the Euro-American subject; it is also metastructural, in that it "sutures," both symbolically and materially, whiteness across specific differences. Consumer utopias and global capitalist flows rearticulate and rehegemonize whiteness. The cultural encoding of the typography of whiteness is achieved by remapping Western European identity onto economic transactions, discursive practices, and cultural formations and inscribing identity into an onto-epistemological framework of "us" against "them" (McLaren 1997a).

To what extent do ethnographers, working comfortably within the ideological coordinates of whiteness, naturalize social relations that support white privilege? By addressing this issue, critical ethnographers can challenge those discourses of whiteness that attempt to occlude the historicity and partisanship—not to mention racism—characteristic of the analysis of social life. Whereas mainstream ethnography often forswears its own ideological constitutivity in discourses of whiteness, the form of critical ethnography that we are envisioning would challenge those discourses in which the researcher's own location is naturalized so as to be rendered invisible. In our view, white ethnography is produced when the social context in which ideologies, cultural practices, and social formations struggling for dominance are not sufficiently questioned in terms of the forms of authority used to legitimate particular representations and interpretations of social life. White ethnography is established in our view when the meaning horizon of the unreflexive white researcher is claimed as valid for all cultures. Critical ethnography necessitates an intersubjective understanding of the cultural movement between insider and outsider positions, between the competing particular and universalizing claims of both researcher and researched. The issue could be reconfigured as follows: How do ethnographers define the context or enunciative space in which the subaltern is invited to become empowered to speak? Consider the issues raised by Behar in her critical ethnography *Translated Woman: Crossing the Border with Esperanza's Story* (1993). Engaging in a serious reflection of the ways in which her life *historias* (histories) of a Mexican woman, Esperanza, might be translated by white North American readers, Behar challenges Anglo-American stereotypes of the acquiescent Mexican woman. Behar writes, "Clearly, any ethnographic representation—and I count my own, of course—inevitably includes a self-representation. Even more subtly, the act of representing 'almost always involves violence of some sort to the subject of the representation'" (1993, 271).

Zora Neale Hurston brilliantly captures the suspicion toward white ethnographers on the part of African American subjects in her book *Mules and Men:*

> Folklore is not as easy to collect as it sounds. The best source is where there are the least outside influences and these people, being usually under-privileged, are the

shyest. They are most reluctant at times to reveal that which the soul lives by. And the Negro, in spite of his open-faced laughter, his seeming acquiescence, is particularly evasive. You see we are a polite people and we do not say to our questioner, "Get out of here!" We smile and tell him or her something that satisfies the white person because, knowing so little about us, he doesn't know what he is missing. The Indian resists curiosity by a stony silence. The Negro offers a feather-bed resistance. That is, we let the probe enter, but it never comes out. It gets smothered under a lot of laughter and pleasantries. [1990, 2–3]

Michelle Fine and Lois Weis further articulate the complex dilemma facing the white critical fieldworker as one that interweaves issues of ethics, epistemology, and agency:

In our texts we ponder how we present (a) ourselves as researchers choreographing the narratives we have collected; (b) the narrators, many of whom are wonderful social critics, whereas some (from our perspective) are talented ventriloquists for a hateful status quo; and (c) the others who are graphically bad-mouthed by these narrators (e.g., caseworkers blamed by women on welfare for stinginess; African American men held responsible for all social evils by White men; police held in contempt by communities of color that have survived much abuse at the hands of police). Do we have a responsibility to theorize the agency/innocence/collusion of these folks, too? When White men say awful things about women of color, do we need to represent women of color, denounce and re-place these representations? If not, are we not merely contributing to the archival representations of disdain that the social science literature has so horrifically chronicled? [1996, 226]

The tropes and tensions of multiculturalism, with its focus on diversity and inclusion, ground much of the work in critical ethnography. The disposition of mainstream multiculturalism is best described as "democratic pluralism." This perspective presumes that there are no predominant interest groups within society, enabling the schools to provide a just balance and fairness in their approach to nonwhite ethnic groups. We argue that critical ethnographers need a new point of epistemological departure. The more that Latino populations are forced to comply with Euro-American forms of discourse, ideological typifications, and social practices, the more they are able to invoke the distinction between *engabachamiento* (becoming white) and forms of discourses that are peculiar to their ethnic practices and location. Because Anglo culture for the most part possesses control over the means of producing social value and material wealth, it is imperative that Mexican immigrants are able to challenge the evidential powers of the dominant Anglo culture. This concern is reflected in the roseate image of diversity that undergirds the liberal ethnographer's analysis of Latino communities. The standard notion of multicultural diversity, we argue, is prefigured in the post-Enlightenment imagination and constituted by the axiom of a globalized, rational civilization and the universalizing ethos of modernity that followed the colonizing thrust of Europe into the non-European world. To what extent is the liberal ideology of diversity actually grounded in the image of an imperial center with racially ordered and marginalized groups added on incrementally and eventually absorbed into the powerful forces of the center?

The center, in this case, serves to regulate the hegemonic processes whereby symbolic and material production are orchestrated such that the subaltern subject is bound ever more firmly to the colonizing culture through the ideological apparatuses of the state—for example, forms of commodity production through signs, symbols, rituals, filmic and televisual representations, and spatial, linguistic, and political formations. Because multicultural perspectives that stress diversity rarely, if ever, begin with a challenge to the invisible dominance of whiteness, we believe that our apprehension is justified. We prefer the concept of "difference" to that of "diversity" because we believe that differences should be understood as historically and ideologically produced within asymmetrical relations of power linked to the extraction of surplus labor under forms of capitalist exploitation. Working from a perspective of "diversity" too often naturalizes white privilege by severing difference from the material conditions of its production and reception within white supremacist and patriarchal capitalist practices. In contrast, the concept of difference enables the ethnographer to analyze the way in which whiteness as an ideological formation operates as a coordinating mechanism that relegates certain cultural and ethnic characteristics and relations as "normal" and others as "abnormal." The contradictions between the professed discourse of inclusion of mainstream multiculturalism and the material and social conditions that favor Anglo-European constituencies (and that, we might add, point to a real politics of exclusion for people of color in general) have led Latino populations to distrust the critical gaze of the Anglo ethnographer. What this suggests is that white ethnographers need to consider their own constitutions as ethnic subjects in reporting on the "differences" of Latino and other populations.

A critical ethnography for Mexican immigrants needs to consider carefully the narrative forms used to capture "difference." Feminist ethnographer Ruth Behar offers this lucid warning:

> If we are to go beyond first world representations of third world women as passive, subservient, and lacking in creativity, then clearly one important task for feminist ethnographers alert to and respectful of the differences between women is to listen well to the stories that other women have to tell, capturing the key images and offering interpretations that mirror the narrative forms they themselves use to tell their life stories. At this juncture in the politics of feminism, it is gratuitous to think that an ethnographer "gets" a less-privileged woman's "experience" by taking down her life story; and it is even more gratuitous to think that her work is done when she has framed the other woman's "own words" with a few comfortable generalizations that make no connections to her own position as the one who brings the story back across the border. [1993, 272]

One provocative, if not epistemologically risky, attempt to move beyond Western Eurocentric narrative formations has been undertaken by Karen McCarthy

Brown in the ethnography *Mama Lola: A Vodou Priestess in Brooklyn* (1991). Brown turns the family story of Alourdes, a Haitian immigrant, into fictionalized short stories that are also "true." She does this because Alourdes's stories do not lend themselves to reproduction by the ethnographer in a written text. The stories themselves have refrains to which Alourdes frequently and rhythmically returns but never in a logical or chronological fashion. Brown's ethnography is constructed out of a polyphonic play of voices, bringing to mind Bakhtin's concept of communication as heteroglot and dialogic. Brown notes,

> I am part of a culture that seeks to capture experience, historical and otherwise, in books. So I write a book about Mama Lola. But in doing so I try to remember that she is part of a culture that serves Gede. Therefore I have tried to make up true stories, ones that are faithful to both Gede and Alourdes. I have tried to create her story through a chorus of voices, much as she creates herself through a chorus of moods and spirit energies. One of the voices that speaks in the book is hers, as carefully recorded and respectfully edited as I could manage. Yet another is my scholarly voice, distanced enough to discern patterns and relationships but not so distant as to create the impression of overall logical coherence. No person's life or culture is, in the final analysis, logical. A third voice is also my own, but this one risks a more intimate and whole self-revelation. The fourth voice is perhaps that of Gede[,] the one who tells the ancestral tales in the form of fictionalized short stories and in so doing plays with truth, seeking to bring it alive for its immediate audience. [1991, 19–20]

We would add a fifth voice to Brown's account, which is that of the reader of her text, so that the polysemy of her ethnography lies not only in the heteroglossia of the voices out of which she constructs her analysis but also in the ways that different socially located readers will activate the meaning potential of the text. Critical ethnographers need to consider when it is appropriate to situate their own voices alongside those whom they are researching and when they might abandon the role of omniscient "translator" of other peoples' lives in order to reveal something of themselves. Behar notes, "It has long seemed to me that most life histories stop short of their goal of decentering Western notions of whose life deserves a place in the world of our letters. We ask for revelations from others, but we reveal little or nothing of ourselves; we make others vulnerable, but we ourselves remain invulnerable" (1993, 273).

In her ethnography *The Good Parsi* (1996), Tanya M. Luhrmann makes a similar recommendation for contemporary ethnographers. Pointing to classical anthropology's history of exploiting and exoticizing the Other, she stresses the importance of understanding the perception of others through patterns established in the ethnographer's own past. Further, she encourages the ethnographer and field subject to move away from the Manichean stance of "us against them" and embrace the subjectivity of the other such that a firm coimplication results. In this way the ethnographer can abandon the role of narrator speaking in a single voice and can begin to fashion a new voice transformed into a complex interweave of textuality within the multistranded time and psychocultural space of history. This brings to mind Gloria Anzaldúa's (1987) concept of *mestizaje* and "border crossing." This suggests to us that the ethnographer needs to assume a mestiza/mestizo consciousness or willingness to reform her or his identity through the crossing of linguistic, cultural, and epistemological borders when engaging with cultural others in research situations. Luhrmann further notes, "Only if anthropology can reposition itself effectively, as an interpreter of a changed and radically reconstituted collection of global polities in which the act of interpretation is not an exploitation but a tool for responsible and effective cross-cultural understanding, can the discipline survive and flourish into the next century" (1996, 239). Of course, we must constantly recall that border crossings are always political and that some borders are open to certain groups while others are excluded, even when they are permitted to "cross over" the barrier. Crossing some borders reconfigures other borders. Borders are never static but, rather, are continually reinitiated. We need to remind ourselves of the lesson of our Chicano/Chicana brothers and sisters when they say, "We didn't cross the border; the border crossed us."

Ethnographers, notes Behar (1993), need to interrogate the sanctioned ignorances of their own ethnographic authority. Reflecting on her history as a Cubana immigrant to the United States, Behar remarks that writing her own ethnography was "a bridge to my own past and the journey my family has made to shift their class identity. How many cultural and class borders I, too, have crossed to end up in the position of being able to turn away the peddler that came to my door, while in all good conscience devoting years to writing up hundreds of pages of another peddler's life story" (1993, 337).

Based on an imperative of solidarity, and offering a counterpoint to existing social relations of exploitation under global capitalism, critical ethnography in all of its experimentations with text, context, and intersubjectivity is in principle not only oppositional but liberatory. It is grounded in what Freire (1995) calls a "pedagogy of hope," whereby individuals and groups can acquire the social knowledge and critical capabilities that are systematically denied to them in a world of market priorities and capitalist production. A critical ethnography is able to reposition already interpellated subjects through new discursive strategies. Critical ethnography is linked to the pedagogical imperatives of social justice and political and economic transformation. Fine and Weis articulate the role of critical ethnographic praxis as one in which "method and voice meet":

> We feel the weight of academics; that is, as public intellectuals, we need to tell the stories from the side of policy that is never asked to speak, to interrupt the hegemony of elite voices dictating what is good for this segment of the population. And yet we feel the need to document the pain and suffering in these communities and the incredible resilience and energy that percolates. . . . We lean toward a way of writing that spirals around social injustice and resilience, that recognizes the endurance of structures of injustice and the powerful acts of agency, that appreciates the courage

and the limits of individual acts of resistance but refuses to perpetuate the fantasy that victims are simply powerless and collusive. [1996, 270]

While no doubt romanticizing their role as ethnographers in their description of themselves as "a well-paid Thelma and Louise with laptops" (1996, 270), Fine and Weis make a good case for exploring the contradictory role played by the critical ethnographer.

One final point needs to be made. In her recent ethnography of Indonesia, *In the Realm of the Diamond Queen* (1993), Anna Lowenhaupt Tsing argues for an ethnography that can bring about global interconnections. She argues that ethnographers need to acknowledge links between their own work and the emancipatory work being done in other countries. In this way, cultural difference—"within shifting and limited frames of meaning"—can be transformed into "a creative cultural intervention in a world we share" (1993, 300). We believe this to be an important point. For instance, when considering the case of Mexican immigrants in the United States, to what extent does the "guest worker" or "ghost worker" system resemble other programs in places such as Germany, where the "armies of invisible people" are the Turks. If, as Marcelo M. Suárez-Orozco suggests, we are entering "the era of postnationalist, supra–nation building" (1998), what similarities can we find between the growth of Latinophobia in Southern California and the recent and ongoing production of fascism and anti-immigrant sentiment in France, Austria, and Belgium? Suárez-Orozco presciently remarks that the grammar of anti-immigrant discourse "is stunningly identical—whether it is deployed in anti-immigrant scripts in Flanders, Paris, or California" (1998). A critical ethnography that vigilantly explores the context of globalization in terms of the way it might be affecting "local" struggles can assist in further exploring how the shifts in globalization of capital are being linked perniciously to discourses alarmingly similar in their hatred of the "Other."

CRITICAL ETHNOGRAPHY OF MEXICAN IMMIGRANTS: THE ETHNOGRAPHER'S PRAXIS

In the recent political context of anti-immigration sentiment and the rapid increase of Latino and Asian populations in this country, educational researchers must acknowledge serious dilemmas and face up to the fundamental challenge of becoming relevant to the pedagogical needs of culturally different student populations. This involves addressing in an uncompromising fashion the issue of white privilege (McLaren 1997b). The study of Mexican immigrants can, in our view, help us illustrate important theoretical points about critical ethnography and white privilege.

A number of scholars feel that the education of Latinos is worse off now than in the previous decade (Portes 1996; Suárez-Orozco and Suárez-Orozco 1995a,

1995b; Valencia 1991). Yet recent studies of academic success of Latino students in high school and their continued efforts to succeed in their adult lives invite reflection on the supportive role of the family and home environment (Diaz Salcedo 1996). The narratives of academic achievement, in the midst of the narratives of inequity for many Latino students, represent a unique success where failure was expected.

The struggle of Mexicans in what is U.S. territory today did not start with the tens of thousands who began to do unskilled labor in the late 1800s. Certainly, many Mexicans were living in the Southwest prior to the annexation of Mexican territory by the Guadalupe Hidalgo Treaty of 1848, but many more have come since. Mexicans have been coming to work in increasing numbers from the beginning of this century. In 1900 the U.S. Census estimated that there were 103,393 Mexican immigrants. By 1910, there were 221,915; by 1920, there were 486,418; and by 31 December 1926, the official count was of 890,746 (Gamio 1930, 2). The exploitation of so-called *inferior* people and the accepted practice of depriving them of certain rights was common during the last century and the first decades of this century. The Civil Practice Act of 1850, which excluded Chinese and Indians from testifying against whites, was extended to Mexicans because they were considered *Indians*, and there was legal segregation against the Indians, in spite of the fact that Mexicans were also of mestizo and Spanish origin. The residential segregation of Mexicans firmly established on the West Coast at the turn of the century became the foundations for the widespread segregation of the 1920s and 1930s; Mexican immigrants were not allowed in public facilities such as schools, restaurants, swimming pools, and theaters (Menchaca and Valencia 1990, 230).

We know of the close correlation between family poverty and children's educational levels and between educational and economic development. Furthermore, the white population is becoming older and decreasing both in the labor force and in schools. In fact, the demographic enrollment predictions of the 1970s were too conservative. In the Southwest, the increased immigration of Latino and Asian populations has shifted in two decades both the total numbers of children in schools and their racial/ethnic balance vis-à-vis the magnitude of the white non-Hispanic population. California will face radical changes before any other state. In 1970, only 30 percent of children in K–12 public schools were ethnic and racial minority students. Finally in 1990, after 140 years of predominantly white enrollment, 50 percent of California public school students belonged to ethnic/racial subgroups. There exists no numerical majority of whites. By the year 2030, white students will constitute about 30 percent of the total enrollment, and Latino students will represent the largest group (44 percent of the total enrollment) (Valencia 1991, 17). Other school demographic projections suggest that the white school-aged population will decrease for the country-at-large while the Latino school-aged population will continue to increase. Latino children (five to seventeen years of age) numbered six million in the national population in 1982 (9 percent of the national youth population); by 2020 they will increase to 19 million (25 percent of the country's youth population). The Latino school-aged population will more than triple in twenty-eight years (Valencia 1991, 18–19).

As Suárez-Orozco has pointed out, the United States is experiencing national hardship. There exists widespread job insecurity, an increase in crime, and a crisis in family values. Anxieties have focused on immigrants and refugees, who are blamed for our problems and our deep and "terrifying sense of home-less-ness" (Suárez-Orozco 1998). Some of this anxiety is related to the vast changes in immigration patterns. To understand long-term population trends and the impact of Latinos, we must examine what we have come to know about Latino immigrants for the last three decades. According to Rumbaut and Cornelius (1995), in 1990 there were 19.7 million immigrants (defined as persons born outside U.S. territory) in the United States (or 6.8 percent of the U.S. population), of which 8,416,924 were Latinos. *Latinos* includes people from Cuba, Colombia, Jamaica, Nicaragua, Haiti, the Dominican Republic, Guatemala, El Salvador, and Mexico. Of these, 4,298,014 were from Mexico. Of all Latino immigrants, 78 percent came between 1970 and 1989 (6.5 million, one-third of all immigrants), and 50 percent came in the 1980s. Only 27 percent of these Latinos have become U.S. citizens, which is understandable given the recency of their arrival, type of work, rural background, and limited assistance. Sixty percent of Mexican immigrants live in California. As has been recognized, a person's educational level seems to predict economic level and employment. The highest rates of poverty are found among the populations with the least education: Mexicans, Salvadorians, Guatemalans, Dominicans, and Haitians. New immigrant children face many difficult problems in their adaptation. According to Suárez-Orozco and Suárez-Orozco,

> Most immigrant families (specifically the Mexican migrant families) must face language inadequacies, a general unfamiliarity with the customs and expectations of the new country, limited economic opportunities, poor housing conditions, discrimination, and what psychologists term the "stresses of acculturation." . . . Despite these obstacles, many migrants often consider their lot as having improved from what it was in their country of origin. [1995a, 325; see also Suárez-Orozco 1998]

In addition, because migrants (immigrants who take low-skill jobs at times in different places for an undetermined period of time) hold to a perception of improvement, they often fail to internalize the negative attitudes of mainstream people toward them by maintaining their country of origin as a point of reference. Indeed, they show as evidence of improvement a pattern of conspicuous consumption in their visits to their villages of origin (displaying new trucks, good clothes, and spending money). The Suárez-Orozcos suggest that immigrants do not see their new lives in terms of the ideals of the majority society but in terms of the "old culture," thus holding to a "dual frame of reference" (1995a, 325).

As children of immigrants become ethnographers, they have to confront serious identity crises and conflicts between their loyalties as members of ethnic communities and as members of an elite of social scientists. In a recent article, for example, Sofia Villenas has expressed some of the conflicts and dilemmas faced by children of immigrants who become ethnographers:

> Geographically, politically, and economically, I have lived under the same yoke of colonization as the Chicano communities I study, experiencing the same discrimination and alienation from mainstream society that comes from being a member of a caste "minority." . . . Racially and ethnically I am *indigena*, a detribalized Native American woman, descendant of the Quechua-speaking people of the South American Andes. Politically I am a Chicana, born and raised in the American Southwest, in the legendary territories of Aztlan. [1996, 712]

Villenas concludes with a remarkable insight, "We[,] the new generation of "native" ethnographers, including myself, increasingly working within and writing about our own communities, we are beginning to question how our histories and identities are entangled in the workings of domination as we engage the oppressive discourses of 'othering' " (1996, 729).

Critical ethnographic practice demands a conscious realization of the risks and epistemological challenges researchers must face (Kincheloe 1991). Our first concern in studying the Mexican immigrant is the necessity of locating the immigrant within the wider practices of domination and imperialism of the capitalist state. Critical ethnographers have employed the concepts of ideology and hegemony in their attempts to explore domination, and we believe these terms are necessary and instructive in the study of Mexican immigrants. Critical ethnographers such as Jean and John Comaroff (1991) have made a significant contribution to our understanding of the ways in which power is inscribed in and through culture, leading to practices of domination and exploitation that have become naturalized in everyday social life. Their analysis can shed important light on the social relations that both constrain and enable the lives of Mexican immigrants to the United States. According to the Comaroffs, *hegemony* refers to "that order of signs and practices, relations and distinctions, images and epistemologies—drawn from a historically situated cultural field—that come to be taken for granted as the natural and received shape of the world and everything that inhabits it" (1991, 23). These axiomatic and yet ineffable discourses and practices that are presumptively shared become "ideological" precisely when their internal contradictions are revealed, uncovered, and viewed as arbitrary and negotiable. *Ideology*, then, refers to a highly articulated worldview, master narrative, or organizing scheme for collective symbolic production. The dominant ideology is the expression of the dominant social group.

Following this line of argument, hegemony "is nonnegotiable and therefore beyond direct argument," whereas ideology "is more susceptible to being perceived as a matter of inimical opinion and interest and therefore is open to contestation." (Comaroff and Comaroff 1991, 24). Ideologies become the expressions of specific groups, whereas *hegemony* refers to conventions and constructs that are shared and naturalized throughout a political community. Hegemony works through both silences and repetition in naturalizing the dominant worldview. There also may exist oppositional ideologies among subordinate or subaltern groups—whether well formed or loosely articulated—that to some extent are able to break free of hegemony. Resistance among oppositional agents can change, subvert, or reject authoritatively proposed cultural meanings. In this way hegemony is never total or complete; it is always porous. According to the Comaroffs,

> The making of hegemony involves the assertion of control over various modes of symbolic production: over such things as educational and ritual processes, patterns of socialization, political and legal procedures, canons of style and self-representation, public communication, health and bodily discipline, and so on. That control, however—as Foucault understood about the generic nature of surveillance—must be sustained over time and in such a way that it becomes, to all intents and purposes, invisible. [1991, 24]

Hegemony and ideology exist in a relation of "reciprocal interdependence." The Comaroffs explain,

> Hegemony, we suggest, exists in reciprocal interdependence with ideology: it is that part of the dominant worldview which has been naturalized and, having hidden itself in orthodoxy, no more appears as ideology at all. Inversely, the ideologies of the subordinate may give expression to discordant but hitherto voiceless experience of contradictions that a prevailing hegemony can no longer conceal. Self-evidently, the hegemonic proportion of any dominant ideology may be greater or lesser. It will never be total, save perhaps in the fanciful dreams of fascists, and only rarely will it shrink away to nothing. The manner in which some of the acts and axioms of a sectarian worldview actually come to be naturalized, or how critical reactions grow from the invisible roots that anchor inequality, is always a historically specific issue. [1991, 25]

What critical ethnographers attempt to reveal, then, is the way in which hegemonic formations are able to persist—often in the face of serious challenges—over time in any given social context or cultural field. In other words, critical ethnographers attempt to reveal how hegemonic practices, systems of meaning and typification, and methods of interpretation have insinuated themselves into everyday life. For instance, in the case of the Comaroffs' own ethnography, *Of Revelation and Revolution* (1991), they were able to investigate the encounter between British missionaries and the southern Tswana peoples of the South African frontier. The Comaroffs analyzed the interplay of structural constraints and situational contingencies that informed the encounter between the colonizer and the colonized and produced forms of agentive power (exercised in purposive acts of the colonizer that express more or less coherent values and meanings and political and material concerns) and nonagentive power (power embedded in conventional ways of seeing and being throughout the diverse forms of the colonizing culture).

There is an additional and productive way of conceptualizing ideology for advancing a critical ethnography for the study of Mexican immigrant families. This position argues that there is no way of experiencing the real relations of a particular society outside of its cultural, semiotic, or ideological categories or criteriologies. Some ideological categories give us a more adequate understanding of power relations than others. Take the work of Althusser as one example. The Althusserian conception of ideology is one in which ideology and hegemony are syncopated. Althusser maintains that ideology "represents the imaginary relationship of individuals to their real conditions of existence" (1984, 36). In other words, ideology produces our symbolic relation to the real. While real relations declare their own meanings unambiguously, within the regime of the "taken for granted," in essence they are ideological because they can only be understood within certain systems of representation. In addition, ideology constitutes individuals as "subjects." This is a powerful formulation because it maintains that ideological relationships produce the illusion that people act out of their own free will. In reality, individuals are not self-determining agents at all; rather, they are produced through discursive, cultural, and socioeconomic processes. Their self-determination is always partial. They have freedom to act—but in contexts not of their own making and populated with the discourses and ideologies of others.

The production of ideology influences individuals to misrecognize their selves as unique and self-determining. Consequently, they are unlikely to understand the production of their identities through social and material relations. According to Althusser, ideological forms of misrecognition of the real relations of domination are transmitted through churches, schools, government agencies, and the media. However, this does not mean that the structural dominance of the ruling class always and forever ensures the dominance of ruling ideas. Ideological strategies have no *necessary* class, race, or gender belonging. In other words, to suggest that the dominant ideology unproblematically reproduces itself—that there is an empirical identity between class and ideology, for example—is unwarrantable. Within this view, hegemony becomes an attempt to create ideological closure through the "winning of consent" of the people—sometimes by articulating their fears and anxieties—to particular ideological perspectives. This is often done through a politics of signification. There is always a semiotic struggle over how discourses are produced. Within the United States, for instance, the meaning of *democracy* is signified in relation to already durable historical meanings and cultural conventions that give the term some ideological fixity. However, in Mexico the meaning of U.S. democracy is often constructed—and, in our view, with great historical accuracy—within a field of discourses that have situated the United States historically as an imperialist nation. In Stuart Hall's interpretation, ideology "sets limits to the degree to which a society-in-dominance can easily, smoothly and functionally reproduce itself" (1991, 112). Yet we stress that hegemony is never fully successful but has to be constantly "won."

By attempting to understand the workings of ideology and hegemony in the lives of Mexican immigrants, the critical ethnographer is able to locate immigrant families who have contradictory relationships with the dominant social order. Immigrant families can be seen as positioned within the larger global division of labor as oppressed groups struggling to overcome their oppression. Yet, from the perspectives of some immigrants, forms of oppression in the United States may be described as of "lower intensity" from an economic standpoint (if they happen to be earning money) or of "higher intensity" from the perspective of how they are perceived by the Anglo majority population (as "illegals" or "crimmegrants").

An understanding of hegemonic and ideological relations—always in relation to social relations of production—that both enable and constrain the Mexican immigrant can help to reveal the conventions—such as commodity, linguistic, and epistemological formations—that suffuse, animate, and regulate everyday life. In this way, the researcher can tease out the contradictions between the world as represented by the ethnographer and the world as experienced by the group being investigated. This is because the relationship between the researcher and the object of research is always historically produced within a nexus of power relations. Knowledge of the social world is always insinuated in human interest and social power, and the power of the ethnographer to define the world for the research subject is an issue that deserves serious consideration.

The process of hegemony can help the researcher to understand how the socioeconomic conditions of individuals and groups persist through succeeding generations—sometimes following some improvement—even among those groups that exercise considerable resistance to their oppression. Here, cross-cultural comparisons might provide some needed insight. Consider the case of what Suárez-Orozco (1998) calls the production of "postnational" space. By "postnational" space, Suárez-Orozco refers to the vacuum that is created when social spaces are subverted, reconfigured, and reconstituted. In such a space, immigrants who come to the United States as part of "guest" worker programs negotiate their identities with a liminal space in which, having been forced to leave one nation, they do not identify wholly with their new culture. Although the economy needs them, they are officially denounced by those associated with the current ethos of anti-immigrant sentiment and Latinophobia. They have been turned into phantoms and ghosts who are not supposed to be in the United States yet are secretly protected in some ways by government officials (who see them as an antidote to labor shortages). Yet these very same officials denounce them in their campaign rhetoric. As Suárez-Orozco (1998) notes, the ghost workers must at once "be there" (to do the impossible jobs) but not be there (be voiceless and transparent). As Suárez-Orozco makes clear, the immigrant workers are necessary to an underground economy that props up the affluent lifestyles of those who live in the bourgeois Anglo neighborhoods and hire undocumented workers to blow-dry their lawns and serve as nannies for their children. Politicians realize the advantage of having Mexican immigrants working here as virtual slaves (who could be exploited more fully?), yet at the same time they officially and unashamedly denounce undocumented workers, support the militarization of the border, and eagerly applaud the police when they capture and beat (and sometimes murder) Mexicans fleeing across the border. In this case, the concept of ideology and hegemony can be employed in order to understand how such a contradictory set of relationships serves the dual purpose of reproducing existing racial and class hierarchies.

An understanding of hegemony can also assist critical ethnographers in postulating counterhegemonic strategies to assist Mexican immigrants in developing a praxis of social transformation. A practice of transformation is one in which Mexican immigrants come to acquire the analytical and conceptual tools to analyze their oppression. This way, they may not only strive to survive and become more selectively "adaptive" to the dominant socioeconomic order but simultaneously work to transform the oppressive living environment that affects not only their own communities but exploited workers in general.

We consider the construction of a critical ethnography for the study of Latino populations within the United States to be an urgent task for current and future generations of researchers. We wish to further sketch some of the characteristics of what such a critical ethnographic practice might look like. Such a critical practice would challenge the authority of the masculine subject of analysis. For instance, Patricia Ticineto Clough (1992) has suggested that the institutional form of discursive authority that accompanies a considerable amount of mainstream ("malestream") ethnographic research subjugates the researcher to an oedipal logic that supports a unified masculinist and heroic identity. A critical ethnography would also attempt to challenge the discourses that tacitly inform the colonial imagination of the researcher whose own self-contained, unified subject position unconsciously forms the privileged reference point for judging research subjects and for legitimating certain imperial discourses that construct those subjects as the *Other*. For instance, in a recent work, Behar comments on the privileged position of the ethnography in the academy:

> When Clifford Geertz writes about "the burden of authorship" or James Clifford writes about "ethnographic authority," they don't say authorship is a privilege to which many of us are not born; we arrive at authorship often clumsily, often painfully, often through a process of self-betrayal and denial. Authorship is a privilege constituted by the gender, sociohistorical background, and class origins, or lately, class diasporas, of the anthropologist doing the writing. [1993, 338]

To respond to this situation, critical ethnographers need to more fully recognize the complexity of relations that constitute the researchers' own socially determined positions within the reality that they are attempting to understand. Different researchers from different disciplines have attempted to develop creative and more eclectic approaches in order to deal with the complex problems of doing research with immigrant populations.

One of the most overlooked domains in situating the researcher's "politics of location" has been that of social class. Critical ethnographers must continue to focus on capitalist social relations and avoid decapitating culture from its deep location within social relations of production. Although capitalism is moving cataclysmically across the stage of history, hurtling along the fault line of the age of consumption with a reckless abandon that threatens at every turn to annihilate justice for the poor, it carries within its engine of destruction the inevitability of its own demise that will cause it to derail itself from the tramlines of progress. Emancipation can be conjured out of capitalism only when the power of capital is broken, only when its virtues are used to crush its vices, only when the range of human activity that capital agitates out of the productive forces is transcended, only when the possibilities immanent within its own calculus of devastation are set free, only when bourgeois monuments to progress tumble and are replaced by revolutionary hope conjugated with struggle, and only when capitalism's a priori foreclosure of moral history is replaced by a vast leap into the social imagination that can overcome the tremulous détente of exploitation between capitalism and democracy and help us to stake our claim to history. For these reasons, it is crucial that critical ethnographers continue their criticism of capitalist social relations.

A PEDAGOGY OF HOPE THROUGH CRITICAL ETHNOGRAPHY

Critical ethnography is risky and painful. At times ethnographers "do not want to know too many of the details. They want to explain social inequality by blaming the victims or in any other way that leaves their accustomed identities intact. They are afraid of being wounded" (Carspecken 1996:170–71). Because critical ethnography is a commitment to praxis, discourse alone is not sufficient. To explain why relatively powerless Mexican immigrant people can create a system of resistance to dominant beliefs, values, norms, and practices can be frightening to many people. Mothers, Mexican immigrant women who defend their cultural integrity in all arenas, especially in the schools, can be even more frightening. A pedagogy of hope based on Vygotskian principles (as we shall see below) establishes the relationship among culture, language, and cognition as the foundation to understand the role of culture in mediating the transmission of knowledge and intellectual growth. The mediation through appropriate cultural symbols in the construction of academic knowledge (or via "assisted performance") must translate instruction into pedagogical practices that permit immigrant children to engage in their own development, to invest their own cultural and linguistic capital, and to advance without prejudice. The research in schools conducted by Kris Gutierrez and her colleagues (Gutierrez 1994; Gutierrez, Larson, and Kreuter 1995; Gutierrez, Rymes, and Larson 1995) is a clear example of critical ethnography with an understanding of the developmental principles that Vygotsky and neo-Vygotskians have established. This research not only disclosed hegemonic structures of teachers but opened new interactional and curricular strategies to capitalize on the linguistic and cultural richness of children's background through an intensive, collaborative, joint construction of knowledge in the classroom.

In spite of the inherent challenges and difficulties faced by ethnographers, critical ethnography with a Vygotskian perspective continues to be one of the most promising fields in the hands of educational researchers committed to sound pedagogy and the full development of immigrant children, for they are new avenues to create a pedagogy of hope in the actual instruction. This type of critical ethnography is based on the principles of assisted performance within the "zone of proximal development" (ZPD) established by Vygotsky and practiced today by neo-Vygotskians. The combined principles of critical ethnography (consistent with Freire's pedagogy of hope) are compatible with, and complementary to, the principles of the sociohistorical school of psychology represented by the work of Vygotsky (and neo-Vygotskians). More specifically, this essay suggests that in order to build an ethnographic research agenda with a relevant pedagogical praxis in schools, one could combine critical ethnography with Vygotsky's theory of human development.

One of the most important contributions of Vygotsky to our understanding of immigrant children's intellectual development and school achievement, especially of those undergoing rapid sociocultural change, is his theory about the relationship between cognitive and social phenomena (1962, 1978; see also Cole 1985; Moll 1986, 1990; Scribner and Cole 1981; Trueba 1991; Wertsch 1981, 1985, 1991). Vygotsky states that the development of uniquely human higher-level mental functions such as consciousness and the creation of taxonomic cognitive structures (required for academic learning) find their origin in day-to-day social interaction. Vygotsky searches in our daily social lives for the origins of human consciousness and higher-level mental functions. According to Moll, if teachers follow Vygotskian principles, they will see literacy as "the understanding and communication of meaning" and will make efforts "to make classrooms literate environments in which many language experiences can take place and different types of literacies can be developed and learned" (1990, 8). Indeed, Moll stresses the idea that "teachers who follow this approach reject rote instruction or reducing reading and writing into skill sequences taught in isolation or a successive, stage like manner. Rather, they emphasize the creation of social contexts in which children actively learn to use, try, and manipulate language in the service of making sense or creating meaning" (1990, 8). Effective teachers who understand the process of internalization that permits students the transition from interpsychological experience to intrapsychological cognitive categories adopt culturally and linguistically meaningful teaching strategies (Cole 1985; D'Andrade 1984; Vygotsky 1962, 1978), that is, strategies occurring within the ZPD of children. The zone of proximal development was defined by Vygotsky as the distance between a child's *"actual developmental level as determined by independent problem solving"* and the higher level of *"potential development as determined through problem solving under adult guidance or in collaboration with more capable peers"* (1978, 86). Furthermore, if we accept the intimate relationship between language and thought proposed by Vygotsky (who sees language as a symbolic system mediating all social and cognitive functions), we must link the lower intellectual development and school achievement of some immigrant children with the abrupt transition from a familiar to an unfamiliar sociocultural environment and, therefore, the lack of both linguistic and cultural knowledge to interact meaningfully with adults and peers. Consequently, no suitable ZPDs are opened up for them by adults or more informed peers, and the discourse and cognitive categories required to function in school are not readily available to them (Brown et al. 1982; Trueba 1991). In other words, it is impossible to create appropriate ZPDs in oppressive and unfamiliar learning environments without the symbolic tools that allow children to make sense of social transactions and translate them into intrapsychological phenomena. However, a bilingual and bicultural teacher who understands the predicament of immigrant children can create appropriate ZPDs, as it will be shown below. The use of these ZPDs requires awareness of not only the relationship among language, thought, and culture but also the principles of critical pedagogy.

The ethnographer not only is an advocate for immigrant children but must discover the rich cultural and linguistic capital of the immigrant family and the optimal use of the cultural and linguistic resources available to children in their own home environments. It is recognized by cultural psychologists and critical pedagogues that the adaptive responses of immigrants vary according to their prearrival experiences. For example, the key factors affecting the educational success of Mexican children are related to the socioeconomic, cultural, and political experiences that shape their sociocultural environments and their skills to handle the traumas they must face in the United States upon their arrival. Let us be more specific. The process of marginalization often associated with school failure and dropout phenomena is often associated with conspicuous poverty and isolation upon arrival to this country. The lack of communication with individuals who speak their language creates a vacuum of support and a deep sense of anxiety over expectations and norms of appropriate behavior. Poverty is associated with the nature of the employment that parents find, which is inherently unstable and not paid well. Another source of poverty is associated with the urgent needs of the family left behind in Mexico, which expects money to be sent home regularly. Immigrants often incur substantial debts in order to pay the costs of going north to find employment.

The ability to learn among immigrant children is related to the home learning environment and their ability to understand in a larger historical context their personal and family rights. This is consistent with Vygotsky's theory of development (1962, 1978; see also Cole 1985; Wertsch 1981, 1991) and Freire's broad concept of literacy (1973, 1995; Freire and Macedo 1987, 1996). Consequently, an important factor affecting the adaptive strategies of Mexican immigrant families is their degree of literacy (in the broad Freirean sense), that is, their understanding of complex social systems and their ability to handle text related to those systems (contracts, government documents, bank, hospitals, immigration office, etc.). The marginalization of Mexican youth is related to their uprooting from their home communities and the rejection they feel in school. Consequently, for them to engage in learning relationships with teachers and more knowledgeable peers (in a Vygotskian sense) is culturally repugnant and the equivalent of siding with the oppressor. They see their parents being abused at work, and they do not buy the notion that the family is better off in the United States. While the point of reference for their parents is Mexico, the point of reference for the youth is not Mexico but, rather, what they see in this country. The marginalization and exploitation of their parents may have begun in Mexico, but the resistance to accept exploitation is an integral part of the self-definition of immigrant youth. Parents' sometimes naive notions about the politics of employment and the organization and politics in schools, and their reaction to societal demands for cultural homogenization and acceptance of an inferior status, are not shared by their children, who feel an ethical responsibility to react and fight back. Much of what happens in gang struggles and street violence is related to marginalization (Vigil 1983, 1988, 1989, 1997). Many Mexican families reflect in their new lives a change not only from one country to another but from a rural to an urban setting. Of course, the added dimension in this country is that in order to acquire the necessary sociopolitical knowledge of appropriate conduct in urban settings, immigrants must first acquire the communicative skills to do so in a second language.

To compound the problem, immigrants often take jobs that are exhaustive and leave them little time to acquire communicative skills in English. The consequences for the children of immigrants is that soon they are forced to play adult roles in making momentous decisions for their parents because the children know some English and understand a bit better the social system. Furthermore, from a Vygotskian perspective, Mexican immigrant children who are socialized in a new linguistic and cultural environment cannot get the assistance that is congruent with their ZPDs and their linguistic and cognitive skills. Thus, their development slows down considerably. This fact has important pedagogical implications for an educational reform that recognizes the need to prepare teachers capable of teaching culturally different children.

Serious problems that may complicate the schooling of young immigrant children upon their arrival in the United States are malnutrition and the neglect of their health. These occur not only in the case of migrant workers but also among urban dwellers who are isolated and cannot afford to pay for the cost of child care. Again, to compound these problems, families who have any members without full documentation feel the most vulnerable and cannot seek help from social agencies, even if they rightfully qualify to receive it. In many instances, exploited workers do not have health insurance or welfare and do not have access to a physician prior to childbirth or even past a few weeks after childbirth. The dismal housing conditions increase the chances of health problems and child neglect. In some cases, even the safety of children is jeopardized in the substandard housing occupied in some cases by drug addicts and vandals. These conditions are also associated with the early recruitment of Mexican children into gangs and the school dropout phenomena.

If, along with the precarious conditions that families live in, the school lacks the resources for or interest in providing special attention to immigrant children, then the chance for academic failure increases dramatically. Families' experience of racial discrimination, verbal and physical abuse of immigrant children on the part of mainstream children, and the predominant opinion among teachers that Latino children are low achievers certainly do not help. These experiences create for immigrant children a complex setting in which they must redefine themselves in the United States, and they often motivate them to reject their own family, language, and culture. This symbolic "self-rejection" and the formation of a new identity do not necessarily result in embracing school and U.S. society. A number of scholars have recently dealt with these problems of adaptation in the context of the school environment (Bartolomé 1996; Bartolomé and Macedo 1997; Delgado-Gaitan 1994; Deyhle and Margonis 1995; Gutierrez 1994; Gutierrez, Larson, and Kreuter 1995; Patthey-Chavez 1993; Wilson 1991). Several scholars, using critical pedagogy, offer as a solution "transformative" strategies for teachers and students (based on Freire 1973 and 1995, see works such as Giroux and McLaren 1994; Freire and Macedo 1987; and McLaren 1995, 1997a, 1997b, 2000, among others).

There is an intimate relationship between the successful psychological adaptation of Mexican immigrant families to U.S. society and the academic success of their children. For example, a recent study in central California (Trueba 1997) shows that the most serious problem faced by the children of immigrants on the West Coast is the alienating experience of transitioning from the local Mexican community middle school to the mainstream high school in a nearby city. Schooling in that city brings a rapid marginalization of these children and adds to their confusion regarding personal identity, cultural values, social acceptance, and their ability to achieve and overall self-worth. Consequently, we feel that if children manage to retain a strong and affirming self-identity and remain as part of the sociocultural community, they can achieve in school. Carola and Marcelo Suárez-Orozco have also shown in their recent study (1995b) that immigrant children's learning abilities and social skills deteriorate the longer they are exposed to American society's alienating environment, which undermines their overall school achievement and adaptation to this society. The traumatic experience of being uprooted, and the confusion about family values and personal survival, coupled with the need for peer support, is bound to lead many youth to become affiliated with gangs (Vigil 1983, 1988, 1989) and to disregard the codes of behavior prescribed by mainstream society.

Frequently, a family takes special precautions to salvage the moral character and overall well-being of a youth by taking him or her back to Mexico for a period of time, to complete his or her education, work under supervision, or marry a local person. There are cases when the entire family returns to Mexico in order to re-educate teenagers in the family's values. This is often associated with a serious reassessment of the family's finances and the risks involved in continuing to work in the United States. The number of repatriated ex-farmworkers in Colima, Michoacán, and Jalisco is increasing rapidly. However, in contrast with the alien-ation of Mexican immigrant children in major cities (such as Los Angeles, Chicago, New York, Houston, and other cities—see, for example, Vigil 1983, 1988, 1989, 1997), those children who live in settings where they can manage to retain their home language and culture, their familiar cultural institutions and networks, seem (at least in some cases—see Trueba 1997) to survive the trauma of schooling in the United States. This, of course, is the result of a carefully exe-cuted plan of education engineered primarily by the mothers who monitor school-ing and defend their language and culture by creating vast networks on both sides of the border, thus supporting their children's strong Mexican identity and their ability to live in a binational and bicultural world. Some scholars (Martin and Taylor 1996) who know intimately the lives and needs of the seasonal farmworker population in California, as well as the demographic trends in the state, have recently outlined their observations and concerns. Immigration of seasonal farm-workers begins with U.S. recruitment during tough economic conditions in rural Mexico and job opportunities in California (Martin and Taylor 1996, 2). Agri-cultural towns in California are rapidly growing as a result of both immigration and the reproductive rates of immigrants. Between 25 percent and 50 percent of residents in these towns have incomes below the federal poverty levels and often live in overgrown labor camps. In these rural communities, the correlation between immigrant population increase and the ratio of children in schools is higher than that between the population's increase and its use of public assistance.

The sense that there is no end in sight to the waves of immigrants is pervasive and creates a contradiction between immigration and integration policies, espe-cially considering that children of seasonal farmworkers raised in the United States do not choose seasonal farmwork. A fundamental question is whether we are allowing unregulated immigration in order to create rural poverty and, if so, what is likely to happen to the children of these immigrants. If the only option left for growers is to import new farm labor from Mexico, then new immigration will bring new poverty and more segregation. If the United States wants to cur-tail immigration from Mexico, it must invest in rural Mexico to develop internal sources of employment so rural Mexican seasonal farmworkers can repatriate.

Repatriation can mean stability and economic security for some families (at least for a while) and provide families with the necessary economic and emotional support that cements their long-term resiliency as immigrants. It can also give children the opportunity to receive an education. Fortunately, not all the circumstances surrounding the education of children from Mexican immigrant families are negative. The fact that so many of them succeed in our schools may be linked to the following factors that enhance their successful adaptation in the United States. The role of women in the maintenance of the home language and culture seems to have played a key role in the successful adaptation of some Mexican immigrant families (Hondagneu-Sotelo 1994; Trueba 1997). Many factors contribute to the retention of the Spanish language: the critical mass of immigrants who speak the language, the frequent visits to the hometowns and cities, and the interdependence between the families living on both sides of the border. The organization of functional networks of these families and their friends has been most instrumental in the survival of families during difficult economic times, but it has also served as a very strong emotional support system to retain a strong Mexican identity in the face of the traumas alluded to above by the Suárez-Orozcos (1995b; Suárez-Orozco 1998). The substantial, although informal, financial cooperative system can also become a powerful political base to demand respect for their educational rights, as was the case in Guadalupe, California (Trueba 1997). Traditional organizations that had a religious character in the Mexican tradition become a strong political enclave and support system in their adaptation to this country (Trueba et al. 1993). In fact, the only way for these families to engage in long-term economic ventures (buying land in Mexico, purchasing homes in the United States, etc.) is through the collective security of the family networks on both sides of the border, collective savings, and a commitment to assist each other in times of crisis. The skills to survive emotionally and economically in the worst of situations continue to be a unique characteristic of many immigrant families, which strategically invest every possible resource they may find. These resources are often obtained through their binational networks. This "know-how," which Freire calls "knowing the world" in contrast with literacy as "knowing the word," is often the key factor in the survival and adaptation of the immigrant family on both sides of the border.

In a recent study in a Mexican migrant community of central California (El Rocío), Trueba (1997) found that the resistance to oppression and the resiliency of immigrant families were enhanced through the maintenance of Mexican culture. In their daily lives, civil and religious ceremonies, and major events—births, burials, weddings, and so forth—family networks functioned via frequent communication with their hometowns in Mexico. Visits from Mexican relatives (grandparents, uncles, aunts, and cousins) forced children to retain their cultural foundations in order to reaffirm their Mexican identity and retain a strong self-concept. Indeed, these children refused to be treated as an underclass by their teachers and the surrounding English-speaking society. Bilingualism was the rule, and academic excellence in both languages was the mechanism to earn respect from teachers. These families articulated a vision for their children's economic futures through hard academic work. It was a vision of resistance to oppression by showing the oppressors that Mexicans are smart and can achieve. It was not an oppositional self-identity in the Ogbuan sense of resigning themselves not to excel in the arenas in which the mainstream population is successful but, rather, one whereby they would do better than the whites in mainstream arenas—in school and professional careers and occupations. The key role in the socialization of Mexican children for academic success was played by women, the mothers who keep a close watch on their children's schooling.

The efforts of women in El Rocío (Trueba 1998) demonstrated an underlying collective organization through networks and long-term economic planning necessary to counteract the inherent instability of farm labor and its meager pay. Economic survival was for these families as important as cultural survival. The integrity of the family life in both El Rocío and the hometowns required very careful use of the family resources. Many of these families had originally planned to return to Mexico and used about half of their income in various investments in their Mexican hometowns (purchase of land, new businesses, construction of homes, etc.). Three factors forced them to change their long-term plans: (1) new economic crises in Mexico, (2) the backlash against immigrants in the United States (see Suárez-Orozco 1996), and (3) the academic aspirations of their children now well adjusted in the United States. Trueba's study reflects an effort in the direction of the type of critical ethnography that we have been discussing. It focuses not only on the oppression of a given population but on their strategies for reaching empowerment; that is, it focuses on schooling and on the actions of parents, teachers, and other adults who have an impact on children's futures and consequently can help children of an oppressed population to escape the trap of underachievement and marginalization. Schoolchildren learn that their own low economic status, clearly resulting from oppressive working conditions, should not destroy their ethnic identity, their aspirations for a better life, or their self-confidence. Trueba (1997) feels that classroom instruction could provide the home language and culture with a legitimacy and high status that enhance a strong affiliation of families to their ethnicity, as well as personal confidence to acquire English as a second language and the academic skills necessary to function in—and transform—U.S. society. In his study, Trueba found that instructional style and its effectiveness in the teaching of mathematics constitute only the beginning for immigrant students' empowerment and their successful adaptation to this country, and that Mexican immigrant women, in particular, express in powerful terms their commitment to the academic success of children as the cornerstone of cultural and economic survival.

CONCLUDING THOUGHTS

Certainly critical ethnography has a utopian moment, one that is not meant to be frozen in certitude but, rather, one that is considered to be suggestive of the struggle ahead. The struggle ahead is never a blueprint we construct through the synthesis of our research. Rather, it is more like a series of possible contingencies and is similar to a critical disposition toward the creation of what Paulo Freire has referred to as "multiculturality"—the "coexistence of different cultures in one and the same space" (1995, 157). According to Freire, no multiculturality arises spontaneously; rather, it "must be created, politically produced, worked on, in the sweat of one's brow, in concrete history" (1994, 157). The most essential characteristic of multiculturality is the struggle for unity within diversity. Such a struggle is a historical creation, involving decision, political determination, mobilization, and organization on the part of each cultural group, in view of common purposes. Thus, it calls for a certain educational practice, one that will be consistent with these objectives. It calls for a new ethics, founded on respect for recognition of people's cultural uniqueness and their right to their "otherness" (Freire 1995, 157). It also calls for a collective struggle on the part of all oppressed groups against capitalist systems of exploitation. We are hard-pressed to find a better definition of the praxis that we would like to see result from critical ethnographic research on Mexican immigrant populations. An appropriate pedagogy for immigrant children brings us to a Vygotskian–Freirean concept of struggle for liberation using the children's language and culture as the most effective semiotic vehicle to invite their active and meaningful participation in their own intellectual and political development without losing their ethnic identity.

The challenge, however, is to combine critical ethnography with a Vygotskian approach to instruction for empowerment. In a genuinely Freirean pedagogy ("knowing the word and knowing the world"), literacy is an essential instrument to reclaim control of one's own life and one's full human rights and dignity. In a Vygotskian theoretical framework, literacy is the essential link between the social and cognitive worlds that permits children to grow intellectually, to learn, and to develop their talents and capacities; but in order to acquire literacy, children need to enjoy full human rights and supportive relationships with "more informed peers" and teachers. For both Freire and Vygotsky, children need to know the world in order to learn the word. Higher mental functions cannot develop unless children enjoy positive social relationships and are not the victims of poverty, isolation, abuse, racism, neglect, or poor health. A Vygotskian pedagogy of hope presupposes the respect for human rights and more: the creation of a positive learning environment in which children become the engineers of their own intellectual destiny and co-construct their future. For Freire there is no liberation or empowerment without active involvement in one's own liberation. Consequently, a Vygotskian pedagogy of hope is truly Freirean in substance, and, in turn, the logical sequel to Freirean critical pedagogy is a Vygotskian developmental approach to teaching and learning. Freedom from racism and oppression does not guarantee learning and development in children, but it is the necessary condition for both. Children's higher mental functions develop on the basis of an environment free of oppression but with the active engagement of joint social and cognitive relationships with those who can help children discover new worlds through new words. In brief, a

Vygotskian theory of development takes off where a Freirean theory of equity and empowerment leaves. The appropriate pedagogies developed on the basis of the ZPD cannot produce the desired outcomes without Freire's principles and the abolition of hegemonic instructional structures and larger social relations of capitalist exploitation. In the end, critical ethnographers must continue to ask themselves what their praxis is all about, what their genuine contribution to the intellectual growth of children is. Critical ethnographers must maintain a serious, consistent, and strong commitment to children's liberation from abuse, oppression, and misery; but such ethnographers must also commit to study further the use of appropriate strategies to maximize the intellectual development of children as they grow in schools and society. Pedagogy does not end in the school; it must continue in the homes, in society, and in all domains of life. Critical ethnographers are just beginning to open up doors and avenues for development. Their understanding of developmental theories is crucial if they are to live their praxis as researchers.

REFERENCES

Althusser, Louis. 1984. *Essays on Ideology*. London: Verso.

Anzaldúa, G. 1987. *Borderlands/La Frontera*. San Francisco: Spinsters/Aunt Lute.

Apple, M. W. 1989 [1986]. *Teachers and Texts: A Political Economy of Class and Gender Relations in Education*. New York: Routledge.

———. 1993. *Official Knowledge: Democratic Education in a Conservative Age*. New York and London: Routledge.

Aronowitz, S., and H. Giroux. 1991. *Postmodern Education: Politics, Culture and Social Criticism*. Minneapolis: University of Minnesota Press.

Bartolomé, L. 1996. Beyond the Methods Fetish: Toward a Humanizing Pedagogy. In "Breaking Free: The Transformative Power of Critical Pedagogy," theme issue, ed. P. Leistyna, A. Woodrum, and S. A. Sherblom. *Harvard Education Review*, Reprint Series, 27: 229–52.

Bartolomé, L., and D. Macedo. 1997. Dancing with Bigotry: The Poisoning of Racial and Cultural Identities. *Harvard Educational Review* 67, no. 2: XX.

Behar, Ruth. 1993. *Translated Woman: Crossing the Border with Esperanza's Story*. Boston: Beacon Press.

Bell, Derrick. 1997. Protecting Diversity Programs from Political and Judicial Attack. *The Chronicle of Higher Education* 43, no. 30 (4 April): 134–35.

Bowles, S., and H. Gintis. 1976. *Schooling in Capitalist America: Educational Reform and the Contradictions of Economic Life*. New York: Basic Books.

Brown, A., E. Campione, M. Cole, P. Griffin, H. Mehan, and M. Riel. 1982. A Model System for the Study of Learning Difficulties. *The Quarterly Newsletter of the Laboratory of Comparative Human Cognition* 4, no. 3: 39–55.

Brown, Karen McCarthy. 1991. *Mama Lola: A Vodou Priestess in Brooklyn*. Berkeley and Los Angeles: University of California Press.

Bureau of the Census. 1996. *Current Population Reports*. June. Washington, D.C.: U.S. Department of Commerce, Economics and Statistics Administration.

Carspecken, Phil Francis. 1996. *Critical Ethnography in Educational Research: A Theoretical and Practical Guide*. New York and London: Routledge.

Clifford, James. 1988. *The Predicament of Culture: Twentieth-Century Ethnography, Literature, and Art*. Cambridge, Mass.: Harvard University Press.

Clifford, James, and George E. Marcus, eds. 1986. *Writing Culture: The Poetics and Politics of Ethnography*. Berkeley and Los Angeles: University of California Press.

Clough, Patricia Ticineto. 1992. *The End(s) of Ethnography: From Realism to Social Criticism*. Newbury Park, Calif.: Sage Publications.

Cole, M. 1985. The Zone of Proximal Development: Where Culture and Cognition Create Each Other. In *Culture, Communication and Cognition: Vygotskian Perspectives*, ed. J. V. Wertsch, 146–61. New York: Cambridge University Press.

———. 1990. Cognitive Development and Formal Schooling: The Evidence from Cross-cultural Research. In *Vygotsky and Education: Instructional Implications and Applications of Sociohistorical Psychology*, ed. L. Moll, 89–110. Cambridge: Cambridge University Press.

Cole, M., and R. D'Andrade. 1982. The Influence of Schooling on Concept Formation: Some Preliminary Conclusions. *The Quarterly Newsletter of the Laboratory of Comparative Human Cognition* 4, no. 2: 19–26.

Comaroff, Jean, and John Comaroff. 1991. *Of Revelation and Revolution: Christianity, Colonialism, and Consciousness in South Africa*, vol. 1. Chicago and London: University of Chicago Press.

D'Andrade, R. 1984. Cultural Meaning Systems. In *Culture Theory*, ed. R. A. Shweder and R. A. Levine, 88–119. Cambridge: Cambridge University Press.

Daniel, E. Valentine. 1996. *Charred Lullabies: Chapters in an Anthropology of Violence*. Princeton, N.J.: Princeton University Press.

De Genova, N. 1997. The Production of Language and the Language of Oppression: Mexican Labor and the Politics of ESL in Chicago Factories. Paper presented at the Spencer Foundation Winter Forum, University of California at Los Angeles, 14–15 February.

Delgado-Gaitan, C. 1994. Russian Refugee Families: Accommodating Aspirations through Education. *Anthropology and Education Quarterly* 25, no. 2: 137–55.

Deyhle, D., and F. Margonis. 1995. Navajo Mothers and Daughters: Schools, Jobs, and the Family. *Anthropology and Education Quarterly* 16, no. 2: 135–67.

Diaz Salcedo, S. 1996. Successful Latino Students at the High School Level: A Case Study of Ten Students. Paper presented at the Graduate School of Education, Harvard University.

Durand, J., E. Parrado, and D. S. Massey. 1996. Migradollars and Development: A Reconsideration of the Mexican Case. *International Migration Review* 30, no. 2: 423–44.

Fine, Michelle. 1991. *Framing Dropouts: Notes on the Politics of an Urban Public High School*. Albany: State University of New York Press.

———. 1992. *Disruptive Voices: The Possibilities of Feminist Research*. Ann Arbor: University of Michigan Press.

Fine, Michelle, and Lois Weis. 1996. Writing the "Wrongs" of Fieldwork: Confronting Our Own Research/Writing Dilemmas in Urban Ethnographies. *Qualitative Inquiry* 2, no. 3: 251–74.

Frankenberg, Ruth. 1993. *The Social Construction of Whiteness: White Women, Race Matters*. Minneapolis: University of Minnesota Press.

Freire, Paulo. 1973. *Pedagogy of the Oppressed*. New York: Seabury.

————. 1995. *Pedagogy of Hope: Reliving Pedagogy of the Oppressed*. Trans. Robert R. Barr. New York: Continuum.

Freire, Paulo, and Donaldo Macedo. 1987. *Literacy: Reading the Word and Reading the World*. Critical Studies in Education Series. Boston: Bergin and Garvey Publishers.

————. 1996. A Dialogue: Culture, Language, and Race. In "Breaking Free: The Transformative Power of Critical Pedagogy," theme issue, ed. P. Leistyna, A. Woodrum, and S. A. Sherblom. *Harvard Education Review*, Reprint Series, 27: 199–228.

Gamio, M. 1930. *Mexican Immigration to the United States: A Study of Human Migration and Adjustment*. Chicago: University of Chicago Press.

Gibson, M., and J. Ogbu, eds. 1991. *Minority Status and Schooling: A Comparative Study of Immigrant and Involuntary Minorities*. New York and London: Garland Publishing Inc.

Giroux, H., and P. McLaren. 1994. *Between Borders: Pedagogy and the Politics of Cultural Studies*. New York and London: Routledge.

Gonzalez, Juan. 1995. *Roll Down Your Window: Stories from a Forgotten America*. London and New York: Verso.

Gutierrez, K. 1994. How Talk, Context, and Script Shape Contexts for Learning: A Cross-case Comparison of Journal Sharing. *Linguistics and Education* 5: 335–65.

Gutierrez, K., J. Larson, and B. Kreuter. 1995. Cultural Tensions in the Scripted Classroom: The Value of the Subjugated Perspective. *Urban Education* 29, no. 4: 410–42.

Gutierrez, K., B. Rymes, and J. Larson. 1995. Script, Counterscript, and Underlife in the Classroom: James Brown versus *Brown v. Board of Education*. *Harvard Educational Review* 65, no. 3: 445–71.

Hall, Stuart. 1991. Signification, Representation, Ideology: Althusser and the Post-Structuralist Debates. In *Critical Perspectives on Media and Society*, ed. Robert K. Avery and David Eason, 88–113. New York and London: The Guilford Press.

Haymes, Stephen. 1995. *Race, Culture, and the City: A Pedagogy for Black Urban Struggle*. Albany: State University of New York Press.

Hondagneu-Sotelo, P. 1994. *Gendered Transitions: Mexican Experiences of Immigration*. Berkeley: University of California Press.

Hurston, Zora Neale. 1990 [1935]. *Mules and Men*. New York: Harper and Row Publishers.

Ignatiev, Noel. 1995. *How the Irish Became White*. London and New York: Routledge.

Ignatiev, Noel, and John Garvey, eds. 1996. *Race Traitor*. New York and London: Routledge.

Kincheloe, J. 1991. *Teachers as Researchers: Qualitative Inquiry as a Path to Empowerment*. London: Falmer Press.

Jessor, R., A. Colby, and R. A. Shweder. 1996. *Ethnography and Human Development: Context and Meaning in Social Inquiry*. Chicago and London: University of Chicago Press.

Leistyna, P., A. Woodrum, and S. A. Sherblom, eds. 1996. "Breaking Free: The Transformative Power of Critical Pedagogy." *Harvard Educational Review*, Reprint Series, 27.

León-Portilla, Miguel. 1995. *La flecha en el blanco: Francisco Tenamaztle y Bartolomé de las Casas en la lucha por los derechos de los indígenas 1541–1556*. Mexico City: Editorial Diana, México.

Lopez, Ian F. Hanley. 1996. *White by Law*. New York and London: New York University Press.

Luhrmann, T. M. 1996. *The Good Parsi: Fate of a Colonial Elite in Postcolonial Society*. Cambridge, Mass.: Harvard University Press.

Macedo, D. 1991. English Only: The Tongue-Tying of America. *Journal of Education* 173, no. 2: 9–20.

———. 1993. Literacy for Stupidification: The Pedagogy of Big Lies. *Harvard Educational Review* 63, no. 2: 183–206.

Marcus, George E., and Michael J. Fischer. 1986. *Anthropology as Cultural Critique: An Experimental Moment in the Human Sciences*. Chicago and London: University of Chicago Press.

Martin, P., and E. Taylor. 1996. Immigration and the Changing Face of Rural California: Summary Report of the Conference Held at Asilomar, June 12–14, 1995. Unpublished MS, *Rural Migration News*.

McLaren, P. 1989. *Life in Schools: An Introduction to Critical Pedagogy in the Social Foundations of Education*. White Plains, N.Y.: Longman.

———. 1993. *Schooling as a Ritual Performance: Towards a Political Economy of Educational Symbols and Gestures*. 2nd edition. New York and London: Routledge.

———. 1995. *Critical Pedagogy and Predatory Culture*. New York and London: Routledge.

———. 1997a. *Revolutionary Multiculturalism: Pedagogies of Dissent for the New Millennium*. Boulder: Westview Press.

———. 1997b. Unthinking Whiteness, Rethinking Democracy: Or Farewell to the Blonde Beast; Towards a Revolutionary Multiculturalism. *Educational Foundations* 11, no. 2 (spring): 5–39.

———. 2000. *Che Guevara, Paulo Freire, and the Pedagogy of Revolution*. Boulder: Rowman and Littlefield Publishers.

McLaren, Peter, and T. da Silva. 1993. Decentering Pedagogy: Critical Literacy, Resistance and the Politics of Memory. In *Paulo Freire: A Critical Encounter*, ed. Peter McLaren and Peter Leonard, 47–89. New York: Routledge.

McLaren, Peter, and James Giarelli, eds. 1995. Critical Theory and Educational Research. Albany: State University of New York Press.

Memmi, Albert. 1965. *The Colonizer and the Colonized*. Boston: Beacon Press.

Menchaca, M., and R. R. Valencia. 1990. Anglo-Saxon Ideologies in the 1920s–1930s: Their Impact on the Segregation of Mexican Students in California. *Anthropology and Education Quarterly* 21, no. 3: 222–49.

Moll, L. 1986. Writing as Communication: Creating Strategic Learning Environments for Students. *Theory to Practice* 26, no. 2: 102–08.

———. 1990. Introduction. In *Vygotsky and Education: Instructional Implications and Applications of Sociohistorical Psychology*, ed. L. Moll, 1–27. Cambridge: Cambridge University Press.

Ogbu, J. 1974. *The Next Generation: An Ethnography of Education in an Urban Neighborhood*. New York: Academic Press.

———. 1978. *Minority Education and Caste: The American System in Cross-Cultural Perspective*. New York: Academic Press.

———. 1982. Cultural Discontinuities and Schooling. *Anthropology and Education Quarterly* 13, no. 4: 290–307.

———. 1987. Variability in Minority School Performance: A Problem in Search of an Explanation. *Anthropology and Education Quarterly* 18, no. 4: 312–34.

———. 1992. Understanding Cultural Diversity. *Educational Researcher* 21, no. 8: 5–24.

Orfield, G., and S. E. Eaton, eds. 1996. *Dismantling Desegregation: The Quiet Reversal of Brown v. Board of Education*. New York: The New Press.

Palerm, J. V. 1994. Immigrant and Migrant Farm Workers in the Santa Maria Valley, California. Unpublished report, Center for Chicano Studies and Department of Anthropology, University of California at Santa Barbara. Sponsored by the Center for Survey Methods Research, Bureau of the Census, Washington, D.C.

Patthey-Chavez, G. 1993. High School as an Arena for Cultural Conflict and Acculturation for Latino Angelinos. *Anthropology and Education Quarterly* 24, no. 1: 33–60.

Population Today. 1996. Population Today: News, Numbers and Analysis. *Population Today* 24, no. 8 (August).

Portes, Alejandro. 1996. Introduction: Immigration and Its Aftermath. In *The New Second Generation*, ed. Alejandro Portes, 1–7. New York: Russell Sage Foundation.

Roediger, D. 1994. *Towards the Abolition of Whiteness*. London and New York: Verso.

Rose, M. 1995. *The Promise of Public Education in America: Possible Lives*. New York and London: Penguin Books.

Rumbaut, Rúben G., and Wayne A. Cornelius, eds. 1995. *California's Immigrant Children: Theory, Research, and Implication for Educational Policy*. San Diego: University of California, Center for U.S.–Mexican Studies.

San Juan, E., Jr. 1996. *Mediations: From a Filipino Perspective*. Pasig City, Philippines: Anvil Publishing, Inc.

Scribner, S., and M. Cole. 1981. *The Psychology of Literacy*. Cambridge, Mass.: Harvard University Press.

Shweder, R. A. 1996. True Ethnography: The Lore, the Law, and the Lure. In *Ethnography and Human Development: Context and Meaning in Social Inquiry*, ed. R. Jessor, A. Colby, and R. A. Shweder, 15–52. Chicago and London: University of Chicago Press.

Spindler, G. D., ed. 1955. *Anthropology and Education*. Stanford: Stanford University Press.

Stallybrass and White. 1986. *The Politics and Poetics of Transgression*. Ithaca, N.Y.: Cornell University Press.

Stewart, Kathleen. 1996. *A Space on the Side of the Road: Cultural Poetics in an "Other" America*. Princeton, N.J.: Princeton University Press.

Suárez-Orozco, C., and M. M. Suárez-Orozco. 1995a. Migration: Generational Discontinuities and the Making of Latino Identities. In *Ethnic Identity: Creation, Conflict, and Accommodation*, 3rd edition, ed. L. Romanucci-Ross and G. De Vos, 321–47. Walnut Creek, Calif.: AltaMira Press.

———. 1995b. *Transformations: Immigration, Family Life and Achievement Motivation among Latino Adolescents*. Stanford: Stanford University Press.

Suárez-Orozco, M. M. 1996. California Dreaming: Proposition 187 and the Cultural Psychology of Racial and Ethnic Exclusion. *Anthropology and Education Quarterly* 27, no. 2: 151–67.

———. 1998. State Terrors: Immigrants and Refugees in the Post-National Space. In *Ethnic Identity and Power: Cultural Contexts of Political Action in School and Society*, ed. Yali Zou and Henry T. Trueba, 283–319. New York: State University of New York Press.

Trueba, Henry T. 1989. Raising Silent Voices: Educating Linguistic Minorities for the 21st Century. New York: Harper and Row.

———. 1991. Linkages of Macro-Micro Analytical Levels. *Journal of Psychohistory* 18, no. 4: 457–68.

———. 1997. A Mexican Immigrant Community in Central California. Unpublished MS, Harvard University.

———. 1998. Mexican Immigrants from El Rocío: A Case Study of Resilience and Empowerment. *TESOL Quarterly* 7, no. 3: 12–17.

Trueba, Henry T., Cirenio Rodríguez, Yali Zou, and José Citrón. 1993. *Healing Multicultural America: Mexican Immigrants Rise to Power in Rural California.* London: Falmer Press.

Tsing, Anna Lowenhaupt. 1993. *In the Realm of the Diamond Queen: Marginality in an Out-of-the-Way Place.* Princeton, N.J.: Princeton University Press.

Valencia, Richard R. 1991. The Plight of Chicano Students: An Overview of Schooling Conditions and Outcomes. In *Chicano School Failure: An Analysis through Many Windows,* ed. Richard R. Valencia, 3–26. London: Falmer Press.

Vigil, D. 1983. Chicano Gangs: One Response to Mexican Urban Adaptation in the Los Angeles Area. *Urban Anthropology* 120: 45–75.

———. 1988. Group Processes and Street Identity: Adolescent Chicano Gang Members. *Ethos: Journal of the Society for Psychological Anthropology* 16, no. 4: 421–44.

———. 1989. *Barrio Gangs.* Austin: University of Texas Press.

———. 1997. *Personas Mexicanas: Chicano High Schoolers in a Changing Los Angeles.* Case Studies in Cultural Anthropology, George Spindler and Louise Spindler, series eds. Fort Worth, Philadelphia, and San Diego: Harcourt Brace College Publishers.

Villenas, S. 1996. The Colonizer/Colonized Chicana Ethnographer: Identity, Marginalization, and Co-optation in the Field. *Harvard Educational Review* 66, no. 4: 711–31.

Visweswaran, Kamala. 1994. *Fictions of Feminist Ethnography.* Minneapolis and London: University of Minnesota Press.

Vygotsky, L. S. 1962. *Thought and Language.* Cambridge, Mass.: MIT Press.

———. 1978. Interaction between Learning and Development. In *Mind in Society: The Development of Higher Psychological Processes,* ed. M. Cole, V. John-Teiner, S. Scribner, and E. Souberman, 79–91. Cambridge, Mass.: Harvard University Press.

Weis, Lois. 1990. *Working Class without Work: High School Students in a Deindustrializing Economy.* New York and London: Routledge.

Weis, Lois, and Michelle Fine. 1993. *Beyond Silenced Voices: Class, Race, and Gender in United States Schools.* Albany: State University of New York Press.

Wertsch, J. 1981. *The Concept of Activity in Soviet Psychology.* New York: M. E. Sharpe, Inc.

———. 1991. Beyond Vygotsky: Bakhtin's Contribution. In *Voices of the Mind: A Sociocultural Approach to Mediated Action,* ed. J. Wertsch, 46–66. Cambridge, Mass.: Harvard University Press.

Wertsch, J., ed. 1985. *Culture, Communication, and Cognition: Vygotskian Perspectives.* Cambridge: Cambridge University Press.

Wexler, Philip. 1992. *Becoming Somebody: Toward a Social Psychology of School.* London: Falmer Press.

Willis, Paul. 1977. *Learning to Labour: How Working Class Kids Get Working Class Jobs.* London: Grower.

Wilson, P. 1991. Trauma of Sioux Indian High School Students. *Anthropology and Education Quarterly* 22, no. 4: 367–83.

Yúdice, G. 1995. Neither Impugning nor Disavowing Whiteness Does a Viable Politics Make: The Limits of Identity Politics. In *After Political Correctness: The Humanities and Society in the 1990s,* ed. Christopher Newfield and Ronald Strickland, 255–85. Boulder: Westview Press.

3

Bilingual Education in an Immigrant Community: Proposition 227 in California

Marjorie Faulstich Orellana, Lucila Ek,
and Arcelia Hernández

On 4 June 1998, a majority of voters in the U.S. State of California endorsed Proposition 227, an initiative that effectively denies bilingual education to 1.4 million English language learners in that state's public schools. Introduced by Ron Unz, a multimillionaire software developer and a former Republican gubernatorial candidate, the measure declares that public schools must teach all children "English by being taught in English" (California Secretary of State's Office 1998, 2). English language learners are to be placed in structured English immersion classrooms for a period "not normally intended" to exceed one year (California Secretary of State's Office 1998, 2); in these rooms "nearly all" instruction should be in English, albeit with curriculum and presentation designed for children who are learning the language. After this exposure, children are to be transferred to English mainstream classrooms. Exceptions are allowed (with possibilities for some form of continued bilingual education, unspecified in the measure) only if parents request and are granted written waivers.

This public policy represents an unprecedented attack on twenty-five years of bilingual program development in California. A 1974 Supreme Court case (*Lau v. Nichols*) established that non–English speakers were denied equal educational opportunities when they were instructed in a language they could not understand, and in 1976 the California legislature passed the Chacon–Mascone Bilingual-Bicultural Education Act. This mandated that all children in the public school system receive instruction "in a language understandable to the student which recognizes the pupil's primary language and teaches the pupil English" (Biegel 1994, 54). Although the Bilingual-Bicultural Education Act officially expired in 1987, school districts continued to provide programs that were consistent with the act; and teacher training programs spent the last decade slowly building up a cadre of

75

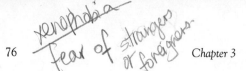

xenophobia — fear of strangers or foreigners

qualified bilingual instructors for the 1.4 million English language learners in the state's public schools.

Proposition 227 rides on the currents of other state initiatives that target immigrants and ethnic minority families and children (Hondagneu-Sotelo 1994): Proposition 187, which aimed to deny public education and health care to undocumented immigrants, and Proposition 209, which put an end to affirmative action in the state's major institutions. Both were fueled by xenophobic reactions to rapid changes in U.S. demographics. The fact that these initiatives were launched in California is not incidental. California is at the forefront of these demographic changes: one-fourth of California residents are immigrants (*Migration News* 1997), and one-third of all California schoolchildren speak a language other than English at home (Cornelius 1995).

The campaign for Proposition 227 was subtle in its manipulation of xenophobia, however, and did not directly pose immigration as a problem. Rather, proponents claimed to speak on behalf of students who were "condemned to this system, in which they spend 80 percent of the school day studying in their primary language" (Ford 1998). The initiative itself centered its argument around issues of equal access to education for immigrants and ethnic minorities. It was introduced with the following words: "Whereas the government and the public schools of California have a moral obligation and a constitutional duty to provide all of California's children, regardless of their ethnicity or national origins, with the skills necessary to become productive members of our society, and of these skills, literacy in the English language is among the most important" (California Secretary of State's Office 1998, 1).

Proponents did not simply claim to speak on *behalf* of immigrants, however. They also claimed support for the initiative from immigrant parents themselves: "Immigrant parents are eager to have their children acquire a good knowledge of English, thereby allowing them to fully participate in the American Dream of economic and social advancement" (California Secretary of State's Office 1998, 1). Advocates for the measure bolstered this claim by citing brief public opinion polls, such as that conducted by the *Los Angeles Times* in October 1997, which indicates that 84 percent of Hispanics surveyed favored the initiative. It was reinforced by the media attention given to a small boycott of bilingual education by parents at a school in central Los Angeles, while parents' protest against the *dismantling* of bilingual education in nearby Santa Barbara was largely ignored.

Public opinion polls, however, at best make general statements about social trends and beliefs. The results are shaped by the way the questions are worded, and they do little to illuminate the *reasons* why those who are polled might hold a given opinion.[1] Through a qualitative study of the ways in which parents and children in an immigrant community in central Los Angeles talk about bilingualism and language learning, we were able to probe issues in more detail than is possible through opinion polls, research surveys, or brief media spotlights on unusual events. This helps to bring the voices of those most directly affected by bilingual education policies like Proposition 227 into the debate.

In our analysis, we situate the attitudes toward English and Spanish of recent immigrant Mexican and Central American parents and their children within the social, political, and historical context in which they were forged. This is a time when many immigrant families in the United States and elsewhere lead transnational lives, actively negotiating between nations as they search for better futures for their children. The boundaries they navigate are linguistic as well as geopolitical.

VIEWS OF LANGUAGE

The research literature on bilingualism and bilingual education makes a distinction that is mirrored in parents' and children's talk about the same issues. In this discussion of "ways of talking about language" we will describe two general patterns: views of language as a "thing" that can be measured and views of language as a social process. We will consider how these patterns emerge in research on bilingualism and bilingual education and then how these views are taken up in talk.

A Measure of Progress

Language is generally treated as a measurable construct in studies of bilingual language acquisition. This research tradition involves recording developmental milestones and measuring aspects of language like vocabulary growth and the use of specific grammatical forms. (See, for example, Dopke 1992; Fantini 1976; Leopold 1947.) Researchers have also measured the "effects" of bilingualism, such as increased metalinguistic awareness and other cognitive benefits (Bialystock and Cummins 1991).

This basic research has helped to establish bilingualism as a phenomenon worthy of scientific analysis. It provides a foundation for evaluation studies, which compare the results of different types of instruction for bilingual students in terms of language acquisition (usually in English, sometimes in the home language as well) and academic progress. (See, for example, Baker and DeKanter 1981; Barik and Swain 1978; Collier 1989, 1992; Ramirez 1992). But most such studies assume a standardized continuum to which all speakers can be compared and give little attention to the sociopolitical or sociocultural contexts of language use.

Researchers acknowledge the difficulties of comparing programs, individuals, or groups because many factors may influence a given set of results. Measurements of progress or development cannot be properly interpreted without considering the social practices that shape language use. Yet great attention is given to studies of outcomes, and they have been used to inform or influence public opinion and educational policy. The results of these sorts of studies were cited by both sides during the campaign for Proposition 227.

A Tool for Participation in Social Practices

The influence of anthropology on language studies burgeoned in the 1980s, spurred by Heath's (1983) generative work on cultural and social class variations in "ways with words." Sociolinguists simultaneously studied the social uses of languages, including among bilingual speakers (Genishi 1981; McLure 1981; Valdés 1981; Zentella 1981). More recent work following in the anthropological tradition examines general language practices in bilingual communities (Valdés 1996; Vásquez, Pease-Alvarez, and Shannon 1994). These studies are largely unconcerned with outcome measures except when they consider the match or mismatch between home language practices and those that are used and valued in other settings, like school. Instead, they seek to illuminate how people use language as a tool to participate in particular communities of practice.

Some sociolinguists have also begun to highlight the uses of language as a tool for constructing and displaying social identities (Bucholtz, Liang, and Sutton 1999; Gee 1996). Most studies of discourse and identity have worked with monolingual speakers. But a few have specifically explored how bilingual speakers signal identities by making choices about when, how, and where to speak each of their languages. Orellana (1994), for example, describes how three bilingual preschoolers moved between Spanish and English as they playacted the characters from popular children's culture (in English) and directed the play, speaking as themselves (in Spanish). Mendoza-Denton (1994) shows how Latino/Latina teens living in Northern California used Spanish to identify culturally as *sureños* (Mexican-identified) or English to identify as *norteños* (U.S.–identified Chicanos). The languages were not neutral media of communication but, rather, important symbols of identity, evoking different cultural and ideological orientations.

In this study we concentrated principally on children between the ages of those studied by Orellana (1994) and Mendoza-Denton (1994). We began with the assumption that elementary school children would be able to articulate some of their views about their two languages and their relative preferences for each, but we were uncertain just how much they might express or when and under what conditions they might do so. We therefore tried asking them directly about their views (in the focus groups and informal conversations); but we also remained attentive to spontaneous comments about language uses whenever we were privy to them.

RESEARCH METHODS AND STRATEGIES

This inquiry into views of bilingualism and language uses is one strand of two larger studies. The first is a comparative case study of childhoods, and children's pathways of development, in three California communities that vary in "race," ethnic, and social class composition, as well as in histories of immigration and language use. In each site we are using ethnographic methods to examine children's understandings of their social worlds, as well as adult practices that shape children's daily lives and possibilities for the future. We are especially interested in processes related to social class, gender, immigration, ethnicity, and racialization during the elementary school years, as well as how these processes shape contexts and pathways of development.

We focus here on one of the three case study communities: an inner-city area in central Los Angeles mostly comprising immigrants from Central America and Mexico. It is served by a large, multitrack, year-round public school that we call "Madison" (a pseudonym, as are all names of people in this article). (See Orellana and Thorne 1998 for discussion of how the year-round schedule shapes daily life in this community.) According to school records, 86 percent of the students at Madison are "Limited English Proficient," and virtually all of the students qualify for free or reduced-price lunches. The majority of the children were born in the United States to parents who fled political and economic problems in their home countries in the early 1980s. Others are themselves immigrants, who arrived recently with family members or rejoined those who came before them.

Orellana served as a bilingual classroom teacher at this school from 1984 to 1993; from 1994 to 1998 she was a participant-observer in and around the school: in classrooms, homes, after-school and vacation programs for children, and other places where children and families can be found. Ek and Hernández worked as bilingual teachers at this and a neighboring school and assisted with participant-observation and other data collection efforts. We draw from multiple data sources collected in this ethnographic project, including over 1,000 pages of field notes written during three years of participant-observation; transcriptions of four focus groups with parents (a total of 19 parents participated); transcriptions of five focus groups with fourth and fifth grade students (a total of 37 children participated); and notes on informal and semiformal interviews with children, parents, teachers, the staff of community programs, and other community workers.

In order to tap into the range of attitudes toward language uses that exist within the Central American and Mexican immigrant community living in central Los Angeles, we also draw from data collected in a second national research project. This study is centered at a state-run preschool, which we call "Children's Center," located a few miles from Madison. Many of the families have children in nearby elementary schools, and the majority of parents work in the downtown garment industry. We base our analyses on transcriptions of five focus groups that Orellana and Hernández conducted with parents. (All parents of the 40 four year olds in the program were invited; 27 participated in all.) These explored children's daily life experiences, home language and literacy practices, parents' hopes for their children's futures, and their visions for children's success.

This essay focuses on how parents and children *talk* about language. It is beyond its scope to detail patterns in children's actual uses of Spanish and English, although we have observed hundreds of children of different ages operating in many kinds of settings (homes, classrooms, the school yard, after-school programs, the local library, fast food restaurants, stores) and interacting with many kinds of people (including peers, siblings, parents, teachers, community leaders, and other public figures). Based on these observations, we can make general statements about preferences for English and Spanish by kids of different ages and in various settings, but we cannot here give the detailed analysis that such a discussion deserves.

Instead, we searched our data (using a computer software program called "Field-note Searcher")[2] for times when participants talked explicitly about language practices, goals for language development, or attitudes toward English or Spanish. We were attentive to these comments throughout our months of fieldwork, and recorded them in our field notes, because we knew they might provide the best means of tapping into "emic" views about bilingualism. In the focus group transcripts, we examined what parents said they wanted for their children's language development. We also considered the language in which particular children opted to conduct each focus group and what they said about their uses of English and Spanish both in and out of school.

VIEWS OF BILINGUALISM IN
AN IMMIGRANT COMMUNITY

Like researchers, parents and children assimilate the ideas of the larger culture and reflect them in their talk. We found that parents and children worked with the same two notions of language that we found in research literature: language as an outcome measure and language as a social tool. Yet these different ways were unevenly distributed between parents and children. Parents focused almost exclusively on language as a measure of progress or of particular outcomes. Children seemed to view language principally as a tool for participating in social groups and signaling particular kinds of identities. Parents expressed concern with children's future options as they might relate to language; while children's uses of language were very much bound up with their views of who they were, what groups they were part of, and their involvement in life in the here and now. We share representative examples of these patterns below.

Parents Talk about Language

During our work on these two qualitative research projects, we were struck by the number of parents who seemed to use their children's ability to communicate in English as a measure of their academic progress. We heard many comments about and comparisons between children based on how much English they did or did not speak. The English capacities of particular children were sometimes measured by their ability to interpret for parents in public settings.

When children appeared to be falling behind academically, parents sometimes wondered if the bilingual program was to blame. Several told how other parents had advised them to take their children out of bilingual classes. For example, Angela Barrientos, the mother of a four-year-old boy at the Children's Center, quoted what other parents had told her: "Cuando están en bilingüe, se atrasan mucho los niños" [When they're in bilingual, the children fall behind]. Flora Ortíz, another parent at the Children's Center, said that she had heard of *children* in bilingual programs that "se enredan mucho" [they get tangled up].

Alma Martínez, the parent of a seven-year-old girl at Madison, had a response to this: "¿Acaso no tiene toda la vida para aprender inglés?" [Doesn't she have her whole life to learn English?]. And Estela Velásquez felt that the parents who were involved in the protest against bilingual education at her son's elementary school were misguided, that it was very important for children to maintain Spanish as well as to study in Spanish so that they would not fall behind academically while acquiring English. She went on at length:

Es facil decir "que se quedan en inglés, porque yo les enseño el español en la casa." Nosotros somos maestros en nuestra casa, en el sentido de educarlos, enseñarlos buenos hábitos. Pero no somos maestros en decirle, "Tienes que aprender estas equaciones." ¡Por que no las sabemos! No sabemos qué es lo que el niño está viendo en segundo, o en tercero. Sabemos, tenemos una tarea de maestros en nuestros hogares. Hablo así con las mamás, y yo les digo, "¿Por qué lo apuntas en inglés? Está chiquito." "¡Porque está chiquito, lo va a aprender!" "No, está mal," le digo. [It's easy to say "they should stay in English because I'll teach them Spanish at home." We are teachers in our own homes, in the sense that we educate them, we teach them good habits. But we are not teachers in these sense of telling them, "You have to learn these equations." Because we don't know that ourselves! We don't know what children should be doing in second grade or in third. We know we have the task of being teachers in our own homes. I talk like this with other mothers, and I tell them, "Why did you put him in English? He's still young." "Because he's young, he'll learn it!" "No, that's wrong," I say.]

Señora Velásquez told of how she let her child choose an English-only classroom but then found that he was staying up until 11:00 at night doing homework with her, "porque la tarea era dificil, porque yo no sé el inglés" [because the homework was hard, because I don't know English]. Her experience led her to believe that her children are better off in classrooms where the language of instruction—and of homework assignments—is one that they can understand. But most parents did not have this point of comparison. When parents had concerns about their children's academic trajectories, it was not easy for them to shrug off criticisms of the bilingual program; they were left wondering if their children's academic problems stemmed from their bilingual placement.

These questions about the bilingual program seem partly influenced by confusion over its design. Parents were sometimes uncertain if their children were even in bilingual programs. (The same confusion existed among children; when we asked if they were in a bilingual classroom, most responded by telling us whether they were "in English" or "in Spanish"—a reference to their reading group placements, not their programs of study.) Ronaldo Padillas, the president of the Parent–Teachers' Association at Madison and a university-educated immigrant from El Salvador whose son had attended the school for five years, told us, "Yo no sé muy bien como trabaja el programa bilingüe; no sé a que grado lo van a trasladar a practicar el inglés" [I don't know very much about how the bilingual program works; I don't know at what grade they are going to move him over to practice English]. (Note, the program at Madison mandates that all children receive English language instruction beginning in kindergarten; but many parents—like the general public that voted for Proposition 227—seemed to think that the bilingual program is conducted entirely in Spanish.)

It is not surprising that such confusion existed because there was considerable variation in the implementation of the bilingual program at Madison. In a number of classrooms that were designated bilingual, English predominated because there was a shortage of certified bilingual teachers at the school. (These classes were taught by monolingual teachers, with a part-time instructional aide hired to work with children in primary language literacy lessons.) All teachers (bilingual and monolingual) varied considerably in how they structured the organization of the two languages in each classroom, depending on their own comfort with Spanish, the skills of available instructional aides, the language practices of children in their classrooms, and, especially, their own beliefs about bilingual education. Nineteen of eighty teachers at Madison, and 48 percent of teachers in the district, said they supported Proposition 227 in a survey conducted by the teachers' union.

Parents' views also seem shaped by recent media attention to the "problems" of bilingual education and the conversations that these news reports generated in the community. We heard many references to information that "salió en la televisión" [came out on television] and to things that unnamed others said ("Dicen que . . . " [They say that . . .]). Yet there were few accessible venues for parents to direct their questions or talk together about their concerns; most relied on the information that classroom teachers provided, and this information varied based on teachers' personal beliefs. A number of parents turned to us to tell them what was best for their children: "Ustedes son los expertos; nosotros no sabemos" [You are the experts; we don't know].

By far the most common sentiment expressed by parents was that they wanted their children to be bilingual when they grew up so that they could get good jobs. Sonia Méndez, the mother of an eleven-year-old girl at Madison, explained, "Va a hacer muchas más cosas que una persona que sólo habla un idioma" [They're going to do many more things than a person who only speaks one language]. Yet, even as they recognized the value of bilingualism, parents tended to emphasize the opportunities that speaking *English* would presumably bring their children. As Wilma Díaz, the mother of seven- and nine-year-old boys at Madison, noted, "Yo digo que tiene muchas oportunidades porque sí puede mucho en inglés el niño" [I tell you that he has lots of opportunities because he can speak a lot of English]. When we asked what those opportunities might be, parents named career positions like doctors, lawyers, and teachers or simply said that their children would be able to make more money than they themselves could. English was seen as the key to this.

Reyna Velásquez, the parent of two middle school girls and a preschooler at the Children's Center, said, "Me hace más felíz que nada" [It makes me more happy than anything] that her daughters can speak English. Isabel Chávez commented, "Yo quisiera siempre que mis hijos hablaran inglés. Yo no sé, yo no sé nada de inglés y lo siento bien orgullosa de que ellos lo sepan" [I would always want my children to speak English. I don't know, I don't know any English, and I feel really proud that they do]. And many parents talked about their own feelings of impotence at not being able to speak English, in contrast to their children. Teresa Maldano noted this explicitly:

> Yo, que aprendiera inglés, quisiera porque es muy importante el inglés en este país. Ya no, pues, el español uno a veces se lo enseña en la casa a los niños, ¿verdad? Pero el inglés es muy importante. Yo, en mi caso yo me he dado cuenta que a mi hijo. . . . A veces me siento tan impotente por no saber el hablar el inglés y por eso quiero que él aprenda inglés. Es muy importante para mí que él habla inglés. [I would like him to learn English, because English is very important in this country. Not that Spanish isn't, but Spanish we can sometimes teach children at home, right? But English is very important. In my case, I have realized this with my son. . . . Sometimes I feel so impotent because I can't speak English, and that's why I want him to learn English. It's very important to me that he learn English.]

Rosa Mariano, the mother of a four-year-old at Children's Center, felt that people who speak English are treated better, even by their fellow Latinos:

> Y hasta recibe uno mejor trato, ¿eh? Hablando en inglés. Por que a veces uno habla español y lo tratan mal a uno. Y yo, por eso, a veces me da, no sé, una tristeza, va, porque ¿por qué? Y a veces siendo los mismos Latinos que a uno, lo tratan mal, por que uno habla español, y si miran que uno habla inglés, ya lo tratan diferente a uno. [And you get better treatment, eh? Speaking English. Because sometimes you speak Spanish and they treat you badly. That's why I sometimes feel, I don't know, sad, you see, because why? And sometimes it's Latinos who treat you badly because you speak Spanish, and if they see that you speak English, then they treat you differently.]

Señora Mariano told how her son internalized the prestige value of the languages; he sometimes told others that he did not speak Spanish, when in fact he did:

> Sí, también los tratan mal a los niños. También hay niños . . . que a veces mi hijo, yo he visto que le están hablando, los niños tal vez son Latinos y que pueden español, pero no quieren hablar español. Y mi hijo le ha hablado, y dice, "No, I don't speak Spanish," le dice. Y el niño pudiendo hablar bien el español, o sea que ya, los dos. . . . Desde chiquitos los están enseñando de que, de que no hablan el español. Y ya los niños, como que ya no, no son, se sienten diferentes también ellos, ya. Se cohiben un

poco también, igual que uno. Eso pasa. [Yes, they also treat the children badly. And the children also, sometimes my son, I have seen that they are talking, children who are say Latinos and who can speak Spanish, but they don't want to speak Spanish. And my son has said to them, he says, "No, I don't speak Spanish," he says. And my son, who can speak Spanish well, or rather, both. . . . From the time that they are little they're teaching them that they shouldn't speak Spanish. And the children, it's like now they're no longer, they're not, they feel different already. They are inhibited a little also, just like us. That happens.]

This prestige value of English, when internalized by families, helped promote a reversal of traditional relationships of power between the generations (a reversal that was reinforced, for example, when children interpreted for their parents, including information that is usually the domain of adults). Parents were proud when their children spoke English and ashamed of their own "slowness" in learning it. They said that even their preschool children commented on the fact that their parents did not speak English—"Mami, tú no sabes" [Mami, you don't know], "Mami, tú no lo dices bien" [Mami, you don't say it right]; urged them to learn English—"Mami, yo quiero que aprenda. Si se hace un grupo de dos o tres o cuatro señoras . . . " [Mami, I want you to learn. If you form a group of two or three or four women . . .]; scolded them for not learning—"Mami, tienes que aprender" [Mami, you have to learn]; or compared them with other adults, like their teachers, who did—"El Teacher lo dice así." We were struck by a comment we heard repeatedly in our focus groups at the Children's Center: "No quiero que sea como yo" [I don't want him to be like me]. This may reflect parents' concern that their children's lives not be as hard as theirs have been; but it gets used in terms of identity—not wanting their children to *be* like them. The way to *be* different is to speak English.

 While parents saw English as a measure of children's success, or their potential for future success in the larger society, they viewed children's ability to speak Spanish as an important index of families' national and cultural loyalties and an implicit measure of parenting skills. We overheard several critical comments about immigrants whose children did not speak Spanish, and parents seemed sensitive to comments (especially from relatives) when their own children's Spanish abilities fell short. For example, Alma González, the mother of four children (ages four, eleven, eighteen, and twenty-one) talked about her embarrassment when her older children visited Mexico and could not communicate with their cousins: "Por que cuando van a México, no saben ni qué. A veces que les hablan, a mí me pasó con mi hijo de que le decían en español y se quedaba por que no decía nada. Y digo, 'Ya ves, tenemos que aprender los dos idiomas' " [Because when they go to Mexico, they don't know anything. Sometimes when they talk, it happened to me that they spoke to my son in Spanish, and he just stood there because he couldn't say anything. And I say, "So you see, we have to learn both languages"]. Her younger children spoke Spanish, but the older ones had lost their abilities over their childhood years. Alma Ortíz similarly noted that when her daughters went to Mexico, "se quedaban así, sin hablar" [they stayed like that, without talking].

Many Madison families are transnational ones, with some members living in the United States and others in their country of origin. More than half of the children in one first grade class, for example, had one or more siblings living "back home." These families are divided because of restrictions on immigration, the costs (financial, emotional, and physical) of traveling to the United States, the timing of families' chain migration processes, and the needs and resources of family members in each nation. For these families, Spanish is essential for connecting through letters and phone calls to those family members left behind.

In looking to the future, children from transnational families may need much more than basic interpersonal communication skills in the home language. Many Madison parents said they were considering returning to their home countries or sending their children back, temporarily or otherwise, while they stayed here to work. This uncertainty about the future stemmed from numerous sources: shifts in immigration policies, the threat of Proposition 187 and other attacks on immigrants, welfare reform, and changes in economic conditions. Eva Morales, for example, was contemplating sending her first grade daughter to live with her sister in Mexico. Her three U.S.–born children received federal assistance, but because of recent changes in the program policies (welfare reform) Eva felt compelled to seek employment, and the only job she could find was as a live-in domestic worker. Ivan Martínez, the father of two high school–aged sons who were born in Mexico and a seven-year-old daughter who was born in Los Angeles, talked about going wherever he had to go so that his children could continue studying; Proposition 187, if enforced, would jeopardize the education of his sons. Parents also considered sending their children back home to avoid the dangers of inner-city living and adolescence in the United States or to give children a different perspective on life. (See Orellana et al. 1998 for further discussion of transnational family practices in this community.)

If children return to their parents' countries of origin, they will need to do academic work in Spanish. Several children in the focus groups talked about attending school in their home countries while visiting there on vacation. They noted that the academic level for their grade was too advanced for them to keep up in Spanish. As one student put it, "I got all Fs."

CHILDREN'S PERSPECTIVES

Parents rarely mentioned the relationship between language and identity, seeming much more concerned with language as a measurement of how their children were doing in a world that they could not fully decode. The children with whom we spoke, on the other hand, did not talk about the role of languages in their futures. They *did* pick up a sense of the prestige value of English and treated

English language ability as a measure of academic achievement. Adalia Gándara, a fourth grade student in the bilingual program at Madison, for example, mentioned that the teachers favored the "better ones"—the children that were "in English." We heard boasts about "passing into English" as a marker of academic status. And Ronaldo Padillas told of his son's question to him, "¿Como puedes saber eso si no sabes inglés?" [How can you know that if you don't know English?], as if English were a measure of intelligence or knowledge.

But most of children's talk about language—especially the spontaneous talk that we were able to record in field notes—revealed a view of language as a tool for signaling identities. They displayed this when we (especially Orellana, an Anglo) spoke Spanish to them. On many occasions they asked, somewhat incredulously, "You speak Spanish? Where are you from?" (In general, the children seemed to equate ethnic identities with national origin, as when they claimed, "I'm from here," rather than, "I'm American," "I'm Mexican," or "I'm Latino.") They seemed especially surprised when they saw Orellana speaking Spanish to her blond, blue-eyed children or heard her address them in their "Spanish" names. (Their father is Guatemalan.) Our observations suggest that language was very much associated with identity, identity was equated in part with national origin, and national origin was marked in the color of skin, hair, and eyes.

A few children made explicit statements about their own language choices based on their claims to particular identities. For example, Andy Espinal, an eleven-year-old boy at Madison whose parents had emigrated from Mexico, reacted when Orellana spoke Spanish to him while playing at an after-school program. Andy said that he did not like to speak Spanish because then people thought he was from Mexico, and he was not; he was "from here." Thorne, Lam, Orellana, and Chabrier (1998) discuss this and other ways in which children construct differences, arguing that differences are constructed in particularly consequential ways when the various strands through which they are marked (e.g., appearance, language, surnames, national origins) line up. By speaking English (and by adopting an Anglicized version of his first name), Andy attempted to disrupt others' efforts to mark him as "Mexican" based on language and appearance.

Robert Durán, an eleven-year-old boy whose family was from Honduras but who presents to (and is located by) a racialized U.S. world as "black" (with dark skin and African features), also said that he did not like to speak Spanish. This was not because it made people think he was from somewhere else; rather, it was because they did not believe he *could* be from somewhere other than Africa. "Everyone says, 'You're black, how come you speak Spanish?'"—and he was tired of explaining. (Robert was not named as "American," however; children in this community used that label only for white people.) Thorne and associates (1998) note that children whose identity strands are not consistent are called on to do more explaining or "identity work." This has seemingly caused Robert to reject the Honduran or Latin part of his cultural heritage; when Orellana spoke Spanish in his focus group, Robert said he "hates the Spanish culture." By speaking English, Robert felt more able to identify with African Americans; he said he likes reading the autobiographies of famous black men "because that's my culture."

David Manolo, another fifth grader at Madison, on the other hand, mentioned in passing that he did not want to speak "only English" because then people think he is "a *gabacho*" (a term used by many Latinos for Anglos). Notably, David is from a Zapotec family from southern Mexico; his parents speak Mixtec and some Spanish, but in moving to the United States David "became" Hispanic, leaving his Zapotec identity behind. He now uses Spanish to identify with the minority culture that he joined when he crossed the border and to differentiate himself from the majority. (We wondered if David might choose to speak Zapotec if he lived in Mexico, as a symbol of resistance to the dominant group.)

In another vein, Adalia Gandara noted that her *father* preferred that she speak English, but she explained his preference like this: "When the conference, my dad said he don't wants me in En—, in Spanish, because, because he don't wants me because I'm from here and I wanna learn." Adalia's father told us that he wanted his children to be bilingual, but he wanted them to emphasize English in school because of the opportunities it would bring them. Adalia seems to have transformed her father's emphasis on English as a tool for future opportunities into a symbol of her identity, marked by her birthplace.

Araceli Nuñez, on the other hand, noted her parents' interest in the instrumental value of English, specifically for translating: "Me dicen que, que es mejor aprender inglés, porque cuando viene, como tenemos en el edificio un manager, un señor que habla inglés y le hablo solo para decirle lo que están diciendo, que ellos no saben inglés" [They tell me that, that it's better to learn English because when someone comes, like in my building we have a manager, a man who speaks English, and I speak to him so that I can tell him what they are saying because they don't speak English]. Araceli did not adopt English as a marker for her own identity; but she had only lived in the United States for less than a year.

In general, we found that children did not talk a great deal about their views of English and Spanish or their use of each language. But our observations of children in many different contexts over a period of several years reveal a gradual but marked shift over the middle childhood years toward a preference for English and a disinclination to use Spanish. When we spoke in English at the start of the year in Hernández's first grade classroom, the children called out for Spanish. When we spoke in Spanish in the focus groups with fifth graders, all but the children who had arrived in the United States within the last year responded in English, and several complained, saying, "Aw, do we have to speak Spanish?" and "I hate Spanish." An analysis of patterns of use is beyond the scope of this chapter, but this trend is consistent with that found by other researchers (e.g., Wong-Fillmore 1991), and it may be a better marker of children's views of their two languages than anything explicit they say.

DISCUSSION

Our research confirms the results of public opinion polls in California: immigrant parents living in Los Angeles want their children to learn English. All of the parents we talked with valued English for their children, and much of their talk about children's pathways to success centered around English language learning. But this does not mean that parents opposed bilingual education. Views on this varied and were shaped by many factors. Most parents (unlike the general public who voted for Proposition 227) recognized that they were not experts on language acquisition processes, and they sought advice from the sources that were available to them: teachers, other parents, and the media.

But we also need to contemplate the *reasons* that parents give for wanting English for their children. Parents seem to believe that if their children speak English, they will get good jobs and be treated well; they want their children to be "American" and not to be "like them." These beliefs reflect a view of language as a measure of something else—of learning, success, and Americanization. They also resonate with views that influenced the vote for Proposition 227: the assumption that English is a solution to all educational problems as well as a force for uniting the United States as "one nation." This perspective may be unwittingly reinforced by research traditions that measure linguistic development under various sorts of instructional designs. Although such research is important for advancing both theory and practice, it diverts attention from larger social, cultural, and political issues, such as the quality of immigrants' schooling, access to resources, and xenophobia and racism in society. It also neglects consideration of the complex positioning of immigrant families that operate across transnational borders and locate their futures potentially in two or more different places.

Children, like parents, seem to see English as a solution to inequity. They believe that they will receive better treatment from teachers and others if they speak English rather than their home language. But children, more than parents—or the voting public—seem to understand that language is much more than a mere measure of achievement; it is a means for marking social placements and displaying themselves to the world. Most of the children that we talked with showed a clear preference for English over their home language. This confirms what Rumbaut (1998) found in a survey of 5,200 immigrant youth in the United States. It reveals children's effort to stake their claims as "American."

Yet being "American" is a birthright for the majority of the children in the Madison community, and this birthright has not protected them from racist treatment in a society that sees all Latinos as foreigners. Our qualitative research helps to situate parents' and children's views of language within the larger social and political context. There is a bitter irony in the fact that Proposition 227 draws support from much of the same constituency that supported Proposition 187. Proposition 227's message to immigrants is "learn English if you want your children to succeed in the United States." Proposition 187's earlier message (and one that resonates through the current climate in Southern California) is "just go home." Some immigrant families, including those with U.S.–born children, are doing just this. But going home, moving back and forth, or simply living in an increasingly globalized world (Featherstone 1995; Hall and DuGay 1997) involves crossing linguistic and cultural borders as well as geopolitical ones. As a society, we would benefit from programs that promote *all* children's development as bilingual, biliterate, and bicultural persons who are able to thrive in and contribute to the world no matter what side of the border (or of multiple borders) they find themselves on.

IMPLICATIONS

Our research suggests that bilingual education advocates need to reflect on how well we have been able to market bilingual education, explain its rationale and benefits, and inform its principal clientele. We also need to consider how the group that it is intended to benefit—English language learners and their families—perceives the policy and makes sense of it. As Spillane (1997, 1998, 1999) has shown in relation to other educational policies, what is communicated to and/or picked up by target groups is not always what policy makers intend. Implementers construct policy messages, and they do not always construct them in ways that are consistent with policy makers' intentions.

Most schools hold meetings that are intended to communicate curriculum design to parents; the number of parents attending such meetings may vary from school to school but is usually only a small proportion of the school population. Information is also sent home in the form of flyers that may or may not make it from children's backpacks into parents' hands. But the principal vehicles through which policies are communicated to parents, and through which parents can ask questions about children's school experiences, are classroom teachers. Teachers thus can serve as either brokers or gatekeepers (Schwille et al. 1983), filtering the information that parents can access. We might do better to acknowledge this role and find ways to support teachers in providing clear, consistent information to parents.

We might also seek alternative ways to communicate information to parents. But in our efforts to inform the constituency that we claim to advocate for, we need to make sure that we are listening as well as talking. It is not enough to tell parents that bilingual education "works" when they have real concerns about their children's academic progress. And it is not enough to tell children that being bilingual will help them get good jobs in the future when they are concerned about how they are treated based on the languages they speak right now. We need to understand both what parents and children want and *why* they want it, and we must consider how these desires influence the ways in which they understand and respond to bilingual policy. We can then seek real ways to address the underlying issues as well as the more surface ones.

Schools might begin to do this by conducting focus groups with community members much like the ones we led during the course of our research. These forums offer a space for people to raise concerns and express opinions. They also potentially allow for the sharing of information and advice. (The research groups that we led were not designed to give advice—though parents invariably asked our opinions. In a different sort of session there might be more give and take of perspectives among parents and bilingual education experts.)

Advocates for Proposition 227 did an effective job of mobilizing parents' sentiments and using it toward their own ends. Advocates for bilingual education could do a better job of mobilizing community sentiments (both parents' and children's) and using them to do what *we* want to do—which is, after all, what parents fundamentally want: to ensure the educational success of English language learners.

NOTES

Acknowledgments. The "California Childhoods" project was supported and funded by the John D. and Catherine T. MacArthur Foundation Research Network on Successful Pathways through Middle Childhood in a grant to Barrie Thorne and Catherine Cooper. The Institute of Human Development at the University of California at Berkeley also supported this research. The study at "Children's Center" was funded by the Center for the Improvement of Early Reading Education in a grant to Robert Rueda, David Yaden, and Laurie MacGillivray. Our thanks go to Barrie Thorne, Elizabeth Martínez, and Jim Spillane for feedback on earlier drafts of this essay. We owe thanks to the children and families of "Madison" and "Children's Center" for sharing their perspectives with us.

1. Different surveys on the issue have produced seemingly contradictory results. For example, the October 1997 poll conducted by the *Los Angeles Times* indicates that 84 percent of Latinos across the State of California favored public school instruction conducted in English, and a *Los Angeles Times* poll of Latinos in one county in California shows that 83 percent favored English language classes for all children when they begin school (Guthrie 1997). But a poll jointly conducted by the Spanish-language newspaper *La Opinion* and the Spanish television station KVEA indicates that 68 percent of respondents favored bilingual education while only 26 percent opposed it. Eighty-eight percent of those who had children in bilingual programs said that such programs benefited their children; only 10 percent were dissatisfied (Rivera 1998).

2. Our thanks go to Gery Ryan of the University of California at Los Angeles for developing and sharing this useful software tool.

REFERENCES

Baker, K., and A. DeKanter. 1981. *Effectiveness of Bilingual Education: A Review of the Literature.* Washington, D.C.: U.S. Department of Education, Office of Planning, Budget, and Evaluation.

Barik, H., and M. Swain. 1978. Evaluation of a Bilingual Education Program in Canada: The Elgin Study through Grade Six. *Bulletin of CILA* 27: 31–58.

Bialystock, E., and J. Cummins. 1991. Language, Cognition, and Education of Bilingual Children. In *Language Processing in Bilingual Children*, ed. E. Bialystock, 222–32. New York: Cambridge University Press.

Biegel, S. 1994. Bilingual Education and Language Rights: The Parameters of the Bilingual Education Debate in California Twenty Years after *Lau v. Nichols*. *Chicano-Latino Law Review* 14, no. 48: 48–60.

Bucholtz, Mary, A. C. Liang, and Laurel A. Sutton, eds. 1999. *Reinventing Identities.* Oxford: Oxford University Press.

California Secretary of State's Office. 1998. *California Voter Information: Proposition 227. Text of Proposed Law.* Sacramento: California Secretary of State's Office.

Collier, V. 1989. How Long? A Synthesis of Research on Academic Achievement in a Second Language. *TESOL Quarterly* 23, no. 3: 509–31.

———. 1992. A Synthesis of Studies Examining Long-Term Language Minority Student Data on Academic Achievement. *Bilingual Research Journal* 16, no. 1: 187–212.

Cornelius, W. 1995. Educating California's Immigrant Children: Introduction and Overview. In *California's Immigrant Children*, ed. Rubén Rumbaut, 378–404. La Jolla: U.S.–Mexican Studies, University of California at San Diego.

Dopke, S. 1992. *One Parent, One Language: An Interactional Approach.* Philadelphia: John Benjamins Publishing Co.

Fantini, A. 1976. *Language Acquisition of a Bilingual Child: A Sociolinguistic Perspective (to Age 5).* Burlington, Vt.: The Experiment Press.

Featherstone, M. 1995. *Undoing Culture: Globalization, Postmodernism and Identity.* Thousand Oaks, Calif.: Sage Publications.

Ford, Peter. 1998. Ron Unz's Alien Initiative. *The New American*, 27 April.

Gee, J. P. 1996. *Social Linguistics and Literacies: Ideology in Discourses.* Bristol, Pa.: The Falmer Press.

Genishi, C. 1981. Codeswitching in Chicano Six-Year-Olds. In *Latino Language and Communicative Behavior*, ed. R. P. Duran, 133–52. Norwood, N.J.: Ablex.

Guthrie, J. 1997. Bilingual Education Split Not on Strict Ethnic Lines. *San Francisco Examiner*, 2 November: C1.

Hall, S., and P. DuGay, eds. 1997. *Questions of Cultural Identity.* London: Sage Publications.

Heath, S. B. 1983. *Ways with Words.* Cambridge: Cambridge University Press.

Hondagneu-Sotelo, P. 1994. Women and Children First: New Directions in Anti-Immigrant Politics. *Socialist Review* 25: 169–90.

Leopold, W. 1947. *Speech Development of a Bilingual Child: A Linguist's Record*, vol. 4. Evanston, Ill.: Northwestern University Press.

McLure, E. 1981. Formal and Functional Aspects of the Code-Switching Discourse of Bilingual Children. In *Latino Language and Communicative Behavior*, ed. R. P. Duran, 69–94. Norwood, N.J.: Ablex.

Mendoza-Denton, N. 1994. Language Attitudes and Gang Affiliation among California Latina Girls. In *Cultural Performances: Proceedings of the Third Annual Berkeley Women and Language Conference*, ed. Mary Bucholtz, A. C. Liang, and Laurel A. Sutton, 478–86. Berkeley: Berkeley Women and Language Group.

Migration News. 1997. Foreign-Born Population and Immigration Up. *Migration News* 4, no. 5 (May).

Orellana, Marjorie F. 1994. Appropriating the Voice of the Superheroes: Three Preschoolers' Bilingual Language Uses in Play. *Early Childhood Research Quarterly* 9: 171–93.

Orellana, Marjorie F., and Barrie Thorne. 1998. Year-Round Schools and the Politics of Time. *Anthropology and Education Quarterly* 29, no. 4: 446–72.

Orellana, Marjorie F., Barrie Thorne, A. Chee, and W. S. E. Lam. 1998. *Transnational Childhoods: The Deployment, Development, and Participation of Children in Families' Immigration Projects.* Paper presented at the Meeting of the MacArthur Foundation Research Network on Successful Pathways through Middle Childhood, Berkeley, 5–6 March.

Schwille, J., A. Porter, R. Floden, D. Freeman, L. Knappen, T. Kuhs, and W. Schmidt. 1983. Teachers as Policy Brokers in the Content of Elementary School Mathematics. In *Handbook of Teaching and Policy,* ed. L. Shulman and G. Sykes, 370–91. New York: Longman.

Spillane, Jim. 1997. Standards Based Reform: What Local Policy Makers Make of the Hoopla. Paper presented at the Annual Meeting of the American Educational Research Association, Chicago, March.

———. 1998. Cognitive Perspective on the LEA's Role in Implementing Instructional Policy: Accounting for Local Variability. *Educational Administration Quarterly* 34, no. 1.

———. 1999. External Reform Initiatives and Teachers' Efforts to Reconstruct Their Practice: The Mediating Role of Teachers' Zones of Enactment. *Journal of Curriculum Studies* 31, no. 2: 143–75.

Ramirez, David J. 1992. Executive Summary of Volumes I and II of the Final Report: Longitudinal Study of Structured English Immersion Strategy, Early-Exit and Late-Exit Transitional Bilingual Education Programs for Language-Minority Children. *Bilingual Research Journal* 16, nos. 1–2: 1–62.

Rivera, C. 1998. Bilingual Classes Get Support in Poll. *Los Angeles Times,* 10 February: B3.

Rumbaut, Rubén G. 1998. Transformations: The Post-Immigrant Generation in an Age of Diversity. Paper presented at the Annual Meetings of the Eastern Sociological Society, Philadelphia, 21 March.

Thorne, Barrie, E. Lam, M. F. Author, and B. Chabrier. 1998. When, and How, Does a Difference Make a Difference: A Case Study of Children and Identity Practices in a California Community. Paper presented at the Meeting of the MacArthur Foundation Research Network on Successful Pathways through Middle Childhood, Berkeley, 5–6 March.

Valdés, G. 1981. Codeswitching and Deliberate Verbal Strategy: A Microanalysis of Direct and Indirect Requests among Bilingual Chicano Speakers. In *Latino Language and Communicative Behavior,* ed. R. P. Duran, 133–52. Norwood, N.J.: Ablex.

———. 1996. Con Respeto. *Bridging the Distances between Culturally Diverse Families and Schools: An Ethnographic Portrait.* New York: Teachers College Press.

Vásquez, Olga, Lucinda Pease-Alvarez, and P. Shannon. 1994. *Pushing Boundaries: Language and Culture in a Mexicano Community.* New York: Cambridge University Press.

Wong-Fillmore, L. 1991. When Learning a Second Language Means Losing Your First. *Early Childhood Research Quarterly* 6: 323–46.

Zentella, A. C. 1981. Language Variety among Puerto Ricans. In *Language in the U.S.A.,* ed. C. A. Ferguson and S. B. Heath, 109–32. Cambridge: Cambridge University Press.

4

Ideological Baggage in the Classroom: Resistance and Resilience among Latino Bilingual Students and Teachers

Elizabeth Sugar Martínez

I will see to it that even if it's just one or two students, they will not go through what I went through, the shame and the distance.

I felt shame . . . a rejection of my cultural identity, of being mexicano, of speaking Spanish. . . . It was a rejection of my identity, something I didn't *want* to be—you know, called a mexicano, a Mexican.

. . . When we arrived [in the United States], we got spit on. They spit on my sister. They did. They beat up on my brother. . . . They would call you names. . . .

On a few humid summer mornings in 1998, I met on campus with six very unique educators to interview them individually. It had been two years since I had met with them last—they were all pre-service teachers then—to conduct interviews for a longitudinal study that will span their career as Latino bilingual teachers. I will track their professional evolution from pre-service training to retirement around the year 2030.

The idea for the study germinated during a conversation with my graduate advisor, Dr. Irma Guadarrama. During the summer of 1996, I was her teaching assistant in an undergraduate course on Spanish language arts methodology for grade school children. Most of the students were Latino bilingual pre-service teachers. During the course, they kept journals in which they made entries related to educational issues. One of the assigned journal topics was to write about some of the positive and negative experiences they had had as students.

A purpose of this assignment was to explore the nature of preservice teachers' experiences and to test Farber's (1995) "ideological baggage" hypothesis. According to Farber, teachers are products of their own schooling process and carry deep within them experiences that affect their classroom behavior. She refers to these experiences as "ideological baggage."

What kind of ideological baggage might these preservice teachers carry with them that would drive their future interactions with students? That is, to what extent might their teaching be different because of what they themselves experienced as students? Their answers to these questions were alarming and intensely revealing. Some of their journal entries describe incidents that made it difficult for me to believe that any educator could treat students as some of these undergraduates claimed to have been treated.

Being somewhat skeptical, I invited the students whose stories I found most poignant to be interviewed so that I could more fully explore what had actually occurred to each of them. Two years later, in 1998, I interviewed the same six individuals again—now, *teachers*—asking them to comment on the remarks they had made in 1996, when they were *students*. My main focus during the second (1998) interview was to find out to what extent these interviewees' own schooling process affected their behavior in the classroom now that they themselves were teachers. Following are excerpts from the initial comments they made in 1996 and their reactions to those comments after their first year of teaching, in 1998.[1]

In 1996, the first interviewee, Magda, had written in her journal about a school field day when she was a first grader. Her teacher had asked everyone to dress in a "spring-like" manner. Magda did not speak much English at the time and had not understood exactly what the teacher meant. Magda had gleaned that it would be a special day, there would be a picnic, and the class would be outside.

When Magda explained the field day to her family, her mother decided that Magda would wear her best dress and patent leather shoes. Magda remembers her teacher's scowl as she stared at Magda from head to toe, "with an expression of disgust on her face," when Magda's teacher saw her the morning of the field day. Her teacher decreed, "That's not a spring dress, and those are not spring shoes." Magda was crushed. She felt awkward and out of place; she thought everyone was looking at her. Magda recalls, "I wasn't able to enjoy my field day."

Notwithstanding the events of that day—and events on other days with the same teacher—Magda said that she learned a valuable lesson and did not feel antagonistic toward her teacher. Her teacher's behavior left an indelible imprint on Magda, and it was instrumental in shaping her teaching ideology:

> It is sad that there are people who don't know how to respect others. In this situation, a teacher degraded a student recently arrived from another country. But something very important in my life is that I've already forgiven this teacher. I do not harbor any resentment toward her because I have learned a great lesson: I will treat my students with respect and love. Never will I degrade them.

At the second interview, I asked Magda to comment on the above (1996) excerpt. She said she had had a "flashback" when reading her remarks, for they mirrored a scene that had taken place in her classroom during her first year of teaching:

This year [1997–98] I had one child who came from Monterrey, México. A sweet girl. A very sad situation at home. . . . I could tell you story after story about "Jay." [Here's one:] We were going to take school pictures. The kids usually wear uniforms, and so they were told that they could wear anything they wanted. All the kids either came dressed in their uniform or wore something a little more casual or a little bit more dressy. . . .

Well, she came in, and I remember that the kids were just kind of like standing in awe. . . . She was wearing this fluffy, ruffly dress and *zapatos de charol* [patent leather shoes], like *I* had been wearing in first grade!

I felt *sorry* for her because the kids were looking at her, and they knew that, "Hey! Jay looks different," "She looks kind of out of place," and, "Let's just stare at her and make her feel bad." But I admired her attitude because she *knew* they were staring at her. She thought she looked beautiful. . . . She felt good . . . I didn't want to bring her down. I could have said, "¡Jay, tenemos que llamarle a tu mamá porque así no te puedes vestir!" [Jay, we must call your mother because you can't dress like this!]. . . .

I knew she felt good, I knew she felt beautiful. I knew she was wearing *her best*, just like I was that day. My mom dressed me up in my best dress, and her mom probably did the same. . . . I didn't want to make her feel bad. I didn't want her to feel the way I had felt that day, and made fun of. So I did tell her, "Qué bonito vestido traes" [What a pretty dress you're wearing]. She felt happy, so I left it alone.

Magda's behavior toward students was based not only on her past school experiences but on her home life as well. She empathized with children who were not receiving enough care and attention from their families. Some of her students had no parents. She contemplated what some of her students might be experiencing, such as never hearing their parents encourage them or verbally express their love for them:

In reading this writing that you have here in front of me [i.e., Magda's 1996 comments], there's one sentence that says, "I will treat my students with respect and love," and I think I've really, really tried to do that. I wasn't raised in a very loving home [with] words of encouragement, words of love—or in a home where one says, "I love you" very often. . . .

I grew up in a good home, don't get me wrong. I guess my parents just didn't have that in them, you know. And so, growing up, I wasn't used to all that loving "huggy-huggy" stuff. So when I got in the classroom, I began to think, "Well, how many of these students probably have never heard 'I love you' from their parents or maybe don't have parents?" and some of them didn't. . . .

I guess that's what I did *different*, you know. I never, never had a teacher—never—to say that they loved me. It's not so hard to do. It's not a romantic love . . . you care for these kids. It's not only your job. You look into their eyes, and you try to see their life and what's going to happen down the road . . . and let them feel that they're someone important.

Magda's commitment to building student self-esteem went beyond her job description as teacher. She gave students her address and phone number and encouraged them to always keep in touch. She wanted to maintain contact with former students as a means to fulfilling her extended classroom role as friend and mentor.

Magda was driven to do all she could to heighten students' sense of personal worth. Her own academic journey compelled her to undergird her little charges with a solid confidence in themselves. The second interviewee, Sara, concurred that it was vital to bolster a child's self-concept. Sara also struggled with feelings of incompetence that were intensified as she encountered negative criticism in school that struck at the core of her identity. A Puerto Rican of African ancestry, Sara explained that she considers herself a Latina, though most people mistakenly assume she is black. When Sara tells people she is a Latina, her identity claim has been challenged and met with antagonism, even among teachers.

During the first interview, Sara explained that when she came to the United States at age eight, she attended a school comprising mainly black and Latino students. She was placed in a bilingual class, but for some subjects, such as social studies and English, she was in a monolingual English class. Sara found that the teacher had difficulty accepting her as a Latina:

> The problem was that the teacher could not understand how it was possible that a girl who was "black" didn't know English. The African American teachers could not understand how this was possible. My teacher began to give me bad grades in school, and I would cry when I had to go to school because the teacher always looked at me in an ugly way and treated me like trash.

When her grades began to drop, Sara's mother took action. At school they told her mother that her daughter was misbehaving in class. Sara's bilingual teacher reported that Sara was not misbehaving and could not understand what kind of conflict the other teacher could be having with her. Sara said it was then that the bilingual teacher and her mother realized that the confrontation was a very serious and personal one between Sara and the black teacher, a problem related to cultural identity. Sara transferred to another school where, with the guidance of supportive teachers, her grades rose again. Nonetheless, Sara had been jolted by the fierce blow to her identity:

> This experience definitely made me question who I was and where I came from . . . something I'd never questioned before. . . . To have teachers question who I was, and tell me I'm something that I'm *not*, was *very* disturbing to me. . . . I was paraded around as some kind of freak— "A child trying to act like something that she *wasn't*."
>
> My life would have been a whole lot simpler if I would have just said, "Oh yes, I'm African American." But because I'm proud of where I come from and I'm proud of my culture, it made it very difficult for me. . . . It definitely affected me a lot. I had to regroup my thoughts and search deep into my family tree and my culture to try to fig-

ure this out. But at the end, I still feel the way I did back then: I'm Hispanic, and Hispanic is what I am, and nobody is going to tell me any different. And I will never, ever let anybody question me like that or destroy the way that I see myself.

When I asked Sara how these experiences would affect her teaching, she emphasized that she would never give up on a student. She had been made to feel like a "nobody." She added, "I just didn't have positive feedback. . . . It affected me a *lot*. I didn't feel I could do it, I felt *dumb*. . . . I felt I couldn't do anything."

Two years later, I asked Sara to comment on the above remarks. She said that during her first year of teaching, she had tried to make her second-grade bilingual students feel "just like everyone else in the school—not that they were the 'bilingual' children and they were separated but [that] they were also students and they were part of the school." I asked Sara to give me an example of how she accomplished this goal, and she talked about the benefits of team teaching with monolingual English teachers:

I did a lot of activities with monolingual [English-speaking] teachers that were willing to help me out with this. My students would write stories in Spanish, and they would go into the monolingual classroom and read them to the students there. The kids got really—they had fun with it, because they were trying to figure out, you know, "What is she saying in Spanish?" and "I want to learn Spanish!" We did a lot of activities together which, in my opinion, made my students feel like they were welcomed and they were part of that school, that they weren't outcasts, and that's how *I* felt when I was in school.

As with Magda, Sara placed great emphasis on assuring that her students felt warmly accepted in the classroom. She affirmed, "I also made sure that they felt safe and loved . . . that they were loved and wanted, which was a big part of how I was [not] treated." And like Magda's, Sara's classroom behavior had been influenced by personal school experiences in the past. Another example of this is manifested in Sara's strong desire to make students more aware of the diversity among Latino cultures:

I want to bring more awareness of different Hispanic cultures. . . . It was my first year, and I was . . . trying to get into the swing of things, [so] I didn't do a lot of things that I would have wanted to. For example, like I said in my previous interview, I'm Puerto Rican, and a lot of people didn't know that Hispanics could have dark skin and the kinky hair! So, I want to make my children more aware of that.

Sara recollected her students' reaction when she first introduced herself to them. They were excited to learn that she was from a place called "Puerto Rico" but had no idea what it was. Sara had a colleague from the Dominican Republic who taught at the same school. Sara observed that even the school teachers did not know where Santo Domingo was located or what language was spoken there, nor did they realize that the Dominican teacher, also dark-skinned, was a Latina, as was Sara.

Sara's desire to instill greater cultural awareness among students was also a concern for Roberto, the third interviewee. He noted that his students had asked him why some black people spoke Spanish. He talked to them about *mestizaje*, or the historical blending of cultures and races in the Americas. He expanded their knowledge about slavery in the United States to include slave trade in Caribbean and South American countries, apprising them of the fact that people of all colors speak Spanish. Roberto added, "I was able to inform them and to open their eyes."

Roberto "opened" his students' eyes to the outside world from the safe and supportive environment he had created in his classroom. Indeed, Magda, Sara, and Roberto all stressed the importance of maintaining a warm and nurturing relationship with students so that the naturally uninhibited and inquisitive spirit in these young children would be free to question, receiving answers about issues related to culture and language without the traumatizing sting of rejection and humiliation that the interviewees had endured. As Roberto explained, "I want them to *want* to come and feel very comfortable in my room, not like I did when I went to school. The children were not intimidated. . . . My first grade teacher would scream every day. Every day."

As I listened to each interviewee, the contrast was acutely pronounced between the kind of teacher they described from their pasts and the kind of teacher they aspired to become. The pain they felt—and that they still feel—has transformed these individuals into a unique kind of educator. Along with the pedagogy they mastered in their teacher preparation program, these new teachers possess an authentic comprehension of their students' cultural frame of reference, not only because they, too, are Latinos but because of the adversity they encountered in school. There is no substitute for firsthand experience. Roberto expressed it simply yet insightfully: "I have a lot of empathy and sympathy for those children."

Not surprisingly, a major theme in Roberto's 1996 interview is cultural sensitivity. In that first interview, he stressed the importance of being familiar with people's cultural background, as he believed that ethnic origin made individuals different in some ways: "People *are* different because of where they come from. Everyone needs to be more sensitive towards that. . . . Because of what I saw within [my teacher] and what I've seen happen to other people, I think that I will always have that cultural sensitivity, more so than I guess someone else would that didn't go through this experience."

The experience to which Roberto is referring took place when he was in first grade. He spoke very little English, and because there was no bilingual program at his school, he was placed in a monolingual English classroom. His teacher seemed to be angry with him because of his lack of English proficiency. Roberto remembers that she would yell at him in front of everyone, "and sometimes simply because I didn't understand what she was telling me, she would take me

out of the room to give me swats with the paddle." First grade was agonizing for
Roberto:

> First grade was really, really hard for me. . . . I felt . . . helpless. . . . [My teacher] had
> absolutely no sensitivity. I can't believe she was teaching. . . . I dreaded her class. . . .
> She would scream at me in front of other classes. . . . I hated this lady. . . .
>   I remember this one incident where we were playing a game ["Telephone Opera-
> tor"], and I couldn't do it because I didn't know what the guy was saying. I said some-
> thing else, and she took me out there in front of—and she started screaming at me
> . . . and then she . . . swatted me. . . . I couldn't relay the [message]—I didn't have that
> ability yet. It was awful. First grade was awful. . . .
>   That experience made me want to adapt and conform to Anglo ways. . . . I wanted
> so hard to be able to speak English and to interact with everyone else, and English
> and Anglo ways were the only way to do that. . . . I want to be a teacher because I
> don't want to see more teachers like [her].

Roberto's desire to "adapt and conform to Anglo ways" was spurred by yet
another episode in the sixth grade when his class had a substitute teacher. The
substitute told students that "the streets were full of wetbacks who didn't work and
lived off others' charity and the government." These allegations were especially
disquieting to Roberto because the substitute himself was a minority. The man
claimed to carry "a revolver in his car because he was afraid that Mexicans would
assault him. . . . The next day some students related to the teacher what the man
had said, but she didn't believe them and nothing was done."

The teachers' messages that it was not desirable to be Mexican profoundly
affected Roberto. For years he combatted an inner turmoil that tore at him from
both sides of his bicultural world, and in the process he learned to hate himself.
His feelings of self-enmity were shared by Olivia, the fourth interviewee. In 1996
she stated, "You don't fit in, and so you try everything you *can* to make yourself
un-Mexican, or un-Hispanic, and make yourself more mainstream." She
recounted that even though she spoke Spanish when visiting cousins in Mexico
or when she saw her grandparents, she understood that it was not always "proper"
to speak Spanish:

> I knew when to speak [Spanish] and when not to. But I felt that you shouldn't speak
> too much in Spanish, or sing too much in Spanish, because you would show too much
> of your culture—that you were still too much associated with your culture. What they
> were trying to do was leave that behind and make you become one big melting pot.
> I see that *now*, but back then I didn't notice that. I realized that I had been displaced,
> or disassociated, when I got to college. I became aware of Mexican American stud-
> ies, of Tejano music, and the music that my parents would listen to as I was growing
> up, mariachi music.

Music is an integral part of Olivia's life, for not only is she a bilingual teacher,
she is a professional singer and recording artist. Her schooling experiences have

had an unmistakable effect on her music career. For many years, the genre of songs she performed were influenced by her feelings of self-rejection, a battle of cultural identity fueled, to a significant degree, by her experiences in school:

> Being that I sing, I've changed my singing style to sing songs in Spanish. Before I would just sing [songs by artists such as] Debbie Gibson—pop music is what I would perform. But now I've gone back to singing in Spanish, which has also made me aware of things that I'd missed out on—writers, singers, or just anything in general that has to do with Hispanic groups—the people that I was supposed to be connected with but was disconnected from. I think it had a lot to do with the school system.

Olivia began school not knowing English. Although her parents spoke English, Spanish was the home language. Olivia lamented, "I learned English as if I'd been yanked and shoved into it. The experience was not positive nor pretty. . . . In kindergarten I had no one—not a teacher, not a volunteer, not a teacher's aide—to help me." She found a classmate who was willing to help her with schoolwork, yet the teacher censured them and would hit Olivia for her attempts to integrate into classroom life:

> There was a girl, who ended up becoming my best friend, who would help me. She would translate the lesson, but afterward the teacher would scold us for speaking without permission. She would hit me with a wooden ruler. She would send me to the corner because I would talk when I wasn't supposed to. But how was I to understand her? It didn't hurt me, but the embarrassment did. . . . Because of this I will see to it that even if it's just one or two students, they will not go through what I went through, the shame and the distance.

Olivia felt that this experience made her realize how essential it was for teachers to allow students to satisfy their yearning to be accepted and valued members of their peer groups. As with Roberto, this is one reason why Olivia chose to become a bilingual teacher: "It has stuck in the back of my mind how I was treated. . . . I felt I needed to do something in order to maybe ease another child's pain and to keep that pattern from happening over and over again." Olivia was fervent about wanting Americans everywhere to try to understand why bilingual education is so important. She summarized, "Hopefully we can send out [a message] to the rest of America [to those] that don't understand why we're bilingual teachers, why we're doing this, and why we have chosen this [profession]."

Two years later, in 1998, I asked Olivia to tell me about her first year as a bilingual teacher. What had she done that she said she would do in her classroom? Preeminently reflected in her responses was an impassioned resoluteness to ensure that her students would never be subjected to the hostility she faced in school. As with all previous interviewees, Olivia's primary concern was for her students' comfort level in the classroom:

I pretty much kept it a really comfortable, very safe, secure environment where they would just not feel embarrassed or feel afraid. . . . And also hearing the Spanish, too—English and Spanish. And making sure that they were very "comfortable," I guess, is a big word. And just having them be able to come to me and ask me things, or tell me whatever's wrong, or if they needed help in something. And that was my main goal, to make sure that someone that needed the help was given the help, despite what language you're asking in.

Because I would see teachers that, you'd see them in the hallway, and a little child comes up to them and asks for help, and they're [i.e., the teachers] nonbilingual, and they'll say, "I don't know what you're saying. Tell me in English." And the child would just stand there, trying to speak in English, and they couldn't.

I know that sometimes the teacher is trying to do it in their best interest, "Well, let me just push them." But there's a certain *way* that you should do it, not in a time of *need* or emergency situations . . . when they're trying to look for the bathroom.

Olivia taught in a school that was permeated by anti-bilingual sentiment, though no one ever publicly expressed opposition to the campus' bilingual education program. She disclosed triumphantly that, notwithstanding the aggression, "I still survived." Olivia admitted she had occasionally made curricular decisions that directly challenged official school policy. She was nonetheless convinced of the soundness of her decisions, for she believed that she—and not the administration—had the best interests of her students in mind: "Nothing bad, I just took it further . . . I tried to include . . . what I thought would benefit [my students]. Sometimes a teacher knows best, and you just need to accommodate and pick what you feel is going to work."

At the end of her first year, Olivia moved to another school where she would have more of a voice in curricular decision making. She was intent on assuring that her students feel comfortable and successful in the classroom. These are equally critical issues for Pedro, the fifth interviewee. The estrangement with which he grappled as a newly arrived immigrant boy from Mexico is perhaps the most extreme of all the interviewees'. During the initial interview in 1996, he talked about his memories of second grade, a time that he remembers as his worst year of school: "When we arrived [in the United States], we got spit on. They spit on my sister. They did. They beat up on my brother. . . . My sister was six or seven when that happened. My brother was thirteen or fourteen. . . . They would call you names."

To aggravate matters, Pedro's teacher, a Latina, had a strong aversion to him. Pedro was dumbfounded; he did not understand what he had done to elicit her reaction. The cruelty she displayed left impressions on Pedro that went far deeper than those she left upon his body:

She used to treat me with a lot of contempt. I remember that for hardly any reason at all she would take me by the arms and would squeeze me, which would leave me with her nail marks in my arms. . . . She also used to hit me with a ruler, and she would do it in front of the entire class. I don't know why she did it. Was it because I was an immigrant? I truly do not know.

When I asked Pedro to what extent his classroom experience would affect his own teaching approach, he responded emphatically, "Definitely I would change it, very differently. . . . I think this teacher was not very sensitive." Pedro speculated that perhaps she lacked multicultural understanding and that "she probably didn't appreciate diversity." Although she was a Latina, Pedro sensed that inside her lurked an anti-immigrant attitude.

By contrast, Pedro's approach with his own students would be "to raise self-esteem and appreciate cultural diversity within the classroom . . . accepting yourself, accepting your culture and other people's cultures and opinions." Because of the ordeals he endured in first grade, Pedro desired a classroom setting for his own students that would be the antithesis of what he had lived through. Never would he want his pupils to be ravaged by the same destructive forces that once worked to annul his fledgling identity:

> Through this experience, I felt shame . . . a rejection of my cultural identity, of being mexicano, of speaking Spanish. I was ashamed of speaking in Spanish to my peers. . . . We [the mexicanos] were also discriminated against by our Mexican American neighbors. It was a rejection of my identity, something I didn't *want* to be—you know, called a mexicano, a Mexican—you didn't want to be called that. This experience added to that, because I knew that the teacher was also Mexican American, and it was a rejection of my culture, my background.

Upon reading the remarks from his 1996 interview, Pedro was satisfied that he had accomplished what he had set out to do in his own classroom. He had envisaged making cultural diversity a prominent theme in daily lessons. He secured a job at a magnet elementary school specializing in international studies. The focus of the program was to integrate awareness of different cultures across the curriculum. A country or region was targeted for study over a period of four to six weeks. During the past year students had traveled, through video, to Thailand, Germany, and among American Indian nations in Alaska. Pedro reported that students greatly enjoyed the curriculum because "they got to see the different children from other countries—how they go to school, what they eat, and of course, some things were funny to them."

Pedro's commitment to multicultural pedagogy corresponded with his goal to build self-esteem among students. Of paramount importance to Pedro was his constant affirmation of students' cultural heritage. To foster self-confidence, he advocated pride in students' native backgrounds:

> I try to build up a lot of self-esteem in the kids and make them feel good about their nationality—whether they're from Mexico, or from Honduras, or from El Salvador. I try to bring out, during my lesson plans, something about their culture, their coun-

try. Something that they can bring out maybe in an art project, or in any lesson I try to integrate something that they could show, something that they could feel proud of. . . . I think if you get the child to believe in himself, that he can *do* something, I think it's just something that—I see [that] that automatically "clicks" [with] them. And if they believe they could do it, they just do it. I think it's just like a barrier that they just have to—I mean, if you tell them, "Hey, you can *do* it," they'll *do* it, and it won't seem like a barrier after they do it. So I think it's something very important, just to *believe* in themselves. I think if they *do* believe it, they could accomplish whatever they want to accomplish.

Pedro sought to cultivate a self-assurance in his students that would engender within them a natural inclination to embrace their Latino origins. A key component to his strategy was to raise the prestige level of Spanish vis-à-vis English. This was also a priority for Jasmín, the last interviewee. She would enthusiastically motivate her students with inspirational accolades such as, "You're going to be a bilingual doctor." The students would respond to her encouragement by making affirming statements such as, "When I'm an accountant, I want to travel to different countries," and she would further confirm their aspirations by declaring, "You will definitely do it if you're bilingual. . . . Don't ever forget your Spanish because that's who you *are*."

Jasmín's regard for her students' cultural ancestry as an asset rather than a liability is in sharp disparity with her teacher's attempt to quell minority language and culture by means of physical force. In 1996, Jasmín remembered how her first-grade teacher would strike her with a paddle when she spoke Spanish. Such encounters forever altered Jasmín's view of punishment in the classroom:

I will never forget how much that paddle hurt me and all the crying that I did. . . . My teaching will be really affected by what happened to me when I was younger. When it comes to punishment, I don't believe in it. I believe there are alternative methods. . . . I think I'll be a very supportive teacher, understanding when it comes to a child's needs and where they're coming from. . . . I'll try to be the most understanding kind of person that I can possibly be.

When I was smaller, you don't know that everyone's different. You just look at everyone like they're the same. This teacher made me realize that I was different, that my family was different, the way I talked was different. I never knew. When I would go home, my dad would tell us to speak Spanish. When I would go to school, my teacher would tell me to speak *English*. Half the time I didn't know what English and Spanish *was*. I was just trying to communicate my needs and my ideas.

As a result of her painful experiences in first grade, Jasmín never again viewed her cultural identity in the same way. She averred, "I knew, from the time I was six years old, that I was different. . . . I was Mexican." She understood that she did not fit in.

After reading her 1996 interview comments, Jasmín reflected on the differences between the classroom environment that her teacher had created and the one Jasmín created for her students. She noted, "I didn't ever punish them for speaking their home language. I just tried to be as positive as I could." The dissimilarity in teacher attitude and philosophy was clearly evident:

> The difference was that when *they* spoke Spanish, I made them feel good about it, you know? The whole year I worked on making them feel confident about the language—about speaking it, writing it, reading it. . . . So when they spoke Spanish, I mean, I was like, "That's *good!*" you know? "That's what you speak at home, that's what we're going to speak here." I told them a lot of different reasons why we should speak Spanish *and* English, why Spanish is so good: "It's your *roots*, it's your family, it's *what* you're all about. It says something *about* you, it's part of you, it's who you are. It's a *whole* bunch of things. It not only will help you communicate with more people, but it will help you in the future. . . ."

Jasmín hoped that teachers at her school would work in concert with her and other bilingual teachers to communicate the idea to bilingual students that knowing Spanish is an invaluable resource, that it is something beneficial. Yet, sadly, she witnessed behavior among colleagues indicating that they did not support bilingual education and even resented it. She was disheartened to see how students were discriminated against in ancillary subject classrooms. To Jasmín, the discrepancy between how her students were treated compared with non-bilingual children went beyond tangible evidence. She could sense the teachers' rejection:

> I mean, I *know* the *different* looks that teachers will give a regular classroom, no matter *how* bad they were. They could be the *worst* as far as discipline goes . . . like throwing paper around, fighting, and stuff like that. But yet they *love them*. They didn't love *mine*, you know? Not that they need the love of every teacher or anything like that. But they didn't like them because of the language they spoke. It made their skin color more *apparent* to them. I could *see* that; I *felt* it.

Jasmín chose not to contradict these colleagues when they advised her to teach her students more English, but she was resolute when she confided to me, "I do what I want in my classroom."

CONCLUSION

The resistance and resilience demonstrated by Jasmín and her fellow interviewees are impressive. Though as children they were mauled by the ideological baggage of misdirected teachers, their own ideological baggage now brims with cultural pride and a firm resolve to effect change in the school system. Their sense of mission is palpable. *They are determined to make a difference in the lives of their students.*

The student community referred to in this chapter makes up an ever-increasing constituency in schools across our country. In fact, rapidly shifting demographics in the United States unveil a new face of the "typical" American. In the fall of 1989, the U.S. Census Bureau predicted that while the white American population will grow by 25 percent between 1990 and 2030, during that same period the African American population will increase by 68 percent; the combined Asian American, Pacific Island American, and Native American populations by 79 percent; and the Latino American population by 187 percent (Barrett 1991).

Latinos and other ethnic minority groups constitute the majority of public school students in two of the nation's largest states. Latino and other minority K–12 students account for over 50 percent of the public school enrollments in California and Texas (García 1991; Valencia 1991). The fastest growing language minority group in the United States is Spanish speaking. Spanish speakers are projected to increase to more than 22 million by the year 2000 (Macías 1993). Latino children represent the future America. Their success is our success as a nation. School, then, should be a place where teachers act as mediators, imparting the curriculum in a way that best fills the needs of the students it serves. Specialized training could be provided by school districts, giving teachers—both veterans *and neophytes*—a voice with which to share concerns and ideas among colleagues. Together, teachers could design curricula tailored to match cultural contexts in which students live and learn everyday.

As a former grade school teacher and university teacher trainer, I am troubled that teaching, in general, continues to be an isolated and isolating profession. We teach in our rooms and rarely, if ever, consult with one another as professionals in a professional forum. I wonder what would have happened if the teachers the interviewees discussed would have been able to meet regularly with colleagues to seek advice for the problems they were having with their language minority students. Would I have written this chapter at all? There may likely have been no journal entries to probe.

Over months and years, a treasure-trove of knowledge is gathered and stored within each teacher. Yet this information most often remains unexamined and, subsequently, underdeveloped. When teachers gather, through discussion and self-evaluation they can make valuable discoveries, such as a change in teaching philosophy, a need to realign goals, or more effective alternatives for dealing with a complicated situation at school. When teachers share their findings, colleagues conjointly benefit from the new insights they have acquired.

Reflecting individually and with colleagues allows teachers to understand more specifically how their ideological baggage affects students. Each student—and teacher—brings a unique set of characteristics into the classroom. Teachers who are aware of these complexities can use them to modify their instructional behavior accordingly. As educators, it behooves us to regularly inspect our baggage with a scrutinous eye. Otherwise, as the interviewees would readily attest, educators are dangerously prone to scarring young minds and hearts for life.

NOTES

All names in this article are fictitious.
1. One of the interviewees, Pedro, had just completed his *second* year of teaching.

REFERENCES

Arias, M. 1986. The Context of Education for Hispanic Students: An Overview. *American Journal of Education* 95: 26–57.

Barrett, P. A., ed. 1991. *Doubts and Certainties: Working Together to Restructure Schools.* Washington, D.C.: National Endowment for the Arts Professional Library.

Brophy, J., and T. Good. 1974. *Teacher-Student Relationships: Causes and Consequences.* New York: Holt, Rinehart and Winston.

Catterall, J. S. 1985. *On the Social Costs of Dropping Out of School.* Report no. 86-SEPI-3. Stanford: Stanford University, Center for Educational Research.

Dixon-Krauss, L. 1996. *Vygotsky in the Classroom: Mediated Literacy Instruction and Assessment.* White Plains, N.Y.: Longman.

Farber, K. S. 1995. Teaching about Diversity through Reflectivity: Sites of Uncertainty, Risk, and Possibility. In *Practicing What We Teach: Confronting Diversity in Teacher Education,* ed. R. J. Martin, 49–63. New York: State University of New York Press.

Freire, P. 1993. *Pedagogy of the Oppressed,* 2nd edition. New York: Continuum.

García, E. E. 1997. The Education of Hispanics in Early Childhood: Of Roots and Wings. *Young Children* 52, no. 3: 5–14.

García, J. E. 1991. Minorities in Texas' Schools Are Majority. *Austin American Statesman,* 7 September: A1, A6.

Good, T., and J. Brophy. 1991. *Looking in Classrooms.* 5th edition. New York: Harper-Collins.

Macías, A. F. 1993. Language and Ethnic Classification of Language Minorities: Chicano and Latino Students in the 1990s. *Hispanic Journal of Behavioral Sciences* 15, no. 2: 230–57.

National Center for Education Statistics. 1997. *Digest of Education Statistics.* Washington, D.C.: U.S. Department of Education.

Valencia, R. R. 1991. The Plight of Chicano Students: An Overview of Schooling Conditions and Outcomes. In *Chicano School Failure and Success: Research and Policy Agendas for the 1990s,* ed. R. R. Valencia, 3–26. The Stanford Series on Educational and Public Policy. Basingstoke, U.K.: Falmer Press.

5

Multicultural Education in Primary Schools in Almería, Spain

Encarnación Soriano Ayala

INTRODUCTION

In recent years Spain has changed from a nation of emigration to one of immigration. Our country is not used merely as a route on the way to the rest of Europe; in fact, 78 percent of emigrants from Africa come directly to Spain. Furthermore, Almería is beginning to lead the provinces in terms of immigration (Checa 1995).

Almería's economy has undergone a great change since the end of the 1970s caused principally by a great expansion in its agricultural sector, especially in the production of intensive crops grown under plastic. According to Jaen, de Pablo, and Carretero (1995), production from these greenhouses currently accounts for over 40 percent of the provincial gross national product and 28 percent of the workforce. The need for unskilled labor has attracted thousands of Africans to this province in search of wages, housing, and a decent place to settle. In this exodus, the men are usually the first to arrive, gradually bringing over the rest of their family members until they manage to gather them all together. They are often young families with school-aged children who need to be sent to an educational establishment. Almería is characterized by the coexistence of various cultural and ethnic groups within the same geographical and sociopolitical area, but the economic position of the immigrant families means that the education of their children becomes the responsibility of the host country. The schools in Almería are facing a new challenge: that of learning to live in a pluralist society, with cultural diversity, tolerance, and respect for "difference." Schools are the ideal place to promote the integration of immigrant children and to lay the foundations for a truly multicultural education.

THE EDUCATIONAL SYSTEM AND CULTURAL PLURALISM

Etxeberría (1992), Juliano (1993), and Rosales (1994) suggest the following phases in the responses given by the educational system to the theme of cultural pluralism:

1. Assimilationist: An objective given high priority is that the children from minority groups quickly learn the language of the majority and become assimilated into the culture of the majority group in the best way possible.
2. Compensatory: The aim is for children from other cultures to overcome any gaps or deficiencies arising from their ethnic origins, so that they may join the culture of the dominant group. An asymmetrical relation of power is established by this process, generating violence and imposing the dominant culture on the minority. The integration of different cultures affects not only the minority groups involved but also the native majority. Social and educational integration must never be seen in terms of losing one's own identity.
3. Corrective: In this phase the aim is to eliminate cases of discrimination and prejudice toward ethnic minorities as reflected in schools, programs, and textbooks.
4. Multicultural: Here the minority cultures are recognized as having equal rights with respect to the majority. This does not involve deciding which culture is superior but, rather, enriching and fully developing these cultures. Multiculturalism defends a symmetrical interchange and seeks to establish communication between cultures in the original conditions of reciprocal interchange—in equality and respect for difference.
5. Intercultural: Here the object is to establish a new culture based on the interchange of cultures, values, experiences, and so on. Intercultural education should give high value to cultural difference as a source of enrichment and should work in terms of difference and not of inequality (García Garrido 1995; Puig I Moreno 1991).

CULTURAL DIVERSITY IN ALMERIAN SCHOOLS: AN ANALYSIS OF THE SITUATION

The main objective of the study is to describe the situation of African immigrants in schools in the western area of the province of Almería: their specific problems and their relations with schoolmates, with teachers, and with the school in general. We attempt to detect the model response (assimilationist, compensatory, corrective, multicultural, or intercultural) that the schools offer to this second generation of foreigners from the African continent. In addition, we endeavor to establish different alternatives and responses, laying down the bases for a joint plan of action with the teachers for forthcoming years.

Methodology: Sample, Instruments for Information Collection, and Procedure

The sample was made up of thirty-three pupils (from a total population of 124 immigrants), the offspring of African immigrants, selected from the three state schools with the highest number of immigrant pupils. In the selection of our sample the following criteria took precedence: that they had a good understanding of the Spanish language and were old enough to understand the questions asked and to provide the information required. In the first state school, the children came from Ethiopia, Morocco, and Senegal, and their ages were between eight and fourteen. In the second state school the children interviewed came from Morocco. Their ages varied between nine and fifteen. Finally, in the third state school, all the children were Moroccan immigrants. The ages of these children were between eight and sixteen. In all three schools the final part of the interview was given to the Spanish pupils in the form of a survey. Head teachers, teachers of immigrant pupils, parents of African and Spanish pupils, and school inspectors were all interviewed.

Various instruments were devised for the collection of information. First, a script for an interview consisting of three parts was prepared for the immigrant pupils. The first part covers information about sociodemographic variables, concentrating on data relating to their families. The second concerns aspects of their conditions of life in Spain: housing, means, possessions, and so on. The third section refers to questions relating to their relationships with teachers and schoolmates. This third part, in the form of a survey, was also answered by the Spanish pupils in three classes.

In order to contrast the data provided by the pupils, the head teachers and teaching staff of the three schools were also interviewed. For this purpose a series of questions was prepared so that these professionals could give us their assessments of the relationships that immigrant pupils form within the school with teachers and other pupils, the advantages (if the interviewee considers that there are any) for the school of having these pupils present in the school, and also the educational needs to enable the school to receive them. We were also interested in the opinion of the Education Authorities, and for this reason we interviewed school inspectors. We questioned the latter about the criteria followed to enroll immigrant children in schools, the resources the schools are provided with, and the advantages and problems of their enrollment in school. It was also fundamental to learn, in addition to the information provided by these sectors, the opinions of the mothers and fathers of both immigrant and Spanish pupils. In order to collect this information we prepared two questionnaires with open questions, whose principal thrust was the relations between these two groups of pupils from the family's point of view.

The in-depth interviews with immigrant pupils, teachers, head teachers, and parents were carried out between the months of March and June 1995. The school inspectors were interviewed subsequently. The interviews with pupils, teachers, head teachers, and parents were completed in one school before passing on to the next (see table 5.1).

Analysis and Interpretation: Immigrants, Schools, Parents, and Needs

The analysis of the data was carried out by contrasting the responses in the interviews given by the pupils, teachers, head teachers, families (both immigrant and Spanish), and the Schools Inspectorate. Not all of the pupils live in complete, nuclear families. Although it is more frequent that the father arrives first on Spanish soil and gradually brings over the older children followed by the rest of the family, only 87.9 percent of the children interviewed have their fathers residing in this country. The number of mothers living in western Almería is even lower: only 81.8 percent. This information is very significant because the children who live solely with their fathers, when their mothers and brothers/sisters remain in the country of origin, lack the care and affection that the mother figure and the siblings normally provide. As regards brothers and sisters, 63.6 percent of the children interviewed have all their siblings in Spain, while 12.1 percent live with only one family member, the rest of their families remaining in the country of origin. The immigrant support teacher told us that "Abdelilah is extremely sad because his family is divided, part here and part in Morocco. He says that he hasn't seen them together since 1990. He misses his mother and sister and hopes they get their visa and can come over."

Table 5.1   Procedure

Phase 1
Approaching the schools
Analysis of school documentation
Initial data collection from teachers and pupils
Phase 2
Sample selection
Drafting the instruments:
Interviews, etc.
Phase 3
Data collection
Phase 4
Data analysis/interpretation:
Contrasting responses
Negotiating results
Phase 5
Diagnosis and proposals for pedagogical reform

Although the children have not been in Spain for more than three years, there are families in which the father has been here for a lot longer: "My father has been here for twenty-six years." Other children assured us that their fathers came twenty-five years ago or less. The work that they carried out in their countries of origin is diverse: "working in the country"; "he was a salesman." Few of the mothers, however, worked outside the home. Despite the diversity of jobs that the fathers had in their countries of origin, in Almería they all work in the greenhouses. As already mentioned, few mothers worked outside the home in their country of origin, but in Almería the number increases: many of them also work in the greenhouses or sort fruit and vegetables in the warehouses; they are also employed in domestic service or in hotels. The ages of the fathers range between thirty-four and sixty-three. The mothers tend to be younger, from twenty-nine to forty-eight years old.

The academic level of the fathers of the children interviewed is quite low, as can be seen from the children's answers: "he can't read or write"; "he can only write his name." The mothers have a lower level of schooling. This information is quite representative, for while many Spanish children receive help from their parents to do their homework, many of the immigrant parents are unable to assist because of lack of means and knowledge.

The living standards of the children interviewed are quite precarious (see table 5.2). None of the families owns its home. These are rented or provided by their employers: 48.5 percent of the pupils live in farmhouses, and 33.3 percent live in houses in towns. The rest live in flats. There are children who said that they live in warehouses separated by curtains, having the kitchens on one side among the boxes and their beds (or, as they say, their bedrooms) on the other. As regards hygiene and installations, the houses do not possess the minimum conditions for a decent standard of living (they need painting and glass in the windows, they have little furniture, and they are very old, etc.). Not every house has a bathroom—

Table 5.2   Immigrant Pupils' Family and Housing Conditions

Family members living in Spain	
Father	87.9%
Mother	81.8%
Brothers and sisters	63.6%
Housing (rented or provided by employer)	
Farmhouse	48.5%
Townhouse	33.3%
Flat	18.2%
Persons sharing the house	
Family only	60.6%
Family and other persons	36.4%
Sharing a bedroom	81.8%

thus, one of the pupils remarked, "I go to the bar, ask for something, and go to the toilet. I have a shower on Saturdays when I play football in El Ejido." Some lack running water, though they all have electricity. All of the houses, except one, possess a television set, but in only eighteen homes is there a washing machine and in twenty-nine a fridge.

Of the pupils, 36.4 percent share the house with persons other than their immediate families: "with my uncle Said"; "with Mohamed's father and Mohamed." Of the children, 81.8 percent share a bedroom, and some even share the bed with brothers/sisters, mothers, or other persons.

A pupil must be motivated to learn, that is, favorable attitudes are required to reach significant learning achievements. We asked the children if they liked going to school. We found the same percentage in both the immigrant and Spanish pupils, although their responses were different. Of the children, 90.9 percent like going to school. The immigrant children justify their answers by saying, "because I want to learn things and learn Spanish"; "they teach me to speak and write, they are very good with me"; "because I have friends and I learn, even though they call me a Moor and hit me." The Spanish children who like to go to school speak in almost the same terms, although they highlight friendship above everything else, together with the desire not to go to work and the aspect of playing with friends at school. Some of their remarks include, "because I can be with my friends, as outside school we all work and cannot see each other and talk"; "because I would rather come to school than work in the greenhouses." The foreign students underline the need to learn, to study, to learn Spanish, to be able to read and write. The Spanish pupils give greater emphasis to relations with their friends, to the enjoyable aspect of school, and to school as an alternative to working in the greenhouses.

Of the immigrant children interviewed 90.9 percent attend school on a daily basis, and 9.1 percent do not attend regularly. This coincides with the proportion of Spanish and immigrant pupils who do not like to go to school: 9.1 percent in both cases. The reasons are various and different between the two groups. The immigrant pupils comment that "the big children hit me and call me a Moor"; "the teachers are crazy." However, the Spanish children say things like, "I don't like exams"; "I don't like to study"; "we only come to learn to write, and we have to study a lot." The foreign pupils express themselves in terms of attitudes to the relations they form at school with teachers and other children. The Spanish children do not bring up problems related to being accepted or to friendships but, rather, to the effort required to complete an exam or the concentration needed to study.

In relation to the question of the need for motivation so that the learning process can be effective, we also asked the children whether they were happy at school: 54.5 percent of the immigrant children replied "always," and 44.6 percent of the Spanish pupils also answered "always." The response "sometimes" decreases from the immigrant pupils to 39.4 percent, and the same reply increases to 53.6 percent from the Spanish pupils. As regards the response "never," this is greater for the immigrant children, at 6.1 percent. When we asked the head teachers,

teachers, and families, all of them assured us that the immigrant children were happy at school. The teachers thought that, considering their difficult circumstances (separated families, precarious lives, etc.), they are happier at school than at home. They also applied this response to the Spanish pupils who have difficult family backgrounds. The immigrant families said that their children were all right at school. In the interviews with the parents we noted that they had great hopes of school as a way of improving their children's living standards, so that they would not have to work in the greenhouses when they were older.

We were interested in the forms in which immigrants are grouped in the classroom. We have discovered that there are no differences in the way that Spanish pupils are grouped, save in the physical space that they occupy (at the front, in the middle, or at the back of the classroom). Only 39.4 percent of the pupils are placed in working groups, 27.3 percent are in pairs, and 33.3 percent are at separate desks. The actual space they occupy in the classroom is different and, by the position of the children's names on the sketch we provided them, we noted immigrant boys and girls at the back of the classroom, next to a Spanish pupil or one of their ethnic group; at the front near the teacher; in the middle of the classroom among Spanish children and others of their ethnic group; and at the back with Spanish children. One pupil told us, "I'm at the back, and nobody is next to me. Fali is in front of me and another boy whose name I don't know."

We thought it appropriate to find out about the relations between the pupils. Their responses were very significant. Of the immigrant children interviewed, 27.3 percent said that they got on well with "all" their schoolmates. The Spanish pupils gave higher figures: 57.1 percent provided the same reply. Of the immigrant children, 48.5 percent said they got on well with "some," and the Spanish children gave a percentage of only 12.5 percent for the same. There was another option only for the immigrant pupils: "with nobody."

When we asked head teachers and teachers about the integration of pupils, they replied, "Well, they are not rejected. There has never been any rejection. The presence of these children in the school hasn't had great repercussions. There haven't been any complaints"; "the relations were very close in the beginning, but as the children got to know them, they began to reject them, and the gypsies reject them more than the others." From the teachers' responses, from observations made in the classrooms, and from an analysis of the school syllabi, we see that there exists an interest that the foreign children learn to speak the language as quickly as possible in order to be able to include them in the activities developed in class that correspond to a determined culture, customs, values, traditions, and language: all belonging to Spanish society.

The teachers informed us that when immigrant pupils enroll, they are behind in their schooling and often have problems with the paperwork. They told us about "children who arrive without any kind of documentation or with their papers only in Arabic." The teaching staff at one school told us that "we don't have the means to know what to do with them as regards didactic level, language, or culture, and the little help which we received from Almería Acoge [a local nongovernmental organization] was taken from us by a phone call from the Education Department." Faced with this kind of situation, we tried to discover whether these children receive more help than the rest of their Spanish schoolmates, whether there is a support teacher available, and what kind of activities they do in the classroom.

The opinion of 60.6 percent of the immigrant pupils is that they do not receive more help from their teachers than the other children; however, this percentage drops considerably in the native pupils: only 5.4 percent express this opinion. The immigrant pupils told us that "they never ask me anything"; "they give us work to do, we work all day, and the teacher works with us and only answers our doubts." On the other hand, the teachers do think that they help the immigrant children more than the others; they said things like, "Yes, he didn't know the language, he's almost got into the rhythm of the class."

Assistance from a support teacher is received by 72.7 percent of the immigrant children. Through a description of the activities that the teachers plan for the support class, we can deduce that their principal focus of interest is that the children learn Spanish as quickly as possible in order to join in the normal activities of the class. They do activities linked to comprehension, production, and communication, both oral and written, of the Spanish language. They do not perform activities in their own languages.

We found different responses from the immigrant and Spanish pupils when we spoke of their participation in class, of the perception they have of whether their teachers and classmates listen to them, and of whether, when they express their opinions, these are taken into consideration by the rest of the class. The immigrant pupils almost polarized their replies: 42.4 percent believe that in a debate situation, they hold the attention of their teachers and classmates. However, 33.4 percent of these pupils take the opposite opinion: their views are "never" considered by the class. Of the Spanish pupils, 57.1 percent believe that their views are "sometimes" taken into account, although a large percentage, 37.5 percent, think that they are "always" listened to. One immigrant pupil said, "We never give our opinions, we say things, but the others don't listen." This same question was put to the teachers, although with a slight difference: they were asked whether "they think that these pupils are heard and whether their classmates listen to their opinions when they speak in class." The teachers replied affirmatively to this question, basing their answers on the interest that the Spanish pupils show toward the customs and views of the immigrant children. Note the discrepancy between the teachers' and the pupils' responses (see table 5.3).

The immigrant parents expect a great deal from school: the education of their children leading to an improvement in their conditions of life so that in the future they will not have to work in the greenhouses like them. The parents believe that their children relate to the other Spanish children outside the school. In addition, they express a preference that their children should have Spanish friends and not only relate with others of the same background. We observed in some of the

Table 5.3   Immigrant and Spanish Pupils' Responses (in Percentages)

	Immigrant Pupils	Spanish Pupils
Daily attendance at school		
Yes	90.9	90.9
No	9.1	9.1
Do the pupils like going to school?		
Yes	90.1	90.1
No	9.1	9.1
Do the pupils feel happy at school?		
Always	54.5	44.6
Sometimes	39.4	83.6
Never	3	1.8
Do they get on well with their schoolmates?		
All of them	27.3	57.1
Quite a few	21.2	30.4
Some	48.5	12.5
None	3	—
Help the children receive from the class tutor		
More than other children	21.2	5.4
The same as other children	60.6	5.4
Help received from the support teacher?		
Yes	72.7	28.6
Do they think that their schoolmates and teacher listen to them when they express their opinions?		
Always	2.4	37.5
Sometimes	24.2	57.1
Never	33.4	5.4

responses given by the African parents a certain "shame" with regard to their own cultures. This is not quite so, but we believe this rejection exists because Spanish people reject their cultures and the immigrant families want to be accepted, even if this means having to assimilate the culture of the dominant group. For example, in one interview a mother said, "Yes, we do have Spanish friends, I don't want Moroccan friends, the neighbor's daughter is always coming round here." As regards relations with the school, some of the families affirmed that they have none. Others assured us that they go to the school frequently and are interested in their children's academic activities.

The Spanish parents who were interviewed think, in general, that their children get on well with their immigrant classmates at school because their children have been brought up not to reject anybody. On the question of the presence of immigrant children at school, they believe that everybody has the right to an education. They maintain that they do not have any contact with the parents of the immigrant classmates of their children, saying that they live far away and that otherwise things would be different.

We requested from the Schools Inspectorate information regarding the enrollment of these pupils, the resources given to schools with immigrant pupils, and the advantages and problems of enrolling children with other customs, languages, and religions. As regards enrollment, they informed us that the only bureaucratic procedure required is an application by the parents to the school. Once the child is enrolled, the grade in which to place him or her is decided with the guidance of a team of teachers. The head teachers we spoke to disagreed on this point, saying that the newly arrived children are placed in classes according to their ages. The Inspectorate considers these children to be classed as pupils with special educational needs, understanding *needs* as social and mutual integration, and thus adaptations in the curriculum are made for them. The latter are necessary, according to the Inspectorate, because the students have not reached the corresponding level in the "curricular contents." The fundamental activity of the support teachers, according to the Inspectorate, is to provide the children with special support, particularly with respect to language acquisition.

The teachers and head teachers believe that the administration should cover the deficiencies that the schools experience when admitting pupils of other cultures, customs, values, and so on, and they request the following from the Education Authorities:

1. Support teachers from the immigrant pupils' country of origin.
2. Training courses in which suitable teaching materials can be prepared.
3. Support staff not only in the schools but also for the families.

Indeed, from the above declarations we appreciate that the teachers feel very neglected by the administration. The latter does not prepare the teachers properly to cope with this new situation. They are not given the necessary material and human resources, and there are no members of staff to serve as a nexus between families and schools.

CONCLUSIONS AND PROPOSALS
FOR PEDAGOGICAL REFORM

Throughout our investigation we have observed that the adaptation of pupils differs from school to school. We recognize that all the schools, in general, favor an assimilationist phase of education linked to a compensatory phase. Second, we have noted the difficulties that the teachers encounter when faced with a class containing one or more children from another culture or with a different language. These difficulties are due, in the first place, to the lack of training they receive to enable them to cope with this new situation and, second, to the insufficient help they receive in the form of special support teachers for immigrant children. The children simply arrive at the schools and without more ado are admitted into classes. The material resources available are minimal, and human resources are even scarcer. What solutions can we provide to promote multicultural education in our schools, in such a way that it is applied at all levels throughout the system? As regards the solutions that the administration can provide, we propose the following:

1. Support teachers who are either Spanish or from the immigrant pupils' countries of origin and who have knowledge of the cultures and languages of these children. These teachers would initially assist the pupils full-time, favoring the use of their mother tongues, teaching them Spanish and also the instrumental subjects. Subsequently, the pupils would be integrated into the classes, though they would continue to receive the corresponding support. Another function of the support teacher would be to work with the class tutor to program courses in common, to monitor the pupils, and to respond to any questions concerning their culture, customs, values, and so on, so as to introduce these elements into the "Curricular Project" and into class programming. A further function of these teachers would be to serve as a link between the schools and the families, helping the latter to participate in school life. They would also be required to look at any difficulties and find possible solutions, thus acting as a support for the pupils at home.

2. The administration should facilitate specific training for those teachers who receive immigrant pupils. This would be carried out, in an initial phase, by means of courses that would include teachers (by zone or by school) with the same needs and which would serve to answer any doubts that they might have in this respect. This would be followed by a second phase of self-training by means of working groups within the schools, whose objective would be to study strategies and prepare teaching materials for use in the classroom.

3. The administration should also introduce a compulsory subject at university level on multicultural education into faculties of education or teacher training colleges. This third point is more related to the initial training of teachers than to their permanent training, something that is covered by our second point. It is appropriate that this theme be tackled from the earliest stages of teacher training.

Regarding the solutions that should be adopted and developed by the schools, we have some suggestions. First, if the multicultural education approach is to work and the curriculum is to be provocative and challenging, teachers will need to be guided. In this way multicultural education should be included in each element of the "curricular project":

1. The development of the capacity for respect and knowledge of the rights of persons should be present in the course objectives. We agree with Rosales (1994) on the necessity to enhance the pupils' awareness of tolerance, sol-

idarity, cooperation, justice, communication, and so on, together with a knowledge of other cultures.

2. The course contents. We should bear in mind that these can be concepts, procedures, attitudes, and values. As to concepts, we agree with Zabalza (1992a, 1992b), Rosales (1994), and Escámez (1995) on the need to teach themes related to cultural values, to ways of life and work, and to the official or nonofficial national and international organizations that regulate the ways in which peoples interact. As much emphasis should be placed on contemporary culture as on historic culture, and groups should be represented as active, real, and dynamic (Gay 1979). Bilingual education can also be provided to all pupils in a school. Trueba comments, "Use of native language is best because critical thinking skills and cognitive structuring are conditioned by linguistic and cultural knowledge that children usually obtain in the home" (1991, 154). As regards procedures, we also agree with Puig Rovira (1994) and Escámez (1995), who propose the use of dialogue between pupils and between pupils and teachers. We must teach children to listen to others and to appreciate their arguments, values, and interests. Dialogue implies knowing how to appreciate different points of view and appraise the information expressed by others. Also, diverse materials should be used to present diverse viewpoints. Pupils should become comfortable with the fact that often there is more than one perspective, and they should learn to expect and seek out multiple versions (Sleeter and Grant 1994). Finally, values that are considered universal should be taught: solidarity, justice, happiness, cooperation, and collaboration.

3. Methodology of instruction and resources. The physical spaces should be changed in the classroom in order to promote communication and allow the immigrant and Spanish children to relate better. To this end, the teacher should arrange work to be done in small groups in which it is essential that the objectives to be achieved are done so by all the members of the group. Debates and discussions should be encouraged. As far as time is concerned, this should depend on the activities and never vice versa. Teachers should help pupils discover their own particular styles of learning for themselves so that they can learn more effectively. To all of this we would add that cooperative and collaborative learning should be favored in the classroom (Slavin 1990). It would be useful if the schools had books and videos dealing with multicultural education.

4. Schools should change the concept of measurement of the learning process for that of evaluation. They should take account of evaluation of the formative type, running throughout the process. This can help to check our work in the classroom, converting programming/planning into mere working hypotheses that are modifiable and adapted to the needs of pupils and teachers.

Second, we should encourage schools to maintain a strong relationship with the family. Teachers must deal with parents' needs for information on effective parenting, on available social services, on school procedures and curricula, and on how to help their pupils. At the same time, effective parent involvement programs acknowledge the fact that parents are the child's earliest and most influential teachers. We believe that we have put forward many proposals and raised many questions that do not warrant us ending our investigations with the present document. This is merely a start that allows us to begin work with the teaching profession and which prepares the way for much needed further research into this field of great interest.

REFERENCES

Bartolomé, M. 1992. Diseños y metodologías de investigación desde la perspectiva de la educación intercultural. In *Educación Intercultural en la Perspectiva de la Europa Unida*, X Congreso Nacional de Pedagogía, 648–75. Salamanca: GRUPOANAYA.

Checa, F. 1995. Migración, riesgos y beneficios. Los inmigrantes africanos en la provincia de Almería. *Demófilo* 15: 103–33.

Escámez, J. 1995. Educación para la tolerancia. *Vela Mayor* 5: 27–35.

Etxebarría, F. 1992. Educación intercultural, racismo y europeismo. Congreso de Educación Multicultural, Ceuta.

García Garrido, J. L. 1995. Interculturalismo: El reto de la educación europea. *Vela Mayor* 5: 6–12.

Gay, G. 1979. On Behalf of Children: A Curriculum Design for Multicultural Education in the Elementary School. *Journal of Negro Education* 48: 324–40.

Jaen, M., J. de Pablo, and A. Carretero. 1995. Un análisis del entorno económico almeriense. *Demófilo* 15: 63–86.

Juliano, D. 1993. *Educación intercultural: Escuelas y minorías étnicas*. Madrid: EUDEMA.

Puig I Moreno, G. 1991. Hacia una pedagogía intercultural. *Cuadernos de Pedagogía* 196: 12–18.

Puig Rovira, J. M. 1994. Diversidad étnico-cultural: Una prueba para la democracia y para la educación. In *Teoría y práctica de la educación intercultural*, ed. M. A. Santos, 97–119. Barcelona: PPU/Universidad de Santiago de Compostela.

Rosales, E. 1994. El reto de la educación intercultural en la construcción del currículum. In *Teoría y práctica de la educación intercultural*, ed. M. A. Santos, 43–67. Barcelona: PPU/Universidad de Santiago de Compostela.

Slavin, R. E. 1990. *Cooperative Learning*. Englewood Cliffs, N.J.: Prentice-Hall.

Sleeter, C. E., and C. A. Grant. 1994. *Making Choices for Multicultural Education*. Englewood Cliffs, N.J.: Merrill Prentice-Hall.

Soriano, E. 1997. Análisis de la Educación Multicultural en los centros educativos de la comarca del poniente almeriense. *Revista de Investigación Educativa* 15, no. 1: 43–67.

Trueba, H. T. 1991. Learning Needs of Minority Children: Contributions of Ethnography to Educational Research. In *Language, Culture and Cognition*, ed. L. M. Malave and G. Duquette, 137–55. Clevedon, U.K.: Multilingual Matters, Ltd.

Zabalza, M. A. 1992a. Implicaciones curriculares de la educación intercultural. In *Educación Intercultural en la Perspectiva de la Europa Unida*, X Congreso Nacional de Pedagogía, 329–51. Salamanca: GRUPOANAYA.

———. 1992b. El trabajo escolar en un contexto multicultural. Congreso de Educación Multicultural, Ceuta.

6

Linking Sociocultural Contexts to Classroom Practices: Language Identity in a Bilingual Hungarian–Slovak School in Slovakia

Bridget Fitzgerald Gersten and Christian Faltis

Wherever your language and your nationhood are disregarded, you are oppressed, no matter how liberal the country may be. [W]here your language is excluded from schools and offices, freedom is taken away from you, from your nation, more than by police or by censorship.
    —Karel Havlicek Borovsky (1821–56) (quoted in Fishman 1997, vii)

Many educational researchers and scholars agree on the need to examine classroom practices in their broader social contexts and macrocontexts. Such examination is particularly important for understanding the particulars of classroom practice in settings populated by immigrant and language minority children (Edelsky 1996; Faltis and Hudelson 1994, 1997; Genesee 1994; Merino, Trueba, and Samaniego 1993; Moll 1992; Pease-Alvarez and Vasquez 1994; Trueba 1993; Trueba and Wright 1981; Vygotsky 1978; Wiley 1996; Zou and Trueba 1998). Issues of bilingualism, language rights, and bilingual education are inextricably linked to the broader sociopolitical and historical contexts (Cummins 1989; Fishman 1967, 1989; Hamel 1997; Macias 1979; Paulston 1997; Phillipson 1990; Skutnabb-Kangas and Phillipson 1997). Studies of bilingual education often overlook the relationships among the macrocontext, classroom activity, and student performance.

On a transnational scale, the contexts of bilingual education are multiple: each bilingual school has a unique set of social, political, and historical circumstances. There are many models and types of bilingual education throughout the world (Baetens Beardsmore 1993; Baker 1996; Baker and Jones 1998; Herriman and

Burnaby 1996). In the United States, the trend is still toward transitional bilingual education, but there are new efforts to introduce and support dual language
programs in which both majority and minority students learn content area subjects in two languages (Christian 1996, 1997).

What are the macrocontextual elements of bilingual schooling? How do they
influence classroom practices, student participation, learning, and biliteracy? The
social context of bilingual schooling involves a complex interplay of attitudes,
beliefs, expectations, and practices of administrators, teachers, parents, and students (Pease-Alvarez and Hakuta 1993). This broader context also encompasses
social, political, and historical contexts that affect language planning, curricular
decisions, and instructional practices (e.g., language allocation or distribution).
An analysis of the macrocontext of bilingual schooling in any setting provides
insights about bilingualism and effective practices for language minority students.
There is a need for classroom-based research that situates first language (L1)
instruction and dual or second language (L2) learning in their macrocontext.
Such contextually based research can help us to uncover and analyze the sociocultural dynamics at play in the development of bilingualism, biliteracy, and
transnational identity among language minority students.

THE MAGYAR MINORITY AND
HUNGARIAN-MEDIUM SCHOOLS IN SLOVAKIA

There are an estimated 15 million Hungarians scattered throughout the world—
a number that is comparable to the population of Australia (Kocsis and Kocsis-
Hodosi 1995). In a European context, Hungarians, or Magyars, are the second-
largest dispersed ethnic group, after Russians; 90 percent of the Magyar
population lives in the Carpathian basin, "on the historical territory of Hungary"
(Kocsis and Kocsis-Hodosi 1995). In Slovakia, Hungarians are the largest language minority—an estimated 11 percent of the total population (Williams
1996). The approximately 600,000 members of this ethnic community vary in
their degree of bilingualism or multilingualism. These demographic realities are
significant: they make Hungarians members of a large diaspora in both Europe and
beyond. This dispersal was the result of numerous sociohistorical events that
caused shifts in political power and territory (i.e., the waxing and waning of various Hungarian monarchies and the Austro-Hungarian Empire, from the year
1000 to 1938). Whether forced or voluntary, this dispersion of Hungarians has
made demands on its members to sustain their language, culture, and identity to
promote conditions for ethnolinguistic survival.

The extended Magyar community in Slovakia is composed of compact and
dense social networks that are geographically distributed in fifteen administrative
regions, located 600 miles along the Danube basin and the present border with
Hungary (Lanstyak and Szabomilhaly 1995). In these mostly rural villages, towns,

small cities, and regional provinces, Magyars constitute an absolute majority or a dominant ethnic group. Hungarian is the primary or first language of local speech communities, though inhabitants exhibit varying degrees of bilingualism in Slovak. Traditionally, there have been official provisions for L1 use at the workplace and at school. Most recently, however, the Slovak government has taken measures to restrict the use of Hungarian at school. The government has done so despite exasperated protests for minority rights from Magyar communities in Slovakia and abroad and austere warnings from international human rights groups (Brunner 1996; Fric et al. 1996; Giarelli 1996; Reisch 1993; Rhodes 1995; Soucova 1994; Spolar 1996; Williams 1996). These tensions reflect challenges met by language minorities in postcommunist Europe.

Hungarian-medium schools in Slovakia occupy an interesting place in the world of bilingual education and language maintenance programs. Their story is a typical one of majority/minority status reversal, not uncommon to other European contexts with shifting borders (Baetens-Beardsmore 1993; Baker 1996; Wright 1995). While Hungarian was the dominant, majority language for nearly 1,000 years, Slovak replaced it as the majority language following political developments after World War I. In this dying breed of schools, Hungarian is the dominant medium of instruction for most content areas, with the exception of the majority language (i.e., Slovak).

In the schools that have survived, the first language (L1), Hungarian, is maintained and developed throughout grades K–12 as the medium of instruction for the majority of content areas in the curriculum, with the exception of the Slovak language (L2). Slovak is taught five hours per week, with an emphasis on performance, play, and oral language development in grades one and two and a focus on literacy, grammar, and language arts from grade three in the elementary school.

One central purpose of Hungarian-medium schools is to preserve linguistic and sociocultural identity at an individual and societal level. Historically, as the Magyar majority status was transformed into a minority position, many Hungarians assimilated into the Slovak mainstream, with a concomitant loss of language, culture, and identity. The Hungarian-medium schools that survive today are oases unto themselves: they are places where language, culture, and identity are celebrated in the school, the classroom, and the arts.

In addition to adhering to the curriculum established for Slovak-medium schools by the Ministry of Education, these schools provide content-based instruction to include Hungarian language, history, and literature. Though Hungarian has historically been the language of home and, at various periods in history, education in numerous schools across present-day Slovakia, the number of schools has decreased drastically from World War I to the present. Some of these schools share building space with mainstream monolingual schools in which Slovak is the sole medium of instruction, except for foreign languages (i.e., English, German, and Russian). In these mainstream Slovak schools, Hungarian is rarely offered as a second or foreign language, and no special provisions are made for language minority children whose mother tongue is Hungarian (i.e., as there is with English as a Second Language programs in the United States). Furthermore, the nationalized curriculum has traditionally limited any particular focus on Hungarian history, literature, or geography.

In most cases, attendance at L1-medium schools is voluntary. In this case, Hungarian-medium schools exist alongside mainstream Slovak schools. In other cases, however, children must attend the closest school to home, even when instruction is available in the nonnative language (e.g., a Slovak child may attend a Hungarian-medium school because there is no Slovak-medium school in the area). Of the total number of public schools and student enrollment in Slovakia, Hungarian-medium schools constitute approximately 10 percent of all public K–12 instruction in Slovakia (Gyurcsik and Satterwhite 1996). A recent statistical survey of Hungarian schools and students in Slovak public schools reported the following data on number of Hungarian-medium schools: kindergarten, 297; grades one through nine, 268; secondary schools, forty-two, that is, eleven grammar schools and thirty-one vocational schools (see Government of the Slovak Republic 1991).

These Hungarian-medium schools differ from other models of bilingual, immersion, dual language, and language maintenance education in various ways. First, all members of the school belong to the Hungarian ethnic minority; consequently, there is no mix of language majority and language minority children. Second, all teachers are Hungarian–Slovak bilingual or multilingual (e.g., German, English, Russian, Ukrainian). Third, there are no curricular provisions or assessment instruments for exiting the L1 program into a majority L2 program. In other words, unless children leave the school, they will continue to learn the majority of content area subjects in Hungarian throughout elementary and/or secondary school (though majority-sponsored legislation has recently been introduced to limit L1 use in content area instruction). Fourth, language allocation (i.e., distributing the use of L1 and L2 across subjects or the school day or week) is not a curricular issue (see Jacobson and Faltis 1990 for a discussion of these issues in U.S. contexts).

In Slovakia, Hungarian-medium schools continue to exist in a state of transition, as enrollment drops and schools close. Moreover, since 1994, the use of L1 across the curriculum has faced threats of being phased out by changes in administrative, educational, and linguistic legislation (Evans 1995a, 1995b; Farkas 1996; Kontra 1995, 1996). In fact, since the Treaty of Trianon in 1920, these schools have continually diminished in number, being replaced by Slovak-medium schools that lack any provisions for bilingual or language minority education. Though language minorities were guaranteed certain rights including L1 education in the constitution of the communist Czechoslovak state in 1968, the situation has deteriorated since the fall of communism in 1989 and the establishment of independent Slovakia in 1993 (Williams 1996).

Some recent political events continue to upset Hungarian language minority rights for L1 use at the workplace and at school. In 1995, a controversial language law was drafted to establish Slovak as the official language of the Slovak Republic. This law placed restrictions on the use of minority languages for official purposes (i.e., at work and at school). Similarly, legislation was drafted that revised the administrative boundaries of the Slovak Republic, eliminating the existence of areas in which ethnic minorities constitute an absolute majority (e.g., Hungarians no longer constituted a majority group on paper once regional borders were redrawn). In 1998, the Slovak parliament proposed additional legislation to restrict further the use of minority languages at school, proposing that Slovak replace Hungarian as the medium of instruction in various content areas, in the interest of improving Slovak language instruction. As educators, parents, and students openly protested the call to use only Slovak on report cards, two principals were immediately dismissed from their functions, despite protests and strikes in ethnic Hungarian communities. Such changes in the sociohistorical fabric have circumstances throughout Slovakia for the ethnolinguistic vitality and attitudes of language minority communities.

THE STUDY

This essay examines details of how the sociocultural context of a bilingual community—and L1 maintenance—influenced classroom practices in a bilingual school in Slovakia, especially in literacy in L1 (Hungarian) and L2 (Slovak) learning. Data for this study come from an eight-month qualitative study that examined the development of L2 writing in one group of Hungarian-dominant children as they attended second and third grade together (Gersten 1997). A multiple case study method was used to investigate the roles of social interaction, L1 use, L1 literacy, L2 proficiency, and social identity in L2 writing development. One teacher was observed over the course of eight months with the same group of students ($N = 27$), in second and third grade (i.e., the teacher taught the same students in both grades). Data collection included detailed field notes of classroom observations; audiotaped recordings; open-ended interviews with students, teachers, and family members; and artifacts; namely, student L1 and L2 writing samples over time and official language policy documents related to linguistic minority education. Though the study focuses on one classroom in a Hungarian-medium school, findings suggest patterns of interest to other bilingual classrooms in Slovakia and elsewhere.

LINKING POLICY AND CLASSROOM PRACTICE

To understand classroom practices and the social worlds of these bilingual learners in Slovakia, it is important to situate their education in sociohistorical and geopolitical contexts. For ethnic Hungarians in Slovakia, L1-medium schooling is the principal means for sustaining cultural heritage, social identity, and language maintenance: any threat to the Hungarian language is considered a threat to Hungarian identity. In this essay, we explore three major areas in which the broader sociocultural contexts influenced classroom practices. These areas include the function and role of culturally bound content area instruction; the connection between L1 literacy and L2 use; and links among writers, text, and the community.

Classroom practices can be linked to the broader sociocultural contexts of Hungarian-medium schooling and expectations shared by parents, teachers, and administrators. The present study shows how various messages about Magyar identity and socialization showed up in classroom practices at school. These practices contained notions about the value of and relationships between L1 literacy, L1 literary traditions, bilingualism, and Magyar identity.

The knowledge base of Hungarian schooling comprises notions about Hungarian sociohistorical heritage, the value of the native tongue and Hungarian literature, the importance of L1 literacy, and the link among language, social interaction, aesthetic appreciation, and artistic expression or performance. These funds of knowledge (Moll 1992) are integral parts of the macro-, transnational context of schooling, which esteems language maintenance, bilingualism, and the social identity of individual and collective members of the Hungarian community. Such historically bound links among culture, language, and identity are important because they emerge in classroom practices in L1 and L2 instruction.

L1 LITERACY, SOCIOCULTURAL HERITAGE, AUTHENTIC LITERATURE, AND MAGYAR IDENTITY

In this section, we present some key notions about the connections among literacy, cultural heritage, authentic literature, and Magyar identity. Members of the Magyar community viewed Hungarian-medium schools as important institutions for language maintenance and literacy development because they provide legitimate space for the native language—and culture—in education. In situations of transnational language contact, the maintenance and protection of the minority language occurs when its value as an expressive means of communication, in speech and in writing, is emphasized in school. One undisputed tenet of the school, the home, and other community institutions is that L1 *identity* is embedded in L1 literacy: using L1 to establish connections with broader sociocultural traditions, events, and social practices.

For the Hungarian students in this study, L1 use and L1 literacy were essential elements of education. Furthermore, bilingualism was taken for granted: children and parents assumed and expected second language acquisition to occur naturally over time because of language contact and formal L2 instruction. Through L1 literacy, children gained access to the cultural heritage and authentic literature that are at the heart of Magyar identity. Drawing from and building on these L1 foundations, children continued the journey of bilingualism and identity as they used L2 for a variety of functions in interaction with peers and their teacher. Within the L1 community, children were socialized into the *strengths*, not deficits, of belonging to the language minority group. These strengths were considered to be the native language itself and the culture and literature of the Magyar community. The children were never considered at risk of failing because they learned through their language and culture.

L1 Literacy

In this Hungarian-medium school, expectations about L1 literacy were a powerful element of the overarching sociocultural context that influenced L2 classroom instruction and learning. The expectation that all children should—and would—learn to read and write, first in Hungarian and then in Slovak, was shared by school, family, and the broader ethnic Hungarian community. Another shared belief was that L1 loss and lack of L1 literacy would weaken ethnolinguistic identity and, potentially, lead to assimilation. One function of this school was, thus, to invite students to participate in their cultural heritage and identity as Magyars *through* the Hungarian language. Because of this, the foundations of literacy were in L1, Hungarian. Once these foundations were in place, formal study of L2 literacy began in third grade, building on the L1 foundations of reading, writing, performance, and structural and textual analysis that constituted the bulwark of L1 literacy.

In what ways did these sociocultural notions influence the curriculum and classroom practices? As the foundations of L1 literacy were established and fortified, the children gained access to an extensive body of authentic L1 literature that is rich in connotation, nuance, and poetic expression. L1 literacy was valued as the key to a significant, sociohistorically relevant knowledge base represented by Hungarian literature. From first grade, the children in this study participated in a rich body of authentic literature, as listeners, readers, and performers. The teacher guided students in experiencing the poetics, beauty, and joy of oral expression; she sought to enhance their understanding of the inherent literary qualities of text.

Because literature was valued in the school and community as an aesthetic and intellectual form of expression, the children were given messages about how their native tongue is an expressive vehicle of thought and emotion. As children became literate in Hungarian, they concomitantly experienced the language of both their ancestors and their community. Because Hungarian is a linguistically complex language, educators and parents believed that children directly benefited from—and potentially contributed to—the rich body of literature only when they accessed that literature through Hungarian.

Another sociocultural expectation was that children would have the foundations for reading in place by first grade, to prepare them for a variety of genre-rich literature of the elementary school language arts curriculum. During first grade, emphasis was placed on a combination of decoding skills and authentic literature.

This included pattern identification, letter recognition, and learning to *read* printed text and *write* in cursive only. Additionally, children practiced decoding and reciting text, orthography, rhythmic patterns, and textual analysis (i.e., form and meaning). The curriculum included authentic literature in the form of poems, riddles, and word play, with emphasis on rhythm and imagery. The teacher made explicit the connections between spoken and written text through group and individual recitation and performance.

In second grade, the children continued to read narrative and expository texts, both prose and poetry, and to perform short texts in class. This performance involved memorization and recitation of poems and songs. When the children in this study began to compose their own texts, they applied knowledge about literary conventions that were familiar to them from literature they had heard and read. Just as they illustrated texts they had heard and read in class, they continued to draw and color their own stories. They also spontaneously performed their texts for peer approval—before, during, and after their completion. In joining the ranks of young authors, they discovered the rewards of joining the literacy club (Smith 1988).

Socioculturally Relevant Content in the Curriculum

In this study, children used L1 literacy to learn about the shared, collective history of Hungarian empires and dynasties gone by, when Hungarians were a majority—not minority—group for almost 1,000 years (i.e., from the year 1001 to 1920). Accordingly, literacy served as a conduit to shared sociocultural traditions. This historical profile includes emperors, kings, queens, monarchies, feudalism, Mongol and Turkish invasions, saints, courts, intrigues, internecine struggles, uprisings, battles, wars, conquests, and resistance. The story of the Magyar nation recounts numerous encounters between eastern and western European cultures; it is also the story of Magyar survival. The expectation that children would become active participants in a dialogue about socioculturally relevant content was shared and supported by teachers, parents, and administrators at this school. The Hungarian collective memory includes a plethora of historical events throughout the ages that have affected the ethnolinguistic vitality and survival of the group itself. These events include shifts in geopolitical borders, forced assimilation, language loss, majority–minority conflicts, and the struggle to maintain institutions that support Hungarian language and identity. This Hungarian perspective on history is one that is not foregrounded in Slovak schools but, rather, retold and reinterpreted through the lenses of majority political perspectives (i.e., the Slovak version of historical events). L1 literacy was a means for children to explore and identify these sociocultural roots through their own perspectives.

Authentic L1 Literature

Authentic L1 literature was an integral component of both the shared sociocultural heritage and the language arts curriculum in this school. The children shared, read, performed, and responded to a variety of authentic literature in the native tongue, including various genres and text types. This included a variety of Hungarian children's literature and other renowned classics rich in imagery, poetic quality, and prosody. These texts constitute an important part of the shared socio-cultural heritage; the writers and poets belong to a rich legacy of Hungarian authors that has evolved throughout the ages. The children also used literature from other western and eastern traditions, in translation (i.e., Aesop's fables, proverbs, multi-cultural folklore). The Hungarian stories, fables, legends, ballads, poems, songs, and essays were not only artistically sophisticated and rich in connotation and allu-sion; they told tales of a shared sociocultural tradition—and samplings of global lit-erature. These authentic texts formed the basis of the L1 language arts curriculum, as children analyzed, discussed, and gave personal interpretations to the intellec-tual, emotional, artistic, and expressive value of literature. As the children explored these texts as listeners and readers, they gained important insights about writing that they applied to their own L1 and L2 composing.

These classroom practices supported notions of the connections between L1 literacy, sociocultural traditions, and Magyar identity in various ways. The chil-dren used authentic literature for multiple purposes: to learn about language, to learn about text, and to gain access to a rich knowledge base about Hungarian his-tory, traditions, accomplishments, and the artistic qualities of the Hungarian lan-guage. Through L1, the children gained access to a shared body of knowledge at the heart of Hungarian identity. In the eyes of parents, the teacher, and other members of the school administration at this school, L1 literacy—and knowledge of Magyar history and literature—was the distinguishing feature of Hungarian identity. Furthermore, L1 literacy paved the way for biliteracy development as the children tackled the written word in L2.

CONNECTING L1 LANGUAGE AND LITERACY TO BILINGUALISM AND L2 CLASSROOM PRACTICES

The principles of L1 literacy, socioculturally relevant content, and authentic liter-ature were not separated from beliefs about L2 literacy development and bilin-gualism; on the contrary, they influenced L2 instruction and learning in various ways. In the broader domain of this school, administrators, teachers, and parents shared the expectation that children would become bilingual and biliterate because L1 and L2 literacy and language use belong to separate and stable diglos-sic domains. They viewed literacy in two languages as a natural and purposeful part of a bilingual's life in Slovakia. Furthermore, these adults shared a belief that bilit-eracy was more likely to occur if L1 were maintained and developed before and after children began to read and write in L2. These beliefs were grounded in shared sociocultural experience, namely, the fact that these adults—and members of their extended families—had undertaken the journey to bilingualism and biliteracy

themselves. This shared belief echoes research findings about how students can
apply to L2 settings what they know about literacy, especially when their language
and academic development are highly developed in L1 (Baker 1996; Bialystock
and Hakuta 1994; Cummins 1989; Skutnabb-Kangas and Cummins 1988).
Because the L1 language arts curriculum focused on authentic literature and
not basal readers, the children had definite notions about structure, content, and
features of various literary genres (e.g., story grammar) when composing their own
texts. Furthermore, the children were frequently invited to give personal interpretations of stories they heard and read in class and at home (e.g., they provided
illustrations for texts they read or composed). This sense of story and an aesthetic,
multiple-media response to text appeared as essential elements in the children's
own writing as they composed *L2* stories, riddles, dialogue journal entries, and
poems (see Gersten 1997 for a further discussion of L2 composing by Hungarian-
dominant children).

L2 Literacy

These beliefs about the relationship between L1 and L2 literacy influenced
classroom practices in this study, especially in L2 composing. First, children came
to the task of L2 composing with very storied lives and a keen sense of the
rhythm, flow, and structure of their native language. This was because of their
exposure to and familiarity with a broad range of text types in L1. Second, the
children had strong notions about the purpose, stylistics, content, and organization of text; as readers, performers, and audience alike, they knew how to structure and craft their own inventive stories. Third, while students in this study
eagerly sought feedback and help from teacher and peers, rarely did any child
resist the opportunity to write or to read what peers wrote. These attitudes
toward and experience with oral and written text in L1 allowed the children to
try their hands at the L2 writers' club with enthusiasm (i.e., create their own stories). Because the children frequently used and *enjoyed* literature in L1 and L2 at
school and at home, they were eager to compose in both L1 and L2. This may be
explained by the children's appreciation of text and the messages about the value
of literacy and literature in the broader sociocultural contexts of school, home,
and community.

Additionally, when children began to compose in L2 in second grade, they
drew on their understanding of how texts work—in reading and in writing—from
literacy in their native language. In this study, children drew on their understanding of spoken and written L1 text to probe peers and teacher about ortho-
graphic, phonemic, syntactic, semantic, and pragmatic features of L2 text.
Because the appropriate language of social interaction at school was L1, the children used Hungarian in the L2 classroom as a means of support in becoming proficient in L2. The children continued to make connections as readers and writers
as they read and wrote longer and more sophisticated texts in third grade.

Authentic L2 Literature

Beliefs about the relationship between authentic literature and literacy development in L1 also supported classroom practices in the L2 classroom. As was the case with L1 literacy instruction, authentic literature in L2 was a key component in L2 instruction for these children during both second and third grade. Similar to the L1 language arts curriculum, L2 instruction emphasized authentic texts that were rich in symbolism, imagery, rhythmic patterns, and word play. In this way, the children further developed language and literacy by reading authentic literature in Slovak. These authentic texts were a combination of classics of Slovak children's literature and renowned authors. Just as the children's L1 literacy education was grounded in the sociocultural roots of the Magyar tradition, their L2 literacy instruction provided opportunities for the children to expand their understanding of stylistics, audience, text organization, and cultural themes through authentic literature (not basal readers). In exploring L2 language and literature, the children participated in a culturally situated knowledge base that was integral to their identity as bilinguals (i.e., they read the authors familiar to monolingual Slovak peers and adults). This bicultural and bilingual experience influenced the types of texts students composed in L1 and L2, as they experimented with their own creations.

LINKING WRITER, TEXT, AND COMMUNITY THROUGH LANGUAGE, LITERACY, AND PERFORMANCE

Findings from this study suggest how bilingual educators view interrelationships among literacy, authentic literature, socioculturally relevant content area instruction, and social identity. These beliefs provide the groundwork for classroom practices in both L1 and L2 instruction. To gain further insight into the relationship between sociocultural contexts and language development, it is important to understand the role of aesthetics, performance, and social interaction in L1 and L2 composing. Language—both L1 and L2—was valued at school for its expressive, analytical, and communicative functions.

A key underlying premise of L1 and L2 use was that language is beautiful: children were expected to view language use as the window to and mirror of one's identity, both as individuals and as members of a collective speech community. Because literacy was viewed as a public, social event that involves the participation and critique of others, reading and writing provided multiple opportunities for social interaction and personal expression. This conceptualization of language as art form reverberated throughout classroom practice: literacy events were occasions for performance of text (i.e., reciting aloud, using nonverbal gestures), sharing with an audience, and garnering respect from peers. The perceived social nature of literacy was a driving force in motivating students to memorize, recite, write, illustrate, perform, and evaluate text in the classroom. As children transformed spoken text into written text in their own L1 and L2 compositions—and written text into spoken performance—they forged connections between a familiar oral tradition and reading and writing.

One related sociocultural goal of L1 education was to instill children with a sense of the beauty and emotional and intellectual power of their native tongue. This was accomplished in the classroom by making explicit beliefs about the beauty, complexity, richness, and expressiveness of the Hungarian language during L1 language arts instruction. To this end, emphasis was placed on inviting children to enjoy literature, to reflect on it, and to extend their love of L1 literacy, verbal arts, and oral expression outside school (i.e., reading books at home; participating in theater, music, and oratory competitions in the L1 community). As the children read, interpreted, performed, and composed texts at school, attention was placed on textual and linguistic features of rhythm, prosody, voice, and tone, as well as the relationship between text and nonverbal communication, audience, and dramatic or artistic representation. This recognition of the beauty of language contributes to the vision of language as having spiritual, moral, emotional, and cognitive functions for the individual and community (Fishman 1997).

This view of the beauty of language and its value as an art form influenced classroom practices in both L1 and L2 instruction. The rationale behind using genre-rich, authentic literature in L1 and L2 literacy development was to engage students in the aesthetic features, poetics, play, and rhythmical beauty of language. The children's textbooks were full of stories, poems, riddles, and narrative and expository text that stimulated both intellect and fantasy. In keeping with the traditional education paradigm, the children memorized and recited many of these texts—especially poems and riddles—for regular scrutiny by peers and the teacher. This practice of memorization and recital was valued in the home, the school, and the community. Oratory and performance skills were key components of competitions, contests, and recitals performed before audiences at school and at local, regional, and countrywide levels. Children spontaneously used these models as they both composed their own stories and read and evaluated texts composed by their peers.

Considerations of text as forms of art and performance were also important contextual elements related to the education of bilingual children in this study. The children were invited to draw illustrations to accompany texts they read or composed in class or at home. As children composed L1 and L2 texts, they drew on their knowledge of cultural expectations about what constitutes a good text (i.e., content, stylistic devices, organization). When the children were given the time and space to compose their own texts, they incorporated symbolism from various media. For example, they combined drawing, talk with peers, and play. They evaluated their own and peers' texts in terms of how closely they approximated conventional norms about the genre they were using (i.e., poems, fables, stories, diary entries).

There was also an aesthetic dimension to composition, as children expressed a need to write neatly, in cursive, and to draw illustrations that were faithful to the real world, conforming to stereotypical representations (i.e., what a princess should look like), or reflective of private or shared worlds of imagination. This attentiveness to the presentation, display, performance value, and aesthetic quality of text was rooted in broader sociocultural expectations. These expectations included taking pride in one's work, establishing a relationship between writer or artist and reader, and text as a representation of self and social identification with a community of speakers.

CONCLUSION

A consideration of the multiple messages of Hungarian-medium schools in Slovakia suggests the power of community, schooling, and language use in questions of identity and language/culture maintenance. In these schools, to be Hungarian means having the desire, means, and potential to tap into the shared sociohistorical traditions of a former empire. L1 proficiency and authentic literacy provide children with keys to a shared transnational identity that they, too, will have the power to pass on to future generations. The message schools send to language minority children is not one of failure, risk, and loss; it is a message of success, survival, and advantage. Group membership is not seen as unworthy but, rather, desirable and comforting. Furthermore, the messages of home, school, and community are in sync; it is the majority group that stands on the outside, sending messages of assimilation and failure to achieve (i.e., to learn Slovak). In contrast to the "at-risk" classification of language minority students of low socioeconomic status in the United States, parents, educators, and students do not adopt a "deficit" model perspective so prevalent in many transnational educational contexts.

REFERENCES

Baetens-Beardsmore, H. 1993. The European School Model. In *European Models of Bilingual Education*, ed. H. Baetens-Beardsmore, 121–54. Clevedon, U.K.: Multilingual Matters.

Baker, C. 1996. *Foundations of Bilingual Education and Bilingualism*. 2nd edition. Clevedon, U.K.: Multilingual Matters.

Baker, C., and S. P. Jones, eds. 1998. *Encyclopedia of Bilingualism and Bilingual Education*. Clevedon, U.K.: Multilingual Matters.

Bialystock, E., and K. Hakuta. 1994. *In Other Words: The Science and Psychology of Second Language Acquisition*. New York: Basic Books.

Brunner, G. 1996. Die Lage der Ungarn in der Slowakei (The situation of Hungarians in Slovakia). *Europaeische Rundschau* 24, no. 1: 47–58.

Central Europe Online. 1998a. *Ethnic Hungarian Pupils Return Slovak-Only Reports*. <www.centraleurope.com>, 1 July.

———. 1998b. *Hungarian Schooling Rights Stay in Slovakia.* <www.centraleurope.com>, 3 July.

Christian, D. 1996. Two-Way Immersion Education: Students Learning through Two Languages. *Modern Language Journal* 80, no. 1: 66–76.

———. 1997. *Profiles in Two-Way Immersion Education.* Language in Education: Theory and Practice Series, 89. Washington, D.C.: Center for Applied Linguistics.

Cummins, J. 1989. Language and Literacy Acquisition in Bilingual Contexts. *Journal of Multilingual and Multicultural Development* 10, no. 1: 17–32.

Edelsky, C. 1996. *With Literacy and Justice for All: Rethinking the Social in Language and Education.* 2nd edition. London: The Falmer Press.

Evans, S. 1995a. Europe Wages a War of Words. *Christian Science Monitor,* 29 September: 7, col. 1.

———. 1995b. Two Tongues Spoil Tale of Cultural Mix. *Times Educational Supplement,* 6 October: 18(1), n. 4136.

Faltis, C. J., and S. Hudelson. 1994. Learning English as an Additional Language in K–12 Schools. *TESOL Quarterly* 28: 457–68.

———. 1997. *Bilingual Education in Elementary and Secondary School Communities: Toward Understanding and Caring.* Boston: Allyn and Bacon.

Farkas, E. N. 1996. Circumventing the State: Securing Cultural and Educational Rights for Hungarian Minorities. *Journal of Public and International Affairs* 7: 52–78.

Fenyi, T. 1990. Hungarians in Slovakia. *The New Hungarian Quarterly* 31, no. 119: 88–94.

Fishman, J. A. 1967. Bilingualism with and without Diglossia: Diglossia with and without Bilingualism. *Journal of Social Issues* 23, no. 2: 29–38.

———. 1989. *Language and Ethnicity in Minority Sociolinguistic Perspective.* Clevedon, U.K.: Multilingual Matters.

———. 1997. *In Praise of the Beloved Language: A Comparative View of Positive Ethnolinguistic Consciousness.* Berlin: Mouton de Gruyter.

Fric, P., F. Gal, P. Huncik, and C. Lord. 1996. *Madarska mensina na Slovensku* (The Hungarian minority in Slovakia). Bratislava: Archa.

Gabzdilova, S. 1992. Schools in the Slovak Republic with Instruction in the Hungarian Language—Present Status. In *Minorities in Politics: Cultural and Language Rights,* ed. J. Plichtova. Bratislava: Czechoslovak Committee of the European Cultural Foundation.

Genesee, F., ed. 1994. *Educating Second Language Children: The Whole Child, the Whole Curriculum, the Whole Community.* Cambridge: Cambridge University Press.

Gersten, B. F. 1997. *Writing in a Second Language: A Study of Four Bilingual Hungarian/Slovak Learners during Second and Third Grade.* Ph.D. dissertation, Arizona State University at Tempe.

Giarelli, A. 1996. Slovakia: Linguistic Bias. *World Press Review* 43, no. 2: 30.

Government of the Slovak Republic. 1991. *Uznesenie vlady Slovenskej republiky z 26 januara 21, 1991 cislo 49, k sprave o stave slovenskeho skolstva v narodnostne zmiesanych oblastiach a o rozvoji a priprave ucitelov,* 47/1991 (Government resolution of the Slovak Republic from January 26, 1991, number 49, as to the administration and condition of the Slovak educational system in ethnically mixed regions and the development and preparation of teachers). Bratislava: Government of the Slovak Republic.

Gyurcsik, I., and J. Satterwhite. 1996. The Hungarians in Slovakia. *Nationalities Papers* 24, no. 3: 509–24.

Hamel, R. E. 1997. Introduction: Linguistic Human Rights in a Sociolinguistic Perspective. *International Journal of the Sociology of Language* 127: 1–24.

Herriman, M., and B. Burnaby, eds. 1996. *Language Policies in English-Dominant Countries: Six Case Studies*. Clevedon, U.K.: Multilingual Matters.

Jacobson, R., and C. Faltis. 1990. *Language Distribution Issues in Bilingual Schooling*. Clevedon, U.K.: Multilingual Matters.

Kocsis, K., and E. Kocsis-Hodosi. 1995. Hungarian Minorities in the Carpathians: A Study of Ethnic Geography. Toronto: Matthias Corvinus Publishing.

Kontra, M. 1995. English Only's Cousin: Slovak Only. *Acta Linguistica Hungarica: An International Journal of Linguistics* 43, nos. 3–4: 345–72.

———. 1996. The Wars Over Names in Slovakia. *Language Problems and Language Planning* 20, no. 2: 160–67.

Lanstyak, I., and G. Szabomilhaly. 1995. Contact Varieties of Hungarians in Slovakia: A Contribution to Their Description. *International Journal of the Sociology of Language* 112: 111–30.

Ludanyi, A. 1996. Preface: The Historical Geography of the Hungarian Nation. *Nationalities Papers* 24, no. 3: 371–76.

Macias, R. F. 1979. Language Choice and Human Rights in the U.S. In *Georgetown University Round Table on Languages and Linguistics*, ed. J. E. Alatis, 86–101. Washington, D.C.: Georgetown University Press.

Merino, B. J., H. T. Trueba, and F. A. Samaniego. 1993. Towards a Framework for the Study of the Maintenance of the Home Language in Language Minority Students. In *Language and Culture in Learning: Teaching Spanish to Native Speakers of Spanish*, ed. B. J. Merino, H. T. Trueba, and F. A. Samaniego, 5–25. Washington, D.C.: The Falmer Press.

Moll, L. C. 1992. Bilingual Classroom Studies and Community Analysis: Some Recent Trends. *Educational Researcher* 21: 20–24.

Paulston, C. B. 1997. Epilogue: Some Concluding Thoughts on Linguistic Human Rights. *International Journal of the Sociology of Language* 127: 187–95.

Pease-Alvarez, L., and K. Hakuta. 1993. Enriching Our Views of Bilingualism and Bilingual Education. *Educational Researcher* 21, no. 2: 4–14.

Pease-Alvarez, L., and O. Vasquez. 1994. Language Socialization in Ethnic Minority Communities. In *Educating Second Language Children: The Whole Child, the Whole Curriculum, the Whole Community*, ed. F. Genesee, 78–102. Cambridge: Cambridge University Press.

Phillipson, R. 1990. *Linguistic Imperialism*. Oxford: Oxford University Press.

Phillipson, R., and T. Skutnabb-Kangas. 1995. Linguistic Rights and Wrongs. *Applied Linguistics* 16, no. 4: 483–504.

Reisch, A. A. 1993. Slovakia's Minority Policy under International Scrutiny. *RFE/RL Research Report* 2, no. 49 (10 December): 35–42.

Rhodes, M. 1995. National Identity and Minority Rights in the Constitutions of the Czech Republic and Slovakia. *East European Quarterly* 29, no. 3: 347–69.

Skutnabb-Kangas, T., and J. Cummins, eds. 1988. *Minority Education: From Shame to Struggle*. Clevedon, U.K.: Multilingual Matters.

Skutnabb-Kangas, T., and R. Phillipson, eds. 1997. *Linguistic Human Rights: Overcoming Linguistic Discrimination*. Berlin: Mouton de Gruyter.

Smith, F. 1988. *Joining the Literacy Club*. Portsmouth, N.H.: Heinemann.

Soucova, D. 1994. Problems of Slovaks and Magyars Living in Mixed Regions of Southern Slovakia in Opinion Polls (Nazory na problemy Slovakov a Madarov zijucich v narodnostne zmiesanych oblastiach juzneho Slovenska vo vyskume verejnej mienky). *Sociologia* 26, nos. 5–6: 496–500.

Spolar, C. 1996. Slovak Leader Fans Bias toward Hungarian Minority. *Washington Post*, 20 November: A23, col. 2.

Trueba, H. T. 1993. Culture and Language: The Ethnographic Approach to the Study of Learning Environments. In *Language and Culture in Learning: Teaching Spanish to Native Speakers of Spanish*, ed. B. J. Merino, H. T. Trueba, and F. A. Samaniego, 26–44. Washington, D.C.: Falmer Press.

Trueba, H. T., and P. G. Wright. 1981. A Challenge for Ethnographic Researchers in Bilingual Education in Bilingual Settings: Analyzing Spanish/English Classroom Interaction. *Journal of Multilingual and Multicultural Development* 18: 243–57.

Vygotsky, L. S. 1978. *Mind in Society: The Development of Higher Psychological Processes*. Ed. and trans. M. Cole, V. John-Steiner, S. Scribner, and E. Souberman. Cambridge, Mass.: Harvard University Press.

Wiley, T. G. 1996. *Literacy and Language Diversity in the United States*. Washington, D.C.: Center for Applied Linguistics and Delta Systems.

Williams, K. 1996. The Magyar Minority in Slovakia. *Regional and Federal Studies* 6, no. 1: 1–20.

Wright, S. 1995. Language Planning and Policy-Making in Europe. *Language Teaching* 28: 148–59.

Zou, Y., and E. T. Trueba. 1998. *Ethnic Identity and Power: Cultural Contexts of Political Action in School and Society*. Albany: State University of New York Press.

7

Wanting to Go On: Healing and Transformation at an Urban Public University

Peter Nien-chu Kiang

This story is not linear or easy to follow. But it is real.
Narratives. Flashbacks. Research Agendas.
This story is very personal. But it is not just my own.
Voices. Pedagogies. Tears.
This story is not yet finished. But please, go on.

MAKING OFFERINGS

"I want to go on."

Her words broke a long silence from the front of the room. A few moments earlier, she had faltered in her project presentation about the experiences of Vietnamese Amerasians and had begun to cry quietly.

Usually, Trang sat in the back with one or two other Vietnamese friends, trying to remain safe and unobtrusive. Had the pressure of speaking her second language in front of everyone in class overwhelmed her? Perhaps she was reliving the memories of her own life in Vietnam. Maybe she recalled how hard it was to arrive here five years ago in the land of her father, still not knowing who or where he was.

"Are you sure?"

"Yes, I want to go on."

She completed her presentation, filled with emotion in accented English, teaching the class about struggle and survival.

On the last day of the semester, I reminded the class of the context and meaning of those words, *"I want to go on."* There are strengths to be shared and lessons

137

to be learned from Southeast Asian refugees, especially in facing and overcoming obstacles.

From the back of the room, Trang looked up for a moment and smiled. Everyone nodded in recognition.

This example of Trang's determination to go on, in spite of her struggle to speak at the front of the room, captures some of the shared learning that has defined my work since 1987 at UMass Boston—an urban, public, doctoral-granting university. I, too, have tried to go on—as a teacher, advocate, and organizer across the fields of education and Asian American Studies. Inspired by students like Trang and her classmates, I offer the following integrative themes of *sharing voices, crossing boundaries,* and *building communities* as a way to introduce my commitments and contributions as a faculty member. I choose not to reproduce the compartmentalized categories of scholarship, teaching, and service that universities traditionally use to describe faculty roles and responsibilities.

Sharing Voices

Much of my work as a researcher and teacher centers on *sharing voices*—creating contexts in which immigrant voices, student voices, women's voices, Asian American voices, and so on, can be expressed and appreciated. The voices of those who are traditionally silenced or structurally marginalized, like the Vietnamese refugee high school student who states in one of my articles, "We don't feel like our voice the authority would ever think of" (Kiang and Kaplan 1994, 116), literally fill my curricula, publications, and projects as well as my classroom and office. The purpose, process, and presentation of my research and writing—whether with Vietnamese children in a bilingual fourth-grade classroom, or Vietnamese American high school students, or Cambodian college students, or Chinese adult immigrant learners in a community-based English as a Second Language (ESL) program—document and authorize student and community voices. In turn, those voices serve to challenge the validity of dominant paradigms (race relations paradigms or models of student persistence, for example) and enable alternative theories to be grounded.

In addition, by sharing voices in the classroom through both the content and pedagogy of my teaching, students consistently "speak up" and "feel heard," unlike in other school settings where they are frequently silent or silenced. This is particularly significant for my undergraduate classes in which immigrant students of color are the majority. In my graduate education courses as well, sharing voices models a student-centered pedagogy and reinforces the importance of drawing from primary sources for content—crucial principles in our teacher education program.

Crossing Boundaries

The structure of my faculty appointment and my teaching responsibilities purposefully cross both disciplinary and bureaucratic, institutional lines. My day-today practice is multidisciplinary on many levels—reflecting the nature of my dual professional fields in Asian American Studies and education as well as my commitment to seek connections across boundaries that isolate subject matter or separate people. In my relationships with colleagues and communities, my own organizing experience, biracial background, and connections to the various worlds of K–12, undergraduate, and graduate education enable me to move comfortably and productively across boundaries of race, culture, gender, and class to facilitate collaboration and forge coalitions.

Building Communities

Nearly every aspect of my research, teaching, and service relate to community building. My studies in Boston Chinatown or with Cambodians and Latinos in Lowell, Massachusetts, for example, explicitly examine the dynamics of immigrant community development, while my research and service within educational institutions invariably point to the importance of communities as a survival strategy for addressing student needs or as an anchor for curriculum transformation. Furthermore, as a teacher, I consciously strive to create community in the classroom, based in part on the mutual understanding and respect that result from *sharing voices* and *crossing boundaries* together. This process has special meaning at an urban commuter school because the day-to-day realities of life facing our students, combined with the institution's resource constraints, limit opportunities to develop a cohesive sense of identity and connections on campus.

CRABS IN THE POT

In using these three themes to frame my tenure statement in 1994, I challenged the problematic "scholarship-teaching-service" design of the tenure review process itself and modeled an alternative approach to make the review more valid and conceptually meaningful, both for my own case and for those of colleagues who would follow me. Admittedly, I was careful to provide adequate documentation of excellence in the separate categories of teaching, service, and scholarship which are traditionally evaluated, but I also explicitly argued that the compartmentalized structure of the traditional evaluation was inappropriate to accurately assess or interpret the intent and impact of my work. By interrogating my own review process individually, I tried to offer a vision to transform it institutionally.

My critical disposition toward the tenure process had hardened many years before facing my own review because of a situation I witnessed at an Ivy League school where students were actively demanding Asian American Studies in the curriculum. The school at that time offered no courses but did have one Asian American in a tenure-track position in international politics who, coincidentally, had been an outspoken activist for Asian American Studies as a graduate student at another elite university. Students had repeatedly asked him to consider offering a special topics course or, at the very least, to publicly support their demands to the administration, but he had become increasingly distant, even defensive. Once, when I visited the campus to meet with the students about their strategies, I found him alone in his office. He sighed, "Can you tell the students to stop coming to me? I just can't deal with them till I get tenure. After that, maybe I can do something, but not now. . . ."

Like sociologist Felix Padilla (1997), who has critiqued this same dynamic among some Latino faculty, I could not have disagreed more with my colleague's assessment of priorities. Not only was there nobody else for the students to approach; but, even from pure self-interest, I told him that this was a fundamental error in political judgment because he was "protecting" himself from the population that would potentially care most about his being there. He insisted on his distance, however, and was denied tenure two years later anyway. Sadly, but not surprisingly, no one rallied in his defense.

At the time, I felt quite self-conscious for criticizing his stance, as if I were his elder, when he was actually half a generation older than me. But I could not accept leaving the students without support, even though I had no affiliation to the campus myself. That moment in his office crystallized a personal vow I made to never sacrifice my own core commitments for the sake of professional status. It also reminded me of hearing community members talk-story about how crabs struggle in a pot—each one crawling over the next, trying to save itself without regard for those it passes over or pushes out of the way. The crabs-in-the-pot metaphor is a warning for us to examine the impact of our individual ambitions and actions in relation to our collective groups, to recognize how we help *or* hurt each other, and to question more fundamentally—*what is the nature of this pot, and how did we all get here in the first place?*

I often raise these questions now as I recruit and mentor new faculty of color. Out of the seven new junior faculty hired in education between 1996 and 1998, for example, all seven were people of color (one African American, three Latina/Latino, and three Asian American). I purposely served on six of those seven search committees myself and am convinced that my presence, perspective, and power (having tenure now) positively influenced the process and outcomes for each case. Gaining critical mass in a mainstream institution is essential, as we all know. But it matters less if we act like crabs in a pot. We need to transform ourselves.

CAN WE ALL GET ALONG?

Another crystallizing moment occurred at a 1993 national conference in Los Angeles on diversifying the university curriculum. I listened to a panel of non-tenured faculty of color from local institutions who vented deep frustration in the wake of the previous year's riot/rebellion. Having responded to relentless demands from communities, government agencies, and the media to provide analysis and assistance in relation to the complex racial, cultural, economic, and political dynamics during that crisis period, they discovered that their heroic interventions counted for little in their annual reviews. Penalized by the traditional reward systems of their institutions, they had each privately concluded that universities were not serious about responding to Rodney King's question of the decade: *Can we all get along?* As a result, communities were left without access to crucial resources and follow up, while a cadre of energetic junior faculty found themselves increasingly cynical about their own roles (Arches et al. 1997).

If those faculty of color, regardless of their own disciplines, had established relationships with their schools' ethnic studies programs, they might have found greater individual support as well as more productive models of community–university collaboration. Although ethnic studies programs are themselves often marginalized by institutional racism in universities, they, nevertheless, represent institutionalized spaces that value faculty and student engagement in communities. Ironically, however, at the national level, references to lessons and models from ethnic studies programs are completely absent from the formal literature on faculty professional outreach or service learning.

Furthermore, if the late Ernest Boyer's (1990) definition of applied scholarship or the late Ernest Lynton's (1995) criteria for evaluating faculty professional service had influenced the reviews of those faculty of color in post-riot/rebellion Los Angeles, the outcomes would certainly have been more positive. Boyer's compelling call to redefine how to evaluate and reward faculty scholarship and other national trends in higher education reform have direct relevance to our individual campuses and our professional lives as faculty of color (Glassick, Taylor Huber, and Maeroff 1997). By connecting our own visions and priorities with these larger policy discussions, we not only strengthen our process of change inside the pot but also find strategies and allies with which to transform the pot itself.

MIS PALABRAS

Still another crystallizing moment emerged in a conversation about curriculum and pedagogy several years ago with Vivian Zamel, the director of our undergraduate ESL program at UMass Boston. Over the years, Vivian and I have had many students in common, and we have collaborated frequently on student and faculty development projects. At the time, Vivian was rethinking her plans for an English composition course with ESL students and wrestling with the question of how much to focus on issues of oppression and inequality as subjects for reading, writing, and class discussion. She wondered, "I'm just not sure if it will be too depressing or discouraging for them."

Reflecting for a moment on my own choices with similar students in Asian American Studies courses, I urged her to be both affirming and honest in analyzing those issues together as a class, even if dynamics became difficult emotionally and seemed out of control pedagogically. The reality of oppression already defined much of our students' daily lives as working-class, predominantly nonwhite immigrants. But those experiences represented rich resources for meaningful teaching and learning. I replied, "It's not like you're making them face something they don't know. Definitely, you should do it."

Much to her credit, Vivian took the risk. By the end of an unforgettable semester of shared learning and inspired writing, the students in Vivian's class crafted a collective poem, titled "Mis Palabras" ("My Words"), that articulates the multiple ways in which they had resisted oppression in their lives. Many found connections with each other's name stories—those experiences in which their names, and, by extension, their identities, had been ignored, disrespected, or changed because of the dominant culture's hegemony. In the process, they touched a hidden dimension of Vivian's own identity and survival that none of us had ever known. Vivian's beautiful given name, she revealed, is *Aviva*, which, in Hebrew, means *Spring*. But, like so many of her students, she had adopted *Vivian* at an early age to be more acceptable to others. Through her words in *Mis Palabras*, I recalled my own story as well.

The Return of Spring
for Vivian Zamel

Aviva shares secrets
returning me to second grade.
Writing our names,
practicing penmanship.
　At least no one has to say it,
　always sounding so funny.
I fill a page quickly.
Use your middle name, too, Mrs. Shapiro commands.
My pencil slows, my hand reluctant.
N i e n—c h u
In the next row,
Gordon Clay steals a glance at my desk
and explodes in laughter.
I hate Gordon Clay. I hate Mrs. Shapiro.
I hate everyone looking at me.
Humiliation lasts forever in a child's heart.
I use my full name
in publications now,
Knowing *Nien-chu* means
Honor your ancestors.
　I think of Aviva.
Mis palabras come to life
as the cold of winter turns to Spring.
　　　　　　　　　　　　　　—Boston, 1993

ON MY OWN

Thoughtful teachers, like Aviva, always strive to make meaningful curricular connections with students' life experiences and prior learning. Similarly, if we wish to authorize the presence of faculty of color in higher education, then we need to recognize the defining power of our own contexts and histories. Long before any of us reaches the university in a professional role, we already have life-times of meaningful experiences—both proud and traumatic—through which we have constructed our identities and developed our worldviews. We have endured many moments of humiliation and isolation, from second grade to Ph.D. programs, in the evolution of our lifelong struggles to survive and transform oppressive environments.

At age nine, I was the youngest member of my elementary school's flag football team, as well as the only Asian American. I went to the first practice hoping to be selected for the safety position where I would serve as the team's last line of defense—a role and responsibility I particularly respected. But the coach saw me toss a ball and directed me to play quarterback. I had not wanted to be so visible but reluctantly complied. A week later in our first game with another school, I called out signals and prepared for the snap from center. Rushing across the line from the other side, someone roared, "Kill the Chink!"

I froze and wondered if they would really hurt me. Though I had grown up hearing racist names many times, no one had ever said "kill" before.

I waited, but no adults intervened, and my teammates seemed not to notice or care. When the game finally ended, I fled the playground without a word to anyone. Once home, I locked the bathroom door tightly and sat alone in the bathtub for nearly an hour. Sitting in cold water, frozen in time, I replayed that moment over and over again—waiting for someone to do something but always finding that I was on my own.

PUMICE AND OBSIDIAN

At the start of my freshman year at Harvard in 1976, three working-class Asian American students who had grown up in the local Boston Chinatown community appeared at the "Minority Freshman Orientation" and were quickly told by the dean of students (who happened to be African American) that they could not participate in the event because they were not "minorities." To challenge the university's official exclusion, the undergraduate Asian American Association was born.

During those years at Harvard, there were no mentors for students of color, no support systems, nothing in the curriculum. We were on our own.

I poured my anger and alienation into activism with others. We called ourselves Third World people, mindful of an earlier generation's visions in Bandung to decolonize the mind as well as the land. On our own together, we shared each others'

cultures and studied each others' histories—finding common roots and connections. Proud of our unity and in love with our colors, our movement shook the campus, and our voices exploded.

We Do Not Mince Words
for Janice Mirikitani

When we say *haole,*
We mean generations of bent brown backs
Harvesting the sugar plantations;
We mean the bones of our forefathers,
Buried with pumice and obsidian
Beneath luxury hotels and military installations.

When we say *bok gwai,*
We mean the golden dreams of sojourners
Carved as memories forever into the Sierras;
We mean the endurance of our mothers
Who stitch in garment factories,
Piece by piece, still chipping away at the granite.
When we say *hakujin,*
We mean families, yellow like the desert sand
That blows freely even behind barbed wire;
We mean the monument at Manzanar
Where our tears mix with rain
From the clouds over Hiroshima and Nagasaki.
When we say *was'ichu s'ichay,*
We mean the devastation of our Red Nations,
The color of Warriors' blood;
We mean the rape of Mother Earth
Where spirits from the beginning of time
Lie uprooted with coal and uranium talus.

When we say *hin dung yi, gringo, shetani,*
We mean the histories and cultures of people of color.
So, when we say your institutions are Eurocentric,
We mean they are genocidal.
You see, in the languages of our homelands,
We do not mince words.
                                   —Cambridge, 1980

GLIMPSES OF THE POSSIBLE

Discovering the poetry of Janice Mirikitani, the songs of Nobuko Miyamoto, the
koto riffs of June Kuramoto, and the work of others in the Asian American movement, I found myself inspired emotionally, intellectually, culturally, and politi-

cally in ways that had been completely neglected, if not actively extinguished, by my "world-class" college curriculum. During the last semester of my senior year, the same period when I wrote my first poem, "We Do Not Mince Words," the university finally approved a one-time-only Asian American Studies seminar for elective credit.[1] The director and associate director of the university's counseling bureau, Kiyo Morimoto and Jean Wu, served as adjunct faculty sponsors. Although internally disorganized and institutionally marginalized, that first seminar offered glimpses of what was possible through a relevant curriculum, a caring pedagogy, and teachers with whom one could identify.

During the next five years, students mobilized to have the Asian American Studies seminar offered on an ad hoc basis four more times at Harvard, twice with Kiyo and Jean and once each with Dorinne Kondo in anthropology and Tu Weiming in East Asian studies. Each semester I helped to plan and organize the course, mobilized students, and assisted with instruction. For the sponsoring faculty, the seminar was usually "extra" in their workloads. Their limited involvement reflected personal and political commitments within rigid institutional constraints. For me, not having any professional affiliations or aspirations at that time, teaching the seminar felt more like sheer love and inspiration. We struggled together to create transformative learning environments to change students' lives (Kiang 1988; Kiang and Ng 1989).

One such student wrote as a freshman in 1983,

> This course has changed the way I see myself and other Asians. For the first time in my life, I feel really good about being Chinese and I feel proud of my heritage. . . . I feel that I had been forced to deny many of the Asian aspects of myself in order to gain acceptance. I still have much to learn, but I think I have taken the first step by breaking out of these unasked for chains.

In spite of the enormous frustration we faced every year—alternately demanding and begging to find a legitimate faculty sponsor for the seminar and an official home in the university curriculum—witnessing this type of impact with nearly every student in every course filled us with determination. *I wanted to go on.*

During those early years of teaching at Harvard, I had no institutional status as a faculty member or even a graduate student. In fact, following my graduation from college, I lived on food stamps while working/volunteering to establish a grassroots educational resource center in Boston Chinatown—the first organization in the community to assert pan-ethnicity (Le Espiritu 1993) in defining itself explicitly by name as *Asian American* rather than *Chinese* or *Chinese American*. During the early 1980s, we produced bilingual slide shows and developed curricula on Asian immigrant issues for adult ESL classes, trained community members in video production for cable television access, organized coalitions to protest anti-Asian racist violence and police brutality, convened conferences and professional development workshops for teachers about stereotypes and Asian American history, and more (Kiang 1985; Kiang and Lee 1982). Our goal was nothing less than making fundamental social

change through the development of Asian American awareness, pride, and unity—
a mission with revolutionary intentions that funders and mainstream agencies never
truly grasped, but which still continues today, after more than twenty years.

HARVESTING IN DESERT SAND

Meanwhile, by the mid-1980s, growing numbers of Asian American students at
many schools east of California were generating new demands for Asian American Studies courses and programs.[2] Schools, like Harvard, that lacked vision or
simply wished to quell student protest typically responded by offering a single
Asian American Studies course, with an adjunct instructor brought to campus
once a week for one semester.

During that crucial growth period, those of us planting the Asian American
Studies field on the East Coast—like braceros and coolie contract laborers following the crops from season to season—rode buses and trains throughout the
week, migrating from campus to campus, to provide students with what might be
their only opportunity to experience Asian American Studies at their schools.
Every week in spring 1988, for example, Shirley Hune rode the Amtrak train from
New York to Philadelphia, while Betty Lee Sung migrated across state lines and
class boundaries between City College of New York and Princeton, New Jersey.
Grace Yun covered the entire state of Connecticut from New Haven, to Storrs,
to Hartford, while I taught three days at UMass Boston, one night at Boston University, and one day at Yale (Kiang 1988, 1995b).

My invited course at Yale on Asian American community development
attracted several leaders of the campus Asian student organizations and motivated
others to become more involved themselves in a range of campus issues related to
ethnic studies, university investment policies, and labor disputes. Although I was
told that my lecturer contract would be renewed if the course was well received,
I later learned that some administrators had privately voiced concerns about my
teaching being "too political" and students becoming "too active." In explaining
to concerned students why they did not invite me to return to Yale for the following semester, however, the department chair simply stated that, in comparison with others, I lacked a doctoral degree.

Yale's decision to not renew my contract represented another crystallizing
moment about politics and elitism in higher education. If I intended to continue
"teaching to transgress" (hooks 1996), then I needed a doctorate for protection and
legitimacy. Until then, I had refused to enter a doctoral program, always believing
that my community organizing experience in Chinatown represented my strongest
qualification for teaching Asian American Studies. Why was training or practitioner knowledge from the community not valued by universities? Certainly it was
more relevant and applicable than my master's program in education at Harvard,
where Asian American perspectives were completely absent from every course I

took and there were no Asian American faculty to work with. My professors had not discouraged me from pursuing Asian American topics in my own research and writing—which I did in every course—but those passions were marginal, at best, within the larger program. Imagining the frustrations I would face in a traditional Ph.D. program dedicated to narrow disciplinary training without attention to issues of pedagogy or curriculum design, I gladly chose to pursue a more flexible but "less prestigious" or "less rigorous" Ed.D. degree in order to focus on the transformative power of learning environments in Asian American Studies.

I returned to Harvard in fall 1989 to get "credentialed" while continuing to teach at UMass Boston. Inspired by students like Trang and supported by a wonderful committee, I turned in my dissertation two years later—a qualitative analysis of the survival strategies utilized by Southeast Asian refugee students to persist in college. In the process, I greatly deepened my own grounded theory about pedagogy and empowerment in Asian American Studies and also expanded my vision of how Asian American voices and perspectives could serve as a powerful force to transform the broader education field. *I wanted to go on.*

NOT VERY NICE COLORS

In fall 1991, with degree in hand, I began a full-time, "target-of-opportunity" appointment in the Graduate College of Education at UMass Boston and started teaching graduate courses in multicultural education and social studies curriculum design, while continuing to offer my undergraduate Asian American Studies courses.[3] I was the only tenure-track faculty of color in the entire College of Education at that time. My appointment signaled the beginning of a dramatic intellectual and cultural shift to realign the mission and activities of the college with the realities of urban schools.

For many years prior, the college's reality and reputation had been exclusionary and out of touch, particularly in relation to students, families, and communities of color who constituted the majority in Boston's public schools. One student described a revealing example of instruction in the elementary education program from that time in the following way:

> The art [curriculum design] teacher left a lasting impression on me. She discussed various art supplies and told the class that she takes all the little black and brown water color paints out of the sets because they were not very nice colors. . . . When I think of this woman, my stomach turns and I feel guilty because I did and said nothing to make her realize how damaging and ignorant her words were.

Another student from that time lamented, "Why would anyone of any background other than white middle class want to attend the current program when they are excluded from nearly every discussion in nearly every class?"

Driving the institutional change process was the college's acting dean, a coura-geous and resilient African American man of faith, steeped in principles of respectful collaboration and urban educational practice. Through a deliberative strategic planning process, reinforced by the dean's calm but steadfast insistence, all aspects of policy and culture in the college were on the table—from the out-dated design, sequence, and assessment of courses, to the lack of diversity within the faculty and student demographic profiles, to the haphazard arrangements with practitioners and school sites. We wanted to transform the entire pot. In addition, through attrition and targeted new hires following a cluster of impending retire-ments, we knew time was on our side. We intended to transform the crabs as well.

Perhaps with good reason, some senior faculty viewed our visions and our pres-ence as threatening. Feeling the chill from several senior *colleagues* and trying to read the power dynamics in my first few department meetings, I remained rela-tively silent until we reviewed a formal proposal for a new course on teaching chil-dren's literature. The syllabus presented "multicultural children's literature" as a one-session topic at the end of the semester, following different literary genres such as poetry, historical novels, and readers' theater. Pushing aggressively for course approval was a full professor who also happened to be director of the teacher education program in which I was based.

Calculating that her retirement would precede my tenure review and remem-bering my vow about not sacrificing core commitments, I asserted in the meeting, and later in a long memo to the department, that we should not approve the course as proposed because the multicultural reality of children's literature needed to be infused throughout the entire course across every genre, rather than being mistakenly and tokenly treated as one of several topics to cover. As teachers of future teachers, I asked, what are the educational practices and principles that we are choosing to model within our own teaching and curriculum design? Not sur-prisingly, the chill in the room grew much more severe. But that moment created space for another junior faculty member to speak up as well—a white male col-league committed to antiracist pedagogy who became my closest ally in strategiz-ing how to implement educational practices that we believed in while also sur-viving the tenure process in our increasingly contentious department. *We both wanted to go on.*

ALL STUDENTS CAN LEARN

Students from that time also acted out the tensions and contradictions in our shifting institutional culture. During my first semester, for example, graduate stu-dents in my weekly social studies curriculum design course openly rebelled after the first class meeting in which I described my broad commitment to antiracist, multicultural education and my specific intent to use the Japanese American internment experience as the focus for a major course assignment to design curriculum units for fifth graders. A core of students actually circulated a petition to have me removed as the instructor, although I later discovered that they had come to the first class already with that intention, encouraged by the teacher education program director. One student outside of that core explained,

> On the first day, I sat in the rear corner of the class and was surrounded by three women who had come in together. According to them, our teacher for the course was not the person we were supposed to have. Maybe, if the class was quickly identified as a disaster, we could get rid of him and have him replaced in time to salvage our education and our futures. That was how my first five minutes of school went. Over the next four or five weeks, my attempts to stay positive were wearing down. I perceived that an element in the class was deliberately trying to sabotage the process, at the same time that I was attempting to become involved in it.

Being a teacher committed to student empowerment, and considering my own background as a student activist, the irony of being the object of student protest challenged me on many levels. As a young teacher, I tried not to take the criticisms personally or obsessively. As a responsible teacher with grading power, I tried not to respond by unfairly punishing those who disagreed with my ideas. As a teacher of teachers, I tried to remain committed to the principle of having high expectations for all students to learn—mindful of realities in urban schools where low teacher expectations, especially for students of color, are daily self-fulfilling prophecies. And as a teacher of color, I tried not to view the problematic classroom dynamics simply as racist resistance by white students who could not accept my position or perspective.

Feeling on my own again, I did not share any of these dilemmas with my colleagues and, instead, turned deeply inward to search for strategies and inspiration. Reflecting on many past transformative teaching experiences with white students, including two remarkable working-class white men who were the first students at UMass Boston to design and complete individual majors in Asian American Studies, I knew I had to reach the class emotionally by directly connecting to their own lives and by touching their hearts as human beings. This helped me reaffirm my decision to use the Japanese American internment experience as a case study to model powerful teaching and learning across subject areas and grade levels—having experienced its impact with undergraduates of all backgrounds in Asian American Studies courses year after year.

Nevertheless, because of the active campaign being waged against me both inside and outside my course, I was unsure if emotional content and a caring pedagogy would be enough to shift the hostile dynamic in the classroom, which also reflected larger issues of race, power, and contention over culture in the college. Instinctively, I responded to the situation in political terms and recalled Mao Tse Tung's basic organizing principle in the Chinese revolution: *unite with the advanced to win over the middle and isolate the backwards.* From that guiding slogan, I regrounded myself in the strengths of my own political training and my skills as a community organizer. Rather than utilizing arbitrary faculty power to crush the core of students challenging my presence, I chose to develop tactics and a strategy to outorganize them.

The students I wanted to reach emotionally were those in the middle. Indeed, most students were there—heavily influenced by the prevailing climate in the college and the strong views of the backwards core but hardly consolidated or actively resistant themselves. Winning them over meant showing, during the second week, that I had listened to their sincere initial concerns that the Japanese American internment seemed to be a narrow focus taking a lot of time in the course, perhaps at the expense of other important social studies topics that they might need for their preparation as teachers. In the third week, I took the direct offensive by showing how teaching and learning about the internment experience are not at all narrow. In that class session, I was able to raise core questions about race, war, loyalty, ethnicity, family, immigration, the Constitution, and the media with curricular connections to economics, politics, geography, history, and psychology, as well as to art, literature, music, health science, and mathematics. I wanted students to see that exploring this one case in depth offered far more powerful learning than skimming the surface of several topics.

Furthermore, by using oral histories, poems, video excerpts, role plays, and reflective writing activities within our own class, I modeled effective teaching methods designed to touch our hearts personally. This moved many students to realize how little they themselves had been taught about the causes and consequences of the internment experience. As a result, they began to reflect more critically and concretely about their own responsibilities to become effective teachers. The internment example challenged and inspired those in the middle to engage with me and the course. *They wanted to go on.*

Meanwhile, to isolate the backwards core of students, I structured many small group activities and discussions that, on the surface, modeled effective collaborative learning/teaching practices but also served to split up the core group members who were otherwise always sitting together, talking among themselves during class, and asserting themselves as a collective force. I also used some of their statements and questions as reference points for class reflection as the semester progressed.

For example, during the second week, one of the resistant students directly challenged my plans with the question, "Maybe you can teach some of this stuff in high school, but not in elementary school. Children don't know anything about war or racism. Why do you have to ruin their innocence?" At the time, I had swallowed my own immediate response of, "Excuse me, whose children are you talking about," and simply replied, "Well, that's a really important question that we're going to examine much more in this course." I returned to that question during the fourth week after some of the lessons from the internment case had been internalized and found several students from the middle who could respond thoughtfully. This fulcrum shift in the balance of classroom dynamics also served to isolate the resistant core. I referenced the same question again at the end of the course to serve as a reminder of where we had started and how far we had come.

UNITE WITH THE ADVANCED

Although my political organizing methods had opened the learning environment sufficiently so that the pedagogy and emotional content built into the course design could reach most in the class, I did not realize until reading students' final reflection papers that I had failed to implement the essential first step in Chairman Mao's framework—*to unite with the advanced.* With tremendous guilt, I learned that I had taken for granted the academic and social needs of those two or three students who were initially thrilled to have an instructor finally offer multicultural perspectives and commitments to urban schools. The lone African American student from the class wrote, "I am not surprised that you as an instructor were greeted with such hostility. . . . I found the atmosphere in this class to be quite uncomfortable, but then again, this is how most of my classes have been."

While appreciating my efforts, she and a white student with longstanding commitments to cultural democracy each wrote about feeling silenced and uncomfortable throughout the semester. I had mistakenly assumed that they saw themselves included in both the content and process of my organizing and teaching, but I had not talked directly to either of them about what I was doing or why. I was so concerned with reaching the middle and neutralizing the resistant core that I failed to affirm and invest in those students who could most benefit from working together with me. The course had not empowered them, and their feelings of frustration and disappointment still move me today to think clearly about my priorities as a teacher and mentor.

Thankfully, the College of Education is a completely different environment now because of retirements, new hiring, and the impact of our transformative visions taking root. Recent graduate program directors of teacher education, special education, and family counseling have all been faculty of color, as are the department chairs for educational leadership and for counseling and school psychology. More importantly, the commitment to urban education is explicit and generally shared by most faculty, staff, and students. At the same time, the students in our M.Ed. teacher education program are still predominantly white—in sharp contrast to the large majority of black, Latino, and Asian students in Boston's schools. Although we are now able to recruit and support significantly more students of color, the urgent reality remains that students who wish to become effective and relevant teachers need immersion in antiracist, multicultural learning environments themselves. This agenda and our capacity to make it happen were barely imaginable just a few years earlier.

Teaching graduate education courses side by side with my undergraduate Asian American Studies courses, however, I constantly confront choices about where to prioritize, what to affirm, and whom to support. Who are the advanced that I must not take for granted? Where can I have the most meaningful impact for both the short term and the long term? Although I have no easy ways to resolve these daily questions, my gut feelings and political sensibilities often converge in choosing to invest in students like Trang, whose simple but profound assertion, *I want to go on*, echoes in these pages. Those are the students who move me most and whose lives and futures I affect most directly and deeply.

MAKERS OF HISTORY

Unlike the elite private schools that dominate higher education in Boston, UMass Boston is the only public university in the local metropolitan area. It attracts a large number of working-class Asian American students, a majority of whom are Chinese and Vietnamese immigrants and refugees who confront the language barrier, cultural conflicts, post-traumatic stress disorder (PTSD), poverty, racial harassment, heavy work demands, and constant family responsibilities. They typically experience profound isolation from both the social and the academic domains within the university while also displaying many strengths, such as problem-solving skills and survival strategies, resilience and motivation to succeed, bilingual/bicultural competencies, and deep desires for peace. Furthermore, they are grounded in the social, cultural, economic, and political realities of the city's Asian American communities because they are members/insiders of those communities themselves. Much of my own writing and teaching in the past decade has focused on creating spaces for their strengths and struggles to be recognized (Kiang 1992, 1993, 1995a, 1995b, 1996a, 1996b).

For example, after taking two Asian American Studies courses, Chanda, a Cambodian woman who lost most of her family in the Khmer Rouge genocide, changed her major from math to women's studies and sociology, with the intention of someday playing a leadership role in her community. Her story is inspiring but not atypical:

> Even when I was here two years, I still did not know what I really want or what I'm good in. But when I took the Asian American Studies courses, then it's like a light come in to define what really I am and what I want. I did not know that I would fight for justice. But when I learn those things, I say that's it! I want to help society to change. Those courses educate me for life, to see how society is structured and operates . . . it makes me think differently . . . if I do not take those courses, I will never understand who I really am or what I want to do in the future.

Chanda's process of survival and personal growth is shared by Sok, a male Cambodian student who discovered himself and his community in our curriculum. He asserted, "Asians help build this society, but the society don't recognize that. We are the makers of history, but we never have courses that tell about that. This class is very important to have."

Beyond the curricular content of our courses, we have crafted inclusive, learner-centered, pedagogical strategies with commitments to models of collaborative, experiential-based, community service learning that respect and respond meaningfully to the cultures and needs of Asian immigrant/refugee students but that also serve as effective teaching practices for students in general. Through staff advising and student word-of-mouth networks, we attract many non-Asian immigrant students, older students returning to school, and students with learning disabilities—all of whom also find precious, comfortable spaces for themselves within our classroom learning environments.

I have argued elsewhere that the content and pedagogy of Asian American Studies courses represent a powerful curricular intervention that facilitates the integration of students (who are often otherwise marginalized) within both the academic and the social domains of the university (Kiang 1992, 1996a, 1997). Because the extent of students' social and academic integration within the university is so closely associated with their persistence and retention (Tinto 1987), the role played by Asian American Studies courses (or other courses/programs/structures in a diverse curriculum with comparable commitments) has profound implications for urban, commuter campuses where enabling students' institutional integration is an urgent and fundamental challenge. The reflections of a Chinese immigrant woman from Hong Kong illustrate what this means concretely: "The courses ended my isolation. I didn't have the courage to participate or to reach out to others before. But the courses enable me to do all that, and to learn about myself, about America, all in one. You learn actively. You always have a question and you look for an answer. You are motivated to learn, and to make a difference."

This process of learning, sharing, connecting, and envisioning new possibilities also engages non-Asian students in powerful ways. A Cape Verdean refugee from Angola explained, "From the class, I said to myself, 'This is it. I want to be a professor. . . . ' It was like a role model to me. It was liberating. I feel stronger. Now if I want to do something, I'll do it. If I have something to share, I'll be able to share it."

Although I choose to describe the effects of Asian American Studies courses through individual voices, this impact cannot be dismissed as anecdotal. Preliminary data from a Ford Foundation–funded study to assess the continuing meaning and long-term impact of Asian American Studies courses in the lives of UMass Boston alumni are crystal clear. These courses have had *overwhelmingly positive* impact in enabling alumni, across all races, to develop and apply specific sets of knowledge, skills, and attitudes that have had direct relevance and meaning across a range of domains, including their jobs/careers, educations, family lives, friendships and interpersonal relationships, community involvements, social awareness, and personal identities.

Our data also sharply contradict assertions within the national debate over multicultural curricular reform that ethnic studies courses/programs have divisive and exclusionary effects. Only 2 percent of all survey respondents, for example, noted that their experiences in Asian American Studies courses made them feel very isolated from the rest of society, compared with 87 percent who experienced this type of effect little or not at all. Similarly, no survey respondents reported feeling much or very much discouraged or bitter about living in the United States as a result of their Asian American Studies coursework. Nine out of ten alumni (92 percent) ranked their Asian American Studies courses as either very good or among the best compared with all the courses they took at UMass Boston. This, in turn, helped 72 percent of the alumni to feel significantly more positively about UMass Boston as an institution.

LEGACIES OF WAR

I came to UMass Boston in 1986 specifically with the intent to create a Center for Asian American Studies, similar in mission to the pan-Asian community-based center I had directed in Chinatown but with the stability and resources of a university setting. Like many urban environments, UMass Boston is tremendously rich in human resources but pathetically poor in the resources of capital and facilities. But the rhetoric and reality of UMass Boston's commitment to an urban, public mission seemed far more compelling than the lack of vision or interest offered by the elite private universities, despite being flush with large endowments. In doing reconnaissance for resources and potential allies on campus, I learned of a remarkable center established by Vietnam veterans during the early 1980s that embodied all of the programmatic elements I hoped to build into the structure of a proposed Asian American Studies center.

Named after Bill Joiner,[4] an African American Vietnam veteran who served as the first coordinator of veterans' services for students at UMass Boston, the William Joiner Center for the Study of War and Social Consequences offered a sophisticated and comprehensive programmatic model that included appropriate campus-based support services for students who were veterans, innovative courses and curriculum resources related to the Vietnam/American war and the social consequences of war more broadly, and applied research and advocacy for veterans issues locally and nationally. The Joiner Center had been established on campus initially with generous line-item funding from the state legislature, due in large part to grassroots organizing and the substantial political clout of the progressive Vietnam veterans movement in Massachusetts (which included, for example, U.S. Senator John Kerry, a founding member of Vietnam Veterans against the War). As I grew more familiar with their deeply grounded visions of peace and justice and their willingness to provide leadership and mobilize resources on campus to educate about the social consequences of the Vietnam/American war, I approached the Joiner Center codirectors with the notion that UMass Boston not only was home to the largest percentage of Vietnam veterans returning to college but also served the largest percentage of

Vietnamese refugee students in the region. If one looks honestly at the complex legacies of the Vietnam/American war, certainly Southeast Asian refugee resettlement
is an essential dimension. Therefore, I asked, could the Joiner Center respond to
Southeast Asian refugee communities and students on campus as an important constituency, alongside U.S. veterans? This was a long shot, I thought, but still worth
raising. Much to my amazement, they agreed and invited me to embark on a process
of research, advocacy, and course/program development related to Southeast Asian
refugee students and communities, which became the foundation for Asian American Studies at UMass Boston and a defining focus for my own commitments.

This is, itself, a remarkable and largely untold story in the history of ethnic studies program development in American higher education. While our Asian American Studies program certainly claims its share of student and community activism
as motive forces in its reason for being, there is no other Asian American Studies
or ethnic studies program in the country that has been so deeply shaped in its
bedrock either by the progressive and humanistic visions of U.S. Vietnam veterans or by the perspectives and interests of Southeast Asian refugees.

At that time, the Joiner Center was also the nexus for many national leadership projects by black, Hispanic, and women veteran activists; advocacy research
on the effects of Agent Orange; and people-to-people exchanges of writers, artists,
doctors, educators, and veterans between Vietnam and the United States. These
were concrete but far-sighted building blocks that paved the way for both the
establishment of the Center for Minority Veterans within the U.S. Department
of Veterans Affairs and later efforts toward reconciliation and normalization of
diplomatic relations between the U.S. and Vietnamese governments. When
political conflicts inevitably arose with organized anti-Communist forces in the
Vietnamese refugee communities that protested the Joiner Center's projects in
Vietnam, we challenged their bitterness through our active involvement with
community-based issues of civil rights and bilingual education, together with the
rationale that veterans' desires to re-establish relationships with Vietnam had little to do with politics and everything to do with their own healing.

Although I formally left the Joiner Center just prior to accepting my tenure-
track faculty position in education, the impact of its leadership and vision
demanded an emotional depth in my work that continues to challenge and inspire
me. I often reflect on the extraordinary confluence of shared interests that the
Joiner Center forged between veterans and refugees and the unexpected ways in
which we have all helped each other to learn, to build, to heal—*to go on.*

Please remember, this story is not linear and not yet finished. Please go on.

LAVA FLOWS

Recently, after spending a late night and all morning transcribing interviews for
a research project, I took an hour break to run and reflect on black lava rocks, feel-

ing the tropical sun amidst the Pacific, far from the snow and ice of winter in Boston. Thinking about how to focus this chapter, I watched a charcoal-colored crab emerge from the shallow tide pool and begin crawling, barely noticeable, on the black basalt. A second and third quickly followed. When their bright black eyes met mine, they stopped for a moment to look deeply and then calmly continued moving together across the lava: no pushing, no walking over one another. They were not in a pot there.

Aloha no. This is Molokai, one of the islands of the Hawaiian Nation, where slogans to think globally and act locally are turned on their heads. Feeling both the traumas and the healing powers of this place, where the demands for sovereignty have profound spiritual as well as political meaning, I am grateful for the opportunity to reconnect with issues, communities, and commitments that grounded my first few years at UMass Boston through the Joiner Center more than a decade ago. *Mahalo.*

I have been transcribing interviews conducted for a research project with Asian American Vietnam veterans, including many living in Molokai, Maui, Oahu, and the other Hawaiian islands. With headphones, a walkman, and a laptop, I replay and relive every moment of each interview. Their voices continue to echo inside me:

During training, "Kill the gooks, kill the slant-eyes." That's the first thing you wake up and see on the walls. "Kill the gooks, cut off their heads." That's how they used to initiate us, you know, just tuning you up to go overseas. That's the way we were taught, kill the gooks or the slopes. And hell, I was the same thing. I used to think about that. You know, 'cause I was Japanese. I thought, don't do that to me, man [laughs]. I'm keeping this green uniform on, man. I'm not gonna put nothin' else on.

We were fighting the people there who looked like me. . . . A lot of them remind me of my family and relatives. A lot of them died and look like my family, you know. There's a lot of resemblance. . . . I remember when these Americans killed all these Vietnamese civilians where these girls remind me of my nieces. They used to wash my clothes. The Americans went in there and killed them. They just thought everybody was Viet Cong, you know. But these girls were unarmed. They're washing clothes at the river. Why even kill them? They're not even harmful to nobody. Stuff like that got me really upset. . . . I had the hardest time for me to get over. And if I see girls that look like those little girls, I have that weird feeling inside of me. [long pause and tears]

The way they [white GIs] treated us make you like always asking are you inferior. They look down on us. After that, I don't like that feeling. When I feel that feeling, I just don't like it. . . . They think they're better than me. I see guys bleed. We all bleed red. I don't care whether you got blond hair and blue eyes or you got black hair, you all bleed red. . . . I don't know. It's too late now. You should have done this [research] twenty-five years ago . . . because, boy, that's a long time to be carrying around all this bitterness.

There's a lot of things that went down in Vietnam that a lot of people don't even talk about yet, and race is one.

Yes. A lot went down in Vietnam, a lot directly related to racism. Asian American men and women who served in Vietnam were on that cutting edge and have much to say. But few have ever been asked.

The four interview excerpts offered here come from the Asian American Vietnam Veterans Race-Related Study, a research project conducted at the Pacific Islander Division of the National Center for PTSD at the Honolulu Veterans Administration, under the direction of Chalsa M. Loo, to document the race-related experiences of American veterans of Asian ancestry (Chinese, Filipino, Japanese, Korean, Okinawan, etc.) who served in Vietnam. By examining how their specific race-related experiences are individually and cumulatively associated with PTSD, the study has profound implications for theoretical conceptualizations and clinical definitions of PTSD, as well as for developing appropriate services, resources, and policies to facilitate healing and recovery from trauma caused by racist victimization (Kiang 1991; Loo 1994, 1998).

WRITE FROM THE PAST, BUT WRITE FOR THE FUTURE

In interview after interview, veterans wished someone had asked these questions about racism twenty-five or thirty years ago—acknowledging how little support they have ever received and how incomplete their own healing processes continue to be, even now. In revealing their trauma stories—many for the first time in their lives—the veterans of Molokai, Maui, and the other Hawaiian islands returned me to what really matters in my work as a teacher, researcher, and organizer. It is all about healing.

Healing. Yes, what I want most to write for this volume is about healing. *Healing and transformation.* In my 1994 tenure narrative, I argued that my work should be evaluated holistically by examining the interrelated themes of *sharing voices, crossing boundaries,* and *building communities.* The theories and practices underlying those themes continue to resonate for me now. But writing today, it is clear to me that the themes of *healing* and *transformation* are even more meaningful signifiers of how I view my role and responsibility in the university. And those themes have been essential and explicit since my first year at UMass Boston when I began to envision ways to connect the principles and passions of Asian American Studies and the Asian American movement with the realities of working-class immigrant and refugee students and communities.

After that first year of teaching Asian American Studies at UMass Boston, I used a poem to articulate my evolving commitments and priorities *"to educate for life."* Like my angry "We Do Not Mince Words" poem from college, I dedicated "Your Words" to the poet/activist Janice Mirikitani, whose work had created space for me as a student when I had needed to develop and trust my own voice.

Your Words
for Janice Mirikitani

Your words return
softly, like a warm embrace
sweetly, like the taste of New Year's Day.
Your words return
with dreams and many memories.

My students now
like Ely and Thanh
slowly shed their silences.

I tell them—
  Writing is healing
  when the walls hide war and devastation
  Writing is transformation
  when the walls are white and echo English Only.

I tell them—
  Write from the past,
  But write for the future.
  Every word
  is a lesson in survival.
And I share your words with them.
Proudly, like albums of family photographs.
Patiently, like a tortoise in movement.
  Awake in the river
  Close to the earth

We, the dangerous
We, the makers of history.
Yes, your words return
and remind me
that *Mirikitani* will always mean *makibaka*. [5]
We carry your words into battle.

—Boston, 1988

BENCHES OF GRANITE

Along Boston's south shoreline, directly beside the entrance to my university, is a memorial for those from this working-class neighborhood who served and died in the Vietnam War. Like many of the sites insp ired by Maya Ying Lin's vision for the Wall in Washington, D.C., this local memorial offers peace and honors lives. But unlike other memorials, the arching granite stones here not only include the seventy-eight names of those U.S. Vietnam veterans who came from this Dorchester neighborhood of Boston—names like Gonsalves, Delverde, Contarino, Rabinovitz, Robertson—they also honor the service of those who gave their lives from the Republic of Vietnam. If individual identities were known, family names like Nguyen, Do, Tran, Quach, and Pham would also be etched here in granite.

In the central circle of the Dorchester Vietnam veterans memorial, four large granite benches show the regions where each of the U.S. I–IV Corps military forces established operations. Inscribed on the benches with map outlines are names like Chu Lai, Nha Trang, Tay Ninh, and Can Tho. Paul Camacho, a sociologist, Vietnam veteran, and research coordinator with the Joiner Center recently told me, "I like to go there and sit sometimes . . . when no one else is there . . . just sit for a minute when it's quiet. I really like those benches. Hey, I was in practically all those places."

The names of those areas in South and Central Vietnam where American men and women served have deep meaning for others in this neighborhood, too. The Asian population in Dorchester grew by nearly 750 percent in the 1980s. Most were Vietnamese, and their growth rate in the 1990s has continued. Often when I run or drive by the memorial, I notice offerings of yellow and red carnations arranged carefully at the base of the monument in the pattern of the flag of the former Republic of Vietnam, which many refugee and immigrant families still claim as their own. In recognizing the names of people and places, the memorial offers veterans and refugees connections to a shared past, just as they now live together in this neighborhood, sharing the present.

It is no coincidence that if one looks up from reading the names to gaze past the memorial's stone arches, the university campus comes into view. UMass Boston continues to enroll the highest percentage of both Vietnamese students and U.S. Vietnam-era veterans of any university in the Northeast region. Veterans, like refugees and immigrants, often take Asian American Studies courses, motivated by their own unspoken searchings, or based on recommendations within their informal but elaborate peer support networks, or simply to fulfill the university's diverse course graduation requirements. Whatever the reasons, our courses—like the memorial—offer an environment within which to recognize common traumas and shared destinies. Both populations sit side by side in classes, each struggling to rebuild lives and establish brighter futures for themselves and their families. *They are going on.*

In a recent Asian American Studies summer course, I took the class on a field trip, first to the segregated Chinese burial grounds at the Mt. Hope public cemetery in Boston and then to the Dorchester Vietnam veterans memorial. At the cemetery, we offered incense and bowed before the graves of Boston's early Asian immigrant pioneers who died alone here without the money or family support to have their bones returned to their motherlands. Witnessing the blatant exclusion and neglect experienced by those earlier generations of Asian immigrants, even after death, offers powerful educational lessons for the living (Kiang 1997).

Moving to the memorial, we then continued with rituals and reflections about peace and healing. A Korean international student offered a song about reconciliation, while a Japanese international student distributed origami cranes she had folded for the class. One of my teaching assistants then reflected with everyone about her family's experiences as survivors and victims of the atomic bomb in Hiroshima, which fell on that same date of 6 August, exactly fifty-two years earlier.

Our concluding ritual was to collectively recite Hiroshi Kashiwagi's poem, "A Meeting at Tule Lake," which he wrote in 1975 to honor a pilgrimage to the Tule Lake concentration camp where he and 18,000 other Japanese Americans had been incarcerated during World War II. In the poem, he asserts that it is right to return to Tule Lake to remember, to be witnesses, to tell the truth of what once happened.

As the summer air turned cooler, we huddled more intimately in a circle. Each of us took a turn to voice a few lines of the long poem—feeling Kashiwagi's intent and our own sense of purpose in being there. We ended together in unison:

> to meet, to share, to learn
> to struggle, to continue.
> I sense an immense feeling
> of continuity
> with
> you—all of you.
> Yes. It's right, it's right
> and I'm glad I came
> back to Tule Lake
> with you.

Following the field trip, one Vietnamese student reflected,

There are many students in class who were Vietnam veterans. There are also Vietnamese students in class whose parents were victims of the war. I hated it because I had to recall so many sad and negative images through videos, lectures, and books as well. There are too much that we've been through, too much that we were suffering for a long period of times. I feel homesick as I see them, like today at the memorial, sitting on those benches. They are something that I try not to remember deeply. However, this is a mixed feeling. If I don't remember the past, I won't be able to tell why I have to leave my homeland, I won't be able to figure out what I expect from myself while staying here to pay back to the sacrifices of my parents. . . . I think we all, as Asians, should know it, should make other people aware of it and remember it, like in the Tule Lake poem. We must remember and tell it; we must acknowledge it and tell it. . . .

IT'S RIGHT TO BE HERE—IT'S RIGHT TO TELL IT

Always take the curved road, if you can; only follow the straight road, if you have to.

—A Cambodian proverb

In reviewing my goals for this chapter, I had many points to make. If I were writing in a linear way, I would now conclude by re-emphasizing the importance of

recognizing one's context and history outside of the university, integrating political organizing strategies with a caring pedagogy in the classroom, not sacrificing
principles for status, and not neglecting or taking for granted the needs of those
who can most benefit from one's investment. But, fundamentally, I am arguing
that faculty of color play unique and desperately needed roles as facilitators of *healing* and *transformation* within universities and communities.

I could have stated the same point directly in a thesis paragraph at the beginning of this chapter. But instead, to reach this point—to say that it is right to be
here—I have traced a curved road. For aesthetic, cultural, and political reasons,
my writing process and product for this book hearken to a traditional Chinese
form (the "eight-legged essay" and comparable forms in other Asian cultures) in
which, if I wish to convey to a reader that the sunset is beautiful, I will never
directly state that the sunset is beautiful. Instead, it is my challenge and responsibility to offer stories, images, metaphors, and markers that indirectly but
inevitably lead one to feel, and therefore to know, without any doubt, that the
sunset is, indeed, beautiful.

So, what is really important to understand about faculty of color in U.S. universities? I am convinced that it is our unstated, undervalued, and constant commitments to facilitate healing and transformation. To illustrate this point and to
end this long, nonlinear story, I offer three additional examples of student voices
from the Asian American Studies summer course mentioned above. At the end
of the course, I asked students to write a letter in which they described something
specific and meaningful they had learned from the course to a real-life individual
important in their own lives. The first letter, by a Vietnamese refugee student, is
addressed to her childhood best friend:

Anh Dearest:
   Hi, how are you? How is school and your family and the restaurant? Everything is
fine with me and my family. You wouldn't believe what I did this summer. I signed up
for a class called Asian Minorities in America at the University of Massachusetts
Boston. I thought this course would be easy so I could kill some of my time, but oh
boy was I wrong. I learn more from this class than all the years of schooling that I
have had.
   You remember our first elementary class up to our high school years, we were never
once taught by anyone about Asians in America. We thought we had learned everything there was to be learn, but guess what? We haven't really learn anything. . . .
   There were a few classes that I could not withhold my tears. When I learn about
the Japanese internment camps, it remind me of the refugee camp that we were in
Indonesia. I remembered we shared the same piece of biscuit and each had only one
pair of clothes for three long months. Our lives then was no better than the Japanese
in the past. Do you see how Asians like us were being treated? Do you see that the
process keep on repeating.
   You know what? I cried most when the professor showed a video of a small boat
with some fifty people escaped from Vietnam and reading from "Lone Pink Fish"
about Vietnamese at sea. Pains rose within me when I saw the faces of those people

and the images that were described in the reading. I am crying now as I write this letter to you. If you seen or read them, you would cry too. I wasn't ready or prepared for such scenes. I tried so hard to bury the pain and hopelessness of the escape for years. I thought that my wounds had heal but when I watch the video and do the reading, I felt like someone had took a knife and slash the healing wound open again. I felt that my tears were no different from the blood that was running down from my wounds.

Although upset, I was glad that the professor showed the video and have such reading. If it wasn't for that, our struggles and hardships would forever remain silence and no one would ever understand what we had to go through.

I guess I should have done my final project on healing and celebrating, rather than defining home. It seems like that is what I need most. The last thing that forever stick in my head is when I went on the field trip to the cemetery and found Chinese graves were separated from the rest of the other race. Anh, can you believe that? Even after you die, you still get discriminated against. You should have seen those ruin graves. I know you would cry. Well, I had try to place an incense on each grave to show appreciation and to warm the dead souls wherever they might be.

Wouldn't it be nice if they had taught us all of these facts years ago. I would like to learn more about how Asian Americans like us today are being treated, wouldn't you? I want to learn more about the history of Asian Americans.

Anh, I hope all of these facts won't shock you. If you want to learn more about these issues, I suggest you move up to Boston instead of staying in Savannah all your life. Make sure you share these facts with your family, other friends, and future children, okay? Miss you very much, and I make sure I teach my children the same. See you soon!!!!

> With all my love,
> Your childhood friend

Others in the summer class who did not share refugee or immigrant backgrounds nevertheless found themselves unexpectedly but deeply engaged in a process of healing and transformation as well. An international student with visa status, for example, wrote a personal letter to her mother in Korea:

Dear Mom,

I know that our family is going through a tough time adjusting to the loss of my brother from a car accident two years ago in Boston. I know that you and dad think about him everyday and you always see something that reminds you of him. But I am taking this class, and this is nothing that I have expected before. I have learned lots of valuable experiences and also learned to be thankful to you for all the things that you have given me and I have taken granted.

Let me explain to you what the class is like. We talk about the roles of the Asian Americans living in the United States, trying to adjust and cope to a new environment. We also talk about racism and discrimination which people experience. One important thing which I have learned is that you can learn from a loss or a tragic experience. For example, there are lots of people in the class who are from Cambodia or Vietnam who came here as a refugee and boat people. They are much less fortunate than I am. They experienced people dying and starving on the boat right next to them. But they seem to use this bad experience into a positive energy. Now, they try harder at what they are doing and try to the best of their ability.

Another example is that they are believing in what they are saying. The class is very powerful and very personal. We often have people cry in class because we are discussing about something that is very personal to each of the individual and they can relate to the hard experiences.

We never talk about my brother's death and the feelings we have and how much we all miss him. But from the class, I learned that it is good to cry and let your feelings out and to talk to someone is very helpful. I could never talk to anyone because it hurts so much, but after taking the class, I learned that it hurts much more not talking about it and just suppressing all my feelings to only myself.

So I think that I have learned many things from the class. Especially that I should be thankful to what I have and try to heal my feelings so that I am able to talk about it. So that I can turn this negative feeling into a positive energy which will help me in the future. So I think that you and I and dad should have a long talk when I go back to Korea during the break. I think it will be very helpful to both you and me. This class gave me the strength to write you this letter. . . . From this class, I think I am more able to cope with my problems or the problems which I will encounter in the future.

Finally, students in the summer class who were not Asian or Asian American also found meaningful connections to the themes of healing and transformation. Their voices and experiences also contributed significantly to the process, as illustrated in this short poem written by a Latina student for her classmates:

The Everlasting Struggle

For you and for me,
Your people, my people
Your race, my race
ONE

Together through history.
Fighting,
Challenging,
Healing,
And
Celebrating.

Let us rejoice
and continue
to overcome . . .

I WANT TO COME AGAIN

Interestingly, those three students were actually enrolled at other local universities—an Ivy League school, a private liberal arts college, and a private music college—but were taking Asian American Studies at UMass Boston during the summer because their own schools did not offer comparable courses. The profound connections they were able to make with themes of healing and transformation, despite not being UMass Boston students, suggest that faculty of color who *educate for life* are needed in many settings beyond their own individual campuses.

When I reflect on my own role within this particular time and space, when I critically analyze these narratives, flashbacks, and research agendas, when I honor these voices, pedagogies, and tears, I think of Trang and others like her, such as Sophorn, a Cambodian woman who graduated several years ago from UMass Boston with a major in sociology. Sophorn now works as a bilingual social worker and youth/family advocate. She will also soon become a mother herself. During the very first class trip to Mt. Hope cemetery several years ago, after most of us had completed our own rituals and reflections, we watched Sophorn who was moving from stone to stone, with great intensity and purpose, offering incense and bowing three times at each grave. When I asked her later what she had been thinking about during those moments, she responded, "My mom was killed in Cambodia, you know, and I never had a chance to say goodbye. I don't even know where she was buried. . . . I'm really glad we came here. It just helped me think about my mom, think about the past, you know. I didn't expect it, but I really felt connected. You should bring the class here every year. I want to come again."

Yes. It is right to be here.

I promise. We will come again.

I know this story has not been easy to follow. I know it is intensely personal. I know it is still far from finished. But it is real and not only my own. And throughout this process—of writing and reflecting, of teaching and learning—the voice of another Vietnamese student, Mai, also still echoes purposefully inside me. Mai is now a bilingual counselor and mother of two children. But nearly ten years ago, at the conclusion of an interview for my dissertation research, Mai resolved, "My dream is just to help the new people aware of what is going on here in this society. They need to get involved in fighting for their beliefs, I mean what they think is right for justice and equality. You know, set up the program or help the younger generation to go on, like get higher education and help their people. That's all I can do."

Yes. Mai is right. In the end, healing and transformation must intersect with justice and equality. We have many legacies to uphold and more pathways to create.

We must go on.

NOTES

All names of students in this essay are pseudonyms.

1. Asian American Studies is an interdisciplinary academic field that documents and interprets the history, identity, social formation, contributions, and contemporary concerns of Asian and Pacific Americans and their communities in the United States. Asian

American Studies has institutional roots nationally in both the campus ethnic studies movements of the late 1960s and the efforts to diversify the curriculum amid sweeping demographic changes of the 1980s and 1990s.

2. The phrase "east of California" is used both informally and officially within the national Asian American Studies field to challenge assumptions that curricular content, pedagogical strategies, programmatic models, and research agendas within Asian American Studies must follow the traditional paradigms and practices of California-based universities, where the field has been historically institutionalized.

3. The "target-of-opportunity" program is a specific affirmative action strategy that I strongly support and acknowledge with appreciation.

4. Bill Joiner died from liver cancer, a disease associated with exposure to Agent Orange, which is consistent with his tour of duty in Guam, where he loaded hundreds of drums of Agent Orange for deployment in Vietnam.

5. *Makibaka* means "to struggle" in Tagalog.

REFERENCES

Arches, J., M. Darlington-Hope, J. Gerson, J. Gibson, S. Habana-Hafner, and P. N. Kiang. 1997. New Voices in University-Community Transformation. *Change* 29, no. 1: 36–41.

Boyer, E. L. 1990. *Scholarship Reconsidered*. The Carnegie Foundation for the Advancement of Teaching. San Francisco: Jossey-Bass.

Glassick, C. E., M. Taylor Huber, and G. I. Maeroff. 1997. *Scholarship Assessed*. An Ernest L. Boyer Project of the Carnegie Foundation for the Advancement of Teaching. San Francisco: Jossey-Bass.

hooks, b. 1996. *Teaching to Transgress*. New York: Routledge.

Kashiwagi, H. 1980. A Meeting at Tule Lake. In *Kinenhi: Reflections on Tule Lake*, ed. Tule Lake Committee, 58–59. San Francisco: Tule Lake Committee.

Kiang, P. N. 1985. Transformation: The Challenge for the Asian American Artist in the 1980's. *East Wind* 4, no. 1: 31–33.

———. 1988. The New Wave: Developing Asian American Studies on the East Coast. In *Reflections through Windows of Shattered Glass*, ed. Gary Y. Okihiro, Shirley Hune, Arthur Hansen, and John M. Liu, 43–50. Pullman: Washington State University Press.

———. 1991. About Face: Recognizing Asian and Pacific American Vietnam Veterans in Asian American Studies. *Amerasia Journal* 17, no. 3: 22–40.

———. 1992. Issues of Curriculum and Community for First-Generation Asian Americans in College. In *First-Generation Students Confronting the Cultural Issues*, ed. Howard B. London and L. Stephen Zwerling, 97–112. New Directions for Community Colleges, 80. San Francisco: Jossey-Bass.

———. 1993. Stratification of Public Higher Education. In *Bearing Dreams, Shaping Visions*, ed. Linda A. Revilla, Gail M. Nomura, Shawn Wong, and Shirley Hune, 233–45. Pullman: Washington State University Press.

———. 1995a. Bicultural Strengths and Struggles of Southeast Asian American Students. In *Culture and Difference: Critical Perspectives on the Bicultural Experience in the United States*, ed. Antonia Darder, 201–25. New York: Bergin and Garvey.

————.1995b. From Different Shores Again. In *Revisioning Asian America: Locating Diversity*, ed. Wendy L. Ng, Gary Y. Okihiro, Soo-Young Chin, and James S. Moy, 207–11. Pullman: Washington State University Press.

————. 1996a. Persistence Stories and Survival Strategies of Cambodian Americans in College. *Journal of Narrative and Life History* 6, no. 1: 39–64.

————. 1996b. Southeast Asian and Latino Parent Empowerment: Lessons from Lowell, Massachusetts. In *Education Reform and Social Change: Multicultural Voices, Struggles, and Visions*, ed. Catherine E. Walsh, 59–69. Mahwah, N.J.: Lawrence Erlbaum Associates.

————. 1997. Pedagogies of Life and Death: Transforming Immigrant/Refugee Students and Asian American Studies. *Positions* 5, no. 2: 529–55.

————. 1998. We Could Shape It: Organizing for Asian Pacific American Student Empowerment. In *Cherished Dreams: Educating Asian Pacific American Children*, ed. Li-Rong Lilly Cheng and Valerie Ooka Pang. Albany: State University of New York Press.

Kiang, P. N., and J. Kaplan. 1994. Where Do We Stand: Views of Racial Conflict by Vietnamese American High School Students in a Black-and-White Context. *The Urban Review* 26, no. 2: 95–119.

Kiang, P. N., and V. W. Lee. 1982. *Our Roots in History*. Boston: Asian American Resource Workshop.

Kiang, P. N., and M. C. Ng. 1989. Through Strength and Struggle: Boston's Asian American Student/Community/Labor Solidarity. *Amerasia Journal* 15, no. 1: 285–93.

Le Espiritu, Y. 1993. *Asian American Panethnicity*. Philadelphia: Temple University Press.

Loo, C. 1994. Race-Related Trauma and PTSD: The Asian American Vietnam Veteran. *Journal of Traumatic Stress* 7: 1–20.

————. 1998. Treatment Issues and Approaches for Race-Related Events. In *Report on the Working Group on Asian Pacific Islander Veterans*, ed. Readjustment Counseling Services, 61–71. Washington, D.C.: Department of Veterans Affairs.

Lynton, E. A. 1995. *Making the Case for Professional Service*. Washington, D.C.: American Association for Higher Education.

Padilla, F. M. 1997. *The Struggle of Latino/a University Students*. New York: Routledge.

Tinto, V. 1987. *Leaving College: Rethinking the Causes and Cures of Student Attrition*. Chicago: University of Chicago Press.

8

Disabling Institutions, Irreconcilable Laws

Concha Delgado-Gaitan

Journaling has been an integral part of my ethnographic research process, a practice that actually began during my high school days. Those days it was a means of maintaining a private identity apart from my parents, siblings, and friends. Later, journaling provided a strategy to gain critical insights about my community fieldwork activities. In my academic research, reflective journaling is an integral part of data collection and tracking where my personal feelings intersected. Little did I know that, as a senior professor at the University of California (UC) at Davis, I would become afflicted with a disabling illness and once again my daily journaling would be the instrument to assist me in making sense of my experience.

Gradually, my physical strength and ability to remain active as a professor diminished. Writing personal reflective narratives enhanced my understanding of the power relations between myself and the university that shaped my identities as a learner and educator. With my journal as my companion, I recognized how my subjective and objective realities became one. Fundamentally, I learned that while I relied on the support of my family, friends, and cultural values to strengthen me and to overcome the illness and retain my position as a professor at UC, the university did not consider my needs; instead, it dealt with my situation only according to its interpretation of the Americans with Disability Act—the bureaucratic law. This was not the first time I had experienced discontinuity between myself and the one institution I trusted.

Schools have played a central part in every aspect of my life. It has been a bittersweet relationship of finding independence, achievement, and a place to learn. At every stage of playing school, the power of knowledge left its imprint on my identity first as an immigrant child eager to embrace everything that education offered, then as an immigrant woman working in the ranks of educational institutions. Boundaries between school and the rest of my life became nearly impossible to discern.

A SCHOOL OF OPPORTUNITY

My parents were international migrants from Mexico and had no opportunity to attend school in either country. When I was a young school-aged child, my parents impressed on me and my sisters the value of schooling and education in general.[1] I both feared and loved school: Although I faced unjust ridicule for not speaking English, the school also provided novelty. Memories still haunt me of spending almost my first entire year at Victoria Elementary School with my head down on my desk at recess because the teacher believed in punishing me for not speaking English.[2] My parents instructed me in ways to overcome adversity; they taught me to appreciate the support of family and friends, to work hard, and to learn all that I could. I relied on these pearls and internalized them as my inner strength—my cultural law. Initial ridicule and prejudice for belonging to a different culture and language group gave way to serious work and a commitment to learn everything I could, in and out of school.

With that determination, at the age of nineteen, I walked through the doors of a second grade classroom at Boggs Track Elementary School in Stockton—this time, as a new elementary teacher. Then, I moved to the Bay Area where I continued working in schools and communities, maintaining my identity as learner. My relationship to my students and the communities where I taught changed me just as much as I am sure I influenced them. Political consciousness was inevitable for anyone teaching in the early 1970s in inner cities. Teaching became a platform to protest segregation, poverty, and the Vietnam War. Schools were both friends and enemies of the communities, and as a teacher I worked for the children and their families.[3] Poor communities were beginning to find their voice and express their disquiet about the failure of schools to teach their children. As a teacher whose professional training underscored that I was the change agent, I joined with the families who proposed complete change to demand the quality of education their children deserved.

My disenchantment with schools and administrators became reason enough to join the leadership ranks. At the age of twenty-eight, I became an elementary school principal, the first woman hired in the south Bay Area district of twenty-six schools. I made it my goal to become the kind of leader that would increase the educational opportunities for poor children. Once again, although my professional role and title changed, my identity as an educator remained unquestioned. My leadership style was democratic but aggressive, and in a few short years I yearned for more time to reflect on the myriad of questions that crossed my mind daily (I had no time to research while I was a principal).

Thirsty for critical reflection, I returned to Stanford for my Ph.D. A career in academia had never been a life-long dream. In fact, as a doctoral student at Stanford, I adamantly rejected the idea of becoming a professor. But my passion for solving a good mystery led to a pursuit of scholarly agendas in research, opportunities typically housed in the bastion of a university.

A NEW LEARNING EMERGES

I was a senior professor at UC Davis, moving fast in my ethnographic field research, publication, and teaching and thick in the university politics. A sudden onset of a debilitating illness that was diagnosed as Systemic Lupus gradually rendered me physically disabled to the point at which I could no longer remain active as a senior professor. In spite of the objective evidence of my health condition, I forged ahead with an insatiable tenacity, attempting to accommodate the physical restrictions visible from the beginning of the illness. My situation was reminiscent of the one-eyed man in the valley of the blind—a story by H. G. Wells that I assigned my class as reading in a graduate seminar. "The Country of the Blind" is a story about a community that has been blind for fourteen generations.[4] They have been cut off from all the sighted world. Names for all the things people could see had faded and changed. They created a new culture, a new language, with new imagination through other senses that became more sensitive. A partially sighted man is lost and finds himself in the country of the blind. He believes that he is superior to them because he is sighted, but in time, he learns to appreciate their life as they convince him that their lives are just as complete without sight. In my newly unfolding experience, I had become part of the blind community and attempted to learn to perform my work as a disabled person. I attempted to convince the university that although I had become physically disabled, I was still a capable professor. My circumstances required specific modifications at the university in the scheduling and the size of my classes, transportation to buildings on campus, and so on.

Away from the university, I conducted fieldwork in Mexican immigrant and Russian refugee communities in Northern and Southern California. Other research collaborations and invited speaking engagements in Alaska, Mexico, and Spain also kept me traveling, but transporting myself to my research sites was a tremendous effort. Even with good research assistants, I begin to feel the strain of traveling, conducting interviews, making demanding observations, and writing. I tried to keep up with the demands of the university, but the fatigue and pain increased, which required more and more time to recuperate after every activity. Canceling research trips and invited lectures became common practice.

Traveling to communities around the country to conduct research decreased, while chasing after miracle therapies and cures accelerated. I experimented with chiropractics, megavitamin therapies, macrobiotic diet, a KM nutritional supplemental diet, yoga, hands-on psychic healing, faith healers, mineral baths, *curanderismos* (Mexican healers), visual imagery, and inspirational lectures. Loved ones gave me ample ideas and suggestions as my abundant tenacity pursued them. However, except for superficial benefits, all endeavors had limited effects.

The implacable reality of my physical identity mirrored my work at the university. A person's ordinary social roles all become temporarily suspended when he or she falls ill.[5] In my case, each passing day required more time for me to get ready to go to work and demanded new energy determined by the changing nature of every new activity. Before I became ill, my fast-paced daily routine could out run the best of them. I could jump out of bed, wash up, throw on my jogging suit, run out the door, do my power walk, run home, jump in the shower, dress, grab a nutritional bar, and drive to work all in the span of an hour. Now, the pace was drastically impeded. I woke up two-and-a-half hours before leaving just to fit in my meditation, go through my physical stretch and strengthening workout, boil my herbs, shower, and eat a hot breakfast, only to feel like I wanted to return to bed; instead I forced myself out the door.

My uncharacteristic late arrival to meetings became a pattern. Mentally, I still operated under the time framework I knew in my former "normal" body identity.[6] I relied on the vanpool for transportation to campus; the van stop was a few blocks from my home. It departed at 7:45 a.m. Ridding the vanpool worked for a while, on days that I could get out the door in time.

Stubbornly, I insisted on maintaining my full-time teaching load, advising students, conducting field research, writing proposals, attending meetings, and publishing. I felt smug. I could defy the illness like I could other physical adversities in the past. It had not defeated me in spite of the medical complications and time delays I faced daily. Everyone encouraged me to keep fighting. I interpreted this as meaning that if I stopped working hard, both at the university and on my healing, that I would be a failure. Fearing that I would never get up again, I maintained my frantic pace. My fear kept my drive alive. I resisted learning how and why I should possibly concern myself with the body. I harbored a fantasy that soon a miracle would materialize.

In January 1992, my symptoms intensified. Dr. Brown, my rheumatologist had warned me that an exacerbation of my condition would mean an increase in medications. My reluctance to submit to increased medical treatment kept me focused on getting stronger. All the while I feared the side effects that medications caused. I was in my office at the university on the day the doctor called me to recommend stronger dosages of steroids and immune suppressants (chemotherapy). What did this mean now? When would all of this end? I wanted my good health restored without chemical intervention. Nervous and scared, I attempted to read my mail, but the phone rang and interrupted. It was Dr. Castaño from Granada, Spain. He and other scholars from the Laboratory of Anthropology at the University of Granada read my books. They invited me to lecture in their summer institute in September that year. I loved lecturing abroad. I explained to them that I could not commit myself to much these days because of serious health problems. They empathized and assured me that the pace would be comfortable for the two weeks. I would teach the topic of international migration with four other international scholars from European universities who would co-teach the seminar with me. Without further deliberation, I agreed to go to Granada in the late summer. A soft voice within me assured me that this was a good omen.

"Great, that gives us a goal to work with. We'll get you stronger by September," exclaimed Dr. Brown. This encouraged me. I was now proficient in asking questions about medications and other therapies. My greatest curiosity was how and why immune suppressants worked differently for Lupus patients as compared with cancer patients. About the time I began chemotherapy, Lukeran, and increased dosages of steroids, a friend of mine had a mastectomy. She received the same drugs. Lukeran and other immune suppressants are sometimes administered to some Lupus patients when steroids alone are ineffective. Immune suppressants helped to control the inflammation by shutting down the immune system. In effect, the system can cease producing antibodies and strengthen itself. The heavy dosages administered to cancer patients were divided into daily dosages. Along with the daily oral chemo, I took with steroids other nonsteroid drugs and handfuls of herbs.

A chemical taste camped in my mouth day and night. Even the tastiest foods failed to eliminate the taste of medications. Thank goodness the Bay Area has a great selection of different international food restaurants—all near my house. The taste of flat chemical in my mouth suppressed my appetite. This sent me on a daily hunt for food with strong distinct tastes in hopes of erasing the metal taste in my mouth. On my way home from campus, doctors' appointments, lab work, or hydrotherapy, I might stop at a Vietnamese restaurant: "An order of sauté chicken with garlic sauce."

"White rice?"

"No thanks."

The next day I might go Mexican: "Chile verde and extra salsa for the beans."

"No rice?"

"No rice, thanks."

Another day I wanted Indian cuisine: "Hot curry chicken and roti, please."

"It comes with white rice."

"No rice, thanks."

A special favorite was Szechwan and garlic eggplant.

"You get rice too."

"No, thanks."

Rice muted the spices and I could not allow anything to interfere with my antidote for the metal taste of medications.

Committed to feeling well, I welcomed each morning with hopeful anticipation that the day would bring a miraculous remission. Morning rituals now included longer prayers before leaving for campus, as well as every night after my writing. I prayed that I would get well just like I did as a child: "I need to feel good, I want my health. Release me from this hell! Give me the money to pay the pile of medical bills that are mounting by the day totaling hundreds of dollars each month." Expenses related to medical care exceeded hundreds of dollars monthly with no relief in sight. Chronic conditions are a financial nightmare with constant doctor visits, lab work, and physical, herbal, and hydrotherapy.[7] I wanted my life back the way it was, *now*! These demanding outbursts expected this God or a

Goddess to remove my pain. My supplications went unanswered—the problem persisted with a vengeance.

Something was wrong. What good did faith do me? Even prayer failed. I, nevertheless, appreciated more than ever the little things family and friends did for me.

ADJUSTING

Contrary to the caring gestures from loved ones, the bureaucratic obstacles on campuses were most unfriendly! My ability to walk long distances at the university to teach my classes became increasingly impaired. The quarter when I first fell ill, I did not need a ride to my class from my office because the registrar's office assigned me to classrooms adjacent to the building where I had an office. I could walk with my cane and pace myself to arrive on time for class. However, the subsequent quarter, I was assigned to a classroom across the campus; it took me almost half an hour of fast rigorous walking to get to my classroom. I called the office in charge of transporting students with physical injuries to class. Evidently, the small carts that transported students with temporary physical injuries was a student service governed by an office financed from student fees and unavailable to professors. I was informed that I had to supply my own transportation to class no matter how disabled I was.

The administrator in that transportation office informed me, "We can give you a ride to your class for a couple of times, but we can't do it for a long term."

"I may need it for an indefinite time."

"Well, when will you be well?" she asked.

"I wish I could answer that question for you, but even my doctors don't know. Meanwhile, I have to teach my class which is a twenty-minute brisk walk from my office."

She responded, "Well, have your administrator send us a letter. I'll present it to our director and we'll get back to you."

Lengthy letters from my division administrators finally persuaded the office of disability transportation to provide services for the remainder of that winter quarter, conditioned on my calling the office each morning before 9:00 a.m. to confirm my ride. Special permission to get handicap transportation ended with the quarter. Their policy no longer permitted me to get a ride to class. The situation worsened the following quarter, when the transportation service refused to transport me to class and claimed that my insurance company was responsible for paying for transporting me from my office to my classroom. The university had no answer for this complaint except to tell me that my insurance company had to provide for my transportation. When I conveyed this to my insurance company, they laughed as they reminded me that the university was responsible for making the necessary accommodations so that I could successfully conduct my work. Not only was I burdened with taking care of my health, but I was forced to make my own arrangements in order to perform my work. I found it increasingly inconve-nient to take the vanpool to the university because I was too fatigued to remain on campus a full day, which was their schedule. This forced me to get on my fore-arm crutches and then drive myself to the different buildings on campus where I had meetings and where I was assigned to teach.

This was only the beginning of the turmoil about classes that ensued every sub-sequent quarter. Inevitably, I was always assigned to teach in classrooms that were located long distances from my office and designated class hours impossible to meet because I felt too debilitated to get up very early in the mornings or stay late enough in the day on campus to teach. Most quarters I fought with the adminis-tration about appropriate scheduling of my classes up to the last minute before class began. This impeded students from taking my course because time and place were often undetermined until the first week of class.

It baffled me that the bureaucratic wheels of the university expected me to find my own transportation to class and forced me to fight for a convenient location and class time. Part of the university's hypocrisy that hurt me during this period was the designation of a special week to call attention to people with disabilities.[8] During that week, they held daily activities including noon-time competitions, in which people who were not necessarily disabled held wheelchair races. "No expe-rience necessary" read the notice inviting participants. A student on the staff of the university student paper contacted me to interview me about my dealings with the university services, given my disability. Weeks passed and the student changed her appointment with me many times until she stopped calling me and stopped returning my calls. What irony! Maybe she knew that I had a rather dismal report about the university's services for disabled professors.

Once the quarter began and I got myself to the designated classroom, I also had to figure out a way to be heard. Teaching large classes of almost 100 students posed more problems than getting transportation to the classroom. Scarcity of funds granted me only a one-quarter time reader. Except for the grading of one minor midterm exam, I ended up doing all of the teaching and grading, as well as lead-ing the weekly discussion groups for my class. More challenges presented them-selves in the classroom. Because my voice had become so weak, I had requested a microphone from the center in charge of equipment, but they could not provide one. They claimed that it took too long to set up and dismantle the equipment and other classes used the same classroom. And so, I stood in front of 100 students without a microphone, trying to manage with the inadequate accommodations. Students became increasingly impatient when I became inaudible and unable to project my voice as my lung muscles debilitated more. My bronchial problems were further complicated as I strained to be heard. Too debilitated to fight the uni-versity, instead I sought the services of the Teacher Resource Center. A consul-tant, Wini, assisted me in my classes by signaling to me when my voice had dropped to the point of becoming inaudible. It was on me to put forth the extra effort to make myself heard.

I was short of breath, with diminishing strength, and finding that I found it increasingly difficult to pace back and forth to hold my students' attention, as I was accustomed to doing. Students complained that I was not lecturing as much as they wanted, and they resented having to hold discussion groups. "This is a waste of time," students commented, "We can't learn from other students."

Feeling more frustrated than I had ever been in my teaching career, I talked with colleagues and friends at the university about ways to remedy the problems that burgeoned from every direction. At the Teacher Resource Center, Wini, one of the specialists, was a refreshing support. She helped me to review the changes I had made in order to succeed in my classroom, given my changing circumstances. We worked very systematically to put everything in writing for students because I had to conserve my voice as much as possible for the lecture. I met with Wini before the quarter began and we reviewed my syllabus. Wini and I planned well-organized small group discussion sessions, and she attended all of my classes to monitor whether my lectures were audible and whether the variety of student activities were well managed.

In spite of my efforts to ensure high quality in my teaching in the face of my immobility, by the beginning of the spring, students' complaints were more commonplace. They were impatient that I could not move the class at the faster pace they expected. They were right in that my voice dragged, I had to pause frequently, and I sat in front of the class because I could not walk back and forth as I had before. Nonetheless, their complaints felt cruel when they showed up in my office with comments like,

> You're too disorganized, and I need an "A" in this class because I don't want this course to ruin my grade point average.
> I got a "B+" in my midterm and I need an "A." You need to present the lecture in an outline form we can follow.
> My paper is an "A" paper and you gave me an "A−." My mother edited it for me, and if you don't change my grade, I'll make a formal complaint.

In my fifteen years of teaching university students, they had never complained so much about my teaching. I felt totally incompetent especially because a couple of colleagues made me their target just as the students had. They viciously criticized me to other students and to colleagues. They believed that I was not a good teacher. Other colleagues in the division had a more holistic perspective about my work because I continued a successful productive pace in my research and publication in spite of my affliction. Feeling more frustrated than ever, I questioned my ability to maintain my academic career along with everything else in life.

One student's visit stands out in my mind as a message that I had to keep going. A Vietnamese student from my undergraduate class on the social and philosophical foundations of education came to me during office hours. I had little energy to sit up and talk to students by 2:00 p.m., but this student's visit was a real gift to me. He introduced himself as a senior student in engineering. He was an immigrant from Vietnam: "I came to talk with you because in class you're always talking about how important it is for students and professors to work together and break down barriers. I've never talked to any of my professors, and so I came to try it and see how it feels."

"And how does it feel?"

"It's OK, I'm not nervous."

"Tell me how you got interested in engineering."

We talked for a while as he shared a moving story about his family's life in this country and their value of education. His visit eased my feelings of incompetence and restored a bit of my confidence.

Evenings at home were a battleground. Would I surrender to demanding academic work or to total collapse? Some days I did both: after a brief few minutes of rest, I forced myself to work until my concentration declined and I fell asleep at my computer.

Working was often preferable because it was a way of feeling competent. When I stopped to rest or listen to music, it required just as much concentration to focus away from my body. However, friends recorded favorite music, which I played sometimes to transcend the pain momentarily. The various pieces affected my mood differently. "Ode to Joy" made me feel calm, as did Steven Pasero's classical guitar. Mexican guitar, like that of El Mariachi del Sol, boosted my energy a bit, but the boost was brief. A friend at the pool where I went for hydrotherapy gave me a tape with favorite vocals like Violeta Parra's "Gracias a la Vida," Streisand's "Memory," Bette Miller's "Wind beneath My Wings," and the Beatles' "There Are Places I Remember" and Sara Vaughn's "Prelude to a Kiss." I was lost in song and words that for selected minutes penetrated deeper than the pain. My delightful music interlude ended with the audiotape as my consciousness returned to the familiar body fatigue, pain, and distress and the thought of work.

Even a new building did not help my situation. The Division of Education was moved to a new temporary building in the 1993 academic year. The building looked like a postmodern shopping mall with all of the false signs of sensitivity to physically disabled people. Specifically, the new building had signs indicating access for "disabled" persons. And, although a ramp existed for wheelchairs to enter the building, there was no access to the restroom. It took two years before the university would install a push-button door in the bathroom that enabled me to enter without further public degradation.

The frustration continued: the doors to offices in the building were fire retardant for the purpose of securing people during a fire, but their weight was too much. Unfortunately, when I attempted to enter the bathroom I was unable to open the door, and I humiliated myself by pounding on the heavy fire retardant door with my cane until a staff member came to assist me.

The mechanics of getting to do my work on campus stressed me, from getting to class, to raising my voice to conduct class, to getting into the restroom. This made me appreciate my home even more. Family and friends called regularly to check on me to remind me that they loved me.

One evening the phone rang. "Concha," came the familiar child's voice, my niece Nikkie. "I got a certificate for best speller in my class today."

"That's great Nikkie, what did you spell?"

"The words I spelled *enormous* and *meticulous*. The other kids couldn't spell them."

"Congratulations dear!"

"What do those two words mean?"

"I've got to look at my list, bye."

Nikkie's call reminded me that my loved ones were the best medicine throughout this ordeal.[9] In spite of the unconditional love that my family and friends extended, the moment-to-moment struggle was mine. At times the external challenges paled in comparison with the inner strife.

In dreams, I saw myself dancing down the same path where I once walked one-hour every morning. I danced gracefully in a long flowing gown, and I awakened feeling so encouraged, thinking, "I will walk again!" My personal journal was privileged to my excruciating pain, which I could not share with others because I felt too much shame to admit how I was being devastated by my illness. My fear of admitting to having this illness was intense. If I admitted to feeling so ill I might make it real. Because there was no known cure, I felt horribly vulnerable, believing that my body might be held hostage forever. My compensatory skills enabled me to maintain a semblance of a normal life as I managed to perform my work by exerting my body. I made bargains with it like agreeing to rest as much as possible on the days when I did not teach or to spend more time with my loved ones. In total, I was unwilling to surrender to my body's cry.

Just keeping the body from totally collapsing required every ounce of mental and physical stamina I could evoke. So I knew that I must help myself as much as possible by getting more rest, more drugs, more physical therapy, and more hydrotherapy. My full attention was on doing whatever I could to place one foot in front of the other. The body had my full attention like never before. The unrelenting physical inconveniences made this a surreal reality unlike anything I had ever faced.[10]

LOSING PERSPECTIVE

Unable to rely on my memory, every meeting with students, colleagues, or research participants required me to write down each time, place and directions to a meeting, and the person's name, title, and physical characteristics. Added to the physical impairment, my increasing memory loss extended the time I spent on every piece of work. Keeping up with research and university business became impossible. Reading, which had once been an effortless and defining activity of my work, quickly became a grueling act. Everything required at least three to five readings to decipher the meaning. On one occasion a colleague came into my office and showed me a published article. She asked me to read it and give my opinion. She came into my office flustered and asked me to read the first page of the article, "Look at this, just read the first page and tell me if this isn't an outrageous line of thinking." I read it slowly, but even then I could not make sense of it because meanings of words eluded me. I asked her to forgive me for the delay, and I continued reading and rereading. Feeling embarrassed and confused, I asked her, "What exactly do you disagree with?" She explained it to me. I could hardly hear her, I was so preoccupied with my concentration and comprehension problem.

My once loved research and teaching became painstaking. Spontaneity was suspended as classes took the form of lectures that I had written out one word at a time. This was appalling because I had always scoffed at passive lecturing as inadequate pedagogy. When I began doing this, it did not feel natural, but I could not help myself. I carefully wrote out every word and armed myself to bombard the class with a recitation of words that sounded more meaningless as days passed. I felt myself becoming increasingly dependent on reading every letter verbatim from my notes. This ritual was accompanied by intense fear, which overwhelmed me when I taught. When students asked questions, I feared not knowing the answer. This was totally foreign because my philosophy had always been that no right and wrong answers exist in any discourse. In my classes, we critically explored issues, and suddenly my twenty-eight years of experience in the field failed me as a resource. Frustration complicated my fear, as I tried to remember common facts, names, dates, and titles of common sources that I had always had at my finger tips. "Maybe there's something wrong, but I can't tell anyone": I could not bear to confirm that this insidious illness was complicating more areas of my body and my work. The shame was more than I could bear. I proceeded with my daily routine hoping that maybe I was just stressed. I questioned my competence, but no one could know. My compensatory strategies were well in place. I consciously tried to divert attention to this new development. Friends teased me about being in a profession in which absent-mindedness was just as accepted as sharp intelligence.

I remained focused on doing my work as best I could in hopes that this nightmare would pass. Work felt so distant and grueling that my desire to heal shifted in purpose. I wanted time to re-create with my loved ones. Everything else seemed more work than I had ever done. All of my time was consumed with doctor appointments, medications, and therapies. This in addition to my academic work cramped my life with no respite.

The increasing memory loss made it more imperative to follow a predictable routine. Months after my initial diagnosis, Dr. Brown recommended that I work out in a heated pool rather than doing weight-bearing exercises. Getting to the heated pool daily was necessary, although it consumed three hours of my time in the late afternoon and evening.

RE-CREATING

By summer 1992, my desperate attempts to strengthen mentally and physically rewarded me. Granada and Madrid finally became a reality. I was able to travel to my destination. I had recovered a great deal of my ability to concentrate and recall. However, I realized that I wrote my lectures verbatim just as I had done months earlier in my university classes when I could not remember. This amounted to many reams of pages, which I had to pack and carry overseas. I complained to a friend that I had to translate all of my lectures for Spain.

"You're creating too much work for yourself," he observed.

"I have to be prepared," I explained

"You're an expert in the field, why are you so preoccupied with these lectures?"

Fear filled my chest, and suddenly the idea of forgetting something tormented me. My confidence had eroded so that it felt necessary to write out everything. Before, I actually did not remember concepts, ideas, and names, among other things. By the time I left for Spain, I felt I had regained about 70 percent of my short- and long-term memory, but I distrusted myself. I had worked rigorously to train myself to use language and memory in a concentrated way. Every moment was a test in which I would force myself to reconstruct words. I wrote lists of words I heard around me when I did not know the meaning. It hurt that my efforts to remember on demand were still strained.

A strenuous flight, lectures, meetings, and travel weakened me considerably, but, overall, I was pleased that I did not totally collapse as my loved ones dreaded. They feared I might regress and reverse the progress I had gained prior to my departure to Spain. I felt confident that maybe I had beaten this illness after all.

Fall quarter classes begin with new expectation in a new building where our division had been moved. We were now located almost on the outskirts of campus near the hog barns. My colleagues commiserated with me on their feeling of isolation from the rest of campus. Although this was a new building, the place resembled a large, cold, and impersonal shopping mall with long hallways and office doors that were designed to remain shut. My ability to stand and teach two classes was applauded by my colleagues who had seen me make great strides. According to lab tests, I was now in remission. I, too, wanted to remain convinced that the illness had passed. I still felt it was up to me. Maybe if I took care of myself, I could remain in complete remission. But in mid-October, a bronchial infection ended my brief week of respite. I was in trouble again and saddened by the continued uncertainty this illness brought. Unpaid bills multiplied, and a routine of doctor visits, medications, and hydrotherapy consumed my day. I stubbornly continued to teach and perform full-time university work in a building that separated me from the center of campus. Just as before, I was immobile, and the university now refused to provide shuttle service for me to classes from this new building because it was not on their route. This I remembered.

Since the onset of the illness, in my dreams I always appeared dancing and walking until the prospect of using a wheelchair became real. One night my nightmare seemed lifelike. Someone pushed me into a wheelchair and told me I could not get out of it. After futile efforts, the chair rolled down a corridor out of control. I could not see where it was going. My screams went unheard. I woke up hyperventilating in panic! These feelings surprised me. I attempted to make sense of this new development. "Scared" and "out of control" describe my feelings well, as I was trapped in my fear of confinement to a wheelchair.

I held onto the prescription as long as I could, wondering if I really needed it and expecting to make a miraculous recovery any minute. Ordering a wheelchair was more of an ordeal than I ever imagined. Above the $1,000 payment to the insurance company as a copayment for hardware, the hassles of insurance paperwork required from the neurologist and me consumed complete days at every step.

The salesman in my home asked, "What color do you want your wheelchair?"

"Color?" I asked. "I thought wheelchairs were all black."

"Not anymore, here's your selection."

Once we decided on the style and its measurements, the salesman spread out a leaflet of colors from which I could select a color. I saw magenta, navy blue, light blue, teal, pink, forest green, and black. Apparently most of the wheelchair was black but part of the rail could be a different color.

"Teal, of course."

"You made a very quick selection."

"You've got to understand half of my wardrobe is teal. Can I have wheelchairs in three other colors?"

"Yes, if you're willing to pay for them."

"Teal will do, thanks."

My attitude strengthened with plenty of inner searching for a way to make my riding a wheelchair a comprehensible development in my healing. A trip around the long hallways in my office building at the university convinced me. I felt a great difference from having to walk the long stretches holding up my listless body on two forearm Canadian crutches. I was actually able to stay on campus an hour or so longer without collapsing.

The overwhelming storm of monthly medical bills for conventional and alternative medicine made me consider that I might just stop all medical treatment. In my frustration, I sat down and began to breathe deeply and meditated for inner guidance on how to deal with this problem. How could I pay all of these bills? No one believes that a full professorship at a University of California campus cannot pay medical expenses for all of the complications related to this illness. The insurance company refused to pay for any alternative medicine, including Chinese therapies, which helped me immensely. It paid only for a few sessions of acupuncture because it believed that acupuncture was for a short-term ailment. I found myself broke and angry about the cost of getting and staying well in this society. Although I could get around in my power wheelchair, I was still unable to work

at full capacity. Remaining functional required a strict regimen of physical therapies, drugs, herbs, acupuncture, and stress management to stay well. The time-
consuming routine prevented me from consulting for extra salary to pay for the
added expenses that depleted my savings.

NEW APPROACHES

Quarter after quarter, I looked forward to summers and sabbaticals in hopes of
replenishing my immune system with lots of deserved rest. In January 1995, I
returned from my sabbatical to teach two seminars. I taught a doctoral seminar
in Davis, and after the first day of class, I wondered how I could manage to hang
in till the end of the quarter. A surprising accolade, however, rescued that quarter. The Spencer Foundation selected me to receive one of the highest awards
given to senior scholars in my field. With the money they awarded me, I was
able to fund five doctoral students to pursue their research for two years. Part of
the gift stipulated that I continue my mentor work with graduate students. We
met regularly to discuss our respective research projects and our writing, but
mostly we shared the humorous and pointed life stories with which we kept our
ideas alive.

Winter and spring quarters, I was scheduled to teach a doctoral seminar for the
California State University (CSU) at Fresno doctoral cohort. Because I could no
longer fly down to Fresno on a regular basis as before, I experimented with Inter-
active Television (ITV). This was a tremendous advantage that enabled me to
teach my doctoral seminars at CSU Fresno without the commute. As I became
more conversant with technology, I frequently commented, "If one is disabled,
this is a great time in history to have it happen. Everything we need is available
on remote control." This was indicative of my attitude. For me, this meant that I
could drive a couple of miles to UC Berkeley and sit in a large room with a square
screen the size of a ten-foot wall. The technician instructed me how to work the
buttons for focus and volume. My students appeared life size on the screen. They
sat around a table, and I could see the full group together. They received the
reverse: my big face bigger than life on their screen. By the second week of class,
students had adjusted to the slight intimidation they felt in having to talk through
a camera. I, on the other hand, appreciated the technology of the ITV medium.
I was not nearly as stressed after hours of class as I always was when I drove one
hour to campus and taught a room full of students. Unfortunately, too many problems existed between UC Davis and UC Berkeley technologies, which prevented
me from teaching my UC Davis classes through ITV.

Experimenting with ITV spurred me to attempt a new physical therapy. In this
third phase of my healing, I noticed an inclination to move slower. I felt more
comfortable with quietness around me than ever before; in fact, I preferred to be
in serene settings rather than in large groups.

At this point, my bimonthly appointments with Dr. Brown consisted of an examination and a report I made on how I managed my daily activities—from physical to metaphysical—to help myself. My written report to Dr. Brown consisted of a list of activities that constituted my healing program.

1. Daily—REST, LOTS OF IT—reduced teaching load and working more time at home than office
2. Daily—hydrotherapy/pool
3. Daily—meditation
4. Daily—Chinese herbs
5. Daily—nutrition—mostly vegetarian
6. Weekly—physical therapy
7. Weekly—Chinese acupuncture

BEYOND EMPOWERMENT

In summer 1995, I returned from one of my summer trips to research and lecture in Alaska. My thoughts were no longer on worrying about what would happen to me or who would take care of me if I remained ill. Alaska always had a calming effect on me. A new potential crisis now claimed my attention. While I was trying to take care of myself so that I could continue performing my academic work, some unsupportive things began stirring at the workplace that admittedly upset me. I was outraged at some university colleagues who circulated a report stating that my leaves as a result of being ill contributed to people having to teach more than their official loads in the division. I retorted with a well-crafted letter, not so much in defense but as an explanation of the errors of the committee members in not considering my side of the problems in the division. They had failed to consult me with their concerns and neglected to mention my many efforts to continue performing my teaching and research, as well as my service to the university. By the time the report was issued, I had only taken one quarter of medical leave in five years, and the rest of the time my leaves had been sabbatical leaves to conduct my research and academic writing. Furthermore, even throughout my illness, I had taught full-time, with the additional burden of reinventing my classes to accommodate my disability, against all the odds that the university's obstacles had presented. And the truth was that no one had ever taught my doctoral classes during any of my sabbatical leaves. I sent thirty letters to various colleagues across campus who were involved in the design and distribution of that committee report. Not one person ever responded to my concerns and questions. The university's silence was another form of insensitivity to my situation. Nevertheless, I felt good that I had asserted my position about the matter; it helped to put things in perspective even if no one at the university accorded me the courtesy of a response.

My fourth academic book is on family and community literacy; *Protean Literacy: Extending the Discourse on Empowerment* was published in fall 1995.[11] This represented a culmination of a decade of academic research that was at the heart of my intellectual investment. With the publication of the book, I felt a sense of completion of a part of my academic career that I had loved but which had to change. I knew I had to alter my research approach. My former community-level ethnographic research, which demanded laborious time and techniques with heavy equipment, had to give way to projects that required more predictable and physically manageable hours and travel. The specifics of my new direction were still a mystery. Nevertheless, I welcomed the change that tugged at me. Until this point, my desire and dreams to explore were dampened. Issues for research and writing quietly intrigued me.

The publication of my new book represented a new affirmation of my accomplishments. I have always worked with families and communities out of a genuine sense of relatedness rather than from a need to change them—to observe, listen, and join with them if invited but not to impose my ideas on them. This is the process of *empowerment* I have discussed in my research; I now saw how genuinely possible that was on a personal level, when we join with others to critically review our experience and by doing so shift the perspective that shapes and redirects our purpose in life.[12]

In the fall quarter of that year, I intended to fully enjoy every minute of my sabbatical, for it would be the last one I would have for years to come. I eased into a steady pace of caring for myself while tinkering with unfinished manuscripts to submit for publication. A surge of energy emerged during the course of one week during which I became obsessed about getting a new house, a new partner, and a new career. When I examined this wish list, I noticed that no mention of my health appeared. I felt more peaceful with myself each day. My health was manageable day by day, but keeping my health stable still consumed most of my time and emotional stamina. I managed my health day by day. I learned to listen to my body's fatigue, pain, and multitude of complicated ailments that remain constant and require time-consuming care. Nevertheless, they were a medicine in and of themselves because they focused my attention on one minute at a time.

I maintained a rhythm of exploration in my scholarly pursuits. Against the university's obstacles to my teaching accommodations on campus and at home, my scholarly commitment flourished in more creative ways. I incorporated my personal autobiographical story in my graduate seminars. I included the students' own biographical accounts to teach culture. At the end of the seminars students wrote, "This was the most meaningful class I've ever taken." The genre proved to be such a successful teaching tool not only for my students but for myself that at the end of the course students wrote, "The self-reflective writing we were assigned in this class made it the most valuable thinking I have ever been challenged to do in academia."

A piece of my writing that was not as well received by the university was a proposal in which I proposed ways to modify my position. As I reviewed my health with my doctors, it became clear that my work demands including driving over two hours round-trip to teach at the university had to be adjusted long term. I needed a way that allowed me to manage as much from home as possible. Working at home on projects like distance teaching, I could pace my activity with sufficient rest periods enabling me to be productive with less stress. I proposed to the university that my position be moved full-time to the Joint Doctorate Program at CSU Fresno that would permit me to continue the distance learning courses I had taught in the program for years with excellent results. I had been an active faculty with the program, and Fresno faculty very much wanted me to continue with the program. During the six years of the health ordeal, I had managed to change the meaning of disability to "diverse abilities" in pursuit of my academic career.

Three months after I submitted the proposal, the university responded. They rejected my proposal and said that if I could not return to work full-time I had to leave the university. They claimed that the university was not responsible for helping me to perform my work from any other place except the physical parameters of the institution. The administration claimed to be within the legal requirements of the Americans with Disabilities Act. They believed that they had helped me by allowing me to select the hours that I could teach on campus. Most sobering was the realization that the illusion of protection, tenure, which I once believed was a semblance of security, in actuality meant nothing during a time when I most needed it. By not allowing me to work in a manner that accommodated the limitations of the illness that physically disabled me, I was forced to leave on disability. Not yet of age to retire, I had to wait until I turned fifty to become a professor emerita.

With perfect hindsight, I have learned how the culture of illness is constructed and how healing itself is also a complex culture. My personal life history has been imperative in understanding my healing. Living with difficult health has taught me about the internal power and insights that my cultural and family values dictated. By listening to that inner wisdom, I adapted to the relentless situation, but it was ultimately the act of letting go of trying to meet external laws—that gave me only a false sense of power—that returned me to my true source of strength.

IN RETROSPECT

My illustrations about academia as a place where learning and teaching were held in high regard eventually disappointed me as I struggled to remain a productive scholar while confronting serious health problems. Ironically, while my scholarly research, publishing, and teaching on empowerment thrived, I found myself in the midst of a situation at the university designed to disempower me. In spite of the circumstances, I felt that I had exhausted every means to accommodate the demands of my career. The university found it more efficient to behave in absolutes, while life presents us mostly gray hues. The university bureaucracy failed to create a means by which I could maintain a position in a workplace that professed to be a "learning institution." Subsequently, I have read the university's promotional magazines in which it attempts to convince the public of its interest in hiring and promoting ethnic minorities, persons of either gender, and disabled people. But, in my case, *diversity* was a meaningless word—in spite of the Americans with Disabilities Act.

Since leaving the university, I have been committed to recovering my health and continuing to pursue learning in a way that I can maintain my health. It is almost like I have come full circle—as a child I never had a dream of "what I would be when I grew up." Rather, I only hoped to do what would allow me to learn and grow. Throughout my career in education, although I resisted school, I fully appreciated my opportunity to learn. After the many positions I have held as an elementary school teacher, a school principal, a curriculum director, and a professor, I am now a professor emerita and still learning.

NOTES

1. A more expanded description of this period of my experience appears in Delgado-Gaitan 1997.

2. Much has been written about the trauma inflicted on students who do not speak English by untrained teachers. One of the most recent publications addressing these issues is Ovando and Collier 1998.

3. See Delgado-Gaitan 1997.

4. See Wells 1910.

5. In the case of a serious illness that requires changes in lifestyle, a person needs to make accommodations to continue surviving for the moment. Ordinary obligations change for the person who is ill, as do the expectations of that person by those around him or her. Two books speak to this issue: Leon Festinger's *A Theory of Cognitive Dissonance* (1962) and John Gliedman and William Roth's *The Unexpected Minority: Handicapped Children in America* (1979).

6. Questions of how ill persons transform their inner perceptions of self are discussed by Erving Goffman in two books: *The Presentation of Self in Everyday Life* (1959) and *Stigma: Notes on Management of Spoiled Identity* (1963).

7. Accommodating one's life to cope with a persistent physical challenge requires more than changing one's attitude and identity; its complexity engulfs every aspect of one's lifestyle, as the following authors comment: Robert F. Murphy, in *The Body Silent* (1990); S. K. Pitzele, in *We Are Not Alone: Learning to Live with Chronic Illness* (1985).

8. A great deal of ridicule of ill people in society stems from fear of becoming ill and incapacitated. The following authors aptly deal with cases of people whose strength is tested under the social stresses that surround them as a result of their illnesses: Murphy, in *The Body Silent* (1990); Goffman, in *Stigma* (1963); and Jessica Scheer, in "They Act Like It Was Contagious" (1984).

9. Physicians have begun researching and writing about the whole person beyond the physical symptoms and the social world that supports healing. Among the most prolific of doctors who speak to patients and their families is Bernie S. Siegel (see 1986).

10. The surreal experiences of people with illnesses that manifest physically are described in a caring manner by Oliver Sacks in *Anthropologist on Mars* (1995).

11. See Delgado-Gaitan 1990.

12. Three books in which I discuss the ramifications of self, family, and community empowerment are *Literacy for Empowerment* (1990); *Crossing Cultural Borders: Educating Immigrant Families in America*, with Trueba (1991); and *Protean Literacy: Extending the Discourse on Empowerment* (1996).

REFERENCES

Delgado-Gaitan, Concha. 1990. *Literacy for Empowerment: The Role of Parents in Their Children's Education*. London: Falmer Press.

———. 1996. *Protean Literacy: Extending the Discourse on Empowerment*. London: Falmer Press.

———. 1997. Dismantling Borderland. In *Learning from Our Lives: Women, Research and Autobiography in Education*, ed. Anna Neumann and Penelope L. Peterson, 37–52. New York: Teachers College, Columbia University Press.

Delgado-Gaitan, Concha, and H. Trueba. 1991. *Crossing Cultural Borders: Educating Immigrant Families in America*. London: Falmer Press.

Festinger, Leon. 1962. *A Theory of Cognitive Dissonance*. Stanford: Stanford University Press.

Gliedman, John, and William Roth. 1979. *The Unexpected Minority: Handicapped Children in America*. Ed. Thomas A. Stewart. New York: Harcourt Brace Jovanovich.

Goffman, Erving. 1959. *The Presentation of Self in Everyday Life*. New York: Doubleday.

———. 1963. *Stigma: Notes on the Management of Spoiled Identity*. Englewood Cliffs, N.J.: Prentice-Hall.

Mizel, S. B., and P. Jaret. 1986. *The Human Immune System: The New Frontier in Medicine*. New York: Simon and Schuster.

Murphy, Robert F. 1990. *The Body Silent*. New York: W. W. Norton.

Ovando, Carlos J., and Virginia P. Collier. 1998. *Bilingual and ESL Classrooms: Teaching in Multicultural Contexts*. Boston: McGraw Hill.

Pitzele, S. K. 1985. *We Are Not Alone: Learning to Live with Chronic Illness*. New York: Workman.

Sacks, Oliver. 1995. *Anthropologist on Mars*. New York: Alfred A. Knopf, Inc.

Scheer, Jessica. 1984. They Act Like It Was Contagious. In *Social Aspects of Chronic Illness, Impairment and Disability*, ed. S. C. Hey, G. Kiger, and J. Seidel, 185–207. Salem, Ore.: Willamette University Press.

Siegel, B. S. 1986. *Love, Medicine and Miracles: Lessons Learned about Self-Healing from a Surgeon's Experience with Exceptional Patients*. New York: Harper and Row.

Wells, H. G. [1910] 1997. The Country of the Blind. In *The Country of the Blind and Other Science-Fiction Stories*, Dover Thrift Edition, H. G. Wells and Martin Gardner. New York: Dover Publications.

9

The Voice of a Chinese Immigrant in America: Reflections on Research and Self-Identity

Yali Zou

Immigration is the driving force behind a significant transformation of American society taking place at the end of the millennium. Few other social phenomena are likely to affect the future character of American culture and society as much as the ongoing wave of "new immigration." The nature of this change is indeed momentous. [C]ensus projections assume that ethnic and racial categories are enduring and more or less static formations. Given ethnic socioeconomic mobility and the high rates of interethnic marriage in the U.S. along with changing cultural models and practices around ethnicity, there is reason to suspect that these categories, fluid and in constant formation and transformation, may be quite irrelevant in three generations.

—Suárez-Orozco 1998a, 5

Coming to the United States from mainland China is an experience that is only partially comprehensible to Westerners and very confusing to immigrants themselves. Not only is the United States a radically different country, but the immigrant's inability to communicate in English can make this experience terrifying. Life in China is full of myths about this country as far away from the truth as Western beliefs about China are. Far from being a racially, socially, politically, economically, or ethnically homogeneous society, China is a complex nation with prevalent philosophies and traditions centered on the family and society.

The purpose of this chapter is to describe my experiences in both China and the United States in order to explore issues of self-identification and the adaptive strategies associated with higher education chosen by immigrants in the United States, as well as how my dual identity impacts my role as an ethnographer. My case may shed some light on complex problems of clashes in cultural values, long-

187

term efforts to excel in academia, and changes in self-identity and the nature of doing ethnographic research. This essay will describe my experiences in China and put them in their historical and political context, and then I will relate my experiences in the United States and discuss how those experiences have influenced my research. Some reflections are offered to the reader. The assumption that prearrival experiences shape immigrants' lives in the host country may find some support in this essay, and suggestions are made as to how an ethnographer can function effectively in two cultures.

CHINA IN THE NEXT CENTURY

By the middle of the twenty-first century, China will have the most powerful economy in the world. The new generations in the post-Mao reform period will vigorously pursue personal wealth in contrast with the current groups of political leaders who fear change. China is, and will continue to be, one of the most complex countries in the world (Starr 1997). It is a country with many different ethnic groups, languages, traditions, and lifestyles. Even the physical appearance of many Chinese people breaks Western stereotypes. The challenge of understanding any of the many ethnic groups, or "nationalities," in China is compounded by the series of rapid demographic, social, economic, and political changes that have taken place in the last half century. Since the People's Republic of China was established, demographic changes have been dramatic. China had a relatively modest population of between fifty and one hundred million between the first and eighteenth centuries. During the Qing dynasty (in the 1770s) the population was about one hundred million. By 1840 it had increased to four hundred million, and when China became the People's Republic of China on 1 October 1949, the population was five hundred million (Poston and Yaukey 1992, 1). By 1990 the population had jumped to 1.13 billion people.

The ethnic, social, linguistic, and economic diversity of Chinese people is overwhelming and complicated. In 1951, China officially recognized fifty-six ethnic groups in China. Among these, the Han was considered the dominant group, both numerically and politically. The other fifty-five groups, the so-called minority groups or nationalities, had, according to the 1990 national census, a population of 91,200,314 people, which was 8 percent of the total population of China. Since 1982, when the Chinese census showed a population of 1,008,175,288, a figure considered extremely conservative by experts (Crespigny 1992, 285), the policy of one child per family was adopted. The fifty-five ethnic minority groups, however, were exempted from this policy. (For a detailed listing of these groups and their geographic distribution, see Trueba and Zou 1994, 61–70.) In 1990 the following five largest ethnic minority groups accounted for over 48 million people:

- the Zhuang in South Central China (with 15,489,630 people)
- the Manchu in the Northeast (with 9,821,180 people)

- the Hui in the Northwest (with 8,692,978 people)
- the Miao in the Southwest (with 7,398,035 people)
- the Uygur in the Northwest (with 7,214,431 people)

In China, 68 percent of the territory is primarily occupied by minority groups. China's borders with Russia, Mongolia, Korea, Pakistan, India, Vietnam, Laos, and Burma run through areas primarily occupied by minorities. These areas are relatively isolated. The privileges given to minority-dominated geographical areas (which constitute "autonomous regions") were granted by the central government in an effort to retain the affiliation of minority groups and the national unity, while at the same time holding onto the Han hegemony. Autonomous regions were offered administrative, legal, and resource control under specific parameters; in fact, the central government retained supervision and control of major resource allocations.

Modern China and the Chinese who immigrate to the United States have experiences and backgrounds that are in sharp contrast to the home values of the United States. Ethnic and racial diversity in China has a history of confrontation and conflict. Ethnic intolerance, often associated with religious intolerance—anti-Buddhism and anti-Manchuism, for example—are present along with preferences for skin color and other physical characteristics. In fact, there is documentation about racial wars at the turn of the nineteenth century that illustrates the practices of racial classifications and extinction (Dikötter 1992). Ethnic nationalism and religious differences clearly separate the Muslim Chinese (probably close to eighteen million of them live in the northwest part of the country—for a detailed discussion, see Gladney 1991).

What follows is a description of part of my life in China, where I lived for about forty years. My intent is to give the reader an idea of how my experiences in China during the Cultural Revolution shaped my value system and educational philosophy. This is the China where I grew up, studied, and worked and to which my self-identity is forever attached. Yet this is also the China that is furthest away from my daily life after having been in the United States for more than ten years.

MY EXPERIENCES IN CHINA

Perhaps no other experience in China had a greater impact on me than working in a rural village for two years during the Cultural Revolution. Being in that village changed my life completely. Although I suffered seriously physically and mentally, it nurtured my deep love for poor peasant children and helped me establish a great relationship with my students' parents, which, in turn, laid the foundation for my future career. Beyond that, I learned how to face challenges and how to develop adaptation strategies. Leaving my comfortable family life in the city for the first time when I was seventeen years old, I was sent like millions of other educated young people to live in one of the poorest villages, where there was not enough food to eat (quite often chaff and wild herbs were the only food); there was no running water, electricity, or gas; and communication with the rest of the world was nonexistent. Everyday I worked physically in an endless field, often for up to fourteen hours under the burning sun or in the freezing winter. In addition, I had to go to mountains to find tree branches for the evening fire and wild vegetables to supplement the community's meals. I was no different from the cow I had been working with. I was never prepared for this kind of life. I was depressed and felt like everything was hopeless. I did not know whether I had any future.

One day I was transplanting rice shoots in a rice field with cold water and had worked for four hours without a break. Suddenly I felt pain in my legs. When I looked at my legs, there were several leeches. I was terrified and fell into the water. I cried and sank into the muddy field. The villagers came to help me and were sympathetic; the leader of the village came to me and said, "Yali, I feel so sorry for you; tell me what we can do to help. What can you do?" I said in despair, "Nothing, just let me die." I felt there was no way to escape from this life. He smiled and comforted me as he sat on the edge of the rice field and asked me, "Can you read?" "Of course," I answered. "Do you want to teach our children?" "Why?" I asked. He told me that no one in the village of forty-two households with 286 people could read a single Chinese character. His dream was that the children in his village would read and write someday. I was shocked by this reality and told him I would like to try. I started to use my simple living tent as a classroom to teach the village children to read, to write their names, to talk, and to express their feelings. The children looked so poor and hungry! Their faces were dirty, and their hair was very long and messy! I wrote to my father and asked him if he could bring a pair of scissors and hair clippers on his next visit to me. When he came with some little gifts and the scissors, I began to cut the hair of these poor children, hair full of lice and dirt. The lice would jump all over me! The children were happy to have their hair cut and their faces washed. They began to trust me and share everything with me. They told me about their families and invited me to visit them.

As I had the opportunity to get to know the parents of my pupils better, I noticed that many of them—although still young (some not yet thirty years old)—were suffering pains in their joints, backs, and waists. Some had pains all over their bodies, perhaps as a result of arthritis or of physical injuries from the hard labor in the field. I realized that I might help them. Because I had serious migraine headaches quite often, I had brought an acupuncture book, some needles, and alcohol to the village in order to help get rid of my headaches. There were no doctors and no medicine at all in the village. I offered my help to the parents who suffered from pain, assuring them that although I did not know enough, I would do my best with acupuncture to help ease their pain. The needles became magical tools. Many parents recovered dramatically; they could move their hands and legs and walk without pain; many even started working in the fields again. Word of my skills passed from village to village. Many people began coming to me for help. They called me the "barefoot doctor," which in Chinese means a person who practices medicine without a formal education or a license.

Because of my excellent performance in the village as a teacher and a "doctor," I was transferred to an urban area, which at that time in China was considered a big promotion because leaving the countryside and going to work in a city was a great opportunity. I went to the Jilin Iron and Steel Plant where I became the inspector for quality control. The plant had 7,000 workers, nine workshop divisions, and one research institute. The Jilin plant was one of the most important iron producers in China (about 60 percent of all iron produced in China came from there). It was managed directly by the Ministry of Metallurgic Industry. Each division had a number of open furnaces with unprotected laborers around who experienced extremely high temperatures and other hazardous working conditions. While I was there, I had the opportunity to talk to the workers and observe firsthand their difficulties. I was moved by their devotion to their work despite unbelievably difficult working conditions. I spoke on their behalf and asked leaders to improve their workplace.

In 1966, because of the Cultural Revolution, China's schools and universities were closed down. All former students and professors went to the countryside "to be re-educated by peasants" as Chairman Mao ordered. Eight years later, in 1972, China reopened the universities and began to recruit students from factories, plants, and villages. I was recommended for the Shanghai Foreign Language Institute. There I learned to speak Albanian and became a governmental interpreter. Later I worked in the Chang Chun Film Studio translating Albanian movies into Chinese. I met and was friends with writers, actors, and actresses, from whom I learned about their concerns, ideas, and creativity. In 1985, I became a professor at the Chang Chun Science and Technology Institute, where I found that for over ten years the schools had never changed textbooks. All the professors could recite the textbooks they used nearly verbatim. The schools suffered from a lack of both resources and new ideas. I started trying different textbooks and compiled readings that made my students very competitive in the provincial learning competitions. The quality of my teaching and the success I obtained in reforming the curriculum earned me provincial and national awards for excellence in higher education.

MY IMMIGRANT EXPERIENCES IN THE UNITED STATES

With ambitious goals and rich experiences in China, I came to the dreamed of promised land—America. I was excited about my bright future in the United States because I believed that I had enough skills and guts to face the tough challenges ahead of me. However, when I came to the United States, I felt totally lost, incompetent, and dysfunctional. I lost my voice (because I could not speak English), my ideas, and even my thinking skills. I could not communicate with people, and I could not even order my food at McDonald's. People saw me as different, somebody unable to do anything. I was depressed and isolated myself from the outside world. I was afraid to meet people. The only way I could express my bitter feelings was by writing letters to my family and friends in China. I told them that "here is paradise because there is everything you want; but also here is hell because you suffer too much." I felt utterly hopeless. Near this time, one of my American friends, whom I had hired in China to teach English at the university, came to visit me. She introduced me to a professor at the University of California at Davis, who encouraged me to study. I did, but I traveled an extraordinarily difficult journey of psychological adjustment in doing so.

In order to support my study financially, I had to find a job. After competing with many applicants, I got a position as an instructor of Chinese at the University of California at Davis. It was my first time standing on the stage of an American institution, teaching American students the Chinese language. I was in a panic. Very soon, however, I discovered that I was considered an authority and the students respected me as a teacher with profound knowledge. In the evaluations of my course, students wrote the following: "Professor Zou is a very knowledgeable and effective instructor"; "She is humorous and resourceful"; "We learned a great deal from her." Teaching Chinese language instilled in me a sense of confidence and power that I needed badly. To be able to say what I wanted, to control the class, to become the professor, and to have Americans struggle to learn Chinese (as I was struggling to learn English) gave me interesting insights into the sort of a dual personality I had begun to develop. On the one hand, I felt as if I was truly in control when I taught my Chinese class. On the other hand, when I was a student in the Division of Education, I felt, for the most part, patronized or neglected. The professors and students had trouble understanding me. They would speak to me slowly, masticating their words, as if I was stupid. I felt humiliated and depressed. For that reason I loved to teach my Chinese class. It gave me a sense of being myself again.

As a Chinese instructor I was a role model, a high-ranking member of the academic community, a person deserving of respect and admiration—a person with social responsibilities and the power to give grades to American students. Furthermore, I was opening a new world of sounds and ideas, of cultural traditions and practices, of history and philosophy for my students. I felt I was useful. I could contribute to the students' learning because I am a very good Chinese speaker, writer, and professor. But after I would finish my Chinese classes, I would start to worry about attending classes as a student myself. I felt confused, anxious, even stupid. In my classes the Americans looked so smart and competent. I felt I could never compete with them. Many times professors did not give me a chance to talk in public. When they did ask me questions, they were always very simple or just about China. One time in a class discussion it was my turn to discuss some issues about human learning development. The professor openly passed over to the student next me. I felt embarrassed and humiliated. I raised my hand and requested that the professor give me a chance to talk. The professor did. This was the first time I felt better about myself because I got the chance to express my ideas. I got fair treatment. After the class many students told me how much they admired my courage. However, I had to accept the fact that, no matter how much I knew, I could not express myself well. I hated feeling that way and feeling confused about the future! Later some professors who had faith in me helped me a great deal by giving me specific roles to perform and asking me to do research with them. Still, in my eyes, American students continued to look so eloquent, so articulate. I would tell myself, "I will never reach that level." My sense of self-confidence was shaken from time to time. I would tell myself, "How can I ever complete this assignment?" I was resolved to give all I had, my very best effort, but I was doing this in a language in which I could not express my most intimate thoughts, though one that I understood well enough to analyze meaning and nuances.

Gradually I began to realize that I benefited from knowing two languages and two cultures. This helped me to get deeper into the structure of the English language and analyze the content of texts better than some American students. That made me anxious to read more and to compare more. I found that comparing the two languages, the two cultures, and the two countries fascinated me and opened up a new world of knowledge to me. I realized I had found something I was really excited about. But I did not know exactly what it was.

One time in a class on ethnographic research, my professor asked me to tell the class about Chinese culture and how it differed from U.S. culture. This question was asked of me quite often when I came to this country. When I was in China no one asked me about this, and I never thought about my culture and how different I was from other people. This made me think about my identity more and about who I am. This reflection was very important for me to help characterize my life, the life of my daughter, and the lives of other Chinese immigrants I know: a predominant trait was resilience or the ability to endure hard labor, stress, and sacrifices and to survive until one succeeds in a task. I spent long nights and many hours of work in the library, in my home, and everywhere I could have a minute to read, write, reflect, and comment. I realized I was passionate in my dedication to the completion of my work. I would go for many hours without food until I finished my job. Why did I do that? What prepared me to stand the stresses and the sacrifices and pursue the completion of my tasks at any cost? Perhaps it was my Chinese background, my philosophy of life, and my experience as a child and young adult, in which I had to endure many hardships in the fields as a laborer and from which I learned survival skills.

BECOMING AN ETHNOGRAPHER: NEW EXPERIENCES

After I took several courses on minority education and ethnographic research, I developed a great interest in minority students' academic motivations and their achievements. I am especially fascinated by the power of ethnographic research. My passion for the poor peasant children and my commitment to help those children led me to read about the Hmong people, who are refugees from Southeast Asia. Hmong people experience tremendous difficulties in adjusting to this new society. However, they are doing extremely well both economically and academically. I admired their brave spirit and their hard work, and I wanted to know more about this group. Through researching the literature, I found that the ancestors of the Hmong people are the Miao people in China (see Trueba, Jacobs, and Kirton 1990).

After a long period of preparation in the United States, in 1992, my main professor and I began an ethnographic research project in China that focused on Miao university students. We did the study both in Beijing, at the Central University for Nationalities, in the heart of the capital of China, and at the Guizhou Institute for Nationalities located in the south central part of China. We selected fourteen Miao students for our study. Seven were from the Central University for Nationalities, and seven were from the Guizhou Institute for Nationalities. The Central University for Nationalities is affiliated directly with the State Educational Commission of China and was established in 1951. It has 2,300 faculty and staff and an enrollment of more than 7,000 students from all fifty-six ethnic groups. The Guizhou Institute for Nationalities was founded in 1951 under the leadership of the Educational Commission of Guizhou Province. It has 2,500 students from eighteen different ethnic groups. The fourteen students we interviewed were all originally from rural areas. Their parents were mostly peasants, although a few were teachers, government officials, and village leaders. All of their families had very low annual incomes. However, the poorest Miao children, as university students and faculty, obtained high prestige as members of mainstream Chinese society and were recognized as leaders in their villages. How did this happen? Where did these poor children get the resources for their studies, and how did they succeed?

In order to conduct the ethnographic research project on the Miao, I obtained a postdoctoral fellowship at the University of Wisconsin at Madison. Being a native Chinese qualified me as an "insider" in China in the eyes of my professors because I was familiar with the Chinese culture and had the authority to interpret it to them. On the one hand, this perception was correct—I had spent forty years in China and knew the country fairly well (I thought). I had grown up in a Chinese middle-class family, and I knew mainstream ideology and lifestyle as a member of the Han people (the mainstream population that comprises 92 percent of the population of China or about 1.2 billion people). On the other hand, I was educated in the United States, I understood Western philosophy, I spoke English, and I dressed like an American. All this gave me the credentials to pass for an American in the eyes of the Chinese. Furthermore, I was armed with cultural ecological theories and ethnographic research methods, and, most importantly, I was funded by a U.S. university.

Before entering the research field, my professor and I reviewed the literature, developed a research design, articulated specific questions to be answered by the research, and carefully planned the implementation of the design through gradual strategic steps. In conducting the research, however, we had to wake up to the reality of our own social identities and cultural roles in China, at least as defined by the Miao people with whom we were working. Consequently, I became aware of my dual identity and was caught in a difficult position. I was both Chinese in the opinion of the Americans and an American in the eyes of the Chinese. But I knew I was neither, or perhaps I was both. That became a serious problem as I continued to reflect on my own identity, although during the research I did not have enough time to think seriously about it.

As I mentioned earlier, because I saw myself as a Chinese person who had lived in China most of my life, I was placed in the category of "insider" with regard to the Chinese culture. However, because I had come from the Han group, which is viewed as the mainstream cultural group and the "oppressor" or controlling group, I could not really claim to have the same way of thinking as those who are ethnically, socially, and economically different, as in the case of the Miao. They have constructed another set of values and perceptions or what is considered to be a "subculture" of Chinese society, and it is different from my own culture. Therefore, all I could do was describe my understanding of what I heard, what I saw, and what I felt in a way of thinking that I socially constructed in settings dominated by the Han people. Furthermore, I constructed these perceptual frames also from the perspective of Western academia. Indeed, the two cultures, the Han culture and Western academia, filtered my views. After five years of intensive study and training in the United States, I went back to China to conduct empowerment research with Miao students with whom I was unfamiliar. Therefore, my dual ideological identity placed me in an asymmetrical power relationship with the Miao students. They viewed me as an educated "Asian American" and consequently as an "outsider" and even "superior" or in a position of power.

When my professor, my American colleagues, and I went to the Central University for Nationalities in Beijing, we lived in a dormitory on the campus in order to be close to the students. Next to our rooms was the Foreign Affairs Office. All of our activities were under the officials' surveillance; they were responsible for approving who could come to see us, where we could go, and in what rooms we could meet. At the same time, however, the officials were eager to provide us with information after we told them we planned to write a book telling Americans about minorities in China. All the information the officials offered to us was official government policy or government propaganda material. We asked the foreign office for permission to meet with the Miao students. After some negotiations, we got the chance to interview and discuss our research project with some of the Miao students. Before we met them, we prepared a set of questions ranging from their personal backgrounds to their opinions about the government policies toward minorities.

The first meeting consisted of fifteen Miao students and two Miao professors. We started asking them questions about their experiences and their journeys from their home villages to the university. At first they kept silent, and they seemed to be anxious about the kinds of answers they could give to our questions. We felt a little embarrassed and did not know what we were supposed to do. Then their professor told us, "Don't feel bad. They didn't prepare for these questions, so they do not know how to answer them." After the meeting we learned that the foreign affairs officials had already prepared the students about what they should say to the Americans. At this time, only three years after the democracy rallies in Tiananmen Square, the Chinese government considered the United States an unfriendly power. Additionally, public expression of one's ideas was closely guarded. Students could not freely say what they wanted to say. In addition, when we arrived in Beijing the Chinese Communist Party Congress had just come to a close. The central theme of the conference was opposition to Chinese intellectual bourgeois liberalism, and the government was worried that students would once again stage demonstrations against the Chinese government. Therefore, the government kept a close watch on the students.

We remembered that on the day the conference ended, we went to Tiananmen Square and saw many military soldiers, policemen, and plainclothes public security personnel watching people's activities. So when we asked questions to the unprepared students, they hesitated in answering. The students did not know what they could tell foreigners and what might get them in trouble. The professor started to enlighten the students and told them in front of us, "You should not worry; you can say what you experienced. For example, you can tell them how the government cares about minority people and gives minorities preferential treatment, so you have a chance to enter college." Then the students started to recall their hardships both in their villages and in school. For example, Mr. Wang, a twenty-three-year-old student from the Guizhou Province, told us that his Han classmates laughed at his poor clothing and quite often he did not have money to buy food (Trueba and Zou 1994, 88–91). As he talked about the hardships that he experienced and his family's difficult life, he began to cry. His story touched both the researchers and the professors.

On another day, a young Miao university professor invited us to observe his class. When he came to our dormitory to meet us, the gatekeeper (a government officer) stopped him and asked him whether he had reported his activity to the Foreign Affairs Office in advance, and the guard would not let him see us. When we came down to the door, we explained to the officer that we had asked the professor to come to discuss one of his courses and his pedagogy in the classroom. Similar red tape and bureaucratic inquiries occurred in situations when phone calls came from the outside, when unexpected students or other visitors attempted to talk to us, or when we tried to change our schedule.

In China, a discussion of oppression cannot be public because it would be considered antigovernment and would subject the participants to incarceration and other sanctions. For the Chinese students, however, the ideological position is that the government is always fair and nobody should view surveillance as oppressive. As we began to think about the consequences of asking people to cooperate with our research, we realized that there was an element of risk and uncertainty associated with critical ethnographic research in a specific context or situation, especially in the context of university students who are often penalized the most for their use of freedom of speech. As researchers, we had to keep in mind that our first responsibility was to the people we studied. Consequently, we had to accept the constraints of the cultural setting in which we functioned. In the end, we kept asking ourselves, How can we, as researchers in a foreign land, pursue our research agenda and still be responsible for the safety of the people we study?

Another dilemma was how as researchers could we best deal with our dominant cultural identity while working with ethnic minority persons? In critical ethnographic research sometimes we unconsciously re-create a context for dominance and tend to impose our values. When we began our research at the Central University for Nationalities, we identified a group of Miao students and professors and organized the schedule for individual and group interviews. We then proceeded to ask our questions regarding their rationales for leaving their villages and becoming university students and professors. We wanted to know how strongly they felt their identity as "Miao" and what roles this ethnic identity had in their motivation to achieve academically. We unconsciously conducted our research without reflecting on the automatic assumption about the "subjects" of our research as if they were "objects." This happened until we started to build rapport with the students and professors and heard the individual stories of poverty, struggle, and oppression that had characterized many of their lives. At that moment we turned our methodology around and began to investigate ways in which we could assist them. Gradually my professor and I were adopted as "honorary" members of their clan. It was only after we traveled 2,000 miles southwest to the Province of Guizhou and interviewed an entirely different group of Miao university students that we realized the fundamental differences between the two Miao student groups (the one from Beijing and the one from Guizhou).

We were interviewed first at length before we could even get to the points we were investigating. The students and professors in Guizhou demonstrated to us that they felt competent and in control of the situation. They described the Miao as a cosmological ethnic or racial group scattered throughout the entire world, and they interrogated us about the treatment of the Miao (Hmong) in the United States. They also gave us their long-term views of economic and industrial plans to move upwardly the entire Miao group around the world and wanted to know if we were ready to invest in such efforts. This experience made us aware that we had mistaken the first group of Miao students as objects of study, instead of as persons. We became humble on our visit to Guizhou, a province that has a high concentration of minority populations. As we turned the discussion to the Miao students' plans for the future, we realized that, instead of answering our questions, they would ask us what we thought they could do to help their own people in the future not only in China but throughout the world. Actually, they changed roles and became the researchers, using us as consultants. They were looking up to us for guidance and practical advice; and they were doing it with a unique global perspective and ambition, talking about the Miao being a cosmic group with a bright destiny and a significant international force. We felt obligated to tell them some success stories of minorities in the United States and how the Miao could use their knowledge to develop natural resources in their areas, to communicate with the outside world to attract investments from the Western world, and to participate actively in public events in order to make the Miao group more visible. They followed our thoughts and developed a lot of new ideas. Mr. Tao Wencen, an eighteen-year-old student, said that after he graduated he would organize county cooperatives and business firms, and later he would use the capital accumulated from the cooperatives to establish a Miao city with hotels, restaurants, and other tourist facilities. Mr. Xiaoping Tao said, "I want to help the Miao people become literate; collect and edit Miao folklore and publish a book; write a book on the history of my Miao village." Mr. Xiong Jianliang wanted to become a village leader and use his intelligence to develop his village (Trueba and Zou 1994, 99–100).

After we finished our research project and wrote a book about what we learned about Miao people, I went back to visit our informants several times. I found out not only that our research encouraged the students to pursue their dreams but that it also helped U.S. students get a better understanding of education. Some of the Miao students we studied now have become university professors and administrators. My American students were moved by the stories the Miao students told, and this motivated them to achieve greater academic excellence.

LESSONS LEARNED: SOME PERSONAL THOUGHTS

The immigration experience is a never-ending venture that continuously redefines one's life and self-concept. For me as a Chinese woman, becoming a permanent resident and getting to know Americans intimately has given me a new view of life and a capability to see the world from different perspectives and in different dimensions. The Eastern and Western worlds are so vastly different and even opposed that a Chinese immigrant (from what I have experienced and seen in others) must make heroic efforts to become flexible, bicultural, and committed to learn every day many new and subtle nuances about the American culture and the English language. Perhaps much of the miscommunication between the East and the West has to do with the lack of ability to learn "new ways of life" and new cultural values. Raising my daughter in this country has opened my eyes to the profound differences in socialization patterns and to the dilemmas faced by Chinese parents in the United States. For me, being a Chinese immigrant is a continued intensive course in acculturation and self-redefinition that will last the rest of my life.

I believe that the foundation for genuine academic empowerment of children of immigrants is a solid self-identity and a clear concept of one's own ethnic community. My daughter and her friends not only are proud of being Chinese but also are proud of understanding American culture and using English with a high level of proficiency. The Chinese community around us is very influential, and the competition for achievement is intense. One of the reasons why I have become very interested in self-identity and academic achievement is that I have lived through the pain of trying to compete with native English speakers, and I have seen my daughter work very hard to become a high achiever.

I go back to China every year in order to teach and conduct research among minority groups. This has been an opportunity to retain a profound adherence to my culture without losing my biculturalism; it has forced me to reflect on my own self-identity and has invited me to revisit some theoretical debates and issues related to immigration in the United States. To mention just a few of these, the complex issue of empowerment among Asian Americans—and the need for a liberation, voice, and appropriate space in the instructional process (see Freire 1973, 1995; Freire and Macedo 1996; Giroux and McLaren 1986, 1994; Gutierrez 1994; Gutierrez, Larson, and Kreuter 1995; McLaren 1995; and others)—is often misunderstood by teachers and academicians. The new Asian Americans of my daughter's generation are not fighting to retain their own ethnic identity and to have a separate voice in schools. They are fighting to acquire an American identity and an equal voice along with other American youth. They will not abandon their own ethnic identity. Their vast networks and frequent communication with other children of immigrants will secure comfort in our own Asian community. But they do not want to be branded different, not even for the sake of recognizing their academic accomplishments.

Regarding the debate on the Asian American "model minorities" (see Ogbu 1974, 1978, 1992), achievement for us Asian Americans, as immigrants, and for our children has been far from easy. It has not been a rapid ascending line to success. On the contrary, we have failed many times but continued to fight. We have had to face our lack of knowledge and experience, but we continue to try because we are building the empowerment of the next generation. Our children struggle, and we force them to continue to try to make more serious efforts. It has not been easy! Specifically, as we try to adapt, along the lines of Gibson's (see 1988, 1997) model of accommodation not assimilation, we certainly retain the most important family values that brought us to this country: loyalty to our ethnic group and parents, commitment to help each other, commitment to always make the greatest possible effort to succeed, and resilience when we fail. The survival and adaptation of Asian Americans in this country is a complex process (see Kiang 1995, 1996; Trueba, Cheng, and Ima 1993). The drastic changes in our multiple identities (Trueba 1999) are directly and profoundly affected by the "transformations" and changes in the children of immigrants and their families (Suárez-Orozco and Suárez-Orozco 1995a, 1995b) and by the global economic and political currents accelerating migration waves (Suárez-Orozco 1991, 1998a, 1998b).

As a committed academician, my questions are the following: How can I deal with my multiple identities as I try to conduct objective research? How do experience, cultural background, and ethnic identity impact the result of ethnographic research? What kind of role should my identities play in ethnographic research? How can I turn my identity and experiences into assets? How should I deal with my own ethnic, cultural, and experiential biases? As have many other immigrants, I have had difficult moments adapting. Yet, in the end, I always come out convinced that my biculturalism has enriched my life. Becoming an immigrant often translates into painful experiences that require healing and understanding. In fact, one of my most recent and profound realizations is that I finally became convinced that often conflict across cultures can be resolved through the culture of therapy. I was feeling torn by two extremely different lifestyles and began to realize that I did not have to be both Chinese and American at the same time within the same cultural environment. My mind was opened when I read about cultural therapy as a means to increase our understanding of value conflicts and resolve such conflicts (Spindler and Spindler 1989, 1992a, 1992b, 1994; Trueba 1994).

In contrast with the philosophy of Paulo Freire, who sees education and the acquisition of knowledge as intrinsically political, the Spindlers feel that the acquisition obtained through anthropological knowledge about our personal ethnic, racial, and cultural identities is not necessarily political and leads to "cultural" reflection, a deeper understanding of value differences, and ultimately conflict resolution. Conscientization (or in the Spindlers' lexicon, cultural reflection) is a means to resolve personal and social problems associated with having the wrong cultural assumptions about other people and their perception of who we are. By learning about ourselves, our "enduring selves" and our "situated selves," and by reconciling them, we can prevent the painful experience of reaching an "endangered self" (confusion and uprootedness from our values). The central concepts of how the enduring self is deeply rooted in the first years of our cultural socialization within the family and community evokes many strong memories in my life. I cannot but accept the fact that my infancy and adolescence as directed by my parents and family left a profound mark on me. Therefore, at the heart of cultural therapy, as I understand it, is the ability to reflect on cultural values, traditions, and personal identity. As a Chinese immigrant, perhaps as many other immigrants have, I have become aware of the need to heal, to piece together my inner self, and to retain my cultural values of both Chinese and American origin (Zou 1998; Zou and Trueba 1998).

I assume that at the heart of cultural therapy as a healing process is the realization that there has to be an acceptance of the self based on a profound historical and cultural knowledge of one's own family. I am aware that in theory, cultural therapy does not assume that each member of humankind needs psychotherapy or that much of the sad state of affairs in the world today is related to social and cultural conflicts. The condition sine qua non for healing from hurts caused by prejudice or bigotry is the possession of a deep cultural knowledge and understanding of human groups and their culturally determined behaviors, as well as an understanding of the mediating role played by language and culture in the acquisition of new knowledge (Trueba 1994, viii–ix). To the extent that I know the nature of my biculturalism and that I use effectively the Mandarin and English languages, I feel at peace, confident, and competent. But the price of this peace has been a great deal of work and persistence to survive failure, to stand up and try again.

REFERENCES

Crespigny, R. de. 1992. *China This Century*. New York: Oxford University Press.

Dikötter, F. 1992. *The Discourse of Race in Modern China*. Stanford: Stanford University Press.

Freire, P. 1973. *Pedagogy of the Oppressed*. New York: Seabury.

———. 1995. *Pedagogy of Hope: Reliving Pedagogy of the Oppressed*. New York: Continuum.

Freire, P., and D. Macedo. 1996. A Dialogue: Culture, Language, and Race. In "Breaking Free: The Transformative Power of Critical Pedagogy," ed. P. Leistyna, A. Woodrum, and S. Sherblom, theme issue, *Harvard Education Review* 27: 199–228.

Gibson, M. 1988. *Accommodation without Assimilation: Sikh Immigrants in an American High School*. Ithaca, N.Y.: Cornell University Press.

———, ed. 1997. Ethnicity and School Performance: Complicating the Immigrant/Involuntary Minority Typology. *Anthropology and Education Quarterly* 28: 315–462.

Giroux, H., and P. McLaren. 1986. Teacher Education and the Politics of Engagement: The Case for Democratic Schooling. *Harvard Educational Review* 26: 213–38.

———. 1994. *Between Borders: Pedagogy and the Politics of Cultural Studies*. New York: Routledge.

Gladney, D. C. 1991. *Muslim Chinese: Ethnic Nationalism in the People's Republic*. Cambridge, Mass.: Harvard University Press.

Gutierrez, K. 1994. How Talk, Context, and Script Shape Contexts for Learning: A Cross-Case Comparison of Journal Sharing. *Linguistics and Education* 5: 335–65.

Gutierrez, K., J. Larson, and B. Kreuter. 1995. Cultural Tensions in the Scripted Classroom: The Value of the Subjugated Perspective. *Urban Education* 29: 410–42.

Kiang, P. 1995. Bicultural Strengths and Struggles of Southeast Asian Americans in School. In *Culture and Difference: Critical Perspectives on the Bicultural Experience in the United States*, ed. A. Darder, 201–25. Critical Studies in Education and Culture Series. Westport, Conn.: Bergin and Garvey.

———. 1996. Persistence Stories and Survival Strategies of Cambodian Americans in College. *Journal of Narrative and Life History* 6: 39–64.

McLaren, P. 1995. *Critical Pedagogy and Predatory Culture*. New York: Routledge.

Ogbu, J. 1974. *The Next Generation: An Ethnography of Education in an Urban Neighborhood*. New York: Academic Press.

———. 1978. *Minority Education and Caste: The American System in Cross-Cultural Perspective*. New York: Academic Press.

————. 1992. Understanding Cultural Diversity. *Educational Researcher* 21: 5–24.

Poston, D. L., Jr., and D. Yaukey, eds. 1992. *The Population of Modern China.* The Plenum Series on Demographic Methods and Population Analysis. New York: Plenum Press.

Spindler, G., and L. Spindler. 1989. Instrumental Competence, Self-Efficacy, Linguistic Minorities, and Cultural Therapy: A Preliminary Attempt at Integration. *Anthropology and Education Quarterly* 10: 36–50.

————. 1992a. The Enduring, Situated, and Endangered Self in Fieldwork: A Personal Account. In *The Psychoanalytic Study of Society. Volume 17: Essays in Honor of George D. and Louise A. Spindler,* ed. L. B. Boyer and R. Boyer, 23–28. Hillsdale, N.J.: Analytic Press.

————. 1992b. The Lives of George and Louise Spindler. In *The Psychoanalytic Study of Society. Volume 17: Essays in Honor of George D. and Louise A. Spindler,* ed. L. B. Boyer and R. Boyer, 1–22. Hillsdale, N.J.: Analytic Press.

————, eds. 1994. *Pathways to Cultural Awareness: Cultural Therapy for Teachers and Students.* Newbury Park, Calif.: Corwin Press.

Starr, J. B. 1997. *Understanding China: A Guide to China's Economy, History, and Political Structure.* New York: Hill and Wang, a division of Farrar, Straus and Giroux.

Suárez-Orozco, M. M. 1991. Migration, Minority Status, and Education: European Dilemmas and Responses in the 1990s. *Anthropology and Education Quarterly* 22: 99–120.

————. 1998a. Introduction. In *Crossings: Mexican Immigration in Interdisciplinary Perspectives,* ed. M. M. Suárez-Orozco, 5–50. Cambridge, Mass.: David Rockefeller Center for Latin American Studies and Harvard University Press.

————. 1998b. State Terrors: Immigrants and Refugees in the Post-National Space. In *Ethnic Identity and Power: Cultural Contexts of Political Action in School and Society,* ed. Y. Zou and H. T. Trueba, 283–319. New York: State University of New York Press.

Suárez-Orozco, C., and M. M. Suárez-Orozco. 1995a. Migration: Generational Discontinuities and the Making of Latino Identities. In *Ethnic Identity: Creation, Conflict, and Accommodation,* 3rd edition, ed. L. Romanucci-Ross and G. De Vos, 321–47. Walnut Creek, Calif.: AltaMira Press.

————. 1995b. *Transformations: Immigration, Family Life and Achievement Motivation among Latino Adolescents.* Stanford: Stanford University Press.

Trueba, H. T. 1994. Foreword. In *Pathways to Cultural Awareness: Cultural Therapy for Teachers and Students,* ed. George Spindler and Louise Spindler, vii–xi. Newbury Park, Calif.: Corwin Press.

————. 1999. *Latinos Unidos: From Cultural Diversity to Political Solidarity.* Lanham, Md.: Rowman and Littlefield.

Trueba, H. T., L. Cheng, and K. Ima. 1993. *Myth or Reality: Adaptative Strategies of Asian Americans in California.* London: Falmer Press.

Trueba, H. T., L. Jacobs, and E. Kirton. 1990. *Cultural Conflict and Adaptation: The Case of the Hmong Children in American Society.* London: Falmer Press.

Trueba, H. T., and Y. Zou. 1994. *Power in Education: The Case of Miao University Students and Its Significance for American Culture.* London: Falmer Press.

Zou, Y. 1998. Dilemmas Faced by Critical Ethnographers in China. In *Ethnic Identity and Power: Cultural Contexts of Political Action in School and Society,* ed. Y. Zou and H. T. Trueba, 389–409. New York: State University of New York Press.

Zou, Y., and H. T. Trueba, eds. 1998. *Ethnic Identity and Power: Cultural Contexts of Political Action in School and Society.* New York: State University of New York Press.

10

Intra-Ethnic Mexican and Mexican American Conflicts: Narratives of Oppression and Struggle for Daily Subsistence

Angélica Bautista

El racismo es una enfermedad del espíritu, del cuerpo, el alma y la mente. [Racism is a disease of spirit, mind, body, and soul.]
—Desorden Público, a Venezuelan urban rock band

There have always been two kinds of original thinkers—those who upon viewing disorder try to create order, and those who upon encountering order try to create disorder.
—E. O. Wilson, *The Atlantic Monthly*, March 1998

The intent of this essay is to reflect on the current theoretical debate about gender, specifically that which involves the historical narratives of two of the most influential discourses in U.S. feminism today: "white/dominant" and "Third World" feminist approaches. To set the stage for this reflection, I will first attempt to summarize some of their most important proposals, placing emphasis on contradictory elements as well as on those points that tend to provide a space of coincidence, with the subsequent enrichment and development of gender theory within academia.

In the second part of this essay, I will try to give a sense of the complexity of gender as a social category, which is intersected in turn by other social categories such as race, class, and ethnicity. I will approach this idea by referring to the specific case of the Chicana feminists' notion of *sisterhood*, which I dare say tends to blur and cover up some of the conflictive power relationships *inside* the Mexican and Mexican American communities. To support this statement, I will provide

some ethnographic data I have gathered that will help me to illustrate the intracultural oppression, discrimination, and exploitation that some Mexican and
Mexican American women experience within the boundaries of their own gender and ethnic group.

According to Friedman (1995), one of the failures of U.S. feminism as an inte-
grational movement has been its concentration on Third World feminists' ideological contestation of the white/dominant construction of womanhood. This
contestation was developed under the category of *difference* among women of different racial, ethnic, and economic backgrounds. Besides emphasizing the hegemonic relationships within the "homogeneous" feminist discourse of the movement, the notion of difference also contributed to the formation of "binary
thinking in the form of white women/women of color or First World/Third World
binaries" (Friedman 1995, 5). If we agree on the relevance of difference as an
important element in the democratization of the U.S. feminist movement, can we
also say that this category has brought a more egalitarian representation/partici-
pation of all groups involved with the movement? Could we assume that *difference* is analogous to fragmentation and, thus, an open invitation toward a paradigmatic form of subjective experiences? How strong can a movement that
experiences such marked ideological/structural dissidence be? Was the proposition of difference the "end" of the U.S. feminist movement? Are we now displaying as feminist ideology the unification of fragmented racial/class subjectivities?

In her essay "On Difference" (1991), Linda Gordon presents a critique of the
various contexts in which the notion of difference has played relevant but different roles. I will mention just two of the most relevant contexts in which this concept has been applied. It is well known that in the beginning stages of feminist
theory, the idea of difference was a powerful tool to

> break with all sorts of universalizing tendencies—male, elite, heterosexual, white,
> Eurocentric. . . . It also became a substitute for several more specific and more criti-
> cal concepts such as privilege, contradiction, conflict of interest, even oppression and
> subordination. . . . Within this perspective, women were battling for ground against
> male preferences, procedures, and standards, and feminists sought to defend their own
> ("different") vision even as they demanded recognition for their ability and produc-
> tivity. [Gordon 1991, 91]

It is important to mention that by this time (the late 1970s), there was a more or
less integrated consensus among the women who were working in the structura-
tion of this feminist public discourse.

In between these two oppositional contexts of difference (I will present the second one right after this comment) and in the development process of a more representative theory inside women's studies scholarship, *gender* became by "widespread agreement the single greatest theoretical premise argued and manipulated
by second-wave feminism" (Gordon 1991, 92). In this new approach, gender was
visualized as a sociocultural construct that "was used to postulate dichotomous

categories and then to valorize the previously devalued female part" (Gordon 1991, 93).

With gender as a prospectus for a grounded theory, scholarship in women's studies began to explore the possibilities offered by this concept, which eventually yielded the second relevant context of difference: *gender difference*. This critical gaze on the understanding of gender "challenges political calls to unity as well as scholarly assumptions of homogeneity, showing that they were often hollow or, worse, illusions among dominant groups that their perspectives could stand for every woman's" (Gordon 1991, 94). This reconsideration of the politics of gender marked a new era within the U.S. feminist movement: for some feminists (Friedman 1995; Gordon 1991) this was the beginning of the movement's fragmentation, whereas for others, mainly for feminists of color, this new gaze meant a heightened awareness of unequal power relationships inside the movement and the possibility of an open forum for the many voices that constituted it.

As Friedman has maintained, this differentiation among women gave rise to binary, exchangeable guilty positions among them: whereas some became "victims," others became "victimizers" (and vice versa, according to the political context of the feminist discourse). As was mentioned before, the notion of difference unleashed the creation and re-creation of dualistic positions that influenced not only political narratives within the feminist movement but also the larger dimensions of academia, specially the humanities and social sciences. The civil rights movement was another powerful agent that reinforced the dualistic picture during the decades of the 1960s, 1970s, and 1980s:

> The power of the civil rights movement and the renaissance in Black women's writing in the last few decades intensified this dualism. White feminists tended to use a mainstream, and racist, white/nonwhite division to create a dualism in which not being white was itself a characteristic. Some influential radical women of color offered another interpretation of that division, arguing for political (if not cultural) unity among "Third World" peoples. "We, the Third World people of Asia, Africa, and the Original Americas . . . victims of racism and ghetto colonies within the United States . . . oppressed because of our color, sex and class. . . . We believe that the sisterhood of Third World people is an integral part of our national liberation struggles." [Gordon 1991, 102]

This whole state of affairs can take us in several directions. On one side, the adoption of binary positions in feminist discourse marked a notorious disjuncture in the feminist project of unification/integration/homogenization among all women and brought with it the following two opposite consequences: the first (positive) was a greater openness to cultural diversity among the multiple racial groups in U.S. feminism; the second (negative) was the weakening of the movement itself. On the other side, the principle of gender difference among women facilitated the incorporation of other social categories onto the political terrain of the now fragmenting feminist movement. Race, class, ethnicity, and sexuality appeared and reappeared as interrelated elements indispensable for a more complex study of gender.

An end result of the feminists' fragmented discourse was the representation of subjective experiences constructed from the perspective of each woman's racial background. In other words, U.S. feminism became a plurality of racialized/colored feminist discourses. What is interesting, and somewhat paradoxical, is that once these various discourses were structured into specific racial narratives, there was a tendency to create homogeneous representations *within* these particular narratives, thus blurring the intersection of class, sexuality, and ethnic distinctions at the intraracial level. This type of homogenization was precisely the crucial point of contention in the initial contestations by the women of color who challenged the early formulations of the white/dominant feminist movement. For the purposes of this essay, I am particularly interested in the political discourse of Chicana feminists, specifically in their ideal/imaginary construction of *sisterhood*. As stated before, this notion of commonalty was, ironically, first brought into being through a process of racial differentiation among women: "Gender difference called up hopes of community among women often named, with the characteristic use of familial metaphor, sisterhood. Differences among women, usually, racial, called up bonds among smaller groups of women" (Gordon 1991, 106).

For me, this idea of sisterhood is problematic in two senses: first, because, as I said, it ironically creates "integration from disintegration." Although there is a logical implication that this idea of sisterhood deals directly with the assumption of intraracial unifying connections, it also conveys a sense of exclusion that promotes and reinforces separation at a very subliminal level. It creates a fence, a frontier, a border that rejects difference, although, paradoxically, it has been originated through it. It is as if this assumption of sisterhood was predicating the following notion: "Historically, we have been discriminated; now that we are together, that we are strong, we have the power to, at least discursively, strike back." In presenting this idea I am in no way neglecting the importance of contesting and denouncing the system of oppression and exploitation that has affected Chicana/Mexicana women in this country; what I am questioning is the basic premise that this reactive feeling might improve us as human beings. I would say that it tends to reproduce resentment and prevent us from looking at further developments within ourselves.

The second problem that I have with the notion of sisterhood is the sense of integration that it claims to foster. As mentioned before, it seems to convey a very homogeneous sense of the Chicana/Mexicana community, but this idea, by and large, operates only in the small world of academia. Unfortunately, women from the community at large seldom have access to this kind of ideology, and, unfortunately as well, women from the academy seldom find time to share this ideology with people from their communities. Some Chicana feminists (Anzaldúa 1987; Castillo 1994) have problematized this sense of "homogeneity" in their communities and have discussed the complexity of cultural patterns that help to produce and reproduce women's oppression by women:

Culture is made by those in power—men. Males make the rules and laws; women transmit them. How many times have I heard mothers and mothers-in-law tell their sons to beat their wives for not obeying them, for being *hociconas* (big mouths), for being *callejeras* (going to visit and gossip with neighbors), for expecting their husbands to help with the rearing of children and the housework, for wanting to be something other than housewives? [Anzaldúa 1987, 16]

Undoubtedly, cultural systems constrain ideology, helping to develop contradictions and oppressive situations even among women. What follows is an attempt to illustrate these kinds of situations as they occur among women who operate in the "real" world, in a space where ideas such as sisterhood do not easily arrive and, instead, the women have to contend with very strong social forces that often position them against each other.

MEXICAN AND MEXICAN AMERICAN WOMEN IN THE STRUGGLE FOR DAILY SUBSISTENCE

About a year ago, I started working on a project that I have tentatively called "Mexican and Mexican American Women: In the Struggle for Daily Subsistence (Race and Gender Conflicts at the Intracultural Level)." The aim of this project is to look at the way new Mexican female immigrants incorporate themselves to the informal labor market in Austin.[1] I am particularly interested in understanding the process of power and cultural negotiation between Mexican immigrants and Mexican American women interacting together in a shared social space: the workplace. This project is concerned with reconstructing these women's experiences of conflict from their points of view; in other words, it will attempt to focus on their own narrative stories and their own understandings of this situation.

What first interested me, as an anthropology student, was trying to understand the process through which new Mexican immigrants begin dealing with a new sociocultural environment, how they readjust their previous senses of symbolic expressive life to the present context, and how this life change may become a problem for their own understanding of their identity as "mexicanos." On this first level, the research would attempt to look at the hegemonic process in which an arriving Mexican culture confronts established Anglo and Tex-Mex cultures, always keeping an eye on what the new Mexican immigrants' sense of social identity will be; thus, I was interested not only in those cultural values that change but also in those that remain and even in new ones that may be generated.

This was, of course, an unfocused and overly ambitious "plan" of research. Even if I had a few years and ample resources to devote to this project (which I do not), its too broad approach would have taken me nowhere. Thus, after an earnest conversation with myself, and after considering the methodological convenience (necessity, in fact) of narrowing the scope of this project, I decided to focus on two very "innovative" categories of study: race and gender.

That is how I came to work with three Mexican female immigrants, looking at the process of power and cultural negotiation between them and the members of the different racial groups with whom they normally interact. Of course, at the beginning of this "new" approach, I was affected by my own bias, and I was waiting, almost eagerly, to hear those spectacular stories about the unequal and unfair power relationships between Anglo and Mexican females. But, to my surprise, after I listened to my informants' first accounts of their power, cultural, and racial conflicts, many of my expectations were frustrated.

Curiously, my three informants agreed that their worst job experiences in Austin had been working for and with Mexican and Mexican American women. My very first reactions centered around the following two initial reflections:

1. The first one is related to my informants' relationships with Anglo-American women. As far as I could see, these were very limited relationships because they were based only on job-related stuff and nothing more. The women assume that all they have to do at their jobs is get there, clean the house, leave, and that is all. And the relationship begins and ends right there. Another factor that contributes to this limited kind of relationship is difficulty with the English language.
2. The other reflection is related to the relationship between my informants and women of their own racial group (Mexican and Mexican American). They tended to define their conflictive relations with some of their workmates and bosses in terms of "envy" and "ill will," respectively. Of course, these conflictive relations should be analyzed from a different perspective: as relations in which elements of power, class, and race, as well as cultural difference in backgrounds, all play a role.

WHO ARE MY INFORMANTS, HOW
WE MET AND WORKED TOGETHER

If among the meaningful ways of understanding ethnographic research there is any room for a beginner,[2] I would cast it as a very creative way of putting subjective feelings next to "objective" findings and then show them all dancing together. Here is my contribution to this sometimes therapeutic way of doing social research.

When I called my first interviewee, a series of feelings and prejudices stirred inside me. I remember being very concerned with finding the best way to explain to her the reason for my call, which made me feel angry at myself because part of my concern was to find a nonacademic language to explain the purpose of my study. This in turn made me reflect on the distance between everyday barrio language and academic discourse, between the world of folks and the world of scholars. Another concern had to do with my personal crisis about being here in the United States: I am not sure why, but I thought that asking my interviewees to reflect on their own problematic situation of being here would provoke a crisis as well in them. So I was telling myself, and blaming myself, over and over, that I did not have the right to do that, that surely these women were living well, and that I would bring to them an uncomfortable feeling after my interviews. Finally, my last preoccupation was about my ability to conduct this project: I have only limited experience conducting ethnographic research. Of course that made me worried about my tools for being able to do this. With all these feelings and concerns, and also with my prejudices about my own culture,[3] I started with Nico, my first interviewee.

I first met Nico at the home of Susan and Jane, who are good friends of my husband and me. At that time (1995) Nico was doing domestic work for our friends, two Anglo-American women who only speak isolated words in Spanish. I remember how my husband and I helped them out by serving as translators between Nico and our friends. Since then, Nico and I developed a good rapport, and we spent some time talking, even when we ran into each other doing grocery shopping at the Fiesta market. So when I approached Nico asking for her help with this project, she agreed readily but had many questions about my research and about my career.

Yola was introduced to me by another good Anglo-American girlfriend. We first met at the Continental Club, where we had gone to listen and dance to old traditional Cuban music. She was staying at my friend's apartment while the friend's husband was in Mexico doing sociological field research. With fieldwork being what it is (lengthy), Yola and I had a chance to meet several other times in social situations, and we started a sort of parties' friendship.

Mary, my last informant, was introduced to me by Yola. Although they had not known each other for long because Mary had arrived in Austin only a few months earlier, she accepted immediately the invitation to talk with me about her short experience as both Mexican immigrant and domestic worker. The next section is a brief introduction to my three informants. Later on we will get to know them better as we discuss their experiences of intracultural race and gender conflicts.

Nico (forty-two years old)

- She was born in Placeres del Oro, in the state of Guerrero in Mexico. In this town, she finished her elementary school.
- This was not the first time she has been in the United States; before being here, she had worked as a farmworker in Florida for four years. During that time, she had two of her four children; the other two were born in Mexico.
- After being in Mexico for ten years, Nico emigrated again to the United States in 1995, following her husband who had been here in Austin for a

year by the time she got here. Since then, she had had two jobs as domestic worker, then worked cleaning offices here at the University of Texas, and currently worked at Taco Bell.

Yola (thirty-three years old)

- She is from Tejupilco in the state of Mexico. In her hometown, she attended high school, and after that she was working in a government agency as a social promoter in rural communities.
- Yola had been here for more than ten years; since she arrived, she had always worked as a domestic worker.
- She has some family here, but for several years she had preferred to live by herself in order to feel more independent.

Mary (twenty-six years old)

- Mary was the most recent immigrant in this group; she had been here for only eight months. She is originally from San Ciro, in the state of San Luis Potosí. She began studies to become a public accountant but never finished because she got married.
- Just like Nico, Mary came here following her husband and left her little girl in her hometown with her parents. She only planned to be here in this situation for a few months, to see if she could get a good job. If this worked out, she would go back to Mexico to get her daughter; if not, she would go back to stay with her.
- In these eight months, Mary had had two jobs as a nanny and one as a domestic worker.

From this very general presentation, I could say that my informants share some characteristics. All are from small rural towns in Mexico, where there are very few opportunities "to become somebody." Life in this kind of town tends to be very structured in terms of cultural patterns; as my two married informants told me, they had suffered very oppressive intragender relationships living in the homes of their parents-in-law. According to kinship rules, they became the oppressed and subjugated daughters of their mothers-in-law. Another shared characteristic is the fact that all of them were living the uncertainty of all undocumented immigrants in this country. In this sense, they all live in "solidarity" with those who share their same situation. It is interesting to note here how, when sharing this kind of solidarity, questions such as race and gender are "transgressed" in favor of the creation of a social network that later on is transformed into a net of help. A final shared factor between them is their domestic labor situation. In Mexico, none of them would even think about this type of work because, besides being very poorly paid, it implies quite a low position in Mexico's social scale. Some labor studies in Mexico have shown that, for the most part, only indigenous women who emigrate to the cities are willing to perform this kind of job.

METHODOLOGY

Methodologically, I decided to work with my informants through three different meetings. In the first meetings, I collected general information about their lives and about how these have changed since they had been here. In our second meeting, I further developed and completed information obtained in the first meeting. Also, in this session I focused the conversation on the categories of "work experience" and "social relations." Finally, the third meeting was dedicated to focus on race and gender issues. For me it was very important to conduct the interviews in a very colloquial way; thus, I also shared with them my experience of being an immigrant, a woman, married, and my only, very frustrating, job experience here in Austin. During the conversations, I tried to make sure that my informants felt comfortable and relaxed. With the exception of Nico, who did not want to be recorded, all the conversations, except the first meetings, were recorded with the women's permission. All our meetings were in their houses, the sole exception being when Yola came to have dinner in my apartment. Our interview sessions took between two and three hours approximately.

FIRST FINDINGS IN THE STUDY

Nico's Case

When I started working with Nico, one of the first reflections that she made was, "Once you are here, working in the United States, it is not uncommon to find people from your own country, or even from your own town, fighting among themselves while working in the same place." With this in mind she shared with me her conflictive relationship with her hometown neighbor. For several months they had been working together at Taco Bell, to which Nico applied thanks to the insistence of this neighbor. After she got it, her neighbor started complicating Nico's job:

> I remember that not long ago, she was pushing me to go to Taco Bell to see if I could get a job there; and I just procrastinated because I was afraid to go and ask for a job. I was afraid that the people there would say NO, but my neighbor always was encouraging me, until the day that I finally decided to go. And I asked her if I could go with her so I wouldn't go alone by myself; she answered to me, "Well, hurry up because I'm leaving right now." Then I got into my house to get my purse, and when I came to meet her outside, I could not find her; she had left. That was a little bit strange; however, I decided not to pay too much attention to this. So I took courage and went by

myself. Fortunately, my boss and I got on well, so I got the job. However, I think that my very easy hiring made my neighbor jealous of me because since then she started giving me a really hard time.

Although Nico and her neighbor never have shared the same shift in this job, this has not been an obstacle for their confrontation. Among her stories, Nico told me that she began to have a good work relationship with her gringo boss and that this encouraged her to try to give her best. Because she was new in the job, she needed some days in the beginning to learn how to prepare Tex-Mex tacos; during these days she started to become friendly with her shift partners. Everything was working well until the day that, for just a few minutes, Nico and her neighbor had a short overlap of shifts and had thus a brief chance to work together in the kitchen of Taco Bell. "There was a day," Nico said,

in which my neighbor and I shared for a few minutes the same shift in this job, but they were enough to begin our problems. I remember I was preparing a taco, and she came to me just looking at the way I was preparing this taco. After I finished, she told me that I had put too much filling in the taco and that I should be careful so that the boss would not see me doing that; if he did, he could get mad at me or, even worse, fire me. I didn't tell her anything. The next day, to my surprise, my boss told me that I was putting too much filling in the tacos . . . can you imagine how I felt? Immediately I knew that she had betrayed me. I got so mad with her; I thought she was a hypocrite because first she was encouraging me to take this job, and after I got it she started giving me a really hard time.

Reflecting on this, Nico thought that her neighbor's behavior was a matter of "envy" by people who more or less share one's same living conditions but who want to be above everyone and thus will do whatever is needed to achieve this upper position. She told me that for her it was very significant that during the time that she has lived here, she has not had any problems with the Anglo-American people; on the contrary, the few Anglos that she has met have been "muy buena gente" (very kind) with her. In this respect, I could recall one of the first hypotheses that I mentioned at the beginning, regarding the lack of intercultural conflicts between these female Mexican immigrants and Anglo-Americans. This has to do, primarily, with the lack of a close relationship between these two groups given their different cultural backgrounds, the language difficulties, and the fact of a power relationship based on a job situation. Another important element is the lack of interaction at the level of everyday life. Living under unsure conditions, not only in the sense of legal status but also in the basic aspects of cultural practices and public culture (again, here language is at the center of this matter), new Mexican immigrants display a tendency toward self-segregation and isolation. I have heard stories about people who just arrived here who are afraid to leave their houses and who sometimes wait months before they finally decide to do it. Thus, the interaction between Mexican immigrants and Anglo-Americans is very limited and sometimes avoided altogether. And, of course, the less interaction there is, the less chances there are for confrontation or conflict.

Mary's Case

She told me that she was from Tampico but that she had been living here in the United States for a long time. That's how we started our relationship; then she told me how I should clean the houses. In my first day I had to clean a big house in only four hours. I don't know how I did it because I never had worked in this before, but I got it done. So this was my test; after that she asked me if I would like to continue working for her and I told her yes.

After a while, as I got to know her, she started complaining that she had a lot of work to offer and that she had many girls like me who were ready to work. But this was only her strategy for putting pressure on me, so I would work hard for her.

This is just the beginning to the story. In this narration, Mary shared with me her worst job experience here in Austin. She was working for a Mexican woman who had a kind of improvised network of domestic jobs. What she did was function as an intermediary: she linked women who were in the same conditions as Mary and found them jobs in exchange for almost 70 percent of their salaries.[4] In the daytime, Mary worked with this person; she had to clean two or three houses in four hours each. According to Mary, her boss was very demanding; she wanted everything to be done perfectly, and she was very condescending with her.

In this subordinating relationship, Mary worked for this woman for almost a month. After putting up with several unfair situations, Mary decided to break off her subordinated position and face her boss:

There was this day when I told her, "You know, you are wrong because you want to treat me like I am nobody." After I told her that, she started telling me that I was very ignorant, that I didn't even know the laws of this country. She got very mad at me and told me that she wouldn't pay me the last eight hours of my work; she told me that even if I called the police she would not, and not happy with that, she also threatened me with calling the INS [Immigration and Naturalization Service].

Of course, this job relation ended in a very bad way. For Mary there was little to lose by getting deported, except, of course, the company of her husband. But she had her little daughter waiting for her in Mexico. So, she was not too afraid when her Mexican boss threatened her with *la migra* (the INS). She was aware from the beginning of the unequal power relationship between herself and her boss; she also was aware of the issue of low wages and labor exploitation. She told me that she could put up with the unfairness of this whole situation, but the one thing she could not stand was being treated badly. Reflecting on her situation, she thought that one of the main problems for Mexican immigrants is the language barrier, and she considered it a powerful obstacle that facilitates the exploitation of new immigrants who do no speak English. She believed that the ability or inability to speak this language should not create social discrimination and exploitation and felt that, independently of the language a person speaks, everybody deserves fair treatment.

Yola's Case

Of the cluster of three, I would say that Yola is the interviewee who best understood the issue of job exploitation of Mexicans working with illegal status. As I mentioned before, she had been employed as a domestic worker for the last ten years, which had given her enough time to reflect on her own working situation:

> Here I feel free and don't feel like I have to hide from the migra. Sometimes it's in my jobs where I have more problems because people who want to contract my services always ask me for my social security number, and I don't have one. So, whenever I find a job I like, and my bosses treat me well, I always try to keep it; but if I get one in which they treat me badly and pay me a low salary, immediately I quit it and look for another one. In other words, I'm not that kind of woman who puts up with everything because I'm undocumented; you know everybody deserves the right to feel comfortable with their job. So, when I have problems with my gringo bosses, I talk back to them when I feel they are treating me badly, I talk to them with the truth, so I can defend myself.

During the time she has been here, she worked for Anglo-Americans, as well as for and with Mexicans and Mexican Americans. The diversity of jobs she has had allowed her to have a good perception of who are the best and the worst employers for Mexican immigrants. During our conversations, she told me that she tries to avoid working for Mexicans and Mexican Americans because they are very complicated people. At least, she said, she could never work for an employer like the one Mary had. She had heard many horror stories about this kind of boss, and she thought that they are very greedy and also willing to take unfair advantage. They want people to work hard for them and then they pay them a miserable wage.

As she just mentioned above, Yola said that she always tries to keep those jobs in which the *patrona* (boss) gives her decent and fair treatment; those in which there are some unfair situations she always runs away from. Yola remembered how at the beginning she used to be very naive because she never stood up to her employers and never tried to defend herself because she was afraid of her illegal working status. So when she started in this type of work she had to suffer some bad experiences:

> I still remember this job I had for like six months; everything was going well until this person, my patrona, wanted me to come to her house on Sunday nights so I could start working on Monday by 7:00 in the morning. But they really wanted me to start

working on Sunday nights, so that when I got to their home I should go directly to the kitchen and clean up all their *mugrero* [filthy mess]. I had to do that several times until the day that I said to myself, "This is not right. Why do I have to start working on Sundays for the same wage of Monday to Friday?"

There was this day that I took courage and talked to my boss: "See Mr. Terry, early tomorrow I'll clean the kitchen because I feel a little tired, so tomorrow is better for me." But he said, "This is not possible because Geo [his wife] doesn't like to see the kitchen so dirty. . . ." But, as I had everything planned, I insisted on my position: "See Mr. Terry, I don't want to clean the kitchen on Sunday nights, I want to begin my work on Monday mornings, as everybody does." But he told me, "In this house you have to start working as soon as you get here on Sunday nights. . . ." Then I answered him, "See, each girl [domestic worker] is different. What you were doing with Hortencia, your last employee, was very wrong because she commented to me that she didn't want to clean the kitchen on Sunday nights but that she was afraid to talk to you about that, so she never said anything. So, from now on, I'm informing to you that I'm going to start working from 8:00 a.m. on Mondays to a determined time in the evenings. . . . Let's take this example, you go ahead and try to get your office employees to work right now, on Sunday night, to see what they would tell you. . . ." He then got really mad at me and told me, "But the thing is that I'm your boss." "You are the boss," I replied, "and I'm a human being, and all human beings have the right to work according with fair schedules." He got even angrier, then his wife showed up very angry too, asking what was wrong in there. Terry answered, "Yola doesn't want to clean the kitchen." After that they talked to each other in English, and I told them, "Calm down, you know, I'll only work for one more week, so I'll give you the chance to look for another person that can put up with you guys, and you will see if this person will accept to clean your kitchen on Sundays night." Then they told me, "It's okay, we'll try to see if we can find another one."

Since this initial bad experience, she had tried to keep only those jobs where the employers offer her decent treatment. Also since then, she had the philosophy to protect herself from job abuses. Now she was concerned with creating a kind of solidarity network between her and her closest friends who share the same job situation; what she wanted to do is, in case that she has two or three houses for cleaning in a given week,[5] ask a friend—who is without work at the time—to clean one of the houses. Yolanda told me that she wanted to do that because one never knows when one will need this kind of solidarity.

SOME FINAL COMMENTS AND PERSPECTIVES FOR THE FUTURE OF THIS PROJECT

The information here presented represents only a minimal part of the conversations I had with my interviewees. For the specific purpose of this essay I selected only those passages that would help illustrate conflicting aspects of relationships between Mexicans and Mexican Americans within a work setting. I am very aware that this project is lacking the Mexican Americans' version and lacking the voices of Chicana working-class women, who are certain to have their own stories about this kind of job situation. For the coming future, I am planning to continue this work, including interviews with Mexican American domestic workers and bosses, in order to achieve a more complete picture.

Looking at race and gender categories with an intracultural scope demands a complex analysis that not only includes perceptions, behaviors, or social and cultural actions but also requires a critical link with the external factors (the *inter*-counterpart) that directly or indirectly affect the *intra*relationships within a social group. Thus, for the study of intracultural conflicts between Mexican immigrants and other Mexican and Mexican American females, the ethnographic approach was fundamental in order to deeply describe my interviewees' perceptions of their job situations and of their relationships with other Mexican and Mexican American women. However, my critical approach would be incomplete if I were to just leave the analysis presented at the level of an internal glance.

It would be unfair, then, to come away with the stereotypical interpretations that my interviewees offered to me about themselves, Mexican American, and Anglo-American women. Intragender conflict perceptions respond not only to individual readings but also to a more generalized or socialized way of constructing collective or group stereotypes. Even if my interviewees had not lived here, they would probably use the same standard stereotypes because the perceptions that these describe are used in a more generalized way.[6] They respond to historical and social determinations of Mexicans and Mexican Americans in the United States. This is why I consider it important to take into account external factors that contribute to the construction and development of social perceptions at the intracultural level. Let us recall, again, what Ruth Frankenberg so aptly points out: "Race as well as Gender are socially constructed categories and, thus, they should be always analyzed as being part of a changing process, and as part of a series of social conditions that determine their meaning through time" (1993, 11). They are both "real" and have tangible and concrete effects on people's lives.

Thus, what we have seen here is not simply or solely a matter of "envy" or "ill will." There is a certain sense of "competitiveness" that the current social and political discourse promotes and which has as one of its results precisely the fostering of intra- and interconflicts among minority groups in the United States in particular and in the whole world in general. This is one of the most successful strategies that powerful conservative groups have long managed to disseminate into the air that we breathe everyday so that we, willingly and with great confidence, keep ourselves busy stabbing each other.

Chicana feminism needs to go beyond the terrain of dualistic positions and seek to reinforce connections with and among the women of its community. The words of Gloria Anzaldúa sum up this point: "We need to de-academize theory and to connect the community to academy. 'High' theory does not translate well when one's intention is to communicate to masses of people made up of different audiences. We need to give up the notion that there is a 'correct' way to write theory" (1990, 26).

NOTES

1. By "informal labor market" I mean jobs related to noninstitutionalized settings; in other words—and for the specific case of this study—I mean jobs that are inserted within informal social networks established by women who labor as domestic workers, office cleaners, and cooking help in fast food companies.

2. See Clifford and Marcus 1986; Coffey and Atkinson 1996; Foley 1990, 1995; Geertz 1973; Malinowski 1944; Rosaldo 1989; and Van Maanen 1995—just to mention a few.

3. While establishing my first contacts I was afraid that my informants would stand me up, in other words, that they would tell me that they wanted to participate in this project and then, "a la hora de la verdad" (at the moment of truth), just tell me a big NO. Fortunately, only one of my four initial contacts did this.

4. This condition illustrates the "subcontracting arrangement" relationship explained in Houndagneu-Sotelo's article "Regulating the Unregulated?: Domestic Workers's Social Networks" (1994b); this category basically refers to the relationship between new immigrant women and women well established in the domestic labor domain. About this relationship, Houndagneu-Sotelo says that "many new immigrant women first find themselves subcontracting their services to other more experienced and well-established immigrant women who have steady customers for domestic work" (1994b, 56). Talking about the convenience of this kind of relationship, she remarks that a "subcontracted arrangement is informative and convenient, especially for an immigrant woman who lacks her own transportation or has minimal English language skills. The pay, however, is much lower that what a women might earn on her own. . . . In an apprentice/subcontracting arrangement the pay can be so low that it renders the experience exploitative and demeaning" (1994b, 57).

5. At times she had had two or three houses for cleaning in a week. Yola said that financially it is better to work this way because she only goes one or perhaps two times per week to clean a home, and then she goes in the same week to clean other houses. Wages earned this way are higher than if one works only in one house the whole week.

6. For a critical analysis of the utilization of Mexican American stereotypes in the United States, see José Limón's article "Stereotyping and Chicano Resistance: An Historical Dimension" (1973). For Mexican cultural stereotypes, see Octavio Paz's book *El Laberinto de la Soledad* (1950).

REFERENCES

Anzaldúa, Gloria. 1987. *Borderlands/La Frontera: The New Mestiza*. San Francisco: Aunt Lute Books.
———. 1990. *Haciendo Caras/Making Face, Making Soul: Creative and Critical Perspectives by Women of Color*. San Francisco: Aunt Lute Press.
Castillo, Ana. 1994. *Massacre of the Dreamers*. New York: Plume/Penguin Books.

Clifford, James, and George E. Marcus. 1986. *Writing Culture: The Poetics and Politics of Ethnography.* Berkeley and Los Angeles: University of California Press.

Coffey, Amanda, and Paul Atkinson. 1996. *Making Sense of Qualitative Data: Complementary Research Strategies.* Thousand Oaks, Calif.: Sage Publications.

Foley, Douglas E. 1990. *Learning Capitalist Culture: Deep in the Heart of Tejas.* Philadelphia: University of Pennsylvania Press.

————. 1995. *The Heartland Chronicles.* Philadelphia: University of Pennsylvania Press.

Frankenberg, Ruth. 1993. *White Women, Race Matters: The Social Construction of Whiteness.* Minneapolis: University of Minnesota Press.

Friedman, Susan. 1995. Beyond White and Other: Relationality and Narratives of Race in Feminist Discourse. *Signs: Journal of Women in Culture and Society* 21, no. 1: 1–49.

Geertz, Clifford. 1973. *The Interpretation of Cultures.* Basic Books, a division of Harper-Collins Publishers.

Gordon, Linda. 1991. On Difference. *Genders* 10 (spring): 91–111.

Hondagneu-Sotelo, Pierrette. 1994a. *Gendered Transitions: Mexican Experiences of Immigration.* Berkeley: University of California Press.

————. 1994b. Regulating the Unregulated?: Domestic Workers's Social Networks. *Social Problems* 41, no. 1: 50–64.

Hondagneu-Sotelo, Pierrette, and Cristina Riegos. 1997. Sin organización no hay solución: Latina Domestic Workers and Non-Traditional Labor Organizing. *Latino Studies Journal* 8, no. 3 (fall): 54–81.

Limón, José. 1973. Stereotyping and Chicano Resistance: An Historical Dimension. *Aztlán* 4, no. 2 (fall): 257–70.

Malinowski, Bronislaw. 1944. *A Scientific Theory of Culture and Other Essays.* Chapel Hill: University of North Carolina Press.

Paz, Octavio. 1950. *El Laberinto de la Soledad.* 1st edition. Mexico City: Cuadernos Americanos.

Rosaldo, Renato. 1989. *Culture and Truth: The Remaking of Social Analysis.* Boston: Beacon Press.

Sandoval, Chela. 1991. U.S. Third World Feminism: The Theory and Method of Oppositional Consciousness in the Postmodern World. *Genders* 10 (spring): 1–24.

Segura, Denise. 1990. Chicanas and Triple Oppression in the Labor Force. In *Chicana Voices: Intersections of Class, Race, and Gender*, ed. Teresa Córdova et al., 47–65. Albuquerque: University of New Mexico Press.

Wilson, Edward O. 1998. Back from Chaos. *The Atlantic Monthly* 281, no. 3 (March): 41–62.

Van Maanen, John, ed. 1995. *Representation in Ethnography.* Thousand Oaks, Calif.: Sage Publications.

Zavella, Patricia. 1991. *Mujeres* in Factories: Race and Class Perspectives on Women, Work, and Family. In *Gender at the Crossroads of Knowledge: Feminist Anthropology in the Postmodern Era*, ed. Micaela di Leonardo, 312–36. Berkeley and Los Angeles: University of California Press.

————. 1997. Playing with Fire: The Gendered Construction of Chicana/Mexicana Sexuality. In *The Gender/Sexuality Reader: Culture, History and Political Economy*, ed. Micaela di Leonardo and Roger Lancaster, 392–408. New York: Routledge.

11

The Use of Cultural Resilience in Overcoming Contradictory Encounters in Academia: A Personal Narrative

Martha Montero-Sieburth

INTRODUCTION

This chapter relates the experiences and contradictory encounters that, as a Latina faculty member, I have faced and continue to struggle with in the most sacred of all educational domains—the U.S. academy. My personal narrative describes how some of the Mexican and Costa Rican sociocultural traditions and educational values that I was raised with have become the cultural resilience with which I have defined my role at different academic institutions. Such resilience has proven to be a resourceful approach beyond simple survival. It has helped me to problem-solve complex situations, deconstruct their meaning, and redefine "success" on my own terms.

These sociocultural traditions, and their socializing influences, prepared me to become the first doctorate-bound female in my family and helped me cope with the demands of academic culture. Thus, one of the purposes of this chapter is not only to describe and explain encounters and contradictory experiences throughout twenty-five years of my academic career but also to identify the ways in which drawing on such Latino cultural resilience can become a source of strength. In documenting such experiences, I hope to pass on the lessons that I have learned so that future generations of academic career–oriented Latinos and Latinas can better prepare themselves for academic life.

Another goal of this chapter is to identify and describe how inequities are sustained and reproduced at different institutions, how we contribute to their reproduction, and how such inequities can be contested and deconstructed. I use the notions of an "educated person" and "cultural production," espoused by Barry Levinson, Douglas Foley, and Dorothy C. Holland (1996), as useful constructs to describe how cultural identities are produced and acquire meaning.

The notion of an educated person is a culturally specific and relative concept that can be used according to Levinson, Foley, and Holland to identify "the historical and cultural particularities of the 'products' of education and thus provides a framework for understanding conflicts around different kinds of schooling" (1996, 3). That is to say, by situating people within their own historical embeddedness and cultural context, we can better understand how they are "products" in the sense of being produced by a definite site as well as how they as products can produce cultural forms.

Cultural production, according to Levinson, Foley, and Holland (1) serves to help us "understand how human agency operates under powerful structural constraints" (1996, 14) and contributes to creating a dialectic between structure and agency; (2) explores "the resources for, and constraint upon, social action—the interplay of agency and structure—in a variety of educational institutions" (1996, 3); and (3) analyzes structural inequalities from a non-Western and nonprivileged perspective in the social and cultural contexts in which they arise. The contestation I speak of is not only about the power relationships and cultural differences that exist between Anglo-European mainstream culture and Latinos but, more significantly, about growing differences between inter- and intra-ethnic groups. As Latinos continue to grow in numbers and visibility, they represent a challenge not only to the dominant Anglo mainstream culture but also to other underrepresented groups whose struggles become intensified as limited resources dwindle.[1] It could be argued that the current emphasis on Ebonics by some African Americans has become a means to obtain some of the funding allocated to bilingual education programs, primarily those addressing the needs of Spanish speakers as a right and privilege that have been denied to African Americans. Under Title I funding, African Americans had been able to garner support for their students, but as it became directed to include Latinos as bilingual funding decreased, it has created terrain for contestation. No doubt there will be growing intensification of such struggles into the next century, and how we respond in nondivisive and conciliatory ways will be particularly important in the academic realm.

ENCOUNTERS WITH SELF AND EDUCATIONAL VALUES

I knew that I was destined to become a teacher from the time I tutored students in English at age thirteen in Mexico and later taught older students shorthand at age eighteen. Whether teaching was a predisposition nurtured by being surrounded by educated professional men in my Costa Rican family or whether I was simply following in the footsteps of my great-grandfather, a renowned educator,

Fam
education

geographer, and historian of Costa Rica from the last century, the fact is that I was drawn to *la mística del maestro* (the mystique or heartfelt commitment of the teacher) at an early age. My own mother's Mexican family, whose parents worked the land and were shopkeepers, did not go beyond the third grade in school. My mother and her six sisters and brothers went only to the fifth grade because, when the Mexican Revolution erupted, schools were closed. Despite these limitations, however, both families maintained a deep respect for the value of education and for teachers.

That mística, well known throughout Latin America, goes beyond subject matter knowledge and a commitment to teach. To be a teacher with mística is to be a teacher soulfully and critically immersed in the practice of teaching. It requires understanding of how teaching actually impacts students and how students come to understand their own engagement in learning. Thus, mística is about the dialectical and dialogical process that ensues when teachers and students connect, when the transference of knowledge as a creatively constructed process, a notion strongly expounded by the late Paulo Freire, is understood.

Because teaching and learning take place in a context, and contexts are socially and culturally constructed, the meanings attributed to becoming a teacher were highly influenced by the values of education I was exposed to since birth. Born and raised in Mexico, yet influenced by Costa Rican culture and later schooling in the United States, I quickly learned how education is valued and honored in each country.

To Mexicans, education has portentous meanings because it is the process by which Mexican youth are socialized not only into civic and national consciousness but, more importantly, into familial and group loyalties. Throughout preschool and elementary grades, children are taught about the history, geography, and culture of Mexico, not simply as memorized facts but as situated social circumstances in which the sense of belonging and unity are nationalistically orchestrated through the enactment of civic, social, and cultural celebrations.

The numbers of civic and cultural celebrations in Mexico have been well documented by anthropologists as part of the "fiesta complex." Well over 100 events are recognized in schools each year, and they serve to recognize not only civic and cultural heroes such as Benito Juárez, Lázaro Cárdenas, Sor Juana Inés de la Cruz, Doña Josefa Ortíz de Domínguez, Emiliano Zapata, and los Niños Héroes (the Hero Children) but also socially binding events such as the Day of the Child, Mother's Day, the Day of the Teacher, Father's Day, the Day of the Flag, and the Day of the Worker, to name just a few. During each of these events, schools prepare children through poetry readings, dances, oratories, and nationalistic speeches.

These rituals serve not only to shape and reinforce the moral commitment and responsibilities of children to their family, school, and country but also to develop the relationships of students to their teachers as lifetime relationships. I still remember Mrs. Maraver, my fifth grade teacher, who demanded precision in our declamations, with just the right intonation and voice projection to emote feeling to our peers. Similarly, Ms. Mustafa, my Spanish sixth grade teacher, maintained strict rules on the orthography of Spanish. Mr. Romero, my sixth and seventh grade history teacher, immersed us in the Mexican–American War, the Treaty of Guadalupe Hidalgo, and los Niños Héroes from the perspective of Mexicans. I came to identify with my school as an extension of my family and culture, so that on the days that we had public displays with the recitations of important heroes and heroines, I came to see myself as living in a larger community and civic national culture. Before I was four, I had learned all of the regional dances of Mexico as well as the *jarabe tapatío,* the Mexican Hat Dance, as a symbol of the national culture.[2]

As adults, Mexicans steeped in such traditions are able to parlay their local and regional knowledge as a means to maintain public relationships and social cohesiveness, but at the national level, such cultural capital is used to symbolically represent a united front, a sense of national unification, despite tremendous economic and social hardships. It is often said that Mexicans *aguantan mucho,* endure a great deal, and do so in spite of their fundamental distrust of politicians and an eroding economic infrastructure. Despite such underlying distrust, Mexicans nevertheless believe in education and invest in schooling as one the most important social, economic, and political human capital returns.

For Costa Ricans, education is the lifeline of democratic life. Since 1848, all Costa Rican citizens have been guaranteed a free, compulsory elementary education, a value taken seriously in a country that has one of highest literacy rates throughout Latin America. Education is such a centerpiece that, for its population of almost four million people, Costa Rica has forty-four private universities and four national public universities. Moreover, as part of ex-President Oscar Arias's legacy to Costa Rica, students since the 1980s have been exposed to computer literacy skills that parallel those in industrialized countries. Seymour Papert of MIT has actively worked in institutionalizing Logo and other computer programs within the educational system. One of the first ecological curricula in Latin America demonstrating how to care for the environment and animals has been disseminated to elementary grades throughout the country; teacher education programs at the universities use Freirean, constructivist, and action-oriented approaches to learning; and practitioner-oriented qualitative research flourishes at different universities.[3] More importantly, education in Costa Rica is inextricably linked to the country's highly developed civic and democratic culture. Children learn to value decision making, group learning, and sharing early on, and parents are highly involved in schools through teachers, school councils, and fund-raising projects. Education is clearly valued in Costa Rica, so much so that the commitment to quality education constitutes one of the largest national expenditures.

Given the explanation of these educational influences, they represent at a personal, instructional, and institutional level some of the core values that foster *responsibility on the part of families and schooling communities for educating and for being educated* as a lifelong process—which is an unknown concept in U.S. schooling. For example, in Mexico, "el ser instruído, no es lo mismo que ser educado"— to be instructed is not the same as being educated. Being educated means more than the learning that takes place in school. It also refers to the continuous social learning that takes place outside of school—with friends, parents, peers, and community members. As one acquires the basis for reading, writing, and arithmetic, one is also learning about how to set up reciprocal social relationships and obligations with peers, teachers, family, extended family, and community members. In such relationships, social behaviors are kept in balance at home and at school by teachers, peers, and family through *consejos*, given advice, as a means to exert pressures toward conformity. Like mothers, who advise children on how to behave, teachers would give consejos on dealing with peers and with one's own inner sense. I often hear Ms. Mustafa telling me, "Más te vale hacer caso, que después estar arrepentida" [You might as well listen than regret the consequences later]. Such dealings help one deal with day-to-day personal and social issues, so that after time, one knows what to expect.

It is no wonder, then, that rules of reciprocity and expectations could readily be understood. The pressure exerted by peers to comply with the groups' social norms, when students misbehave in Mexican classrooms, is enough to keep behaviors in check without the intervention of the teacher. Verbal threats by peers, such as, "Ya veras" [You'll see] or "Me la vas a pagar" [You'll pay for it], suffice to keep even sixty students on task.

Similarly, socialization in Costa Rican schools is not only about learning but also about becoming a proud *tico* or *tica* (endearment terms for a Costa Rican male and female) who identifies with the school community as an extension of the family. Wearing the uniform of one's school, singing the school song, and competing in group sports or academic tryouts represent the type of symbolic loyalty that ties children to parents and school community. Within the communities at large, families tend to sustain both the conformity and loyalty that are taught in schools and unconditionally support the endeavors of teachers, who in turn use these shared social mores to control the behaviors of children in their classrooms. This does not suggest that everyone in Costa Rica conforms automatically but, rather, that there is value placed on teaching a child how to be *buena gente*, a good person, which places one in good social stead and allows one to sustain and balance all types of negotiations as an adult. It should be noted that this works well in a country such as Costa Rica, where, because of the great degree of intermarriage between families, social civility rather than confrontation becomes important.[4]

Among the most valued rules and behaviors for Mexicans and Costa Ricans as well as many other Latinos is the sense of *respeto*, respect, which is acknowledged as both a right and a privilege.[5] Adults as well as teachers and elders are owed respeto, but children are also taught to demonstrate respectful behavior and to expect to be respected. Among one of the most known statements in Mexico is

Benito Juárez's motto, "El respeto al derecho ajeno, es la paz" [Respecting the rights of others is peace]. The role of a teacher is inherently respectful in and of itself, and the teacher is endowed with an aura of expected respectful behaviors that extend beyond the knowledge and wisdom of being educated to include social relationships, compromises, duties, and responsibilities between teacher and students. A *profesor/profesora*, a term usually attributed to teachers in secondary schools or at the university, also carries this same sense of respectful relationship building between student and teacher. Beyond the qualifications of authority and knowledge, respeto also conveys social mores and behaviors. University faculty, or *catedráticos*, those who officiate *cathedra*, often carry their lectures from the academy to the nearest coffee shop, where teacher and students continue to dialogue, expanding the social learning of the class as well.

Thus, it can be seen that the role of teachers as well as faculty carries with it a sense of authority, status, dignity, and honor, which are ascribed to the profession and are embodied in the types of relationships that develop. Similarly, the learner learns to confide in the *maestro*, or professor, as a trusted mentor. While the roles may not be reciprocal at first, as needed exchanges between student and teacher occur over time, social and lifelong relationships that balance the authority-deference relationship develop. For example, it is not uncommon for maestros or profesors without housing in some of the most remote villages of Mexico or Costa Rica to be locally housed and fed. Their valued role in teaching children is symbolically recognized with gifts such as fruits, plants, and clothing. Moreover, as teachers become known within a community, they are overtly recognized as social and educational mentors resulting in long-term familial relationships with obligations. It is not uncommon for teachers to become the *compadres* or *comadres* (godfathers/godmothers) of children within a family. Thus, the family may include teachers. For me, that notion of well-earned respect, honor, and dignity attributed to being a teacher has often been called into question throughout my academic career in the United States. How one earns and maintains respeto in the academy is worth exploring.

ENCOUNTERS WITHIN THE ACADEMIC PROFESSION

When my family emigrated to the United States so that my father could continue to specialize in medicine, I did not realize that I would live a borderless existence. At the time that I grew up in the 1950s and 1960s in the United States, Latinos were referred to as the "other," white, of Spanish surname.

The physical borders between Mexico, Costa Rica, and the United States became blurred as we moved over 100 times between each country and each state. My brother and I lived and studied in Mexico and the United States, and we vacationed in Costa Rica, learning to continuously adapt and renegotiate each culture's demands, language requirements, social class differences, and academic and social competencies. For over twenty-five years, the continual *ir y venir*, coming and going, created opportunities to adjust from urban to rural settings, from bustling city life to secluded hospital life, from being in the midst of things to being on the periphery, from being called a *pocha* (a Mexican who has been Americanized)[6] to being called a "taco bender, spic, bean eater, and greaser," and most importantly, from code switching from Spanish at home to speaking English in school. I became what Hugh Mehan has described as "competent" in negotiating the rules for group membership in several cultures. In adapting, I drew on each culture's strengths and derived from each the acceptable behaviors and norms that later allowed me to develop what I call cultural resilience to cope in academia. Each culture contributed influences that are still with me today.

Caught between the cusp of changing Mexican traditional values of the 1950s and 1960s and the legal and social independence guaranteed to Costa Rican women since the 1800s, I found myself gaining political control over my life to make decisions that many of my female counterparts were denied. In the closed traditions of my Mexican family, where males were favored over females, I experienced the strength of my maternal grandmother, aunts, and mother. My grandmother could defy the authority of the minister of her church by quoting the Bible with greater insights and understanding than he. Uneducated but experienced in life after having eight children and being left to raise them on her own, she encountered obstacles with stoic tenacity. My three aunts, fearless of their husbands' blustery behavior and some of their infidelities, challenged them openly, so much so that I considered them to be *muy fregonas* (quite competent). My own mother rebelled in silence yet used her beauty and wit to gain power over her two husbands. Thus, the feminism that I understood from them was not about becoming "like a male" but about being feminine, enjoying the art of dressing up, wearing make-up, being coquettish, and handling males subtlety while having needs met.

From my Costa Rican side, I experienced the effects of feminism early on. I enjoyed the freedom Costa Rican women experienced in being their own persons, making legal contracts, and having their well-being and status historically protected by law. Women in Costa Rica, expresses Clotilde Obregón Quesada, "retained their maiden name in marriage and, from the eighteenth century on, children carried both their mother's last name and their father's. This custom has permitted Latin American women to retain their identity and to avoid the trauma of being legally obligated to use the husband's name" (1997, 54–55).

I also witnessed democracy at work, seeing well over thirteen different parties at national elections, the development of people-initiated communities, children addressing issues of decision making in schools, and democracy linked to education in schools. I was influenced not only by a strong feminist stance but by the democratic ideals that Costa Ricans live by. My sense of obligation, concern for ideals, and the freedom that I emphasize in my teaching are most likely owed to these influences.

Beyond these single strong impressions, I was profoundly impacted by both countries' emphasis on the overt nature of the extended family, celebratory rituals saturated with folk histories, and lived experiences, the richness of mestizo cultures blended from the mixtures of European, African, and Indian backgrounds. In all of this, I found the "grounding" of my experiences in history, much like the historicity that the late Paulo Freire often spoke about. That historicity is about defining and situating oneself in a given context, but it is also about the history that one creates as one becomes aware of one's role in deciphering actions to be taken within social, economic, and political spheres. Such grounding carries the meaning of a sociohistorical past into the present. It is that history that I believe also helps define identity, one's self-awareness and critical consciousness.

That grounding has given rise to the cultural resilience that I speak of, of influences past and present, born out of the struggle between cultures of domination and subordination, class and language differences. Such resilience has no doubt become the basis for the emergence of my academic career. I became the first in my generation to break ground as a Latina faculty member teaching at different private, ivy, and public institutions. During the 1970s, I was the only female administrator in a private international university in Mexico. I had to contend with the honors attributed to men but not to women in such positions, for most females were relegated to clerical positions. Being fully bilingual in English and Spanish, I became the link to the vice-presidents and president of the university because I developed programs that attracted several hundred foreign students and became quite profitable for the university. But even in such an important role, the attitude shared by my Mexican male counterparts was that there were limits to what I as a woman could do. When I hired a young female secretary who under Mexican law would be able to receive child care benefits for three months if she became pregnant, I was asked to fire her by the president of the university, to thus avoid any payment of future maternity leave. I refused to do so by demonstrating that there had been sexual harassment of several of the secretaries by the vice-president and that I would go public in a highly religious state. On that basis the president allowed me to keep the secretary, and I continued to challenge the status quo. Yet the struggle between what I could demand as a female and what the males could require and do became a constant battleground. I felt that the institution was simply not ready to understand the significance of gender in its midst and entrenched hierarchy, and I decided I could no longer endure the war.

As visiting professor at the University of Costa Rica, even though I am Costa Rican and have extensive family connections, I was not taken seriously as a qualitative researcher until I presented my own political stance. As the first to introduce qualitative coursework to faculty and practitioners, I was under suspicion, first, because I criticized the center-to-periphery decentralization of the country under regionalization and, second, because I was assumed to hold leftist political views, given the nature of the exposure of action research throughout Latin America and the perception that such research was conducted mostly by leftist or communist educators. The fact that my Costa Rican family had highly religious and conservative members as well as socialist and leftists activists who were Troskyite Marxists made it altogether more difficult to be seen as a committed pedagogue and not a political activist. Once I began the courses and students emerged fluent in qualitative research knowledge and skills, the suspicions subsided.

As painful and difficult as these encounters were, I was culturally equipped to deflect the political posturing and to present myself as a researcher in a positive light. It was not until I studied for my doctorate that the "implicit culture of academia" with its unstated rules and norms made a greater impact on my life and personal career.

Entering the domain of the academic rites of passage for the dissertation proved to be a stressful experience. Although my major field was administration and curriculum, I had a concentration in bilingual education that was the focus of my dissertation. Yet, because it was a separate program, conducting ethnographic research, framed by the new sociology of education on bilingual education, was not considered legitimately traditional.

I spent a year and a half changing committees until I was able to find a chair who saw value in the research I was conducting within a Latino community. The fact that I wanted to draw data from a Latino community was viewed by some faculty as a major obstacle not only for reasons of objectivity but also because some of the members of the committee felt uncomfortable in supporting the fieldwork of Latinos they knew little of except through what they read. In fact, the year I completed the degree, the chair of my dissertation, an immersed critical pedagogue, was denied tenure. His neo-Marxist philosophy was used as an explanation, but the fact was that he was extremely popular with students, published extensively and internationally, and had gained a following because of his critical pedagogy. I nevertheless went through four different committees and received a doctorate based on a dissertation that my chair considered to be ahead of its time for its incisiveness in analyzing bilingual education from the perspective of critical theory.[7]

The aftermath of the doctorate was anti-climatic—not only was my research based on the advocacy of bilingual education, a political minefield in Massachusetts despite it being the first state to start bilingual education programs in 1971, but even in the 1980s its validity as a field was still questioned. More evident was the competition in finding available tenure-track positions in a city of colleges and universities like Boston, even though promises of affirmative action hiring were openly stipulated by each institution. I began teaching as an adjunct faculty in several of the adjacent colleges hoping for the door to open in academia.

I quickly learned that, as a part-time instructor, the access to institutional affiliation and the rights and privileges accorded full-time faculty were not available, so I opted for combined administrative/teaching positions in order to have greater opportunities. I became the "first Latina" to teach and administer programs in several Boston-based colleges during the late 1970s and early 1980s. Yet while such opportunities have provided entry into academe, they have also had dire personal and professional consequences.

ENCOUNTER AND CONTRADICTIONS IN ACADEMIC LIFE

One of my first teaching experiences in higher education in the United States was at a large metropolitan private university, where I began as a specialist in a federally funded program that provided bilingual education in-service training throughout the New England area. After completing the initial interview for the position with the director of the program, I was told I was not hired because I was not Puerto Rican, even though I had all the necessary competencies, including a study of Puerto Ricans as part of my master's degree. While I readily understood the reasoning behind the director's reticence to hire me and was aware of the majority status of Puerto Ricans within the Latino population of the commonwealth during the 1970s, I contested the decision on the basis that it was the same excuse used by whites to deny jobs to Latinos, blacks, and other underrepresented groups. I tenaciously argued my point and was hired the next day by the director. Yet I was left with the quandary of what I needed to do to prove myself among Puerto Ricans. I believe that as Latinos we were all struggling to attain the same rights and privileges in the United States. So I decided to turn the situation into a challenge. I would attempt to understand the differences and nuances that existed among Puerto Ricans, Mexicans, Central Americans, and South Americans in greater metropolitan Boston; thus, I would become even more knowledgeable of the lives and struggles of Puerto Ricans in the United States.

After such an encounter, I became aware of issues that had to do more with class and less with ethnicity at small private institutions in Boston. The fact that I did not come from a working-class background, was not a Chicana, did not have migrant experiences, and spoke English without an accent made it difficult for some of my Anglo counterparts to situate me given their basic stereotypes of Mexicans as poor, non-English speakers, uneducated, and from working-class backgrounds. When I spoke of my Costa Rican background, I was inevitably thought of as being Puerto Rican, demonstrating my colleagues' total lack of geographic knowledge. Notwithstanding, I grew to expect this unsophisticated knowledge base from Anglos and was willing to teach about my origins, but I was not prepared to face a similar situation with my Latino counterparts.

Being a Mexican and Costa Rican in New England, and particularly greater metropolitan Boston, made me a "minority within a minority" because the numbers of Mexicans and Costa Ricans are relatively small compared with that of Latinos from the Caribbean and Central and South America.[8] When I identified as a Latina from Latin America, I was often relegated to being Hispanic, a term that began to be used generically in Boston during the 1970s. Many of my Latino counterparts who had been raised in the United States seemed to characterize me in terms of their own internalized stereotypes, basing their perceptions on media images and lacking much of the historical, cultural, and linguistic knowledge and grounding of Mexico and Costa Rica. It became evident that, to be a Latina, holding onto cultural roots in Mexico, Costa Rica, and even Europe, speaking Spanish, and using the colloquialisms that I grew up with were not readily admissible norms of my more assimilated Latino colleagues. Speaking Spanish was in some cases viewed as an affront, and I was reminded that I was being impolite in speaking Spanish in the presence of English speakers, obligating me to use only English in most of my communication.

I came to recognize that the cultural resilience, which I proudly view as fortitude, was perceived as a mechanism that distanced my colleagues and carried with it social class implications. Learning to discard the formal *Usted* of Costa Rica and Mexico for the informal *tu* of the Caribbean and highland Mexico seemed more appropriate. I also learned to downplay my father's social class background in order to equalize my status with my peers, although I share more in common with them through my Mexican family background. I proudly wore outfits such as the *huipil* (an embroidered tunic used by Mexican Indians) or the *jorongo* (poncho) because they represented part of my symbolic identity, making me feel comfortable and empowered, yet my colleagues saw this as quaint and picturesque, making me feel odd.

Experiencing such reactions made it poignantly clear that even though we were Latinos/Latinas, the fact that our experiences were rooted in different social spaces, times, and historical, linguistic, and cultural contexts made our *sense and essence of being Latino/Latina* quite different. While my demeanor expressed the cultural resilience of traditions and socialization from Mexico and Costa Rica, my Latino counterparts responded solely by reifying Mexican and Latino cultures as artifacts derived from media depictions, for example, Mexican sombreros, food, and costumes.

This leads me to believe that Latinos who have internalized colonialism, accepted the subjugation of Latino culture vis-à-vis dominant Anglo culture, accepted the linguistic imperialism of English only and the devaluing of ethnic status, come to superficially know their own Latino cultures. The emic interpretation of deep and meaningful cultures remains hidden.

Furthermore, I believe that some Latinos readily accept the monolithic representation of Latino cultures without question because it provides a degree of entry into American society as one of many and also allows Latinos access to a democracy based on being "classless, ahistorical, and atheoretical," issues that attract those doubting their identity but contribute in the final analysis to diminishing their cultural resilience. Within the current black-and-white dynamics of race, Latinos remain invisible, unlikely of being known in their own right despite their ever growing sheer numbers. On the one hand, their subjugation through incorporation to white mainstream culture is maintained by the enculturation of schools based entirely on economic outputs. The promise of the American

Dream—that attending school, learning English, and completing high school will yield opportunities and jobs—makes it easy for Spanish to be rejected in favor of English as the more significant status language with greater currency in the economic job market. Along with this enculturation is the assimilation that is occurring through the impact of modernization and adaptation to technological changes. Only the English-speaking medium is used in much of cyberspace communication. On the other hand, Latinos who are not grounded in their own language, cultures, and histories of their past may unwittingly end up supporting the erosion of their own cultural resilience. Clearly one cannot assume that all Latinos in the United States *consciously know or comprehend the meaning of their cultural roots or history*, see the advantage of speaking Spanish beyond acquiring linguistic competence as power, and use such culture and traditions as grounding for their social and economic struggles.

The deculturalization that has taken place for Latinos in some contexts is such that, when I address cultural values as being formidable resilience to dominant cultures, I am more likely to be judged as being "traditional" and, hence, atypical. That is to say, for some of my Latino counterparts, the artifact approach to culture has superseded the more powerful symbolic and interpretive meanings of Latino culture, the linkage of history to present and the embracing of Latinoization of U.S. life.

Yet as challenging as these encounters continue to be, decoding the underlying culture of small women's private colleges as a Latina has been fraught with contradictions. It is at these colleges where contradictions between the "assumed communities of learners" clash with the entrenched institutional racism. In such colleges, the assumption exists that because they are small and populated mostly by women, a community of sensitive and committed individuals to education, the nature of the environment will tend to represent women's caring values and ways of knowing. What is often not understood is the way that the institutional culture has evolved in such places, and oddly enough, the basic pattern evident in such colleges is that of more traditional colleges, with men most often being in the positions of power (deans, department chairs, provosts, etc.) and women ascending into the power spaces they are allotted (chairpersons, lead teachers).

At one of these small private institutions, I team taught a basic teacher education course with faculty of African American, Anglo, and Jewish backgrounds. The majority of students, mostly white women preparing for careers in teaching, conducted most of their field experiences and practica (supervised teaching) in urban and suburban schools. When disagreements over absences during religious holidays, getting higher grades, and the demands of academic learning were evident between students and faculty, the African American faculty member and myself readily became the targets of student demands. Rarely were the other faculty implicated, and the issues were usually viewed as "our problem," until the team acted as a "united front" that students could not divide and conquer.

Another less evident but influential contradiction is how some colleges define the experiences of their students as being urban. As part of their practica, students were to have a suburban and urban student placement. I found students being placed in suburban schools and working with METCO (an urban educational program that assigns inner-city students to suburban schools as a means to level the playing field) students who were bused in to gain "urban experiences." Being placed in urban schools presented yet another contradiction. The college sent students out in a van to the urban schools but selected only those that were not perceived as being "dangerous." Many of the inner-city schools with good safety records were not even known to the faculty until I took some students to visit such schools. Thus, the containment of students from experiencing perceived violence in inner-city schools by not allowing them to do their practica except through safe environments begs the question of why we even have a program that addresses urban needs when it is basically sanitized.

Another common contradiction appears to be about how peoples' roles are perceived within the college. While I was hired as an expert in curriculum, multicultural education, bilingualism, and teacher education at one of these women's colleges and to teach subjects that by their nature are contentious, controversial, or radical, and when I lectured and discussed institutional racism or provided a political critique of why systems maintain the status quo, I was labeled as being "radical and confrontational," making me the culprit for creating change. Ironically, my coursework in multicultural education was directed at intellectually challenging student attitudes and perceptions, a role that, as a member of an underrepresented group, one is expected to fulfill. Yet when such teaching extends beyond the class to include other faculty in the workplace, such efforts could be curtailed and "silenced" because they run counter to the college's institutionalized socialization. After a while the fear of being seen as being petty for attempting to create positive change prevails, and one's best intents are drowned.

It should be noted that, at women's colleges, gender differentiation may be even more insidious than that by ethnicity or race. I found the oppression experienced by white females by other white females in power to be as traumatic as white males oppressing women. In such small colleges, seniority gained over years of political survival provides an entitlement to women that is akin to that of males in powerful positions. Incoming faculty, therefore, are made to feel that their demands must be earned over time. When I requested an office with a window, I was told that even the most senior members had waited close to fifteen years to move out of offices that were closets compared with the new offices with windows. I was made to feel that I had no right to complain but was begrudgingly given an office.

Yet the responses of my colleagues represented much of the oppression that women imposed on each other under a system in which the male deans spent their time checking in on how well the department staff, made up mostly of women, was working. During the board of overseer's visit to the college, the dean announced that on any given day he could come to our department and see all of us working hard, even during weekends.

Working in such an environment made me aware of how some mainstream women prove much of their feminism by assuming male-like behaviors, choosing to be workaholics and setting up the same rules for other women that males have set for white women. This is where I have heard the commonly stated adage, "I choose my battles carefully and try to win the war."

The fact that I called into question much of the purpose of our work as busy-work and asked for conscientious reflection about what we wanted our program to be created polarization between those who were powerful and the more silent majority. Questioning an institution and why things are the way they are proved to be too challenging for the top female administrators, whose response was "to keep you in line." The option I chose was to leave the school after only one year.

In another instance, at a prestigious private institution where I was hired because of my *qualitative research background and experiences in working in poor communities within the United States and abroad,* I was openly told that I should not expect tenure as a minority. While at the time such a statement sounded harsh, it was in fact strikingly true. Years later I realized I had not acquired the cultural capital from undergraduate college—where I would have been socialized into its specific closed culture—to teach at this institution. Those colleagues who did receive tenure, for the most part, had graduated from this institution with their doctorates and had attended undergraduate school at this institution. They were privy to a social network that they could call on for support as they ascended in academe. In fact, when I was hired, I was the only finalist who was an outsider.

At the time I did not pay much attention to social and political climate because I believed I had been asked to join the faculty for my qualifications and background. I did not think about tokenism simply because I brought community skills that the institution sorely lacked. Yet, during my stay, I was evaluated on the basis of my academic output and not my practitioner or community knowledge. One colleague inquired, "Why are you wasting time recording teacher's issues and agendas in the community, when the real knowledge comes from established theories?"

Similarly, the fact that I was a generalist in this position, which allowed me to move from the world of curriculum theory to multicultural education and to international education, I thought made my work attractive. Yet, throughout seven years of teaching, I was questioned for not being a specialist in one single subject or area of interest.

As a Latina, part of my professional persona had been developed by "knowing the world around me," that is, by being immersed in educational issues in relation to the wider economic, social, political, and cultural influences that affect their development. Nothing of what I have done in education has been in a vacuum, and nothing has been without understanding my own ideological stance. When I suggested to one of the administrators that my teaching was about uncovering students' ideologies, I was told that my teaching should be solely about content because ideology might be considered only in terms of Marx's notion of ideology, which was negative. The fact that everyone has an ideology was simply passed over. When I suggested to the same administrator that to impose curriculum as a universal structure, given the different contexts for learning in which it occurs, may in fact lead to the control of learning, I was told that I simply needed to maintain the curriculum as constant, modifying the methods for different types of learners. These reactions led me to understand that my multilayered thinking, problem posing, and problematizing of issues, using Freire's notion, instead of problem solving, ran counter to the unilinear, positivist, functionalist, and outcome-driven production of knowledge that my colleagues considered substantive.

Heterogeneity as a concept and practice posed yet another striking contradiction. I was asked to develop courses around multicultural education, emphasizing the heterogeneity of U.S. cultures, and some field experiences. To that end, I attempted to bring the community perspective into the courses through different speakers and community site visits; thus, I branched out into communities not adjacent to the campus but, rather, areas that had not been explored, and I initiated fieldwork with diverse schools and community-based organizations. While my students thrived from such experiences, I was told by colleagues that I was creating problems for myself in working in the most problem-ridden schools. Missing for them was the fact that it was in those schools and communities where the "action was." For delving into such experiences, I earned the title of being a "clinical" rather than theoretical instructor and heard sharp status distinctions being made between both.

The late Paul Nash, an expert on higher education, pointed out to me that, given my background and aspirations, a fit between my own ideologies and that of the institution I taught in would not likely be possible. He explained that an institution's own ideology, policies, and practices exist solely to maintain the homogeneity of the institution at all costs, even though such institutions profess acknowledgment and acceptance of differences and heterogeneity through "forced" recruitment of faculty from underrepresented groups. Such institutions, he pointed out, expect faculty to fit "their agendas," exacting compliance and conformity of their implicit, yet highly conservative culture without anyone "rocking the boat."

My naivete was such that I did not realize that my mere presence and ideology rocked the boat. When I decided to use my hyphenated name, denoting my married status, instead of my maiden name, I did not realize it would be questioned. One faculty member in my department suggested that the computer could not use so many letters and that my second name would be difficult to pronounce because it was German. Yet it was only when I spoke to another colleague with a hyphenated name that she made me realize that the questioning was about the value I brought to the institution as a token Latina versus an ethnically mixed Latina. My premium was greater using my maiden name. The university could then certify that it had attracted a true "Latina" to meet its affirmative action standards.

I also did not realize that to use confrontation instead of aggression, which I had learned through assertiveness training, would serve me wrong at this institu-

tion. I complained bitterly to an administrator about being left out of the cata-
logue in my first year of teaching after having submitted the required information.
He suggested that I not make a fuss but instead produce flyers showing the requirements of the course and including my own background information that could be
dispensed to students as they shopped around for courses during the first weeks of
the semester. I wondered if the same would have been asked of other faculty.

I also confronted my own department colleagues about not going into schools
where I felt the real "action of teaching and learning" was taking place. I found
myself alone in the process of enacting university-to-school collaboration, even
though a program of this nature was created several years later to cash in on the
master's degree market.

Such minor but significant issues began to have a cumulative effect on me. Trying to find colleagues who would explain "what was going on" or "why" was not
easy. I learned to survive without needed collegial support and learned to find
mentoring outside my own institution. By submitting articles for publication and
attending conferences, I found colleagues who supported my work and served as
mentors. Yet the loneliness I experienced became more accentuated when I heard
other colleagues speak about being supported through writing groups, as well as
feedback and tenure focus groups.

Considering I had gained the right to be promoted to associate professor after
the first five years, and backed by my chair, I requested promotion to associate professor. After undergoing an arduous process, in which the committee assembled
did not represent any of the areas of my expertise—because one faculty member
was anti–multicultural education, another had newly joined the program and did
not know my work, and the third, while in my general area, was a psycholin-
guist—I was denied promotion. During the review process, two other women were
also seeking promotion, but unlike these women, I was asked by one of the administrators to submit additional work beyond the twelve publications I had submitted. I was also asked to demonstrate that I was on two advisory boards and had
published a book. When my chair protested to the administrator about "when and
where had the criteria changed since it had not gone through faculty council," the
administrator backed off. The chair, upset by the process and embracing me, commented, "This is such a racist place."

The administrator of the school informed me when I inquired about the reasons for denial that not only did my research "lack quality" but my department
had not been fully supportive. To this day, I still do not understand the institution's meaning of quality. Its essence eludes me, for by all research reports, the
notion of quality is tenuous, symbolic, and subjective. The lack of support from
my own department was far more painful. As I searched for answers, I became
aware that my slot was at stake because the department chair of my program was
being denied any additional slots. I was not aware of the negotiations that had
taken place among the senior faculty of the department to support another faculty member's tenure at all costs and the compromises that were made in order

to not lose my slot. The faculty decided not to support me, I found out, because, as one member later admitted, I needed to be the "sacrificial lamb." When I confronted my supervisor as to why I was even supported by her to start the process of promotion, her response said it all—"Nothing ventured, nothing gained." After several months of despair, I turned inward and searched my own cultural resilience to consider what my Mexican grandmother, Librada, would have done. I sought legal counsel and demanded the right to seek promotion within the year. Ironically, the work I submitted was the same as the previous year, but this time I personally requested that my chair and a Latino member be part of the committee. The aftermath was bittersweet. The promotion went through during midyear, but my contract was terminated that summer. I stayed on as a visiting professor for another year to complete research I had begun, and I left the institution feeling my own personal sense of success amid what appeared to be perceived as academic failure.[9]

My current role at a public university has presented me with new challenges, some of which carry the same institutional meaning as those at the private institutions but are couched within different political, sociocultural, and economic domains. The institution has enormous economic pressures, limited funding, and scarce human and material resources yet prides itself in its urban mission; innovative doctoral, master's, and undergraduate programs; and image of being "the poor man's Harvard." Students who attend this institution come from all walks of life and from diverse ethnic groups. Yet, despite the university's urban setting and reputation for diversity and the fact that, among its research and policy institutes, the first to receive state funding was that directed to Latino concerns, the Latino faculty and students have not fared well despite the enormous growth of Latinos in the state over the past ten years.[10] Recent hires have raised the Latino faculty count close to twenty-seven in all disciplines, yet only three male and two female professors are tenured, with none in education.[11] Latino students account for less than 6 percent of the total 1,200 students enrolled at the undergraduate and graduate levels.

Once again, I have become the first Latina in education at this institution, a role I had hoped in the 1970s and 1980s would have earned the right for other Latinos to enter the academy, but it seems that even though the decade of the 1970s was touted as the decade of the Latinos, it is only in the 1990s and into the next century that they are coming into their own. As I move into my fourth year of teaching, I have also readily taken up the advocacy of Latinos by becoming the adviser to the Latino student–run organization, a member of the Latino Studies Program, and a faculty member who is vested in recruiting Latinos into the doctoral and master's education programs. Within these four years, the experiences and contradictions I have encountered are worthy of exploration.

It is ironic that while I was considered to be a clinical instructor at the private university because of my community schoolwork, at this institution I have already earned the title of being the "theoretical professor" for my teaching of critical theory. Such contradiction points to the way that *contexts tend to define the individual rather than how one defines oneself within contexts*.

At the same time, several unresolvable tensions that have to do more with the program's role within the institution are evident. These tensions are between theory and practice, the academic versus practitioner role, students' recounting of "war stories" and "doing research," maintaining academic rigor and practical common sense, and transitioning the realities of urban school life with that of academic civil cultures. Such tensions are played out in class by students who leave the realities of everyday work to confront theory and thinking in their evening classes. Academic rigor, viewed as complex, distancing, and demanding of their time, has been referred to by students as "rigor mortis." Common complaints of "too much work," "too many demands," and "complex readings and writing" bespeak the disregard with which some of these students approach academia. What prevails is a culture of incivility and disrespect, which for lack of a common community culture becomes expressed through angry channels. Their resistance is manifested through outspoken remarks, complaints, and diatribes, shared not only with faculty but with each other. The tribulations and "war stories" of their workdays outshine the theory they are learning. Their issues are about concrete problems, requiring quick fixes and short-term solutions. When issues about "race" become a major concern in class discussions, although they are put on the table through moments of "honest talk," they are not purposefully pursued, expiring as futile exercises. Students demand, "Just tell me what to do, and I'll do it," under the weight of academic demands and anti-intellectual denunciations.

Witnessing such behaviors, I am reminded of how distant the mindful respect with which I was raised appears to be in this context. Such behaviors raise questions about how new programs can be introduced to practitioners in a way in which they can legitimize their own workplace knowledge and at the same time see the value of academic theory and practice. It also raises questions about the type of leadership that can be developed whereby students do not repudiate their own social and intellectual responsibility for learning. At the same time, it raises for me questions about my role in creating spaces where students are able to work through their own personal and professional issues in the program and how, as a change agent, I can help students deconstruct the very positivistic systems that have denied practitioners access to knowledge while they reconstruct more humanistic opportunities for themselves and their students to learn.

Beneath the bravado, I recognize the students' fear of the unknown, fed in part by the lack of intellectual nurturing from their schools and peers and from their own grounding of knowledge and skills. For many students, the glamour of obtaining an advanced degree and being in the academy are advantages that they readily buy into based on the society's obsession with credentials as status symbols. However, such an emphasis replaces the necessary grounding in knowledge, skills, and attitudes required by the academy. Ignored are skills on how to critically read and decode the language of critical discourse, attitudes on how to work as cohort group members with sensitivity, and knowledge about how to access and use the social and cultural capital of the academy, which they have not been privy to in their backgrounds or workplaces. Under the aegis of graduate work, students come together to learn without having developed their own raison d'êtres for analyzing urban schooling. The demands and pressures of their workdays tend to spill over into our classes, and students and faculty begin the arduous process of teaching and learning without any common processes or culture of transition being in place.

In this milieu of contested knowledge, faculty members rely on the written blueprint of the new programs, which profess to teach about leadership in urban schooling through participatory and democratic processes. However, how faculty actually live out such commitments in their teaching, workplace relationships, and obligations seems to be a contradiction of sorts, given the fact that the lives of these programs tend to be inserted within a traditional and inflexible academic hierarchy. Ironically, the creation of innovative programs of a practitioner-driven nature may be to legitimate the knowledge of teachers and principals using inquiry-based research, but they are nevertheless influenced by the more quantitatively driven requirements of the academy. Students in such programs become caught between the adaptive and evolving culture of practitioner-driven knowledge and the deconstruction of linear and traditional expectations for such programs within the institution.

In such situations, the contradictions are as evident for students as for faculty. Letter grades, for example, are required by the academy, even though coursework reflects dialogical individual processes that are subjective and could be considered under a pass/fail system. The more seasoned faculty within the institution, even though well intentioned, and without meaning to create power differences, unknowingly set up situations in which there are differences, condescending relationships, and little in-depth learning of each others' strengths.

Just how information is gathered, used, and allocated and by whom and with what outcomes within academic circles set up power differences and are a case in point. For example, the newness of the program has not yet allowed us to develop individual or group protocols for expressing concerns between faculty and students, except for those that exist as grievance procedures by the university. Therefore, students may direct their concerns to program directors, chairs, or department heads without ever having talked to their faculty beforehand. Such use of information not only places faculty who hold the information in privileged positions over other faculty but also assigns a particular status to such persons. This may be an uneasy situation, especially for incoming faculty, who have not uncovered the implicit culture of the institution and must resort to learning through default, and for underrepresented faculty members whose supervisors are all white.

Another common situation is one in which one faculty member in meeting with another faculty member and student attempts to clarify issues by assuming the role of counselor, providing feedback on each point of the discussion. While they may believe that they are genuinely helping decode students' messages to another faculty member, they end up placing themselves in positions of power through their brokering or negotiating. The underlying assumption is that the other faculty member cannot speak for him- or herself. This is particularly disconcerting when the person in power is white and the person being helped or informed is a "minority." Conversely, in other situations when, as perceived "minorities," faculty are solicited for the expertise they have, knowing exactly what their role is warrants clarification. For example, I was asked to review a proposal that had already encumbered monies by a white researcher at this institution. When I objected to the project's reification of three single attributes for Latino families and refused to attach my name unless the research design was reorganized, I was told by the researcher, "All I need for this proposal is a Hispanic name."

Similar contradictory situations have also arisen with my Latino counterparts at this institution. While it is the first time that I have been at an institution where there are Latinos other than myself, I have found that the sense of community solidarity, which I have known in other contexts, is unknown, highly politicized, and emergent. All things being equal, I realize that with the few slots available in academia and the low numbers of Latina academicians, there is a greater preponderance of Latino males in most of the positions of power. Thus, while through my presence I add to the visibility and number of Latinos on campus, I am still competing as a female and as a perceived minority for such slots. Being the first and only one in a given area places me at a disadvantage because there is no platform—as there is among African American or mainstream women—for emergent Latinas in academia and there is no Latina network to which I can belong.

This requires that I develop political rather than ethnic coalitions among Latinos on campus, and as a "minority within a minority" (Mexican and Costa Rican within the context of Puerto Rican and Caribbean majority), I need to develop strategies that cross over ethnic and gender lines and present me as part of the unified front. In this respect, the stakes are usually higher than they are among white faculty given the political and cultural arena. To be able to more than survive, I need to maintain a strategy that is balanced, whereby I am viewed first and foremost as a professional in my own right and whereby I am not viewed as too "traditionally ethnic," using Latino culture and language exclusively, or "too knowledgeable"—placing myself above the group, for this can be viewed negatively and have exclusionary consequences. Thus, even within the context of Latinos, I need to continuously redefine myself and reconstruct the parts of me that fit the context.

I expect that as Latinos gain secure positions within academe, the way that Spanish language and culture come to be used will be significant, especially if there is to be continuity and affirmation of cultural resilience. I find it hard to sit through meetings where Latinos conduct the creation of coursework and scholarly production all in English without using Spanish language and culture. I have made it a policy in my classes to accept short and reflective papers written in Span-ish from Latino students (except for their final papers). This becomes a means for me to retain and sustain the cultural resilience of my students. Just as Freire pointed out in the case of Guinea Bissau after its independence, substituting the language of the oppressor for a people's indigenous language was a return to the dominant and subordinate relationships and epistemological paradigms of the oppressor with the oppressed. I, too, find that the replacement of Spanish by the use of English solely in all of our university conduct is perhaps one of the biggest contradictions Latinos face.

In sum, as I continue to feel my way over the past few years through the initial culture shock of learning about this university's implicit culture and its multiple contradictions, I also need to reflect on how I contribute to perpetuating much of the status quo of the institution through my actions and teaching. This leads me to consider the significance of the constructs of "an educated person" and "cul-tural production."

LESSON TO BE SHARED AND REFLECTED ON:
FROM PROBLEM SOLVING TO PROBLEM POSING

Given the encounters and contradictions that I have narrated, the notion of an educated person espoused by Levinson, Foley, and Holland (1996) becomes a use-ful construct because, through its application, the conflicts around schooling that I have observed can be understood not only in terms of their historical and cul-tural situations but, more importantly, in terms of the responses that I have made. My responses may in fact contribute to engendering new cultural forms.

As an educated person who believes in the cultural resilience derived from my own historical and cultural embeddedness in Mexican and Costa Rican values and influences, the culture of the academic world can be viewed in terms of its need to maintain conformity and homogeneity. By its very nature, academia is homogeneous, and any departure from its commonplace norms may be viewed as "radical." What goes on outside of the walls of academe is not central to the insti-tution because it has ensured its own perpetuation through maintaining an ideo-logical stronghold of its faculty and of its normative culture. Faculty members in such institutions play out the academic politics fostered by a unified and tradi-tional academic hierarchy, embedded in vested interest groups in power and not derived from community consciousness. In such private or public institutions, academia becomes an entrenched structure advancing those holding onto its nor-mative culture and repudiating those who present challenges, whether through agency or social actions. Simply being the "other" becomes risk taking, accentu-ated by one's ethnicity, language, culture, and background. The more one acqui-esces and fits into the norm without contestation, the more likely the rewards. But the more one challenges the institution through epistemological and ideological actions, the more likely one is viewed as being contrary, rebellious, and insubordinate. Finding supportive networks in and outside of such academic structures allows one to respond beyond survival to create problem-posing responses. These responses, strategized to pose issues rather than solve problems, allow faculty to become involved in creating spaces for change, contributing to heterogeneous growth from multiple perspectives and ensuring the development of negotiation strategies and conflict resolution skills.

I responded initially through survival, meeting the demands of the institution and attempting to "fit" myself into the academic mind frame. At one point in my career during the height of the "War on Poverty of the 1960s," I even accepted the research paradigms that focused on Latinos as "problems in need of fixing." Yet, by the early 1970s and into the 1980s, influenced by the aftermath of the civil rights movement, the Chicano movement, and the Vietnam War, as well as the research that had been conducted in urban black communities, I began to shift my research paradigm from the perspective of mainstream researchers to that of Latinos and the very people represented in such studies. Epistemologically, I could no longer accept a universal paradigm untempered by specific cultural contexts and experiences. Most recently, I have begun to carve out meanings of success in academia on my terms by posing what the "real" issues are and how I chose to respond to these. I have begun to uncover the implicitness of academic culture, and I have published several articles that focus on the intersection of self and research (Melendez and Montero-Sieburth forthcoming; Montero-Sieburth 1996, 1997). Of the lessons I have learned, I share the following thoughts and explanations.

1. Deconstructing the "Other" to Become "Self"

For those of us who choose academic lives, the required rites of passage are a repetition of the rites required in deconstructing the "other" to become the "self." That is, just as when Latinos need to explain themselves to others, it also takes time for perceptions of others to change about who one is and how one wants to be perceived. It also means that such changes do not occur without intent or purpose. Therefore, to the degree that one is willing as the "other" to compromise, give in, or contest academic perceptions of self, such a process cannot take place in a vacuum and without necessary social and academic networks that extend beyond the institution's own ritualistic norms. It does require finding a cadre of academicians and mentors who are willing to support one's endeavors and to guide one along the way. (See the research in Castellanos 1996; Gomez and Fassinger 1995; Gorena 1996.)

2. Decoding the Implicit Culture of Academe by Making It Explicit

Learning how to decode the implicit culture of academia and making it explicit requires, first, identifying the types of rituals that are overt and describing the general values and patterns that these rituals embody and, second, uncovering the implicit rituals and underlying patterns that may not be evident but nevertheless serve within the institution to maintain the status quo. In such discovery, Latinos may learn more out of default or after the fact than because they are told what to expect. Third, once the disparities between explicit and implicit cultures are made evident, the job of deconstructing these patterns by transforming them through positive group action becomes a necessity. In sharing personal narratives, how "pseudoliberal" behaviors in the name of fairness can cover autocratic decisions of upmanship and condescension may be learned. It also means that the skills for refuting the tokenism of universities, in which Latinos may be situated as "the first Latina/Latino to teach about Hispanics and their culture," may be developed. For example, refusing to be a featured presenter on panels, admissions committee work, and recruitment, in which one is regarded as the Latino to represent all Latinos, may actually advance the cause of Latinos more than being the one-of-a-kind for all. It may also help analyze what is at stake in the university's commitment to underrepresented groups and how such processes help mitigate some of the guilt from past actions. (See the research in Gándara 1995; Padilla 1998; Padilla and Chavez 1995; Reyes and Halcón 1988.)

As such uncovering takes place, it is also important to find cultural brokers or *padrinos* or *madrinas*, who are mentors, willing to advise, advocate, and promote one's interests. While they may be from the mainstream simply because of their numbers, rather than Latinos, they may nevertheless need to be seasoned bicultural strategists who are agents of transformational change.

3. Decoding Intragroup Differences from Intergroup Differences

While differences between groups tend to be accentuated in academia, particularly under tokenism, the more significant differences may be found within the same group. One can readily understand the position of the "other" and even of racists simply because they are evident, but it is more nebulous and intricate to decode the differences within Latino groups and what other Latinos motives are with regard to one's own role.

Because trust is hard to develop in the context of academe, it becomes even more important to understand and to hone in on the subtle differences that may exist among individuals within the same Latino groups. Such understanding may enhance the camaraderie that is needed to further the professional careers of Latinos.

4. Drawing from and Using Cultural Resilience

Whether one is an acculturated or assimilated Latino, knowing how and when to draw from the strength of cultural resilience may be more useful as a strategy of empowerment, particularly in academia. Understanding the importance of core values within Latino groups, their historical contributions, and their social capital can help situate the less important games played out in academic politics. This is not to say that Latinos need to reify their culture but, rather, that they need to learn to draw the power of their own identity from historically and theoretically grounded meanings. For example, using the folkways of doing things within Latino culture may be more effective in changing given situations in academe than the directness and formality of mainstream culture. I have given several lectures to American and Latino audiences on the meaning of Cinco de Mayo from the perspectives of Mexicans because I lived in Puebla, Mexico. In such presentations, I attempt to recapture the historical and cultural sense of self-determination and nonintervention that Mexicans defined after the battle with the French invaders in Puebla, along with the role that Chicanos in the United States have in regard to U.S. political and cultural policies for education, health, and economic development. By doing this, I am able to shift the idea of celebration or fiesta to their more significant historical, political, and cultural meaning and to what this says in terms of epistemological and paradigmatic values.

5. Identifying the Production of Inequities: Their Reproduction and Maintenance at the Institutional, Instructional, and Interpersonal Levels

Inequities will continue to be produced within academia because of its sustenance of homogeneity and monoculturalism. Latinos presenting oppositional realities, whether at the interpersonal and interactional level, in terms of instructional materials and formats, or in relation to institutional concerns such as racism, genderism, and so on, will no doubt find themselves working alone if they are one-of-a-kind representatives or may be able to engender and invite like thinking from other constituents. The difficulty is how to garner the support of individuals around issues of privilege when some may find themselves in such positions. Contesting inequities on the basis of racism disengages those who most need to be engaged. Therefore, when Latinos are able to share their own vulnerabilities and biases, those in the mainstream may be more likely to engage. How we produce and reproduce inequities through our own roles is a critical type of discovery that when shared even with trepidation with others levels the playing field. Support groups of the type that help with scholarly writing can also be directed at funneling some of the critical observations of inequities in the workplace.

6. Distinguishing between Individual and Group Attainment of Latinos in Academia

Leadership in academia is a newfound area for many Latinos who are more accustomed to experiencing such leadership in their communities. While males may be more prone to rise to power within those communities, it is the women who usually back their efforts. Thus, the inequality of more male Latinos in academia, compared with female Latinas, can be understood on this basis. However, as more and more Latinas rise to power in communities and in academia, and men begin to share their power, the obligations and responsibilities to community and academia present a dilemma. The question of whether the educational advancement of Latino individuals overrides that of the advancement of the group as a whole needs to be critically examined.

I have learned that *it is individual Latinos and not Latino groups who ascend in the academy*. For some of the individuals, ethnicity and community work get in the way and are viewed as limited platforms of power. Yet, for other Latinos, the sense of community becomes the drive for attaining faculty status in "the name of the community." Thus, there are those individuals who may use the community for their advancement without serving the community as such, and there are others who maintain a foot in the community as well as in academia through research and projects.

It is also a matter of how the academic institution approaches community relationships from their own perspective. I have grown disenchanted with the idea that universities can best serve Latino communities and their community-based agencies. In fact, my own research on Latino parental involvement indicates that the best efforts from the university may be to transfer needed skills such as research knowledge and action to parents within the community: that is, taking the university to the community rather than the community to the university.

If Latinos are to provide role models for youth from the community who aspire to become professors, then the issue of how community interests can be weighed by faculty against academic demands becomes a difficult decision of "either/or." *Can Latino faculty be in the community at the same time that they are attempting to advance teaching and research on Latinos? Can community members comprehend the role of single Latino faculty conducting research on their behalf?*

To undercut such questions, I propose a strategy that goes beyond the individual gains of faculty to one that crosses identity, gender politics, and the power dynamics of Latino majority groups. I acknowledge that, while the rise of individual Latino stakeholders with power in and brokerage of the academic system may allocate some visibility and representation, even as one-of-a-kind representatives, "What impact and consolidation of other Latino faculty can such individuals engender beyond themselves?" and "How can that faculty member respond to community needs?" are critical questions worthy of serious consideration.

CONCLUSION

The narrative I have shared in this chapter is intertwined with the use of cultural resilience as a strategy and tool for recovering one's identity in the midst of academic homogeneity. That cultural resilience needs to be known, learned, and studied so that the human agency that it creates can be understood in terms of how it operates within powerful structural constraints. In my case, it has been the grounding that I have made by accident and choice in maintaining Spanish language and keeping Mexican/Costa Rican cultural values alive against the pressures of cultural assimilation and acculturation and academic homogeneity. While such values, influences, and beliefs have served me to adapt in different cultural contexts, they have also created a means for me to dialogue within the context of institutional structure. I have attempted to bring to the academy my own agency of many years in the community. Now it is the academy, in terms of its resources, that I attempt to bring to the community, for it is only in such a context that the perspectives of Latino parents and community members can be known. In this regard, Levinson, Foley, and Holland's use of *cultural production* is appropriate because it allows for a vision to be developed from a nonmainstream perspective, which is often missing from such analysis.

As I contemplate the future, I realize that only by developing a pedagogy of resilience based on the mística of my past will I be able to foster the changes I have identified above. Clearly I face a new challenge in teaching graduate working students in urban schools, many of whom have different social and cultural capital than the academy and our faculty expect. In understanding their highly complex and multilayered situations, I will need to uncover their situated complexities by not only talking about research but doing research with them—understanding their contexts, discourse, and practitioner thinking. At the same time, I will need to develop "hands-on" approaches to education and provide them with practical opportunities to uncover their issues. Nevertheless, a even greater challenge will be how to understand the transformative nature of participatory research within an institution like mine, which is constrained by its own power hierarchy and limited resources. This will demand more than changing the curriculum or providing innovative research; it will require faculty who live and model such changes themselves.

As I continue to teach and learn, I am reminded of the learning that spurred me toward an academic career and taught me how to face what appeared to be insurmountable odds. That same learning, drawn from my own sense of identity, affirmed by the cultural resilience that has been with me throughout my life, will no doubt continue to help me overcome the obstacles of future encounters and contradictions in academia.

NOTES

1. As a point of fact, according to Hernandez, Siles, and Rochín (2000), with the aging of Americans, the sustenance of social security is in jeopardy if the younger generations, mostly Latinos, are not actively productive. While in 1950 there were seventeen persons working for every retiree, by 2020 that number will be 1.7 persons working per every retiree.

2. Mexico has an extensive child care system in place for government workers, whereby the children are housed in the same buildings as their mothers. I enjoyed eating lunch with my mother and being taken home by her from my *guardería* (caretaking facility) at the end of her workday. As soon as we children could walk, we were taught all of the dances of Mexico by the child care providers. When I was four, I danced before the president of Mexico, Sr. Ruiz Cortines, in one of our many presentations.

3. I introduced qualitative research in Costa Rica during the 1980s, and the team of researchers with whom I worked over the years recently presented their longitudinal study of urban-marginal schools at the American Educational Research Association meeting in San Diego, California, in 1998. Other types of qualitative research of a constructivist nature have also been developed at other Costa Rican universities.

4. In the historical development of Costa Rica, intermarriage between second cousins was allowed by the Catholic Church because there were few women who came to the New World with the agriculturalists who left Spain, and, thus, a great number of families are interrelated. A consequence of such interrelated marriages has been genetic ailments, which can be traced in some of the Costa Rican families. For example, the Monge family suffers from deafness, and other families have predispositions for illnesses over several generations.

5. Anthony Lauria describes the notions of respeto and *relajo* as cultural attributes of Puerto Rican demeanor in the 1960s, yet they are pervasive norms that are shared by all Latin Americans and Latinos.

6. *Pocho* or *pocha* has been used for Americanized Mexicans or Americans of Mexican heritage. However, it carries a negative connotation of having "sold out." See Jorge Mejía Prieto's *Así habla el Mexicano* (1997).

7. The dissertation was based on the perspectives of bilingual teachers in which each presented different approaches to teaching limited-English-proficient children. To do justice to situating bilingual education, I couch the research in the theories of the New Sociologists of Education, ethnographic theory and method, and the ensuing debate on bilingual education.

8. While the numbers of Mexicans in the New England area purport to be small based on the 1990 Census, which effectively enumerates a total of 32,000 Mexicans in New England, the fact is that their numbers are growing through (1) secondary migration from California, Illinois, and New York and (2) the arrival of undocumented workers who work in the food and cleaning industries. Today, according to the Mexican Consulate in Boston, there are close to 15,000 Mexicans in the greater metropolitan area, compared with the 7,000 reported by the 1990 Census, and close to 50,000 for the New England area. The number of Costa Ricans appears to be close to 3,000 in the commonwealth, for few leave Costa Rica. Costa Ricans are found in several communities—Malden, Chelsea, Lowell, and Lawrence—and are represented in the majority by black Costa Ricans.

9. The denial of tenure at this institution for several white faculty has not been without psychological and physical consequences for me. While they have been able to continue with their teaching and research and have received tenure elsewhere, their experiences at this institution have taken their toll.

10. The Latino population in the state has risen in some cities and towns well over 400 percent from 1980 to 1990, and current secondary immigration patterns of Latinos from California and New York are impacting the growth of several towns. It is estimated that the population of Latinos now is about 500,000.

11. In 1998–99, I received tenure, becoming the first Latina in my area to do so.

REFERENCES

Anderson, Gary L., and Martha Montero-Sieburth, eds. 1998. *Educational Qualitative Research in Latin America: The Struggle for a New Paradigm*. New York: Garland Press.
Castellanos, Jeanett. 1996. The Relationship between the Chicana/Latina Value System

and High Education: An Ethnographic Study. Paper presented at the American Educational Studies Association Meeting, Montreal.

Gándara, Patricia. 1995. *Over the Ivy Walls: The Educational Mobility of Low-Income Chicanos*. New York: State University of New York Press.

Gomez, Maria J., and Ruth E. Fassinger. 1995. Career Paths of Highly Accomplished Latinas. Paper presented at the Annual Convention of the American Psychological Association, New York, April.

Gorena, Minerva. 1996. Hispanic Women in Higher Education Administration: Factors That Positively Influence or Hinder Advancement to Leadership Positions. Paper presented at the Annual Meeting of the American Educational Research Association, New York, April.

Hernandez, Rudy, Marcelo Siles, and Refugio Rochín. 2000. Latino Youth: Converting Challenges to Opportunities. In *Making Invisible Latino Adolescents Visible: A Critical Approach Building upon Latino Diversity*, ed. Martha Montero-Sieburth and Francisco Villarruel. New York: Garland Press.

Levinson, Barry, Douglas Foley, and Dorothy Holland. 1996. *The Cultural Production of the Educated Person: Critical Ethnographies of Schooling and Local Practice*. Albany: State University of New York Press.

Mejía Prieto, Jorge. 1997. *Así habla el Mexicano. Diccionario Básico de Mexicanismos*. Mexico City: Editorial Panorama.

Melendez, Edwin, and Martha Montero-Sieburth. Forthcoming. *Latinos in a Changing Society*. New York: Greenwood Publishing Group, Inc.

Montero-Sieburth, Martha. 1996. *Beyond Affirmative Action: An Inquiry into the Experiences of Latinas in Academia*. Mauricio Gaston Institute, John W. McCormack Institute of Public Affairs at the University of Massachusetts at Boston, *New England Journal of Public Policy* 2: 65–98.

———. 1997. The Weaving of Personal Origins and Research: Reencuentro y Reflexión para la Investigación. In *Learning from Our Lives: Women, Research and Autobiography in Education*, ed. Anna Neumann and Penelope Peterson, 124–49. New York: Teachers' College Press.

Montero-Sieburth, Martha, and Francisco Villarruel, eds. 2000. *Making Invisible Latino Adolescents Visible: A Critical Approach Building upon Latino Diversity*. New York: Garland Press.

Padilla, Raymond. 1998. Chicana/o College Students: Focus on Success. Unpublished MS, the Hispanic Association of Colleges and Universities.

Padilla, Raymond, and Rodolfo Chavez, eds. 1995. *The Leaning Ivory Tower: Latino Professors in American Universities*. Albany: State University of New York Press.

Obregón Quesada, Clotilde. 1997. Contradictory Aspects of Costa Rican Women's History during the 19th Century. In *The Costa Rican Women's Movement: A Reader*, ed. Ilse Abshagen Leitinger, 52–60. Pittsburgh: University of Pittsburgh Press.

Reyes, María de la Luz, and John Halcón. 1988. Racism in Academia: The Old Wolf Revisited. *Harvard Educational Review* 58, no. 3: 299–314.

12

Confronting the Walls: Border Crossing, Gender Differences, and Language Learning in Academe

Gisela Ernst-Slavit

INTRODUCTION

In Gloria Naylor's novel *The Women of Brewster Place* (1983), the characters live on a dead-end street closed off by a brick wall. The wall separates Brewster Place from the rest of the community. It makes apartments dark, it creates shadowy and unprotected spaces where painful events occur, and it concocts feelings of isolation and despair. The brick wall is thus a symbol of the ways in which social structures create barriers and constrain choices and opportunities. For faculty of color, the structures of academe pose constrains similar to those created by the wall. Indeed, on some occasions, the constricted nature of academia can appear unbearable.

In this chapter I share stories and turning points that have strengthened my identity and enriched my work in academic settings. By talking and writing about my own trajectory, by sharing carefully constructed masks that hide my fears, and by confronting my "lived experiences" (Greene 1988), I engage in a cathartic and solitary journey: cathartic because it allows me to swirl around my own memories while locating them parallel to others within larger structural frames; solitary because it enables me to join the parade of others who have or are currently engaged in confronting the inequalities that dwell in academic halls. This process of cultural reflection on one's own ethnicity, race, class, and status is what Trueba (1994) and others call "cultural therapy." This effort allows individuals to come to terms with their own reality in the surrounding cultural context with the purpose of healing. This conscious awareness and acceptance of my own roots and circumstances has been pivotal in finding ways to survive within the confines of academe.

The first section includes a discussion of how perpetually imprecise generic racial labels reduce people's identities to neat and unrealistic categories. It is imperative that those in the academy embrace multiple identifications and border-crossing activities that defy those static racial divisions. Ultimately, by accepting and promoting "new cartographies of identity and difference" (Giroux 1992) will we be able to reformulate sociological theories of cultural identity and, thus, expand and enhance our perspectives by including the voices of marginalized populations.

Reflections about the gendered nature of academe are presented in the second section. Discourse styles, teaching approaches, and research methodologies are not the only areas in which gender differences become evident in academe. Throughout history, male voices and perspectives that exclude one-half of the population have nurtured the fund of human knowledge. The work of psychologist Carol Gilligan, who discovered that famed researchers such as Erik Erickson and Lawrence Kohlberg worked with all-male samples from which they derived universal principles, endorses the idea of an authentic female moral perspective based on an ethic of care and responsibility. For many of us, this idea provides new understandings and a source of empowerment.

In *Black Skin, White Masks*, Frantz Fanon states that "to speak means to be in a position to use a certain syntax, to grasp the morphology of this or that language, but it means above all to assume a culture, to support the weight of a civilization" (1952, 11). These lines for me have a special meaning, as I have for years struggled with the challenges of not being a native English speaker in a nation where many believe that the Bible was originally written in English. In the third section I discuss my struggles with learning the language and culture of this my new home amid lay and academic environments that consistently remind me that I am not ready, in Fanon's words, to support the weight of this civilization.

IDENTITY CONSTRUCTION, ETHNIC LABELS, AND BORDER CROSSING

There is no pure culture. Itinerancy is the rule.

—Paul Gilroy

I was born in Lima, Peru; my upbringing was typically colonial and Catholic. I was expected to get a good education and marry well, perhaps even to a non-Peruvian, as my mother had done before me. I attended private schools, lived in a handsome neighborhood, and was surrounded by a protected haven of mostly well-educated friends and acquaintances. Like other Peruvians, I am a *mestiza*, the product of the encounter of two continents, of two races, the daughter of an Austrian father and a Peruvian mother. Like many others, I had European names and Peruvian looks, spoke more than one language, and was proud to be a Peruvian—who also had knowledge about and appreciation for her father's homeland. Being Peruvian and European allowed me to have one foot in one camp and one foot in the other. Because I did not quite fit in, it gave me the possibility to ease in and out of those circles.

In spite of my good fortune, I also encountered my share of problems, sorrow, and broken dreams. This is why, like many others who leave their familiar lands in search of better lives, I, too, left mine. I had little money but lots of hope, confidence, and a clear sense of national identity as a Peruvian woman. Therefore, I left familiar lands unaware of the need for clear labels to identify my ethnicity, race, and culture. Soon after my arrival in Florida, I did what many other foreign students have to do to go to college: fill out multiple forms. It quickly dawned on me that my avowed national identity was of little relevance to the society at large. Instead, I recurrently realized that I was seldom a Peruvian and most often a "Hispanic," "legal alien," "Latino," "Spanish speaking," "South American," "Spanish," or, even worse, "Other." So within this context of official forms, institutionalized inquiries, and government requirements, I was faced with having to find an appropriate label to describe my identity. Often I felt I did not quite "fit"—especially when I had to answer questions about my ethnicity or race. Simple questions like the one below generated a host of challenges to my own identity.

Ethnic Origin (mark one)
_ *White (not Hispanic origin)*
_ *Asian or Pacific Islander*
_ *Black (not Hispanic origin)*
_ *American Indian or Alaskan Native*
_ *Hispanic*
_ *Other*

These constructions seemed useless. Actually, they inhibit understanding because most individuals, in spite of their collective amnesia, do not "fit" within these discrete categories. In my case, none of these labels really suited me. For example, given the categories mentioned above, I could have marked the first option because I appeared as "white" in both of my passports (Peruvian and Austrian). Yet, at the same time, that option would be incorrect because I had no doubt that I have something that could be called "Hispanic."

I also thought about marking *American Indian* because, in fact, I was born in (South) America and there is some Indian blood in my mother's genealogical tree (even though she might not admit to it). But *American Indian* was truly not a good label for me because it does not speak for all my other influences (e.g., my mother's ascendancy from Spain, my father's Austrian and German blood, the fact that I do not speak the languages or share the cultures of Peruvian Indians). So my only other option was *Hispanic*, but because I had to use my European passport in the United States (because it included my visa and my "alien" number), I felt that neither of these categories encompassed my national and cultural identity.

My confusion kept going in crescendo as the smorgasbord of categories changed—from form to form and from institution to institution—and I often found myself spending considerable time trying to select the most appropriate label. After several months and many more forms, I opted to leave the question unmarked (when possible) or to mark "Other" (if there was such an option). On some occasions, depending on my mood, when the question asked for "race," I would write "Chihuahua," "German Shepherd," or "unknown" on the blank line next to "Other." Because there was often an indication that this information was optional, I did not feel any remorse for perhaps skewing some demographic data. On the contrary, this subversive action allowed me to show my dissent toward questions that limit my individuality to a generic label.

Do classifications recognized by the U.S. Census Bureau offer us a useful way of understanding our national and cultural experiences? Do terms such as *black*, *Asian American*, and *Hispanic* have any real substance to them, or are they really the creation of media czars and political impresarios? An examination of the official definition of *Hispanic* (according to the 1990 U.S. Census) might prove useful: "A person is of Spanish/Hispanic origin if the person's origin (ancestry) is Mexican, Mexican-American, Chicano, Puerto Rican, Dominican, Ecuadorian, Guatemalan, Honduran, Nicaraguan, Peruvian, Salvadoran; from other Spanish-speaking countries of the Caribbean or Central or South America; or from Spain" (U.S. Bureau of the Census 1988, 51).

The ethnic label *Hispanic* began to be used heavily by state agencies in the early 1970s to refer to all people in this country whose ancestry is predominantly from one or more Spanish-speaking countries. As a result, millions of people of a variety of national and cultural backgrounds are put into a single arbitrary category. No allowances are made either for our varied racial, linguistic, and national experiences or for whether we are recent immigrants, longtime residents, or belong to an associated territory. Ethnic labels, like all names, are constructs, abstractions of a reality. In this respect, social scientist Suzanne Oboler (1995) argues that perhaps the inevitable use of ethnic labels includes singling out particular socially constructed attributes, whether related to race, gender, class, or language. These attributes are assumed to be common to the group's members and are used to homogenize the group—regardless of whether this designation corresponds to the reality of the group to which the label is attached. The use of the "Hispanic" label to refer to those who are of Spanish-speaking origin is problematic because it excludes a considerable sector of the population in Latin America for whom Spanish is not a first language. Many "Hispanic" immigrants come from regions that are not necessarily predominantly Spanish. This is the case of those who speak Nahuatl and Tiwa in Indian villages in Mexico; Kanjobal and Jacaltec in the southern part of Guatemala; Quechua and Aymara in the highlands of Peru and Bolivia; Guaraní, Chulupí, and Mascoi in the Chaco region of Paraguay; and Tukano and Tuyukaf in the swamps of Venezuela and Colombia; as well as others from predominantly non-Spanish-speaking regions. Thus, given that their native language may not be Spanish, it is inaccurate to call these people of "Spanish-speaking origin."

Furthermore, as Berkeley social scientist Carlos Muñoz (1989) writes, the term

Hispanic is derived from "Hispania," which was the name the Romans gave to the Iberian Peninsula, most of which became Spain, and "implicitly emphasizes the white European culture of Spain at the expense of the nonwhite cultures that have profoundly shaped the experience of all Latin Americans" through its refusal to acknowledge "the nonwhite indigenous cultures of the Americas, Africa, and Asia, which historically have produced multicultural and multiracial peoples in Latin America and the United States" (1989, 11). It is a term that ignores the complexities within and throughout these various groups.

Although these feelings of not fitting in coupled with my status as immigrant intensified as I was asked questions about my ethnic identity, I kept reminding myself of the privileges that come with being one of those people able to ease in and out of different groups, what Renato Rosaldo (1993) calls "border crossers." Fortunately, I am not alone in this journey; an increasing number of social scientists are using different labels to address the diversity of racial, ethnic, and cultural identities. For example, Gloria Anzaldúa (1987) describes "border culture" as the result of the merging of two worlds. Borderlands are those unintentional, multicultural spaces where cultures meet, where those living on the edges discover similar shared beliefs and rituals and are able to construct new ones. "From this racial, ideological, cultural and biological cross-pollination," writes Anzaldúa, "an 'alien' consciousness is presently in the making. . . . It is the consciousness of the Borderlands" (1987, 77). Other terms used to give voice to emerging visions of identity include "cultural bricolage" (Lipsitz 1991), "cultural fusion" (George 1993), and "unity of disunity" (Berman 1982). These languages of possibility are attractive to many of us who are constantly crossing borders and who actually enjoy the richness encountered when moving in and out of different circles. These new constructions, according to David Wellman (1996), allow people to feel at ease in border cultures because their identities are not discrete and finite. In his words, "Border cultures produce identities that are neither singular nor static. In these locations, multiple cultural identities are invented, and people slip in and out of them without being called upon to renounce their initial identifiers" (1996, 37). Perhaps that is why I consider my crossings as options and opportunities but, more importantly, as vital for my personal and academic growth. Ultimately, the diversity of backgrounds, cultures, and perspectives that inhabit the borderlands is more than a choice for me. It is a way of life, an affirmation, and a matter of cultural survival.

ACADEME: NOT AN UNGENDERED, DISEMBODIED FIELD

For we have to ask ourselves, here and now, do we wish to join the procession, or don't we? On what term shall we join the procession? Above all, where is it leading us, the procession of educated men?

—Virginia Woolf

By the end of my first year in graduate school my initial sheer joy was somewhat evaporating as I began to perceive my department as a "guy gulag." All my professors were male, did heavy work as consultants in developing countries (like my own), and, although extremely thoughtful and culturally aware, were male researchers "helping" others in developing countries. In addition, the papers and books we read—mostly on international development education and national literacy programs—no longer brought that initial excitement and challenge that new ideas and visions promote. Not surprisingly, male authors—mostly from the United States—wrote most of the materials we read about educational efforts in countries like mine.

As I tinkered with the idea of pursuing a Ph.D. and joining the academic ranks, I encountered the same dilemma Virginia Woolf encountered sixty years ago. I could not—and did not want to—join the procession of male professors. Not because they were not good scholars or teachers; they were indeed well published and attempted to make their classes interesting. Perhaps it was because the content of the courses they taught, the pedagogy they used, and the ideologies and expectations they espoused no longer appealed to me. I soon realized that the inability to align myself with them was because of an acknowledgment of the position I occupied as a Latina woman and a student, as an immigrant, as a person who has encountered oppression from both sides—as oppressor and as oppressed. For example, the faculty in my department were born and raised in a First World nation (i.e., the United States), whereas I was born and raised in Peru, a Third World nation; their degrees were from prestigious universities (e.g., Stanford, Cornell, Harvard), unlike our solid but not widely recognized institution; the faculty and the literature used a constrained set of technical terms to refer to painful realities that I could not avoid describing with deeply emotional impressionistic discourse.

In retrospect I see that, like other students born in developing countries, I, too, was struggling with some of the professors' understandings of the social wounds and injured spaces populating our Third World nations. Our own trajectories and limitations, determined in part by our gender, ethnicity, background, status, and ideologies, appeared in the forefront as we constructed knowledge quite differently from our professors and the majority of our peers—so different, indeed, that at times we felt marginalized. As the work of postmodern feminist thinkers suggests, "position, perhaps more than any other single factor, influences the construction of knowledge, and . . . positional factors reflect relationships of power both within and outside the classroom itself" (Maher and Tetrault 1994, 22). Part of the problem was that the premises of the intellectual discourse that pervaded our readings, lectures, and discussions was paternalistic at times or did not bode well with our efforts to claim and maintain affiliations with our roots, cultures, and political postures.

During my third semester, I finally figured out that academia was not an ungendered, disembodied neutral field, that universities were not immune to prejudice, and that research can indeed be biased. Two important events contributed to this understanding: reading Gilligan's book *In a Different Voice* (1993) and my first class with a female professor.

The work of psychologist Carol Gilligan has afforded many a new way of looking at the academy. While working at Harvard with Kohlberg and Erickson, Gilligan observed that these two widely known and respected scientists used all-male samples for their research—from which they drew universal conclusions. This was, of course, no different to what Freud and Piaget had done before them. Although I agree that knowledge is power, accessing this new information about the work of such renowned psychologists crushed me. All of a sudden my undergraduate degree in clinical psychology appeared suspicious of deep biases. My solid and lengthy undergraduate degree was strongly built upon Kohlberg's twenty-year research on moral development, Erikson's work on self and identity, Freud's psychoanalytic premises, and Piaget's studies on cognitive and moral development. I was surprised and shocked. Suddenly, the university began to feel like many of the public institutions in Latin America I was familiar with—designed to favor few and alienate many—rather than "a place of promise and possibility" (hooks 1994, 4).

Fortunately, during that time I enrolled in a class with Cynthia Wallat, the only female professor in the department. Her course, "The Social Psychology of Education," not only introduced me to a new way of looking at classrooms—through the use of sociolinguistic and ethnographic lenses—but also provided a link between my previous experiences as a teacher and school counselor and the course content. An important goal in this class was the examination of studies that attempted to understand how contexts of learning in classrooms and schools influence the nature of the teaching and learning processes by doing intensive ethnographic work with a focus on classroom discourse. The works of Cazden, Gumperz, Hymes, Philips, Heath, and others provided us with a new set of lenses to examine how certain social and discursive classroom practices afford or deny students access to particular forms of learning.

But the content was not the only aspect that made this course different from others. The style also reminded me of some of the courses I had taken during my undergraduate work in Peru. Basically, I felt as though the course was designed around students' abilities and needs. Every class felt like an exciting journey—never boring and always critical. Every Tuesday, we moved further away from what Freire (1970) calls a "banking system of education," the uncritical assimilation and accumulation of information, to a somewhat "subversive" approach (hooks 1994) whereby we questioned ideas both emotionally and rationally. In class, the instructor shared anecdotes about the authors we were reading; students shared their own experiences as both students and teachers; and, as a group, we criticized conventional research methodologies, searched for alternative methods of inquiry, and discussed some of the trials and tribulations of academic life.

In looking back, it is clear that male and female professors also used different discursive styles in their teaching. While male professors favored discourse that is more competitive, abstract, and based on the belief that authentic knowledge is acquired through distance and objectivity, female faculty included personal anecdotes and relational modes of thoughts. Deborah Tannen, in her bestseller *You Just Don't Understand* (1990), has highlighted these differences in men's and women's conversational styles. Tannen's analysis triggered a reappraisal by women of the relative merits of cooperative as opposed to competitive strategies in conversation. She calls women's talk "rapport talk" (as connecting) and men's talk "report talk" (as informing). In hindsight, I can now understand that the apathy I was developing toward my graduate work may have been associated to the lack of "connectedness" I felt in some of the classes taught by male faculty.

Exposure to a different way of teaching afforded us students the opportunity to experience and compare different ways of accessing information and different ways of knowing (Belenky et al. 1986). I no longer had the feeling of estrangement so pervasive in earlier semesters—on the contrary, I felt like an active participant in the pedagogical process. This class was a true learning community in which everybody's voice was heard, their presence recognized, and their perspectives valued.

In retrospect, Gilligan's book and Wallat's class transformed my attitudes and my prospects to join academe by pointing out a myriad of possibilities. Rather than attempting to unreflectively join the procession by becoming a passive thespian in academe or to altogether reject the university as a place of possibility because I was failing to tolerate the contradictions between the academic discourse and my own ideology, a third option emerged: In order to pursue a doctoral degree and later attempt to access the world of academe, it was imperative to encounter a program that would nurture and challenge students, promote critical reasoning and action, and espouse communal learning. The classrooms I longed for would have faculty who "acknowledge their own limitations and those of the educational system, react with feelings of moral and ethical outrage, reflect upon both limitations and feelings, and become change agents and advocate on behalf of their students" (Ernst and Statzner 1994, 203). I did not find such a program but found instead outstanding teachers and mentors. My search has not ceased though. Now, as a tenured faculty, my quest is to create those kinds of nurturing and critical spaces for my students.

THE PERILS OF NOT BEING
AN AUTOCHTHONOUS ENGLISH SPEAKER

So, if you want to really hurt me, talk badly about my language.

—Gloria Anzaldúa

Like many other assistant professors, I jostled with producing paper presentations and publications in order to get tenure. Part of the problem involved having to produce manuscripts in a format that fulfilled academic requirements. My struggle was increased, however, because I had to do it in a language that is not my first.

As a teacher, most of what I do is through talking, listening, reading, writing, and communicating with others. What is problematic is that most of what I say or write is in a language that is still, after more than decade, foreign to me. I sometimes find myself staring at a blank sheet of paper when I have to write a formal letter or a paper or prepare a presentation. Many writers go through writer's block, so I am not alone in this struggle. But it is not only writing—I often stumble when I have to speak in public, and I am always scared when I have to voice my opinion in front of those who speak a so-called Queen's English.

In many educational settings—including my own institution—there are those who avoid communicating with or dismiss the utterances of unfortunate souls, like me, who happen to display some traces of a foreign accent. As a child I was never shy; as an adult I am seldom quiet, but as a doctoral student I became consistently withdrawn, and as a beginning assistant professor I became extremely cautious.

My struggles with English began not so much when I emigrated to this country but when I entered my doctoral program. There, in a university located in a state with one of the largest populations of Spanish speakers, I was the only teaching assistant with an "accent." Indeed, everyone had an accent, but mine was "unauthorized" because it was a Spanish accent.[1] Not being an autochthonous English speaker raised some flags for many in the department—especially the chair, a former English teacher. I knew about their concerns even before I moved to begin my doctoral program. Yet this knowledge did not prepare me for what happened with my very first paper in the program.

Before the fall semester started, all teaching assistants were required to enroll in a three-week intense summer course to master the theoretical premises that guided the teacher education program in which we were going to teach. In an effort to be accepted by my peers and faculty, I attempted to portray myself as a doctoral student of worth; I burned the midnight oil as I read, more than once, every article required and suggested in our reading list, prepared useful outlines, and drafted thoughtful questions. Yet, as the only dark-skinned person in that group and the one with a foreign accent, I was consistently reminded that I was not one of them. Unlike my peers, I had not taught in the state, and I was unfamiliar with the surrounding public schools and the idiosyncrasies of the state educational jargon. Furthermore, I felt trapped when I had to juggle sounds to articulate my peers' names—there was a Jo, John, Joan, Jean, and Jo Ann within this class. Despite the challenges, I felt a clear sense of accomplishment at the end of the day. I was amassing a great deal of knowledge, I was learning how to differentiate Joan from John (with the help of a tape recorder), and I was making some new friends. All was well until I turned in my final paper. While my peers got theirs back within a week, I received mine two weeks later—not in my mailbox, like everyone else, but through a faculty member who later became my adviser. Although I got an A on that paper, the course instructor expressed her concerns about my writing skills—especially because it appeared that I did not know the basics such as "after a period there is a capital letter." As my adviser was trying to tactfully explain the circumstances, pain and anger plagued me: "How can someone think that I don't know when to use a capital letter? Doesn't this professor know that punctuation is used similarly across Indo-European languages?" I felt a heavy weight on me. All these weeks I had tried my best to make a good impression, to reveal myself as a strong doctoral student. And now this instructor was expressing a serious concern about my ability to pursue a Ph.D. I was locked in an oppressive silence.

While staring at my paper, I realized that the printer (an old dot matrix with a worn ribbon) was not printing below the line; that is, commas became periods, *g* became *a*, *y* became *v*. Hence my mistake was to turn in my paper without reading it one last time—I only checked the format (e.g., widow lines, page order, and alignment). The instructor, after seeing a period (which was typed as a comma) in the middle of a sentence, associated that mistake with a language problem (because I was not a native English speaker), which, in turn, suggested to her that I was not doctoral material.

Though I may hesitate on the correct interpretation of certain aspects of my experiences in graduate school, one thing is beyond doubt: the incident with my first paper carved a profound scar. "What a way to begin my doctoral program," I thought. My confidence decreased, my willingness to share my writing disappeared, and I panicked every time I had to write on the chalkboard. Whenever possible, I offered to do presentations, gather materials, and take oral exams to avoid writing. At the onset of my doctoral degree, writing had become a painful, solitary, and oppressive activity.

Luckily, Ginger Weade, my doctoral adviser, was always interested in what I had to say, not only in how I said it. My participation in her research projects allowed me to commune with all the stages of designing, participating in, and publishing a study without having to do much serious writing. As my assistantship allowed me to work and publish with other faculty, my confidence increased, the barricades diminished, and I began to believe I could learn how to write—even though I could only produce one sentence for every two hours of work. From then on, writing became an arduous and challenging endeavor that filled many hours with bitter feelings and wondrous moments.

It was particularly pacifying to discover that others, whose mother tongue was English, had similar problems (although to a lesser degree) and had written about it! I could clearly identify with Pamela Richards' chapter in Howard Becker's *Writing for Social Scientists* (1986) regarding the risks involved in writing and the large amount of writing that has to be done in order to produce a few good sentences. In her words, "What I seem to be learning as I spend more time writing is that the risks are worth taking. Yes, I produce an appalling amount of crap. . . . And occasionally I produce something that fits . . . something that captures exactly what I want to say. Usually it's just a sentence or two, but the number of those sentences grows if I just keep plugging away" (1986, 119).

And then came the dissertation. During the last semesters of my doctoral program, I worked intensely within the confines of my research study. I was still not willing to share my writing, but I began sharing preliminary findings from my study in other classes or symposia. The affirmative feedback from my audiences—mostly peers and faculty—gave me a great deal of confidence. Later, as I presented parts of my unfinished dissertation at the annual meetings of the American Anthropological Association and the American Educational Research Association and again received positive feedback, I realized that there might be some value in my work. Now I just needed to figure out a way of putting it into print. At this point two powerful writings proved invaluable: Van Maanen's *Tales of the Field* (1988) and Zaharlick and Green's chapter "Ethnographic Research" in the *Handbook of Research in Teaching the English Language Arts* (1991). While the first piece offers a readable and lighthearted treatment of the rhetorical devices used to present the results of fieldwork, the latter makes a clear differentiation between the "context of discovery" and the "context of presentation" in ethnographic research and suggests avenues to move from one context to the next. They were exactly what I needed! I know how to conduct a study, and now I needed to learn how to write it.

In spite of the help from Van Maanen and Zaharlick and Green, writing my dissertation was, as for many, a major struggle. Fortunately, though, I had an adviser who meticulously read every page of the many drafts, suggested conceptual changes, and gave me carefully crafted advice as to why and how I should change a sentence's construction or why my commas were too numerous. Although writing my dissertation was at times a painful process, it also triggered what became one of the highlights of my doctoral program: my relationship with a mentor who gave me unswerving support throughout the program, helped me scaffold my confidence, and guided me, step by step, through writing in English for academic purposes. *Gracias* Ginger.

The point of this story is not, however, to suggest how some in academe lack even basic knowledge of language differences. Nor is it to expose my weaknesses. Rather, I am using this narrative to suggest how vulnerable we are when our work, writings, and thoughts are tacitly judged because of our ethnicity or language backgrounds. It also explains how, along the way, I met people who were expecting me to fail, perhaps hoping I would fail. Yet these instances were also teachable moments. I learned, at some point during my doctoral program, that if writing demanded so much effort and time, I should send manuscripts to top journals. In the worst-case scenario, I thought, papers would get rejected—but at least I would have useful and pointed advice from reputable reviewers (of course, this is not always the case). So while in graduate school I began sending papers to top-rated journals. I was not that successful—only the papers written with my professors (mostly written and edited by them) got published. However, the efforts were not in vain, for I did gain practice in writing letters to the editors, revising papers, and, what I believe is more difficult, learning how to read—with aplomb—lengthy singled-spaced comments about the weaknesses of one's own work.

By the time I began my career as assistant professor, I had already tasted the sweetness and bitterness, depending on the case, that accompany the trajectory of a manuscript sent for publication. This knowledge was priceless during my first years in academe. I knew exactly what to do (e.g., find a journal, read guidelines, prepare a manuscript, and write to the editor) and was aware of the process that follows a manuscript submission. Hence, by the time I went up for tenure, writing was still a struggle but no longer a devastating enterprise.

SOME FINAL THOUGHTS

In the final act of *The Women of Brewster Place* (Naylor 1983), the brick wall becomes the focus of collective action. In a communal and solidaristic effort fueled by wrath and rebelliousness, the residents of the street destroy the wall that restricted their views, constrained their opportunities, and limited their life chances. This kind of activism, of collective action, is necessary to change the social structures that limit and suppress opportunities for many whose voices have been silenced in academia. Collaboration with others in various disciplines and with differing viewpoints has been pivotal in affording those of us in the borderlands opportunities to learn, grow, and produce without losing sight of our identities and ideological stances. My close colleagues and friends are more than just peers; they are as vital to me as pollinating bees are to my flowers. Without them, growth and advancement would be impossible. Close to my heart are also those who over the years, knowingly or unknowingly, played a crucial role in encouraging, launching, or supporting my academic endeavors. These mentors are exquisite role models, who have influenced my thinking and research agendas, challenged my actions or, at times, my complacency, and consistently given me sound *consejos*.[2] Ultimately, these colleagues and mentors are the true forces leading or supporting the destruction of walls constructed by class, race, language, and gender and are the solid columns that scaffold the construction of critical and dynamic borderlands.

NOTES

A version of the section "Identity Construction, Ethnic Labels, and Border Crossing" was discussed in "País de Mis Sueños: Reflections on Ethnic Labels, Dichotomies, and Ritual Interactions" (Ernst 1998).

1. The term *unauthorized language* is used to reflect the limited value assigned to languages and dialects not accepted as viable and legitimate within the institutional realm. For a discussion on language use and authorized language, see Bourdieu 1991, Bourdieu and Passeron 1990, and Ernst-Slavit 1997.

2. Delgado-Gaitan (1994) defines the Spanish word *consejos* as nurturing advice.

REFERENCES

Anzaldúa, G. 1987. *Borderlands/La Frontera: The New Mestiza.* San Francisco: Spinster/Aunt Lute.

Becker, H., ed. 1986. *Writing for Social Scientists.* Chicago: University of Chicago Press.

Belenky, M., C. Blythe, N. Goldberger, and J. M. Tarule. 1986. *Women's Ways of Knowing: The Development of Self, Voice, and Mind.* New York: Basic Books.

Berman, M. 1982. *All That Is Solid Melts into Air.* New York: Simon and Schuster.

Bourdieu, P. 1991. *Language and Symbolic Power.* Cambridge: Polity Press.

Bourdieu, P., and J. Passeron. 1990. *Reproduction in Education, Society, and Culture.* London: Newbury Park.

Delgado-Gaitan, C. 1994. The Power of Cultural Narratives. *Anthropology and Education Quarterly* 25, no. 3: 298–316.

Ernst, G. 1998. País de Mis Sueños: Reflections on Ethnic Labels, Dichotomies, and Ritual Interactions. In *Distant Mirrors: America as a Foreign Culture,* ed. P. DeVita and J. Armstrong, 60–67. Belmont, Calif.: West/Wadsworth.

Ernst, G., and E. L. Statzner. 1994. Alternative Visions of Schooling: An Introduction. *Anthropology and Education Quarterly* 25, no. 3: 200–07.

Ernst-Slavit, G. 1997. Different Words, Different Worlds: Language Use, Power, and Authorized Language in a Bilingual Classroom. *Linguistics and Education* 9: 25–47.

Fanon, F. 1952. *Black Skin, White Masks.* New York: Grove Press.

Freire, P. 1970. *Pedagogy of the Oppressed.* New York: Seabury.

George, L. 1993. Gray Boys, Funky Aztecs and Honorary Homegirls. *Los Angeles Times Magazine,* 17 January: 14–19.

Gilligan, C. 1993. *In a Different Voice: Psychological Theory and Women's Development.* Cambridge, Mass.: Harvard University Press.

Giroux, H. 1992. Post-Colonial Ruptures and Democratic Possibilities: Multiculturalism as Anti-Racist Pedagogy. *Cultural Critique* (spring): 2–39.

Greene, M. 1988. *The Dialectic of Freedom.* New York: Teachers College Press.

hooks, b. 1994. *Teaching to Transgress: Education as the Practice of Freedom.* New York: Routledge.

Lipsitz, G. 1991. *Time Passages: Collective Memory and American Popular Culture.* Minneapolis: University of Minnesota Press.

Maher, F. A., and M. K. T. Tetrault. 1994. *The Feminist Classroom.* New York: Basic Books.

Muñoz, C. 1989. *Youth, Identity, Power.* London: Verso.

Naylor, G. 1983. *The Women of Brewster Place.* New York: Penguin.

Oboler, S. 1995. *Ethnic Labels, Latino Lives: Identity and the Politics of Representation in the United States.* Minneapolis: University of Minnesota Press.

Richards, P. 1986. Risk. In *Writing for Social Scientists,* ed. H. Becker, 108–20. Chicago: University of Chicago Press.

Rosaldo, R. 1993. *Culture and Truth: The Remaking of Social Analysis.* Boston: Beacon Press.

Tannen, D. 1990. *You Just Don't Understand: Women and Men in Conversation.* New York: William Morrow, Ballantine.

Trueba, H. T. 1994. Reflections on Alternative Visions of Schooling. *Anthropology and Education Quarterly* 25, no. 3: 376–93.

U.S. Bureau of the Census. 1988. *Development of the Race and Ethnic Items for the 1990 Census*. New Orleans: Population Association of America.

Van Maanen, J. 1988. *Tales of the Field: On Writing Ethnography*. Chicago: University of Chicago Press.

Wellman, D. 1996. Red and White in White America: Discovering Cross-Border Identities and Other Subversive Activities. In *Names We Call Home*, ed. B. Thompson and S. Tyagi, 29–41. New York: Routledge.

Woolf, V. 1938. *Three Guineas*. New York: Hartcourt Brace.

Zaharlick, A., and J. L. Green. 1991. Ethnographic Research. In *Handbook of Research in Teaching the English Language Arts*, ed. J. Flood, J. Jensen, D. Lapp, and J. Squire. New York: Macmillan.

13

Myth or Reality: Publish or Perish

Li-Rong Lilly Cheng and Kathee M. Christensen

Asian Pacific Americans originate from Pacific Asia or are descendants of Asian Pacific Islander immigrants. Numbering 8.8 million in the United States, Asian Pacific Americans (APAs) are the fastest growing segment of the U.S. population, representing 3.3 percent of the nation and 10 percent of California. Fifty percent of APAs in the United States reside in the State of California. They are fast becoming an influential presence educationally, socially, politically, and economically. There has been significant growth in the Asian Pacific Islander population in the United States, from less than 1 percent of the total population in 1970 to an expected 4 percent in the year 2000, a projected growth of 400 percent in thirty years (Gardner, Robey, and Smith 1985; Rueda 1993).

Approximately 40 percent of immigrants to the United States in 1990 were from Pacific Asian countries (U.S. Bureau of Census 1993). Over the last two decades the United States has experienced a great influx of migrants, immigrants, and refugees from Latin America and Pacific Asia, especially from Southeast Asia. The greatest increase in immigration has been by Asian Pacific immigrants. The 1990 census (1993) reported that there were 7,273,662 Asians and Pacific Islanders in the United States in 1990 (2.9 percent of the population), as compared with 3,500,439 in 1980 (1.5 percent of the population), representing an increase of 107.8 percent, excluding undocumented aliens. Currently, more than 300,000 Southeast Asian students are in the K–12 programs in this country. With the takeover of Hong Kong by the People's Republic of China in 1997 and changes in U.S. immigration policies regarding the quota of immigrants from the People's Republic of China and Hong Kong, this number is expected to increase.

The Asian American school-aged population has increased more than six-fold from 212,900 in 1960 to almost 1.3 million by 1990. In 1990, 40 percent of APA children were first generation, indicating the recentness of their time of arrival. Historically, Asian Pacific Islander groups have been immigrating to the United States for more than two centuries, with the first records of arrival of Chinese dating from 1785.

Since that time more than seventeen Asian groups have immigrated to the United States. The most numerous APAs have origins in China (Taiwan and the People's Republic of China), Hong Kong, Japan, Korea, India, Vietnam, Cambodia (Kampuchea), Laos, Guam, the Philippines, India, Pakistan, Bangladesh, Malaysia, Indonesia, Singapore, and Samoa. Since 1975, over one million refugees from Southeast Asia have settled in the United States, but in recent years many refugees from Eastern Europe, the Middle East, Africa, and the former Soviet Union have also come to the United States. Refugees and immigrants from Asia and the Pacific Islands come from a variety of historical, social, educational, and political backgrounds. Some are affluent, well-educated, voluntary immigrants, and some are preliterate refugees.

In order to understand the APA immigrant/refugee experience better, in-depth study of each group is required. For example, the Chinese have been around for a long time, yet the Chinese diaspora is still not well understood. The diaspora of Chinese across the world has taken over 39 million overseas. Though the majority live in Southeast Asia, over 4,000,000 reside in North and South America. Of that number, approximately 1,645,000 live in the United States (U.S. Bureau of Census 1993). With communities concentrated in major urban metropolises, Chinese Americans are most likely found in cities such as San Francisco, New York, and Los Angeles. Among the early immigrants to the United States from Pacific Asia, Chinese immigrants came as laborers in the first big wave in the nineteenth century. Much scholarship has been done on the experiences of these Chinese Americans with the "Gold Mountain" of California and other western states. Included in this history have been a series of anti-Asian immigration bills that severely curtailed Chinese immigration for decades until World War II alliances relaxed some of these restrictions. However, it was not until the Immigration Law of 1965 that Chinese immigration to the United States dramatically increased. Among this earlier group of immigrants, many—including former chancellor of the University of California at Berkeley Tien and Nobel Laureates Paul Chu, Yang, Lee, and Lee—continued their graduate study and research in the United States and chose to enter academia. Southeast Asian refugees came in the mid 1970s, and not many are in academia, yet there is a great need for them in the educational system. East Indians and Filipinos have generally better English preparation, and some have chosen to be academicians. Their voices are often not heard. In an attempt to address some of these gaps in scholarly study, this essay intends to highlight relevant information in five vignettes of APA faculty and their experiences in surviving academia.

In 1998, an article coauthored by a few Asian leaders appeared in *Asian Week*. It urges Asians to create a cohesive political voice and to gain political power. The following is copied from *Asian Week*:

Political Power: A Common Goal

Although Asian Americans, having come from many regions in Asia, have many differences, we must unite on a joint quest for political clout to get rid of the glass ceiling hanging above us, and in that process help make America, our beloved nation, "a more perfect Union." When compared with other nations, the United States is the most open and inclusive. But even in America, it's up to a small minority composed mostly of immigrants, namely us, to organize politically to gain equal opportunity. That's not so much our view as it is the consensus of historians who have studied American history. Indeed, a Kennedy Library exhibit illustrates that very view. Prominently displayed on a wall in the library is a quote from a famous scholar, which states: "The history of America is the history of the immigrant underclass using the political process to climb up to the equal class." The exhibit uses the history of Irish immigration, coupled with the family history of the Kennedys, to illustrate how the Irish used the political process to gain equal opportunity. The exhibit goes on to point out that this was also how Polish and Italian immigrants, who mostly arrived after the Irish, gained equal status. The exhibit concludes by stating that this is how Jewish Americans, African Americans and Latinos are fighting for equal opportunity today. Some Asian Americans don't understand why immigrants need political power just to enjoy equal opportunity. After all, this is America, where "all men are created equal." However, we must realize that human beings tend to overlook inequity against others unless it is made glaringly clear to their consciences. Indeed, human beings may even institute or perpetuate inequity against others if it works to their advantage. Slavery was one example. Discrimination against Irish immigrants was another. The internment of Japanese Americans during World War II was yet another. The edge in opportunities enjoyed by men over women is a more recent one. The glass ceiling above Asian Americans is another. Asian Americans have only one-third the opportunity of Americans of any other ethnic group to rise to management positions in the academic world, the corporate world and even in government. Even in the federal government, where one least suspects discrimination, there is a low glass ceiling for Asian Americans. Of the 250-plus Cabinet positions at or above the rank of assistant secretary, Asian Americans hold only two of the lowest positions (Bill Lann Lee, as acting assistant attorney general for civil rights, along with Robert Gee, the assistant secretary of the Department of Energy). Of the 845 serving federal judges, only seven are Asian Americans. To illustrate the disparity: we represent 3.5 percent of our nation's population (and 10 percent of California's), but we hold less than 1 percent of policy-making positions in the federal government. Had such statistics applied to blacks or Jews, the media would have screamed "discrimination." Our federal government would have threatened to withhold funding from offending institutions unless they took immediate corrective action. But since the malfeasance applies to Asian Americans only, and even the federal government condones it, no one seems to care. But we should care. Have you wondered why Jews and blacks fare so much better than us? Is it because each, as an ethnic group, is larger in numbers? No. There are only 6 million Jews in the United States, as opposed to about 10 million Asian Americans. Is it because each, as an ethnic group, gives more generously to politicians? No. African Americans don't give a lot of money to politicians. Then why is there such a big difference? It is because Jews and blacks know that political clout comes from internal political cohesion, and from using political carrots and sticks during presidential elections. Look at the American Israel Public Affairs Committee, a Jewish organization stationed in Washington,

D.C. Although powerful, the group prefers a low public profile. However, if a federal or presidential candidate is not endorsed by AIPAC, that politician will have little luck raising money in the Jewish community. That's internal cohesion and political "carrots and sticks" for you.

In addition, Jewish Americans vote 8 to 2 in favor of political candidates who share the concerns of many Jewish Americans. In New York, where there is a large Jewish population who are mostly registered as Democrats, the Jewish vote can often deliver New York's convention votes for a Democratic candidate in the presidential primary. It could also mean delivering the state's 33 electoral votes—second only to California—to the next president of the United States.

African Americans also display great internal political cohesion when it comes to presidential elections. They vote 9 to 1 for the Democratic presidential candidate in most cities. That is the carrot. Nowadays, a Democratic presidential candidate is not likely to be elected without a large turnout of African Americans in Illinois, Michigan, New York, New Jersey and Pennsylvania. Hence, when black political leaders are dissatisfied with what the Democratic party is doing for their community, they threaten not to help turn out the black votes in the cities. That is the stick.

Asian Americans most likely can acquire the same kind of political voice, if we learn to develop internal cohesion and use political carrots and sticks during presidential elections. While Jews are heavily concentrated in New York, with 33 electoral votes, most of us live in California, which has 54 electoral votes. About 10 percent of California's voters are Asian Americans. If we vote 8 to 2 for the presidential candidate who shares our concerns, we could swing the state's electoral votes and perhaps the presidency. When the votes of Asian Americans are of such pivotal importance to the outcome of presidential elections, the two political parties, induced by self-interest, shall share our concerns. Mind you, the glass ceiling above us is not there because we don't work hard. Asian Americans are known for our work ethic. The glass ceiling is not there because we are uneducated. The percentage of Asian Americans with bachelor's degrees is twice as high as that for the nation as a whole. The glass ceiling is there because the political atmosphere permits it, just as the glass ceiling was once there for women and blacks. If we go back far enough, the glass ceiling was there even for the Polish, Irish and Italians, when the political atmosphere permitted it. A political problem requires a political solution. So that is why we suggest that Asian Americans mount a joint quest for political clout—to climb from the immigrant underclass to the equal class.

The 2000 presidential election is just around the corner. Do we want to exercise the rights guaranteed to us by the Constitution—power in the ballot box—to gain equal opportunity? We suggest that Asian Americans should do this, if not for ourselves, certainly for our children. Let's form a grand coalition of Asian American communities, not just of activists, but of people from all walks of life. Every man, woman and child must pitch in if we are to become equal partners in the making of the American Dream, and in the process help make America "a more perfect Union."

Woo is a former Democratic lieutenant governor of Delaware; Tien is a former chancellor of UC Berkeley; Chennault, a Chinese American Republican, is president of TAC International; Lin is national president of the Organization of Chinese Americans; Ho is a professor of system engineering and applied math at Harvard University; and Tang chairs the Committee of 100. [Woo et al. 1998]

The above piece from *Asian Week* points out a number of key points that often apply to Asian Americans and Asian Americans in higher education. Asian Pacific Americans in the United States have observed a shared reality. That is, the glass ceiling phenomenon is a strong and an unfortunate reality. APAs in academia find the following patterns:

1. Asians in academia typically stay in teaching positions, and only a small percentage of them move into administration and positions of power.
2. Because there are few APAs in higher education, there are even fewer Asians available to mentor new academics.
3. Many Asians believe in meritocracy but do not understand that tenure and promotion are political processes even though academia may call them reviews of academic competency.
4. Racism toward APAs in higher education is pervasive and unusually powerful because APAs are expected to be better and more competent than people in other groups because they are seen as "model minorities"; of course, along with that comes jealousy and mistrust toward Asians.

The following vignettes offer a glimpse into the lives of Asian faculty on U.S. campuses. Each of these persons joined the faculty to fulfill a dream, a dream of academic excellence and stability. All of them carry the widespread Asian tradition of profound respect for the professions of university professor and administrator. Some achieve and survive academia through blood, sweat, and tears. Others give up. Most, however, show resilience, and here are their stories.

VIGNETTE 1

Lisa grew up in the Philippines where she was born in 1939. When she was a little girl, Japanese soldiers came to her village. In fear of being raped and killed, Lisa and her family hid in the river using pipes from the reef to breathe. She suffered serious infections of her urinary tract and later in life found out she could not get pregnant. Lisa was a top student in class and eventually finished college with a degree in nursing. She chose to study and work abroad and settled in Washington State. She attended graduate school there and stayed in the dormitory. The first winter was very harsh for Lisa. She was cold but did not ask for more blankets. During the Thanksgiving holiday, she was alone in the dormitory with no place to call or go. She cried through Thanksgiving, and, finally, the supervisor of the dormitory found out she was all alone and invited her for Christmas. Lisa worked two jobs and sent some money home. Despite all the hardship, she managed to finish her training and found a nursing job in a hospital. She did not mind working late and did not mind working overtime. She had a wonderful reputation, and eventually she chose to work in the burn unit taking caring of the most serious patients. She was devoted to her work and was chosen as an exemplary nurse.

Lisa met her husband while taking a cruise to the Bahamas. They fell in love, and she asked permission from her family to marry Larry. After the wedding, Lisa moved to Virginia. She decided to go back to school and later received her doctoral degree. Fortunately, she found a tenure-track teaching job and was very happy. Lisa and Larry were both active in the community. She spent time working with the Filipino Nurses Association and received a few grants from the World Health Organization (WHO). She wrote and published many articles in professional journals and was involved with writing projects for the WHO. She gained enough recognition and prestige that she was elected as the president of the National Organization for Filipino Nurses. She also helped to organize conferences on nursing care in the Philippines. She received funding to serve as a consultant for the Philippines. When she presented the invitation to her chairperson, she was told that the department could not spare her for a few weeks because the accreditation team was coming and she would need to be there (she was the only faculty member who was other then Anglo in her department of twenty-five faculty).

On her campus, there is a merit increase system, and faculty could apply for it. Lisa felt that, with her excellent track record, she would stand a chance. She applied and was told that she had very high ratings, yet she did not get it. She applied three years in a row, and still she did not get it. It dawned on her that she might be the subject of discrimination. On her "lily-white" campus, Lisa stood out like a "sore thumb." The walls of her windowless basement office were decorated with plaques and certificates of recognition and appreciation. No faculty members ever came to visit, only students. They were in awe of all the accolades Lisa had received. They admired her nursing skills and her compassion. She would spend hours and hours on student projects and theses. She also volunteered to take on committee work for the department and to work with students in the community. Her academic records were impeccable. With great confidence, Lisa prepared her portfolio for faculty tenure and promotion. She had consulted with a few senior faculty about her portfolio, and they all felt that she would have very little problem attaining tenure and promotion. To her shock, she was told that she lacked scholarship, and her tenure application was denied. She could not believe what had happened, so she decided to appeal the case. One day, as she walked up the stairs from her basement office, she overheard a conversation about her between several faculty members. One said, "Did you hear that Lisa was going to appeal?" A second person said, "Not in her lifetime will she ever get tenure here. I will see to it that she fails. She does not belong here. She is so different." A third person said, "The journals that she published in are not good, and some of them are foreign journals, and you know that they are of inferior quality." Lisa could not endure this any longer. She was so shaken by this conversation that she quickly retreated back to her office and sat there for the remainder of the afternoon. She finally left her office, when she felt that it was safe to leave. On the way home, she cried. She kept thinking, "What did I do to her to deserve this? Why do I not belong? What makes me different?" She felt a deep sense of hopelessness and help-lessness. Although she knew that her colleagues in her department had not pub-lished and done research, she felt that they were discriminating against her and she was numb. That night, she told her husband about what she had heard and that she was deeply wounded by this experience. Her husband told her to stand tall and be strong. Returning to work the following week was most difficult because Lisa knew that quite a few people in her department did not want her there. How does one feel when one is not wanted?

Several months later, Lisa was invited to give a presentation in Hawaii. Her research was cutting edge and her presentation was outstanding. Right after the conference, she was offered two jobs, one in Hawaii and one in New York. This boosted her ego and made her stronger. She returned to campus and decided to keep on fighting for her rights. Unfortunately, she was not able to find a mentor who could help her by talking through these experiences. She was on her own, with only the support of her family members. They, of course, believed in her ability, but they were not knowledgeable about the university tenure system. Lisa went to the administrator on campus whose responsibility was to support and mentor new fac-ulty. As a white male, he found it hard to understand her situation. He told her he would check into it, and he did talk with her department chair regarding the situ-ation. He was unable to see the discrimination that Lisa felt. His report to her indi-cated that she should try again for tenure. Lisa went to the dean of the college and found no support in that office. She went to the affirmative action office, received some general advice, and followed up on all suggestions. Eventually, she turned to the faculty union, as a last resort, and discussed her options for filing a grievance. The union representative helped her to complete the official paperwork and sub-mit it. The person who received this paperwork was none other than the adminis-trator whom she had contacted previously for help—the white male in the Faculty Affairs Office. The circle was complete, and Lisa felt more ostracized and defeated than ever before. Unfortunately, Lisa also found that the union was not able to help her because, though the organization can bring to the attention of administrators the issue of racial discrimination, the group cannot make changes. Lisa felt disem-powered; she had gone through all available university channels but there was lit-tle hope that she would receive promotion. The discrimination Lisa was battling came from faculty members who had the power to decide on her tenure, and many of those faculty members had not looked at their own racism. These individuals also hid behind the university's bureaucracy.

VIGNETTE 2

Stephen was born and grew up in Oakland, California. His father left his home in the four-village area of Canton, China, to come the United States at the age of fifteen. After he made some money, he went back to his village and brought back a bride. The family owned a small food store in Oakland selling mostly Chinese foods. Stephen did very well in school and went to Berkeley, where he received excellent grades. While Stephen was in high school, he had felt attracted to and interested in members of the same sex. It became clear to him that he was gay when he went to college. He met a young Anglo male in New York who became Stephen's partner. Stephen's mother, who did not speak English, kept asking Stephen about marriage. He did not have the heart to tell his mother that he was gay. He also heard negative comments from his mother about the gay population. He was fearful that in revealing his true identity and sexual orientation, he would be punished and upset his parents. He kept his gayness in the closet. Eventually he earned a bachelor's degree in French. He then went to France to study for two years and became fluent in French. He returned to the States and started teaching French. After several years of teaching, he felt a need to advance himself, and he chose to go into the field of second language acquisition. He went to New York and pursued a doctoral degree. During his study in New York, he also taught part-time at the university. His students found him exceptionally effective as a teacher and said so in their evaluations. Although Stephen had traveled extensively, he still wanted to return to the Bay area to work so that he could be closer to his family. So he began to apply for teaching positions in the Bay area right before he handed in his dissertation. Several universities responded to his application immediately, and he was excited. He made a few trips to the West coast, but the most desirable area was in the Bay area. He was well prepared for his interviews and gave very good presentations. He felt that he needed to be more open about his sexual orientation, so, during his interviews, he asked a few questions about campus support for gays and lesbians. All of the campuses he visited said that they would find out. However, only two actually followed through and called him about the support system for gays and lesbians. Stephen felt that he was competitive and should be able to get an offer from several of the universities he visited. Interestingly, he was offered a position in Texas with an ultraconservative faculty. They mentioned nothing about the gay and lesbian support. In fact, they said they did not have such support and had never heard of any. Stephen declined the offer. He waited for a very long time for offers from California, but he did not hear from them.

The following was actually what happened during the interview process in the Bay Area. Stephen found out about this years later. One person on the search committee knew him and revealed to him what had occurred. During the personnel search committee meeting, Stephen was rated very highly on teaching and research potential. His Asian heritage was considered a plus because many students were of Asian Pacific Island descent. Stephen was selected as a finalist along with one other candidate and invited for a final interview. He brought his male partner with him. During an informal dinner party for Stephen, two Anglo male members of the search committee were openly hostile to Stephen and his partner.

At the next search committee meeting, they expressed the opinion that gays were not welcome at the university and said, furthermore, that they would never allow a gay man to be hired in this particular department. They effectively influenced the search committee vote, and Stephen was eliminated from the list of finalists. The excuse provided was that he was not yet finished with his dissertation. However, everyone knew that he would finish his degree well before the start of the fall semester when he was to begin his teaching assignments. The homophobic senior professors had been successful in discriminating against this promising young scholar.

VIGNETTE 3

Mai was a child when the Vietnam War started. She lived in a village not too far away from Danang. When she was a young girl, she worked for the Viet Cong. People in her village sympathized with the Viet Cong. They would help dig tunnels from their kitchens leading to the outskirts of the village. Mai would often spy for Viet Cong. She was captured a number of times and was interrogated and tortured. She did not have a lot of formal schooling during that time, but her father taught her to read, and they often read together at night. She was always interested in learning, and whenever she saw a book, she would grab it and began to read. Her brother moved to Saigon as a young man. Eventually, he left for the United States as a refugee after April 1975. Mai's family was sponsored by her brother and arrived in Camp Pendelton in 1980. Mai met her husband there, and soon after they were settled in San Diego. She knew how important it was to learn English, and she quickly enrolled in an adult school. She was so eager to learn that she soon found out about community college. She went to Mesa College in San Diego, and later her family moved to L.A. Her husband worked as an auto mechanic for a shop owned by a Vietnamese businessman. Mai went to California State University (CSU) in L.A. and earned a bachelor's degree. She was very interested in teaching. Because there was such a great need for Vietnamese-speaking teachers, she received an emergency credential to teach. As a teacher, she was frequently asked to give presentations about Southeast Asia, and she became very good at giving presentations. She also felt the need to receive further education. She decided to go to school part-time and continue working full-time. This put a severe strain on her and her family. Her husband complained constantly that she was not home and no food was prepared. She often bought fast food, pizza, hamburgers, and frozen TV dinners. This created a tremendous burden on her, and her mother-in-law became very disenchanted with her. The lack of support from her husband and her family made it impossible for her to continue her relationship with her husband. To her great sadness, she agreed to a divorce and to let her husband take care of their son. With encouragement from her mentor, who was the department chair of her program, she went on to pursue a doctoral degree in education. She knew full well that her family, her own mother and brothers, did not support this idea. Mai still went to school to prove to herself that she could do it. After so many years of struggle, she finally "made it" and received her doctoral degree. She applied for a position at one of the CSU campuses where she was told that there were no tenure-track openings but that they were happy to hire her as non-tenure-track faculty. Not knowing what that meant and delighted with the opportunity to teach at the university, Mai quickly accepted the offer. She taught full classes and three to four courses each semester. She had to supervise student teaching and was driving all over the city to supervise. She found herself totally fatigued and unable to find time to do research. This went on for five years. Then, when there was an announcement for a tenure-track position in her department with a multicultural emphasis, she felt eminently qualified for the position and immediately applied, thinking that she had given the department so many years of service and that they all knew her very well. In Vietnam, someone in a similar position would undoubtedly get the job because the person had given so many years of service to the university. She thought she would stand a strong chance of being chosen. In fact, most of the faculty had heard her lecture several times in the past. She did not spend much time on preparing for the interview, and when she arrived at the lecture hall, she realized that she was not prepared for a formal presentation to the faculty. The presentation was weak, and she appeared to be unprepared and incoherent. She had to fish for her transparencies and could not answer the questions from the floor. She did not have references from the current literature ready to cite.

What happened during the deliberation about this candidate? The faculty met and deliberated about Mai's application. It was quickly decided that she was not ready for a tenure-track position for the following reasons:

1. She had no record of scholarly publications.
2. She did not seem to have an understanding of the current literature in the field.
3. She did not appear to take the interview process seriously.
4. She had been around a long time, and the department really needed "new blood."

Her cultural experience was limited to Vietnamese, and the department wanted someone with broader experience, even though it had literally depended on her to fulfill the university's obligations to the community and to the credential program. The department was willing to take advantage of Mai's ability to teach a full load, but only in a non-tenure-track position. She was not given any mentoring by the department, nor was she given adequate time for scholarly research. Mai, herself, was too busy doing her teaching and supervision to notice that she was not being given equitable treatment with regard to career advancement.

VIGNETTE 4

Helen was born in Canton, China, right after World War II. Her parents left for Hong Kong when she was very little, and she was taken care of by her aunt. She went to primary school in Canton and then, with great difficulty, was able to be reunited with her family in Hong Kong. She went to a very good high school in Hong Kong and was accepted by Stanford University. She went to Palo Alto, studied biology, and received a scholarship to study at the University of California at Los Angeles (UCLA). She finished her doctorate and went for one year of postdoctoral training at Johns Hopkins University.

She got a job at the Centers for Disease Control (CDC) in Atlanta and was doing research there. A teaching opportunity opened up and she applied. She did a good job in the interview and was eventually offered the position. She was quite happy to make a transition into teaching. The first year on campus was an extremely hectic one for her. Her student evaluations were very poor. Comments included, "I cannot understand her"; "She is not clear on the assignments"; " She seems inaccessible"; " Her communication style is poor"; "The instructor is not organized"; "The lectures are boring"; "The class was a waste of time"; "I never understood what she meant"; and "Her grading was hard and unfair." Helen's speech quality is intelligible with a slight influence of her native language. Helen was crushed when she received those evaluations. At the same time, there were a few students who felt that she did a good job as a teacher, but they were in the minority. She went to her department chair and asked for help. Her chair suggested that she visit some classes and observe how other faculty members taught. She became unsure of herself and questioned her own teaching style. She went to observe other classes and learned from the various colleagues of her department. No faculty offered to mentor her. Helen also wanted to become more involved in her professional associations. She submitted a proposal to speak at her national conference. The proposal was accepted, but it did not go well. A few people from the audience questioned her quantitative methodology, and she did not answer the questions well. She lost a lot of confidence and became even more doubtful about her ability.

The following fall quarter, she had to prepare for her personnel review, and she did not know what to include. She submitted what she thought was appropriate documentation and found out later that her colleagues had spent days and weeks and had even hired student assistants to put their portfolios together. In comparison to theirs, hers looked pitiful and inadequate. A small group of senior faculty members on the personnel committee in her department discussed her portfolio, and their comments included, "She has a real problem in communication"; "She cannot write"; "She is so different, and she does not fit"; "She is a poor teacher"; "She does not have research potential"; and "She speaks poorly." The personnel committee wrote a scathing letter to her essentially telling her to "shape up or ship out." Upon receipt of the letter, Helen was totally speechless. Tears ran down her face, and she could not control herself. A faculty member walked by and, finding her in such a state, calmed her down and offered to help her. Together they went through her work and accomplishments, and she was reassured that she had a good record. They outlined a strategy to improve her teaching. She reread the letter and decided to write a letter of rebuttal. This letter was sent to the department chair and the dean. A week later, a letter from the dean's office arrived on her desk acknowledging the receipt of her rebuttal and providing support for her. She felt a little better and decided to continue teaching on that campus. She also sent her work to be published in professional journals such as *Science* and *New England Journal of Medicine*.

When it was time to apply for tenure and promotion, she sought the help of two faculty members in the department and one from outside the department. They went over her portfolio and gave her valuable suggestions. These three faculty members told her that they also went through a tough time getting tenured. With their support and encouragement, she presented a much stronger case. It was very difficult for her to "toot her own horn" because all her life she had been told to be humble and to not talk about herself. In the Taoist philosophy of her family upbringing, it was not recommended to fight for one's rights or to talk about oneself. One is encouraged to seek peace and harmony and not personal gain. This is in direct contrast to the Western way of being assertive and seeking to fight for the rights of people. The fundamental question that the personnel committee wrestled with was whether or not Helen could be effective at the university. Until this point, little attention was given to helping her succeed. The members of the department, concerned with their own teaching and research projects, expected that Helen would seek assistance on her own. They had given her a "warning" in the form of a weak review. Students had pointed out her lack of effective communication. Who was responsible for her failure to improve as a professor? Should there be mentors, formally appointed, to work with new faculty? Is the department responsible for supporting new faculty, or should they be allowed to "sink or swim" on their own? The committee identified this as a moral dilemma.

There was little recourse for Helen, at this point, because much damage had been done. The chair of the committee met with the chair of the department, and presented the conflicting points of view expressed by the committee members. Some felt that Helen had failed to meet the minimum standards for tenure. Others felt that she had arrived with no idea of how the system of the university functioned and that the university had failed to educate and support her in her progress through the maze of that system. The problem was not a simple one. The department chair, wisely, suggested that they meet with the dean of academic affairs to discuss not only Helen's situation but the situation of other junior faculty who may not have understood the challenges of gaining tenure in a large and impersonal state university. Because the university policy file states a strong commitment to hiring faculty from diverse ethnic and cultural backgrounds, the university could not, in good conscience, continue to penalize these recruits for their lack of sophistication with a complex and inbred "old-boy system." This story has not yet reached a conclusion. Helen was granted an additional probationary year by the dean of the faculty. The faculty governing body is debating the issue of policy to support the success of junior faculty. The conclusions that they reach will have a profound effect on the recruitment, hiring, and retention of faculty in the twenty-first century.

VIGNETTE 5

Laura was born in GuanZhou, China, the daughter of a diplomat. Her father went to Taiwan in 1949 leaving his family of six children and a wife behind. Laura spent four years in GuanZhou under the Communist regime. Being a landlord family, a family of wealth owning large pieces of land, they were considered corrupted and evil. They were chased out of their home and became homeless. The family tried to find shelters with friends and family members, but most of them shunned them. One of Laura's brothers died of sickness and starvation. They lived from day to day by finding food in the fields. She learned to pick roots, leaves, and wild grass for food. Many nights they would stay in caves using heated stones to warm themselves. Four years later, they were able to leave China and were finally reunited with her father.

As a diplomatic family, they moved from country to country; they lived in Europe, Thailand, Saudi Arabia, and South America. Laura finally chose to study in the United States and earned a doctoral degree in history with a minor in art history. She met her husband in graduate school, and both of them graduated about the same time. He was offered a position at a university in the Midwest, and Laura followed him. She also found a teaching job in another university. She spoke English and French fluently and began to help her university in branching into programs in Europe. She would often take groups of students to Europe and soon was invited to apply for a position as the dean of extension. She felt qualified for the position, and after several rounds of interviews, she was selected as the dean. In her position as the dean, she was given the authority to develop a variety of programs and often traveled to different parts of the world. Her previous experience as the daughter of a diplomat helped her to gain communicative competence in dealing with persons from diverse backgrounds. Her experience as a homeless child also taught her to work hard, to be humble, and to not take anything for granted. Her academic credentials and her linguistic ability made her marketable for a job that required interpersonal skills, communication, innovation, persistence, creativity, and audacity. She was quite happy and busy. She was the only Asian administrator on her campus, and she saw very few Asians in professional meetings of university administrators. A few Asian faculty members would go to her seeking support. She was surprised to hear their stories and felt frustrated that they were mistreated. She decided to form a strategic alliance with

Asian faculty on her campus. They would meet regularly over lunch to talk about their frustrations, and they also helped each other with publication and writing. Laura would often critique the papers they wrote, ripping them apart and putting them back together, going line by line and paragraph by paragraph. She spent an enormous amount of time mentoring faculty and helping them succeed in the tenure process. When prospective Asian faculty applicants came to the campus to interview, her group would often meet with them and share with them their experiences. Laura gained a reputation on her campus as "mother Laura" as she continued to empower others. Years of strain from her work, travel, family, and commitment to equity made her so tired and burned out that one night, on her way home, she fell asleep and drove off the road. She was found by a police officer and was taken to the hospital. The medical examination revealed a heart condition, and Laura was told to rest and take time off from work.

Lessons learned include "you can't be any good to others, if you are not good to yourself, or people will take advantage of you whenever they can; and although it may help them, it may not be very helpful for you." Mentors are not necessarily Mother Teresa types.

CONCLUSION

The title of this chapter suggests that faculty of Asian Pacific Islander descent are surviving. The vignettes, however, suggest a different scenario. Asian Pacific faculty members are not achieving tenure-track positions that allow opportunities for tenure and promotion. They are used frequently to fill part-time faculty positions. When they are hired in tenure-track lines, they are given huge teaching and advising loads that limit time for research and publication. They assume that they will be rewarded for hard work and time spent in teaching and advising. Mentors are rarely available to explain the reality of academic life: that is, publish and receive grants if one intends to become tenured and promotable. Clearly, the Asian Pacific community must acknowledge and meet the discrimination that faces them at the university. This so-called model minority will need to challenge the system in ways that are not expected. According to Cho, there is evidence from case studies that cases that challenge "the fairness of tenure or promotion denials to Asian Pacific Americans are shaped by assumptions of the victims' passivity" (1996, 37).

Progress toward successful promotion and tenure can be derailed by subjective assumptions that can and should be challenged and reversed. Assumptions regarding the passivity of the Asian Pacific population are fueled by the arguments of Schlesinger (1992) and D'Souza (1995), who claim that Asian Pacific Islanders do not succeed because their cultures teach them to work hard and not complain. This stereotype must be replaced by an alliance of Asian Pacific Islanders who form collaborations with other groups and, together, speak out against injustice and discrimination, especially in the workplace. Expansion of the research on how ethnic stereotyping has limited the advancement of Asian Pacific faculty may help this group to confront and dispel apparent myths.

Efforts to recruit, hire, and retain Asian Pacific faculty must become a challenge and a cause across the entire campus community. If a university is truly committed to faculty diversification efforts, there must be a diversification plan constructed and supported by the faculty and administration. A report published by the CSU Office of the Chancellor (1994) indicates that Asian Pacific Islanders were the most underrepresented in senior and executive management in the CSU system. Therefore, a high-ranking administrator, who understands the implications of this underrepresentation at the hiring level, must be assigned to guide and implement the diversification plan. Nicely worded documents and mission statements will not achieve equitable hiring and retention practices without a solid infrastructure of administrators and senior faculty who support diversity. The person who oversees recruitment and hiring, as well as the development of a faculty mentoring program, must be supported by the campus community. A presence in the Office of Academic Affairs is mandatory. A presence on the president's cabinet is mandatory. Opportunities for dialogue among new faculty and experienced faculty mentors are mandatory. Even with all of this external support, Asian Pacific faculty will not be successful unless the community itself presents a strong image. All of these components, working together, will provide an environment in which diverse faculty members, including faculty of color, women, faculty with disabilities, and gay and lesbian faculty, can expect to be treated fairly and equitably. We should ask for and accept no less.

REFERENCES

California State University (CSU). 1994. *Asian Pacific Americans in the CSU*. Long Beach: CSU Office of the Chancellor.

Cho, S. 1996. Faculty in Higher Education. In *Proceedings of the Ninth Annual Conference of APAHE,* ed. S. Cho. Sacramento: Asian Pacific Americans in Higher Education.

D'Souza, D. 1995. *The End of Racism*. New York: The Free Press.

Gardner, R. W., B. Robey, and P. C. Smith. 1985. Asian American: Growth, Change, and Diversity. *Population Bulletin* 40: 1–44.

Rueda, R. S. 1993. Meeting the Needs of Diverse Students. Paper presented at the Multicultural Education Summer Institute, San Diego State University, July.

Schlesinger, A., Jr. 1992. *The Disuniting of America—Reflections on a Multicultural Society.* New York: W. W. Norton and Co.

U.S. Bureau of Census. 1993. *1990 Census of Population: Asian Pacific Islanders in the United States*. Washington, D.C.: U.S. Government Printing Office.

Woo, S. B., Chang-Lin Tien, Anna Chennault, Michael Lin, Larry Ho, and Henry Tang. 1998. Political Power: A Communal Goal. *Asian Week,* 2 July.

14

Beyond the Politics of Schools and the Rhetoric of Fashionable Pedagogies: The Significance of Teacher Ideology

Lilia I. Bartolomé and Enrique (Henry) T. Trueba

The commitment to educate immigrant and low-status populations constitutes the heart of American democracy. Selected exclusion and shrewd politics on the part of high-status populations are an attempt to retain power and privilege. The voices we have heard in the previous chapters invite serious reflection toward a reconstruction of ethnohistorical realities. Reconstruction is important to some because it provides the human species with a justification for being and doing what we are and do; it is an effort to justify actions, goals, use of power, and the retention of high-status positions by dominant groups. But reconstruction is even more important to others because it provides them with the foundations to challenge stereotypic or unfair accounts that can challenge the status quo, the current distribution of power and privileges. Social, cultural, and economic changes begin by challenging historical accounts regarding equity, justice, fairness, and traditional wisdom.

The valuable contribution of this volume consists precisely in giving the readers a tool kit to challenge the existing distribution of resources and power. The information and value perspectives needed to question the status quo and to explore a fair distribution of privileges also pave the way for an active participation of underrepresented groups in American democratic institutions, especially in higher education. Because political, religious, and educational institutions constitute the quintessence of Western civilization and of American democracy, we believe that a better understanding of the politics of education and our discussion of the power of ideologies that ultimately silence oppressed groups are of central importance. This final chapter brings to a conclusion our discourse on immigrant experiences in the United States. The authors write from many different stand-

277

points because they are (1) immigrants who describe their own past and current struggles in this country, (2) researchers interested in the theoretical and empirical study of immigration phenomena, and/or (3) educators responsible for teaching immigrant students and thus facing many challenges.

Much of the current discussion regarding preparation of teachers of education focuses on "best practice" as a means to address the academic needs of immigrant students primarily viewed as "limited-English-proficient" students. This narrow focus often neglects the fundamental role that teacher ideology plays in the instruction of culturally different students. To be more specific, the need for clarity of political beliefs, practices, and commitments is as important as the actual pedagogical strategies used in instruction. Hegemonic structures in classroom instruction work effectively in penalizing linguistically and culturally different students, especially students of color.

In addition to the tendency to view immigrant education as a purely technical or methodological "problem" vis-à-vis the "limitations of students," responses by educators often reflect an outdated assimilationist ideology suggesting that all immigrants, regardless of race/ethnicity and prior socioeconomic status level, must eventually assimilate and blend into the dominant white, Eurocentric culture.[1] Implicit in this ideology is the acceptance of the existing social, political, and economic hierarchy that is viewed as appropriate and fair and consequently need not be questioned by educators. Educators operating under this assimilationist ideology argue that the resulting socioeconomic order is based on merit and, consequently, if nonwhite immigrant students want to move up the ladder and achieve as much as their white counterparts, all they have to do is simply learn English and adopt mainstream cultural values.

This myth about an easy way to mainstream America is clearly contradicted by experience. We have only to look at those African Americans, Native Americans, and Latinos who have been forced by social pressures to become either monolingual in English or dominant in standard English. They had hoped that English-language proficiency and cultural assimilation would guarantee them first-class citizenship. Yet they continue to face with profound disappointment racism, neglect, and prejudice in their daily lives.

It is important to understand that, while teaching strategies and techniques are important, focusing chiefly on technical issues often distracts teachers from the very real ideological and political dimensions of teaching immigrant students. Educators of immigrant and U.S.-born low-status students need to, first and foremost, develop both political and ideological clarity in order to become more effective in their instructional efforts.[2]

"Political clarity" can be defined as the process by which individuals achieve a deepening awareness of the sociopolitical and economic realities that shape their lives and their capacity to transform them.[3] In addition, it refers to processes whereby individuals come to better understand possible linkages between the macropolitical, economic, and social variables and the microclassroom instructional activities and performance of subordinated groups.[4] Thus, it invariably requires that educators struggle to link sociocultural structures and schooling.

A related concept, "ideology," refers to the framework of thought that is used by members of a society to justify or rationalize an existing social (dis)order. Thus, "ideological clarity" refers to the process by which individuals struggle to identify both the dominant society's explanations for the existing socioeconomic and political hierarchy and their own explanations of the social order and any resulting inequalities. Ideological clarity requires that teachers' individual explanations be compared and contrasted with those propagated by the dominant society. The juxtaposing of ideologies, hopefully, forces teachers to better understand if, when, and how their belief systems uncritically reflect those of the dominant society and support unfair and inequitable conditions.

We believe that teacher education programs that enable prospective teachers to, first, recognize the existence of the political and ideological dimensions of education and, second, to increase their political and ideological clarity will produce the type of intellectual practitioners we urgently need to teach in the ever increasing culturally and socially diverse urban schools of today. It is our belief that uncritical prospective teachers often end up blindly following lock step methodologies and promulgating unexamined beliefs and attitudes that often compound the difficulties faced by immigrant and U.S.-born low-status minority students in school. It is important to reiterate that while we strongly agree that educators of immigrant students must be well versed in language acquisition theory and practice, management, and organization, as well as a variety of instructional approaches, it is important to understand that, in addition to these technical skills, they must also be ready to struggle with the greater political and ideological challenges that face them in their attempts to work with immigrant and U.S.-born low-status minority populations.

The following sections of this chapter expand on the argument in the following fashion. First, the historical negation of the political and ideological dimensions in the field of teacher education is discussed. Second, selected research sources on effective teaching are presented, particularly how the research suggests that teachers who possess some degree of political and ideological clarity are more likely to successfully counter dominant culture assimilationist and deficit ideologies in order to better serve their immigrant and U.S.-born low-status minority students. Third, general recommendations are offered for improving teacher preparation programs so teachers can deal with the issues of politics, ideology, and ethics in education.

THE POLITICAL AND IDEOLOGICAL DIMENSIONS OF TEACHING: "NAMING" AND INTERROGATING HURTFUL IDEOLOGIES

The issue of teacher ideology and the role that it may play in teachers' thinking and behavior in education, especially in the education of low-status immigrant

minority education, has usually been ignored or negated in most teacher education programs as well as in much of the teacher education literature.[5] Historically,
the preparation of teachers has been treated as chiefly a technical issue. Although
there have been experimental teacher education programs in the past to develop
teachers as critically minded intellectuals or "transformative intellectuals," the
dominant tradition has tended to be one that equates teacher preparation with
training and the imparting of technical skills in instruction, management, and
curriculum.[6] Despite this reality, the significance of teacher political and ideological orientation on teaching has not been sufficiently acknowledged as relevant
to the task of teacher preparation.

Educators need to "name" ideology for what it is. Given our history of negat-
ing the political nature of education as well as the existence and significance of
teacher ideology, it is not surprising to witness that, despite these being key issues
in current immigrant education discussions today, there is no general overt recognition of this reality by those engaged in the debate. Furthermore, although there
have been, and continue to be, efforts to examine teacher beliefs and attitudes,
there have been few systematic attempts to examine the political and ideological
dimensions of teachers' "beliefs" and "attitudes" and how these worldviews are
part of a particular ideological orientation. Indeed, teachers' beliefs and attitudes
have been treated as apolitical, overly psychologized constructs that "simply"
reflect personality types, individual values, and predispositions that have little to
do with the existing larger political, social, and economic order. Teachers' beliefs
and attitudes regarding the legitimacy of the greater social order and of the resulting unequal power relations among various cultural groups at the school and classroom levels have, by and large, historically not been acknowledged as significant
to improving the educational process and outcome of immigrant and U.S.-born
minority students.

However, even without utilizing the term *ideology*, the literature suggests that
prospective teachers tend to uncritically and, often, unconsciously hold beliefs
and attitudes about the existing social order that reflect the dominant ideology.
Unfortunately, this reproduction of thinking often translates into teachers'
uncritical acceptance of assimilationist and deficit-based views of linguistic
minority students. We believe that the assimilationist and deficit ideologies held
by most white teachers and many nonwhite teachers have had and continue to
have detrimental consequences in the education of nonwhite immigrant and
U.S.-born linguistic minority students. The combination of the assimilationist
belief system with a deficit ideology can be an especially deadly one because it
rationalizes disrespecting minority students' native languages and primary cultures, misteaching them dominant culture and English, and then blaming their
academic difficulties on the students' "pathological deficiencies."

The reality is that most prospective teachers have not been forced to critically
reflect on their ideological orientations and "bring with them, unintentional or
otherwise, racist and xenophobic views with the potential to corrupt teacher-stu-

dent interactions and academic instruction."[7] The restricted perspectives by which some teachers view their students are usually a product of their own personal theories, internalized beliefs, and values that reflect their own formative and restricted life and cultural experiences and influences. However, they often do not recognize beliefs and attitudes as reflecting the dominant ideology but, instead, view them as "natural," "objective," and "commonsensical"—in other words, the norm.[8] Despite the reality that one's ideology serves as a lens that filters new information or knowledge, conventional teacher education programs usually fail to acknowledge its existence and treat pre-service students as blank slates who simply need to learn the latest in teaching and discipline techniques to function effectively in the immigrant and minority classroom.

The dramatic increase in poor, nonwhite, and immigrant students in U.S. public schools also signals the urgent need to understand and challenge the ideological orientations of prospective teachers in teacher education programs. Within the next two decades we expect to have in the classrooms of public schools in most large cities a net majority of African Americans, Latinos, Asian Americans, and Native Americans. In 1945, the U.S. population was 87 percent whites, 10 percent blacks, 2.5 percent Hispanics, and 0.5 percent Asians. By the year 2050 whites will make up 52.8 percent; Hispanics, 24.5 percent; blacks, 13.6 percent; and Asians, 8.2 percent.[9] One current challenge is to adequately prepare the overwhelmingly white, female, and middle-class pre-service teacher population to work with subordinated student groups that are quickly becoming the majority in many of the largest urban public schools in the country.[10] While the nation's school population is made up of approximately 40 percent minority children, nearly 90 percent of teachers are white.[11] In addition, social class differences between teacher and student continue to widen. For example, 44 percent of African American children and 36 percent of Latino children live in poverty, yet more teachers come from white lower-middle- and middle-class homes and have been reared in rural and suburban communities.[12]

Furthermore, there are also significant differences in teacher-student language backgrounds. The majority of teachers are English monolingual, while estimates of school-aged limited-English-proficient students in the public schools range from 5 to 7.5 million.[13] Even in bilingual education, the majority of teachers are white, which points to the common misperception that nonwhite teachers fill the majority of bilingual teacher slots. The reality is that only 10 percent of teacher positions are held by Latinos.[14] In addition, while Hispanic students constitute two-thirds of limited-English-proficient students, only 15 percent of bilingual teachers are Hispanic.[15]

Given these changing student demographics, it becomes evident that all teachers, not just bilingual and English as a Second Language teachers, are responsible for preparing immigrant and U.S.-born minority children. And, given the social class, cultural, and language differences between teachers and students, it becomes especially urgent that teachers critically understand their ideological ori-

entations with respect to cultural and class differences so they can begin to comprehend that teaching is not a politically or ideologically neutral undertaking.

Although the need to help teacher and prospective teachers "name" and interrogate their ideological stances is urgent, it is not an easy task. The reality that
educators unknowingly accept and support the status quo even when it can potentially harm their students is unfortunate, but it is not surprising given, as Bourdieu
states, that

> teachers are the products of a system whose aim is to transmit an aristocratic culture,
> and are likely to adopt its values with greater ardor in proportion to the degree to
> which they owe it their own academic and social success. How indeed could they
> avoid unconsciously bringing into play the values of the milieu from which they
> come, or to which they wish to belong, when teaching and assessing their pupils?
> Thus, in higher education, the working or lower middle class student will be judged
> according to the scale of values of the educated classes which many teachers owe to
> their social origin and which they willingly adopt.[16]

Research on prospective teachers' beliefs, attitudes, and preferences suggests
that teachers prefer to teach students who are like themselves in communities
that are familiar to them. Most pre-service teachers very clearly state that they do
not want to teach in inner-city schools or work with minority or immigrant students.[17] Approaches for preparing prospective teachers to deal with increasing
cultural and linguistic diversity in schools can, with few exceptions, be described
as fragmented additions to the existing teacher preparation curriculum. While
most teacher education programs have begun to acknowledge issues of cultural
and linguistic diversity, they usually do so by requiring only one or two courses in
multicultural education or electives that discuss cultural, ethnic, or gender
issues.[18] Few programs have seriously attempted to infuse or permeate the existing teacher education curriculum with key concepts that require prospective
teachers to critically examine and interrogate their ideological orientations as
part of their learning process.[19] Critics of "fragmented" multicultural education
claim that it fails to seriously address issues of structural and ideological inequality or to challenge prospective teachers' ethnocentric and culturally parochial ideologies. Because of these limited and superficial attempts to prepare teachers for
meeting the needs of immigrant and U.S.-born minority children, there is little
opportunity for the teachers to begin to develop political and ideological clarity.

However, in our view, instead of falling prey to a form of hopeless cynicism that
infantilizes teachers, we propose a radical transformation in teacher preparation
whereby political and ideological clarity are prioritized. We believe that the
restricted perspectives by which some teachers view their immigrant and U.S.-
born minority students are not fixed and irreversible. Teachers' actions and beliefs
that eventually contradict the dominant norms serve as evidence that the individual is a creator as well as a recipient of values. Many members of the dominant
culture, as well as members of subordinated cultures, are open to recognizing the

political dimensions of teaching, questioning the status quo, and working toward creating more just and democratic educational conditions for all students.[20] In fact, we believe that what we have learned from effective teachers of immigrant and U.S.-born minority students can enhance our thinking about the types of concepts and learning experiences for prospective teachers in all teacher preparation programs in order to achieve greater political and ideological clarity.

EFFECTIVE TEACHERS OF IMMIGRANT AND U.S.-BORN MINORITY STUDENTS: WHAT DO WE KNOW?

Past efforts to identify the characteristics of exemplary teachers suggest that successful teachers share anti-deficit ideological orientations.[21] In addition, the teachers in these studies question, in one form or another, the "correctness" or "fairness" of the existing social order and actively work to prevent its reproduction at the school and classroom levels. Current work by Bartolomé and Balderrama suggests that effective educators of immigrant and U.S.-born minority students, for a variety of reasons, have developed the understanding that education is a political act that can either support the status quo or challenge it.[22] The researchers describe five common ideological beliefs shared by the educators in a predominantly low-socioeconomic-status minority high school in a Southern California border town where approximately 75 percent of students go on to college. In this chapter, we will discuss two educator ideological beliefs, which include the rejection of both (1) an assimilationist orientation and deficit views of immigrant and minority students and (2) white supremacist and romanticized views of white middle-class (mainstream) culture. In addition, we describe the educators' cultural border crossing experiences—during which they personally experienced or witnessed someone else's subordination. These three findings are briefly elaborated on in the following section in order to illustrate the power of teacher ideological clarity in working with subordinated student populations.

Educator Rejection of Assimilationist and Deficit Views of Immigrant and Minority Students

An important belief shared by these educators was their rejection of deficit views of immigrant and minority students in general and Mexicano/Latino students in particular, as well as their refusal to assume an assimilationist stance in educating them. In fact, these educators promoted native language instruction so that students, in the words of one teacher, "can learn academic subject matter appropriate to their grade level and . . . maintain positive self-esteem and cultural pride." In rejecting assimilationist views, the majority of these teachers voiced their belief that cultures in contact (such as Mexican Americans and Anglo-

Americans in contact in the Southwest) should inform and transform the other, with each cultural group taking the "best" from the other culture and discarding the "worst" from its respective culture.

Furthermore, one of the teachers in the sample, Mr. Tijerina, explained that effective teachers of Mexicano/Latino students and other minorities have to be conscious of cultural and ethnic differences and of their own racist tendencies and beliefs. He explained that to be effective teachers of minorities, "You have to like people of color—you have to authentically like dark colors, you have to love brown [people]!" He explained,

> I think we have the feeling here [at Riverview] that minorities aren't inferior. I think there's a difference between patronizing in some schools where they really think a person is inferior to some degree, but, "Hey, you can make it if you try harder." The white people here—I don't think they feel that here. I think that they feel that our kids are equal—they have the same brains as kids in [more affluent, predominantly white schools such as] Playa Dorada, or Buena Vista, or any place else. They do have the same brains—only the background is definitively disadvantaged—for lots of reasons.

The educators consistently voiced the common belief that the disproportionate academic problems among immigrant and U.S.-born minority students are not a result of their cultures, languages, or some innate racial pathological disorder. In fact, the participants distinguished between the very real poor and often restrictive life circumstances their students lived and their students' innate potential. These educators understood that their students "do have the same brains" but, through no fault of their own, have experienced difficult life conditions that are often the direct result of living in poverty. They see their students' chief problem as that—as not having money—however, they do not restrict their students' academic potential because of their low socioeconomic standing. They appear to believe, as Paulo Freire eloquently states, that students' lack of familiarity with the dominant culture "does not mean . . . that the lack of these experiences develop in these [students] a different 'nature' that determines their absolute incompetence."[23] Instead, these educators consciously reject deficit explanations and look to utilize, build on, and infuse into the school culture the numerous cultural strengths that they see their working-class, immigrant, and U.S.-born minority students bring to school.

Deromanticizing "Romanticized" Views of the Dominant Culture

In addition to rejecting deficit views of minority students and assimilationist approaches to dealing with cultural diversity, the educators in this study questioned the superordinate status typically conferred on "mainstream," middle-class, white culture. One teacher, Mrs. Cortland, debunked beliefs about the superiority of white, middle- and upper-middle-class culture when she spoke of the hypocrisy, dishonesty, arrogance, and disrespectful behavior often exhibited by many of the affluent white students she had worked with in the past. She pointed out that while white students, their parents, and their teachers delude themselves about just how superior the students are in comparison with poorer, nonwhite students, she found many of the white students to be seriously lacking in numerous human qualities such as respect and empathy for others. She shared her views, acquired when she began to substitute teach at the district's more affluent high school, as follows: "I never had one kid ever, as I was walking across the campus, come up to me and say, 'Are you new here? Can I help you? Do you need help in finding the room?' "

Furthermore, she observed,

> They [the students and their teachers] played this "game": "all these students are smart and wonderful." And the kids would come and go, "We'll pretend we are smart and wonderful." And, I mean, the lady I took over for . . . I think she had a nervous breakdown. They never told me, but I walked in and the first class was, what they called, 122 English and it was all Anglo kids. [When the assistant principal left me in the classroom], they [the students] all stood on their desks and sang, "Ding-Dong the Witch Is Dead" and thought it was funny.

Mrs. Cortland and Mr. Tijerina shared their belief that many aspects of middle-class, white culture serve to dehumanize people of color and promote the erroneous and arrogant belief that whites are superior. Mr. Tijerina argued that if the mainstream would adopt traditional Mexican values of respect, humility, and acceptance of difference, our society might become more humane and reduce feelings of disconnection and alienation that so many of its own members feel.[24]

The educators in this study consciously challenged and rejected romanticized perceptions of white, mainstream culture. Their attitude seemed to be that they "knew better" than to believe unrealistic and uncritical views of white middle-class culture. Too often, the norm in schools and in society is to compare poor, nonwhite students with an invisible, yet highly romanticized, white middle-class standard. The educators in this study were neither impressed by nor subscribed to myths of white supremacy or, conversely, myths about Mexican or working-class inferiority. On the contrary, they very realistically named the invisible center—middle-class white culture—and pointed out numerous undesirable aspects of it; they worked to maintain their minority students' cultures and prevent their uncritical assimilation of the negative Anglo cultural elements.

Educators as Cultural Border Crossers

Given their own life experiences as "cultural border crossers," these educators reported having lived with or witnessed the arbitrariness and unfairness of low-status accordance at some point in their life histories.[25] For instance, the high school principal, Mrs. Peabody, attributed her early cultural border crossing experiences to growing up as one of a few whites in inner-city, predominantly African

American, Pittsburgh. As a working-class white girl growing up in an African American community, she explained, she learned about the advantages of cultural pluralism early on. Although she experienced firsthand what it means to be relegated to low status, given her position as a "minority" white person in her African American community, she recognized the lifelong privilege and preferential treatment she received by virtue of being white. She told of her exposure to racism and discrimination as chiefly a result of her close work with people of color. She also shared her belief in allowing people of color to "use" her position as a white person (and, therefore, the perception of her by other whites as a more legitimate spokesperson) to carry their messages. Mrs. Peabody shared her conscious decision to utilize her privileged position as a white woman to become a change agent in school settings.

All of the educators in this sample experienced, at some point in their lives, opportunities to cross cultural and social class borders. These "border crossing" experiences, however, did not resemble the types of border crossing opportunities that white, middle- and upper-middle-class individuals often experience when they travel abroad or when they "visit" lower-class, predominantly minority urban areas. During these more typical types of border crossing experiences, white individuals often become unconscious "voyeurs" who view their new situations through never-acknowledged assimilationist and deficit ideological lenses. In addition, they usually do not consciously recognize their positions of dominance and higher status vis-à-vis the poor and nonwhite people they encounter. Often, as a result, they emerge from these experiences evermore bound to their unquestioned classist and white supremacist ideologies.

The border crossing experiences of the educators in this sample varied from typical "white border crossing" in that these individuals either personally experienced or witnessed others' subordination. For a variety of reasons, the reality of asymmetrical power relations among cultural groups became evident to them. Given their "baptism of fire" during their border crossing experiences, these educators better understand asymmetrical power relations among cultural groups and consciously assume the role of cultural brokers so as to better serve immigrant and U.S.-born low-status minority students.

The educators in this study understand that teaching is not an apolitical undertaking.[26] Although the educators varied in terms of political and ideological clarity, they, nevertheless, understood that immigrant and U.S.-born minority students are often, through no fault of their own, viewed and treated as low status in the greater society and in schools. These educators questioned narrow meritocratic explanations of the existing social (dis)order that implicitly suggest that Mexicano/Latino students occupy the lower end of the hierarchy because of a lack of merit and ability. The educators listed a number of factors that often eclipse issues of merit and ability such as racism and monetary limitations.

In addition, these educators rejected deficit and assimilationist ideologies imposed on their students. They recognized aspects of working-class, immigrant, and U.S.-born minority cultures as extremely positive and desired that their students maintain their cultural values. Similarly, while they recognized the need for their students to critically appropriate aspects of mainstream culture, they rejected romanticizing middle-class white culture and did not expect minority students to uncritically and blindly assimilate into it.

Given their life experiences as cultural border crossers, they recognized how low status is often unfairly assigned to members of lower-class and nonwhite groups. Thus, these educators understood their role as cultural brokers as key in assisting students from subordinated populations to succeed in mainstream culture in general and in academic culture in particular. They take very seriously their responsibility to provide students with the cultural knowledge and strategies needed to succeed academically in psychologically harmless ways. These educators' political clarity, solidarity with students, and sense of ethics made them true advocates and cultural brokers for their students so that they might "equalize the unequal playing field."

CONCLUSION AND GENERAL RECOMMENDATIONS

In conclusion, we would like to close this chapter by making general recommendations regarding the types of knowledge areas that prospective teachers need to acquire in order to become more politically and ideologically clear educators. The implications of the research on effective teachers of immigrant and U.S.-born minority students, though limited, requires that we go beyond simplistic and unidimensional recommendations for creating more effective teacher preparation programs. Nonetheless, despite space restrictions, we make the attempt to offer general recommendations that we believe really reflect the ideological stances and practices of the effective teachers discussed in the previous section.

It appears from the literature that effective teachers of immigrant and U.S.-born minority students have acquired political and ideological clarity, possess a great deal of courage, see themselves in solidarity with their subordinated students as well as their communities, and possess a clear and unwavering sense of ethics. What is not clear is how these teachers acquired such an understanding and commitment to immigrant and U.S.-born minority education. While it may be true that these individuals may have gained this clarity not in teacher education programs but through individual life experiences, it is our belief that efforts can be made in teacher education programs to better understand and teach to prospective teachers the significance of four key knowledge areas—teacher political and ideological clarity, courage, solidarity, and ethics—for effectively working with subordinated populations. Though these four general knowledge areas are fundamental to teacher education, we believe that they are seldom explicitly addressed and taught in schools of education.

Although there are numerous teacher preparation programs in existence that provide many learning experiences with the potential to help prospective teachers increase their political and ideological clarity, as well as confront issues of courage, solidarity, and ethics, very few programs are structured to insure that these key areas are present across the course of study. For example, many teacher education programs require that their students visit, observe, and student teach in culturally diverse and low-socioeconomic-status communities. In addition, a number of programs also present their students with opportunities to study abroad in order to develop bilingual and bicultural competencies. Despite good intentions, students are generally left to their own devices in terms of "making sense" of their cross-cultural and cross–socioeconomic class experiences. Often, students who participate in these cross-cultural and cross–socioeconomic class experiences become "cultural voyeurs" who unconsciously make sense of their new situations through unacknowledged assimilationist and deficit ideological lenses. Thus, students often emerge from these experiences evermore bound to their unacknowledged and unquestioned ethnocentric ideologies.

Bartolomé, one of the authors, recalls working with a group of prospective bilingual teachers who had spent a year abroad in Mexico City and returned to the United States to complete required coursework. These students, a majority of them white and middle class, were well-intentioned individuals who returned from Mexico City expressing disillusionment with aspects of Mexican culture. They shared having witnessed or experienced acts of sexism, classism, and racism (against indigenous Mexicans by lighter-skinned mestizo Mexicans). Without a theoretical framework for interpreting their experiences, the students unconsciously fell back on ethnocentric ideological perspectives.

Many of the students expressed relief at being back in the United States because they believed that sexism, racism, and classism were less of an issue than in Mexico. Had their perceptions been left unexamined, the students could have come away with an incomplete analysis and understanding of their experiences abroad. The goal of the year abroad program included producing teachers who would emerge bilingual, bicultural, and sensitive to cultural differences in order to effectively teach immigrant children in bilingual classrooms. Yet merely providing students with cross-cultural opportunities and not providing some type of critical framework for perceiving and interpreting new experiences can end up neutralizing a teacher education program's academic and cultural goals.

Bartolomé's response was to encourage the students to critically reflect on the hurtful and dehumanizing experiences that they witnessed or personally experienced during their year in Mexico. She explained that, as outsiders of the culture, they had been in a unique situation to clearly perceive the dominant social order and its manifestations of unequal treatment. She urged them to remember how painful and humiliating it feels to be unfairly accorded, through no fault of one's own, a low position of status and then treated accordingly. Bartolomé challenged them to decide whether or not they were willing to commit to work against such oppressive and undemocratic practices present in our own society and in our schools. She also urged them to question whether their opinions as middle-class white Americans that "racism, sexism, and classism are less important issues in the United States" would be countered or confirmed by poor people, people of color, and women in this society.

Our point in sharing this experience, what we consider to be a good teacher education program, is not to criticize specific aspects of the particular program but to illustrate the point that there are a number of teacher education programs that already offer their students valuable courses and educational experiences but lack a clear and coherent mission for insuring that students consistently and critically reflect on and question their ideological orientations vis-à-vis nonwhite and non-middle-class students. What is needed in many teacher preparation programs is commitment, on the part of administrators and educators, to weave key concepts such as political and ideological clarity, courage, solidarity, and ethics across the existing curriculum in order to better prepare prospective teachers to become effective teachers of all students but, in particular, of low-status immigrant and U.S.-born minority students.

Prospective and current teachers must develop ideological and political clarity that will guide them in their denouncement of a discriminatory school and social context so they can protect and advocate for their students. In addition, this clarity will also serve to help them move beyond the present so as to announce a future in which social justice and a humanizing pedagogy are always present in our classrooms.

According to Paulo Freire, beyond technical skills, teachers should also be equipped with a full understanding of what it means to have courage—to denounce the present inequities that directly cripple certain populations of students—and effectively create psychologically harmless educational contexts.[27] He challenges us to become courageous in our commitment to defend subordinated student populations even when it is easier not to take a stand.

In addition to ideological and political clarity and courage, prospective teachers must see themselves in solidarity with their students and their students' communities. They must understand the meaning and risk of solidarity so as to protect the dignity of their students. Again, actions of solidarity require politically and ideologically clear, courageous individuals as demonstrated by many of the effective teachers discussed in the previous section.

Finally, schools of education should also create spaces where the development of an ethical posture informs not only the technical acquisition of skills but also one's position vis-à-vis the human suffering that certain populations of students face in their community and in their school. All too often, in our quest to become "culturally relativistic" and "politically correct," we fail to discuss the ethical and moral dimensions of our work as educators. Regardless of the diversity of "cultural" opinions found in any school of education, concepts such as "equality," "democracy," "fairness," and "justice" need to serve as ever present anchors across the teacher education curriculum so as to remind prospective teachers that teaching is ultimately a moral and ethical undertaking. Such an undertaking requires a high level of commitment and political clarity so as to enable educators to learn what happens in the world of their students, their dreams, and their struggles.

In addition to the mastery of the content of one's field of specialization, political and ideological clarity becomes a decisive factor in a person's effective teaching and learning. Just as one cannot be a successful teacher without rigorous content preparation, one cannot be effective pedagogically without the political and ideological clarity that would force one to ask the a priori political questions, What content, against what, for whom, and against whom? Thus, the role of a teacher can never be reduced to a facile and mechanistic transmission of selective content.

NOTES

1. *Assimilationist ideology* as used here is treated as synonymous with the "Anglo conformity model," which refers to the belief that immigrants and subordinated indigenous groups should be brought to conform to the practices of the dominant Anglo-Saxon culture.

2. *Low-status* refers to the low political, social, and economic standing of nonwhite and uneducated immigrant groups in the United States. The term is used to distinguish the former immigrant groups from high-status immigrants who are often "white," educated, and possess the necessary social and academic cultural capital to do well in school settings and to assimilate into the dominant culture if they wish to do so. Although the term *low status* can be considered synonymous with the concept of "subordinated" minority group (as described below), we utilize a distinct term when referring to newcomers to U.S. society, so as to recognize Ogbu's distinction between "caste" and "immigrant" minorities. It is our position that low-status immigrants, because of their ethnic/racial makeup, low socioeconomic standing, and lack of mainstream cultural capital, are often perceived by members of the mainstream as similar in status to U.S. domestic minority groups such as African Americans, Chicanos, and Native Americans.

3. For a more detailed discussion of the concept "political clarity," please see L. I. Bartolomé, "Beyond the Methods Fetish: Toward a Humanizing Pedagogy," *Harvard Educational Review* 64, no. 2 (summer 1994): 173–94.

4. *Subordinated* refers to cultural groups that are politically, socially, and economically subordinate in the greater society. While individual members of these groups may not consider themselves subordinate in any manner to the white "mainstream," they nevertheless are members of a greater collective that historically has been perceived and treated as subordinate and inferior by the dominant society.

5. For examples of past studies that examine the relationships between teachers' biased beliefs and their classroom practice, see J. Brophy and T. Good, *Teacher–Student Relationships* (New York: Holt, Rinehart and Winston, 1974); and "Teacher Behavior and Student Achievement," in *Handbook on Research on Teaching*, 3rd edition, ed. M. Wittrock (New York: Macmillan, 1987), 328–75.

6. Henry Giroux and Peter McLaren define a "transformative intellectual" as one who exercises forms of intellectual and pedagogical proactive praxis, which attempts to insert teaching and learning directly into the political sphere by arguing that schooling represents both a struggle for meaning and a struggle over power relations. We are also referring to one whose intellectual practices are necessarily grounded in forms of moral and ethical

discourse exhibiting a preferential concern for the suffering and struggles of the disadvantaged and oppressed. See Giroux and McLaren, "Politics of Teacher Education," *Harvard Educational Review* 56 (1986): 215.

7. R. Gonzalvez, *Resistance in the Multicultural Education Classroom*, unpublished MS, Harvard Graduate School of Education, 1996.

8. Gonzalvez, *Resistance in the Multicultural Education Classroom*.

9. U.S. Census Bureau 1996, cited in M. M. Suárez-Orozco, "Introduction," in *Crossings: Mexican Immigration in Interdisciplinary Perspectives*, ed. M. M. Suárez-Orozco (Cambridge, Mass.: Harvard University Press and the D. Rockefeller Center for Latin American Studies, 1998), 6.

10. M. L. Gomez, "Teacher Education Reform and Prospective Teachers' Perspectives on Teaching 'Other People's' Children," *Teaching and Teacher Education* 10, no. 3 (1994): 319–34.

11. National Center for Education Statistics, *American Education at a Glance* (Washington, D.C.: Office of Education Research and Improvement, 1992).

12. N. Zimpher, "The RATE Project: A Profile of Teacher Education Students," *Journal of Teacher Education* 40, no. 6 (1989): 37.

13. B. McLeod, "Introduction," in *Language and Learning: Educating Linguistically Diverse Students* (Albany: State University of New York Press, 1994), xiv.

14. See R. Sanchez, "Mapping the Spanish Language along a Multiethnic and Multilingual Border," in *The Latino Studies Reader: Culture, Economy, and Society*, ed. A. Darder and R. D. Torres (Malden, Mass.: Blackwell Publishers, Inc., 1998).

15. S. Nieto, *Affirming Diversity: The Sociopolitical Context of Multicultural Education* (New York: Longman, 1992).

16. P. Bourdieu, "The School as a Conservative Force: Schools and Cultural Inequities," in *Knowledge and Values in Social and Educational Research*, ed. E. Bredo and W. Fernberg (Philadelphia: Temple University Press, 1982), 399.

17. American Association of Colleges for Teacher Education (AACTE), *Metropolitan Life Survey on Teacher Education Students* (Washington, D.C.: AACTE, 1990); Gomez, "Teacher Education Reform and Prospective Teachers' Perspectives on Teaching 'Other People's' Children"; K. Zeichner and K. Hoeft, "Teacher Socialization for Cultural Diversity," in *Handbook of Research in Teacher Education*, eds. J. Sikula, T. Buttery, and E. Guyton (New York: Macmillan Library Reference USA, 1996), 525–47.

18. K. A. Davis, "Multicultural Classrooms and Cultural Communities of Teachers," *Teaching and Teacher Education* 11, no. 6 (1995): 553–63.

19. C. E. Sleeter and C. A. Grant, "An Analysis of Multicultural Education in the United States," *Harvard Educational Review* 57 (1987): 421–44; Zeichner and Hoeft, "Teacher Socialization for Cultural Diversity."

20. E. Garcia, "Effective Instruction for Language Minority Students: The Teacher," *Boston University Journal of Education* 173, no. 2 (1991); R. T. Jimenez, R. Gersten, and A. Rivera, "Conversations with a Chicana Teacher: Supporting Students' Transition from Native to English Language Instruction," *The Elementary School Journal* 96, no. 3 (1996): 333–41; R. Rueda and H. Garcia, "Teachers' Perspectives on Literacy, Assessment and Instruction with Language-Minority Students: A Comparative Study," *The Elementary School Journal* 96, no. 3 (1996): 311–32.

21. L. I. Bartolomé and M. Balderrama, "The Need for Politically and Ideologically Clear Educators: Providing Our Children with 'The Best,' " in *The Best for Our Children:*

Latina/Latino Views on Literacy (New York: Teachers College Press, in press); T. Beaubouef, "Politicized Mothering among African-American Women Teachers: A Qualitative Inquiry," Ph.D. dissertation, Harvard Graduate School of Education, 1997; Garcia, "Effective Instruction for Language Minority Students"; Jimenez, Gersten, and Rivera, "Conversations with a Chicana Teacher"; Rueda and Garcia, "Teachers' Perspectives on Literacy, Assessment and Instruction with Language-Minority Students."

22. Bartolomé and Balderrama, "The Need for Politically and Ideologically Clear Educators."

23. Paulo Freire, *A Pedagogy of the City* (New York: Continuum Press, 1993), 17.

24. Mr. Tijerina explained that these values and worldviews are also present in other immigrant, nonwhite cultures such as Filipino, Vietnamese, Pacific Islander, and Central American—populations also represented in the high school.

25. *Cultural border crossers* refers to individuals who demonstrate the ability to understand and participate in various social and cultural realities or "Discourses." *Discourse* refers to "a socially accepted association among ways of using language, of thinking, feeling, believing, valuing, and of acting that can be used to identify oneself as a member of a *socially meaningful group*, 'social network,' " or culture (James P. Gee, *Sociolinguistics and Literacies: Ideology in Discourses* [London: Falmer Press, 1990], 143, emphasis added). In other words, a Discourse is like an "identity kit" of sorts that participants adopt or are expected to assume. The identity kits vary in terms of status and power (e.g., the discourse of white male doctors versus the discourse of Mexican male farmworkers).

The individuals in this study engaged in border crossing experiences in which they became clearly cognizant of issues of unequal power relations across cultures and subordination.

26. Bartolomé and Balderrama, "The Need for Politically and Ideologically Clear Educators."

27. Paulo Freire, *Pedagogy of Freedom: Ethics, Democracy, and Civic Courage* (Lanham, Md.: Rowman and Littlefield Publishers, Inc., 1998).

Index

293

About the Contributors

Encarnación Soriano Ayala holds a Ph.D. in educational sciences and is professor of research methodology in education at the University of Almería, Spain. Her initial field of investigation was in learning strategies applied to mathematics, and some of her publications include "La enseñanza de las matemáticas en el primer ciclo de al educatión primaria" (1997) and "Enseñanza y aprendizaje de las matemáticas en educación primarian. Diseño y evaluación de programas" (1999). Since 1994 her research has centered on multicultural education and her publications included "Immigrantes entre nosotros" (1999) and "La escuela almeriense:nun espacio multicultural" (1999).

Lilia I. Bartolomé is an associate professor of education in the Teacher Education and the Leadership in Urban Schools Doctoral Programs at the University of Massachusetts at Boston. She has published extensively in the areas of literacy, multicultural education, and critical pedagogy and has authored *The Misteaching of Academic Discourses: The Politics of Language in the Classroom* (Boulder: Westview) and coauthored (with Donaldo Macedo) *Dancing with Bigotry: Beyond the Politics of Tolerance* (New York: St. Martin's).

Angélica Bautista obtained her M.A. from the anthropology department at the University of Texas at Austin, where she is currently finishing her Ph.D. She has worked as a researcher at the Centro de Investigaciones Sociales in the University of Colima, Mexico, where she participated in several projects of national scope, including *La Telenovela Mexicana* and *La Formación de las Ofertas Culturales y sus Públicos en México*. She is coauthor of *Cuéntame en qué se quedó. La Telenovela como Fenómeno Social* (ed. Trillas, 1994). Her research interests include Chicano/Chicana studies, the immigration of Mexican women to the United States, and the labor market for women of color in the United States.

Li-Rong Lilly Cheng is a professor of communicative disorders and assistant dean of Global Program Development of the Office of the President at San Diego State University. She is a past president of the International Affairs Association, a related professional organization of the American Speech-Language Hearing Association (ASHA). She is also a fellow of ASHA. Dr. Cheng is the recipient of the 1997 ASHA Award for special contributions to multicultural affairs. She is the current president of the Chinese American

Education, Research and Development Association. Dr. Cheng has written numerous publications and has lectured all over the world.

Kathee M. Christensen is a professor in the Department of Communicative Disorders at San Diego State University, where she coordinates the teacher preparation program in education of the deaf. Dr. Christensen is the past president of the National Council on Education of the Deaf and the recipient of the Frederick C. Schreiber Distinguished Service Award from the National Association of the Deaf. She coedited *Multicultural Issues in Deafness* (Longman, 1993) and is the editor of *Deaf-Plus: A Multicultural Perspective* (DawnSignPress, 2000). She has written numerous articles on education of learners who are deaf or deaf-blind. Her research interests include trilingual education, multicultural issues, nonverbal communication, and cognitive development in learners who are deaf or deaf-blind.

Concha Delgado-Gaitan is an award-winning ethnographic researcher and scholar on oral and written traditions in immigrant communities. She is the author of three books, *Literacy for Empowerment, Crossing Cultural Borders* (with H. Trueba), and *Protean Literacy*. She is the coeditor of *School and Society* (with H. Trueba). Dr. Delgado-Gaitan has also published over forty book chapters and articles in scholarly journals, among them, *Harvard Educational Review, Anthropology and Education Quarterly*, and *American Educational Research Journal*. She is a writer in the Bay Area.

Lucila Ek is a doctoral student in the Urban Schooling division in the Graduate School of Education and Information Studies at the University of California, Los Angeles. Her research interests lie in the areas of language, literacy, culture, and identity. She is particularly interested in how these issues shape the educational experiences of Latino/Latina immigrant students. Lucila was a bilingual classroom teacher from 1992 to 1997.

Gisela Ernst-Slavit earned her Ph.D. at the University of Florida in 1991 and currently is an associate professor at Washington State University at Vancouver. Her research interests include teacher education, oracy and literacy development, bilingual and English-as-a-Second-Language education, and the use of ethnographic and sociolinguistic perspectives in the study of classrooms. She is a past president of the Washington Association for the Education of Speakers of Other Languages, has received the Public Awareness Award from the Washington Association for Language Teaching, and has published in *Anthropology and Education Quarterly, Linguistics and Education, TESOL Quarterly, TESOL Journal, Qualitative Studies in Education, Hispania, The Foreign Language Annals*, and *The Reading Teacher*, among others.

Christian Faltis is professor of bilingual and second language education at Arizona State University in Tempe, Arizona. In 1999, he was visiting professor at the University of California, Berkeley in the Graduate School of Education. Professor Faltis was a Senior Fulbright Scholar in Honduras, and has taught and lived in Latin America, Spain, and Tunisia. An author of more than sixty articles and ten books, his most recent publication (with P. Wolfe) is *So Much to Say: Adolescents, Bilingualism & ESL in the Secondary School* (Teachers College Press, 1999).

Bridget Fitzgerald Gersten is the English language officer for North Africa. She was a Fulbright Scholar in the Czech Republic, and holds a doctoral degree from Italy, where she lived for ten years. Proficient in six languages, Dr. Gersten has taught English as a second/foreign language since the 1980s. She is editor of *Tips from the Classroom*, *TESOL Journal*, and is active in bilingual and ESL education.

Arcelia Hernández is a bilingual teacher in the Port Hueneme School District in Oxnard, California. She received a master's in public policy from Claremont Graduate University where she also worked as an associate faculty member in their School of Education. Her research interests center around the effects of public policies on immigrant children's experiences in education. She was a bilingual classroom teacher in Los Angeles from 1993 to 1997.

Peter Nien-chu Kiang is an associate professor of education and director of the Asian American Studies Program at the University of Massachusetts at Boston. His current research focuses on the impact of ethnic studies in the curriculum, leadership development with Asian American youth, and documenting the experiences of Asian Pacific American Vietnam War veterans. Dr. Kiang's work with Asian Americans in both K–12 and higher education have been honored by groups such as the National Academy of Education, the Massachusetts Teachers Association, the Massachusetts Association for Bilingual Education, the NAACP, and the Anti-Defamation League.

Donaldo Macedo is professor of English and distinguished professor of liberal arts and education at the University of Massachusetts, Boston. He is the author of many books, including *Literacies of Power* and the forthcoming *Ideology Matters*, coauthored with Paulo Freire.

Elizabeth Sugar Martínez, who received her B.A. and M.Ed. from the University of California at Los Angeles, is currently a University of Houston Ph.D. candidate in curriculum and instruction. She has taught K–12 and university students in the United States, Italy, Japan, the Marshall Islands, and Lithuania. Her research interests include teacher training, bilingual education, and critical pedagogy.

Peter McLaren is a professor in the Division of Urban Schooling in the Graduate School of Education and Information Studies, University of California at Los Angeles. He is the author, editor, and coeditor of over thirty books on critical pedagogy, multiculturalism, the sociology and anthropology of education, the politics of education, and Marxist theory. His recent books include *Che Guevara, Paulo Freire, and the Pedagogy of Revolution* (Rowman & Littlefield), *Critical Pedagogy and Predatory Culture* (Routledge), *Revolutionary Multiculturalism* (Westview), and *Schooling as a Ritual Performance* (3rd edition, Rowman & Littlefield). A political activist, he lectures worldwide on the politics of liberation. His works have been translated into twelve languages.

Martha Montero-Sieburth is an associate professor at the Graduate College of Education at the University of Massachusetts at Boston, in the Leadership in Urban Schools Doctoral Program, and in the Educational Administration Masters Program. Her recent publications include *The Struggle for a New Paradigm: Qualitative Research in Latin America*, co-edited with Gary Anderson in 1998, and *Making Invisible Latino Adolescents Visible: A Critical Approach Building upon Latino Diversity*, with Francisco Villarruel in 2000.

Marjorie Faulstich Orellana is an assistant professor in the School of Education and Social Policy at Northwestern University. Her research interests center around language, literacy, and power in sociocultural practices and Latino immigrant children's experiences in urban school communities. She was a bilingual classroom teacher in Los Angeles from 1983 to 1993.

Carola Suárez-Orozco is the codirector of the Harvard Immigration Project. She is also a senior research associate and lecturer in human development and psychology at the Harvard Graduate School of Education. She coauthored (with Marcelo Suárez-Orozco) *Transformations: Migration, Family Life, and Achievement Motivation among Latino Adolescents*, the recipient of the Society on Research in Adolescence's 1995 Best Book Award. With Marcelo, she is also the author of *Children of Immigration* (Harvard University Press, in press). Currently, the two are editing a six-volume series called *The New Immigration* for Garland Press.

Marcelo Suárez-Orozco is professor of human development and psychology, co-director of the Harvard Immigration Project, and chair of the Interfaculty Committee on Latino Studies at Harvard University. His recent books include *Children of Immigration* (with Carola Suárez-Orozco, Harvard University Press 2000) and *Cultures Under Siege: Collective Violence and Trauma* (with Tony Robben, Cambridge University Press 2000).

Enrique (Henry) T. Trueba has a Ph.D. in anthropology from Pittsburgh University. He has an endowed chair as Rubén E. Hinojosa Regents Professor at the University of Texas, Austin. He has written many articles and books on ethnic minority children: on Mexican Americans, *Healing Multicultural America: Mexican Immigrants Rise to Power in Rural California* (Falmer Press 1993, with Rodriguez, Zou, and Cintrón); on the Hmong or Miao of China, *Power in Education: The Case of Miao University Students and Its Significance for American Culture* (Falmer Press 1994, with Yali Zou); on ethnic identity, *Ethnic Identity and Power: Cultural Contexts of Political Action in School and Society* (SUNY Press 1998, with Y. Zou); and *Latinos Unidos: From Cultural Diversity to the Politics of Solidarity* (Rowman & Littlefield 1999). This book obtained the 1999 Gustavus Myers Outstanding Book Award.

Yali Zou is the founder and director of the Asian American Studies Center at the University of Houston and an associate professor in the Department of Educational Leadership and Cultural Studies. She obtained her M.A. and Ph.D. in education from the University of California at Davis and has conducted ethnographic research in both China and the United States. She has written a number of articles, and, as an author and editor, she is also responsible for four books on ethnic identity and multicultural issues. The two most recent are *Power in Education: The Case of Miao University Students in Its Significance for American Culture* (Falmer Press, 1994) and *Ethnic Identity and Power: Cultural Contexts of Political Action in School and Society* (State University of New York Press, 1998). Dr. Zou is currently working on two books: *Chinese Culture in America* and *American and Chinese Look at Each Other: Cross-Cultural Perspectives*.